BEFORE COLONIZATION

COLUMBIA STUDIES IN INTERNATIONAL ORDER AND POLITICS

COLUMBIA STUDIES IN INTERNATIONAL ORDER AND POLITICS

Stacie E. Goddard, Daniel H. Nexon, and Joseph M. Parent, series editors

The Columbia Studies in International Order and Politics series builds on the press's long tradition in classic international relations publishing while highlighting important new work. The series is founded on three commitments: to serve as an outlet for innovative theoretical work, especially that work which stretches beyond "mainstream" international relations and cuts across disciplinary boundaries; to highlight original qualitative and historical work in international relations theory, international security, and international political economy; and to focus on creating a selective, prominent list dedicated to international relations.

Beyond Power Transitions: The Lessons of East Asian History and the Future of U.S.-China Relations, Xinru Ma and David C. Kang

Governing the Feminist Peace: The Vitality and Failure of the Women, Peace, and Security Agenda, Paul Kirby and Laura J. Shepherd

States and the Masters of Capital: Sovereign Lending, Old and New, Quentin Bruneau

Making War on the World: How Transnational Violence Reshapes Global Order, Mark Shirk

Before Colonization

NON-WESTERN STATES AND SYSTEMS IN THE
NINETEENTH CENTURY

Charles R. Butcher
and Ryan D. Griffiths

Columbia University Press
New York

Columbia University Press
Publishers Since 1893
New York   Chichester, West Sussex
cup.columbia.edu
Copyright © 2025 Columbia University Press
All rights reserved

Library of Congress Cataloging-in-Publication Data

Names: Butcher, Charles R. author | Griffiths, Ryan D. author
Title: Before colonization : non-Western states and systems in the nineteenth century / Charles R. Butcher and Ryan D. Griffiths.
Other titles: Non-Western states and systems in the nineteenth century
Description: New York : Columbia University Press, 2025. | Series: Columbia studies in international order and politics | Includes bibliographical references and index.
Identifiers: LCCN 2024059899 (print) | LCCN 2024059900 (ebook) | ISBN 9780231219358 hardback | ISBN 9780231219365 trade paperback | ISBN 9780231562652 ebook
Subjects: LCSH: State, The | Comparative government | Asia—Politics and government | Africa, West—Politics and government—To 1884 | World politics—19th century | International relations—Philosophy
Classification: LCC JC248 .B88 2025 (print) | LCC JC248 (ebook) | DDC 320.1095/09034—dc23/eng/20250305
LC record available at https://lccn.loc.gov/2024059899
LC ebook record available at https://lccn.loc.gov/2024059900

GPSR Authorized Representative: Easy Access System Europe, Mustamäe tee 50, 10621 Tallinn, Estonia, gpsr.requests@easproject.com

Cover design: Milenda Nan Ok Lee
Cover image: The Print Collector / Alamy Stock Photo

CONTENTS

LIST OF FIGURES AND TABLES   vii

ACKNOWLEDGMENTS   ix

Chapter One
Billiard Balls and Bull's-eyes   1

Part 1. Theoretical Framework and Beginnings

Chapter Two
The Birth and Death of States Before the League of Nations   23

Chapter Three
The Comparative Dynamics of States and Systems   55

Part 2. Regional State Systems

Chapter Four
East Asia   77

Chapter Five
South Asia   107

Chapter Six
Maritime Southeast Asia   137

Chapter Seven
West Africa   163

Part 3. Synthesis

Chapter Eight
Lessons from the Case Studies   195

Chapter Nine
Systems of Decentralized States   219

Conclusion   241

NOTES   253

BIBLIOGRAPHY   291

INDEX   317

FIGURES AND TABLES

FIGURES

FIGURE 1.1. Annual number of states in the world per COW and ISD data, 1816–2016   6
FIGURE 2.1. World map of states per COW data, 1816–1920   34
FIGURE 2.2. Number of states per the ISD, 1816–1920, within the borders of contemporary states   39
FIGURE 2.3. Global state births and deaths per the ISD, 1816–2016   40
FIGURE 2.4. State births and deaths in Africa and the Americas per the ISD, 1816–2016   41
FIGURE 3.1. System of centralized states: the billiard ball model   57
FIGURE 3.2. System of decentralized states: the bull's-eye model   58
FIGURE 4.1. States and population densities in East Asia per the ISD, 1816–1920 and 1800   79
FIGURE 4.2. Cities in East Asia, 1750–1900   86
FIGURE 4.3. Battles in East Asia, 1700–1920   88
FIGURE 4.4. Battle locations in East Asia, 1750–1920   91
FIGURE 5.1. States and population densities in South Asia per the ISD, 1816–1920 and 1800   109
FIGURE 5.2. Cities in South Asia, 1750–1816   113
FIGURE 5.3. Battles in South Asia, 1600–1920   117
FIGURE 5.4. Battle locations in South Asia, 1750–1850   118
FIGURE 6.1. States and population densities in maritime Southeast Asia, 1816–1920 and 1800   139

FIGURES AND TABLES

FIGURE 6.2. Cities in maritime Southeast Asia, 1750–1900   147
FIGURE 6.3. Wars in maritime Southeast Asia, 1700–1920   149
FIGURE 6.4. War locations in maritime Southeast Asia, 1750–1910   150
FIGURE 7.1. States and population densities in West Africa, 1816–1920   166
FIGURE 7.2. Cities in West Africa, 1750–1900   170
FIGURE 7.3. Numbers of active war years in West Africa, 1700–1900   173
FIGURE 7.4. War locations in West Africa, 1700–1900   174
FIGURE 9.1. Diagram of a bull's-eye state   221
FIGURE 9.2. Heteronomy   231
FIGURE 10.1. War participation per state-year per COW and ISD data, 1816–2007   252

TABLES

TABLE 2.1. Regional Patterns in State Formation and Death, 1816–1920   44
TABLE 2.2. State Deaths in Africa   48
TABLE 2.3. State Deaths in Asia   51
TABLE 2.4. State Deaths in Europe and the Americas   53

ACKNOWLEDGMENTS

We have acquired many debts in the making of this book. Ben Goldsmith, Jason Sharman, and Jesse Dillon Savage have been keen supporters from the beginning. Members of the Department of Government and International Relations at the University of Sydney gave terrific advice at important points in the early days, including James Der Derian, Charlotte Epstein, Graeme Gill, Justin Hastings, Diarmuid Maguire, Ferran Martinez i Coma, Gil Merom, John Mikler, Pippa Norris, Sarah Phillips, Madeleine Pill, Aim Sinpeng, Frank Smith, Rodney Smith, Adrian Vickers, Natasha Wheatley, and Colin Wight. Key parts of the book were written during research visits supported by the Department of Government and International Relations at the University of Sydney and the School of Politics and International Relations at the Australian National University, for which we are thankful.

The data collection for the book (International System(s) Dataset, version 2) could not have been accomplished without a Discovery Grant from the Australian Research Council (ARC). That grant helped support a great team of graduate researchers: Marigold Black, Keshab Girl, Jiye Kim, Aden Knaap, Haneol Lee, Christian Novak, Jeremy Simpson, Nik Skon, and Chris Watterson. We also acknowledge financial support from the Norwegian University of Science and Technology (NTNU) and the European Research Council (ERC) under the Horizon 2020 Consolidator Grant program, which was crucial to the coding of states and in-depth research on their features. We thank Ludovic Devos, Alice Dalsjø, Indrit Gradeci, Kari-Anne Helland Barland, Sofie Grønset, and Jan Helge Røskar for their outstanding research efforts.

We thank Lars-Erik Cederman, Jason Sharman, and Ayşe Zarakol for their participation in a book workshop in August 2022. They pushed us to streamline and redesign the book in many ways that made for a much better product. We also thank Austin Mitchell for excellent feedback and a close reading of the book toward the end.

A number of other colleagues have served as sounding boards over the years. Nisha Fazal, Kristian Skrede Gleditsch, Seva Gunitsky, George Lawson, Charlie Miller, Andrew Phillips, Hendrik Spruyt, and Megan Stewart have been present in the intellectual development of this work. Early encouragement from Bill Thompson helped us to hold the course. A previous version of the book was presented at the Hertie School Centre for International Security, and we received excellent feedback from Anita Gohdes, Marina Henke, and Julian Wucherpfennig, among others. We also thank Jan Teorell, Amanda Cheney, Augustin Goenaga, Martin Hall, Johannes Lindvall, Ted Svensson, and members of the STANCE project for excellent feedback throughout the development of this manuscript and especially for hosting us at workshops at the University of Lund in 2019 and 2021.

NTNU and Syracuse University have provided a home for much of the writing. We thank the Violence, Instability, and Peace (VIP) research group at NTNU, which was a source of intellectual inspiration and encouragement throughout. We also thank the LEGACIES research team, especially Kari-Anne Helland Barland, Sofie Grønset, Oda Bringa, Christoffer Andersen, Jan-Helge Røskar, Stine Reitan, Cristina Monzer, and Marius Wishman for "fun facts" and inspiring and energizing discussions about historical states that were essential to refining the ideas in this book. We thank Matt Cleary, Colin Elman, Peg Hermann, and Brian Taylor at Syracuse University for feedback on the book and related grant proposals as well as general publishing advice.

The ideas in this book build on several earlier publications, and we thank the editors and anonymous reviewers of our articles in *International Interactions*, *International Studies Quarterly*, *Review of International Studies*, and *International Theory*.

ACKNOWLEDGMENTS

We thank the editorial team for the series International Order and Politics at Columbia University Press, including Caelyn Cobb, Stacie Goddard, and Joe Parent. Dan Nexon was particularly crucial in the development of the book, not only for his insightful work as an editor and scholar but also for his earlier support for our *International Studies Quarterly* article "Between Eurocentrism and Babel" (2017), which laid much of the theoretical groundwork for the book.

Finally, we thank our families, who have moved across continents during the writing of the book. Ryan Griffiths thanks Ali, Henry, and Bea for their support, patience, and constant source of entertainment and diversion. From Charles: to my parents, Laurenza and Rob, for so many dinners, surfs, coffees, and quizzes, for always backing me. To Reuben and Luke for keeping life grounded in *this* century and focused on what matters. And, above all, to Kate for her unwavering belief, encouragement, and love over many years and countries, without which none of this would have been possible.

Chapter One

BILLIARD BALLS AND BULL'S-EYES

Traces of extinct state systems are everywhere. A visitor to Indonesia today can tour the palace of the sultan of Yogyakarta on Java or the royal water palaces of the Balinese rajas of Klungkung and Karangasem. Before the Dutch, these states were independent. Relics of their former prestige line the attached museums, from monochrome photos of foreign dignitaries to diplomatic correspondence to weapons of war—imprints of states and systems that existed before Europeans swept across Asia and Africa, colonizing in their wake and enclosing the earth's territory into a single interstate system for the first time.

What was the world like before colonization? Consider this snapshot of different state systems around the world in the year 1820. West Africa was in a period of ferment. The Oyo Empire (~1600–1836) was in decline, just as the Sokoto Caliphate (~1804–1903) ascended. In maritime Southeast Asia, Balinese kingdoms switched from selling slaves to selling rice. In five years, the Sultanate of Yogyakarta (1755–1830) on Java would fall to Dutch invaders. In South Asia, regional states such as Punjab, Bahawalpur, and Gwalior that had blossomed after the Mughal collapse were now fighting for survival as the British marched west from Bengal. In East Asia, the Qing Dynasty was the focal point in a highly developed Sinocentric order that included Korea, Vietnam, and Japan. Each of these vibrant systems would endure for the better part of the nineteenth century.

However, for much of the accumulated work in international relations (IR), they might as well never have existed. The field of IR has a problem. It is a field that aims to explain broad patterns in world politics, such as the processes of state formation, the nature and frequency of conflict, and how order emerges among states across a range of issue areas. To answer these questions, IR scholars have looked back into history to draw general lessons and construct universal theories. Yet for the most part they have examined one state system, the European system, which expanded to become the global system by the early twentieth century. But other state systems existed during this period that are less well understood. Their exclusion amounts to an external validity problem for IR given that universal theories have been generated from one case study (the European system) instead of from a set of comparative case studies. To achieve its goals, IR needs to expand the analysis to include other historical locales.

When the field of IR has looked beyond the West, it has too often done so through the lens of several received wisdoms. A strong one in the realist tradition of IR is that states elsewhere were just like Europe—they had clearly defined borders and internal hierarchy.[1] If these states were not as developed as their Western counterparts, it is because they did not experience the centuries of warfare that forged robust political structures in Europe.[2] A different wisdom, equally Eurocentric, is that the rest of the world was stateless and that Europe was the only state system. As we show in chapter 2, this wisdom has been transmitted by the dominant sources of quantitative data on states and systems in the nineteenth century. A very different wisdom is that political order outside Europe was fundamentally different. Rather than states surviving in conditions of anarchy, polities existed in a more feudalistic context where power was fluid and cut across borders. According to this view, there is no sense thinking of these polities as independent states with control over their external relations because the internal/external distinction did not hold. These three received wisdoms are contradictory, and all of them cannot be right.

In his work on war and change in world politics in the early 1980s, Robert Gilpin identified the "need for a comparative study of international systems."[3] Similar calls have been made by other scholars,[4] and, after decades of neglect, English-language IR has finally begun to examine non-Western and precolonial state systems.[5] In his call for a new agenda for international studies, Amitav Acharya argues that we need to examine non-European regional systems and orders and include societies that have hitherto been ignored. He states that IR scholars should aim for a pluralistic universalism that applies to all but recognizes and respects global diversity.[6] In a sense, the IR scholarship must break free from its traditional Eurocentric provincialism.

However, a major obstacle to getting beyond the West in this comparative sense has been the lack of data. That is, if we want to fix the problem and compare across regional systems, we need to start with an accurate register of other states and systems. Until now we have lacked such a register. As an illustration of the problem, consider this simple question: How many independent states existed in 1820? The question of how many states there are in 2024 is relatively easy to answer because we have globe-spanning, sovereignty-attributing institutions such as the United Nations (UN) (before that, the League of Nations) that admit aspirants to the club of states.[7] There is uncertainty on the margins—that is, are Kosovo, Taiwan, and Palestine states?—but most will agree that there are between 193 and 196 independent states today. However, the existing work in IR has not produced an accurate number for 1820. A commonly cited figure is 23 states, given by the Correlates of War (COW) project.[8] Yet all the states in the COW list were in Europe and the Americas, and vast regions of the globe are elided. Were these regions truly stateless?

Historians, anthropologists, area specialists, and some historically oriented IR scholars and comparativists paint a different, albeit scattered picture. We hear about empires such as the Borno Emirate that were the size of France, monarchies with standing armies such as Dahomey, confederations of military regimes like the Maratha Empire, warring city-states in Sulawesi, and rogue traders who created their own countries in places such as Chad and Borneo. We also hear about China and its hierarchical relations with its neighbors, but the COW state list neglected it, too, adding it as a state only beginning in 1860. What explains this disjunction? The answer is not that polities outside of Europe were not states. Rather, the ways IR scholars have defined states are too exclusive and too Eurocentric.

Importantly, we do not mean that there is no scholarly work on states in these neglected regions. Quite the contrary, a rich stock of knowledge has been produced in other disciplines. A historian of Africa would probably find little that is surprising in our descriptive rendering of the West African system in chapter 7, and the mandala states we describe in chapter 6 would not be new to an anthropologist of Southeast Asia.[9] Scholars have long drawn upon historical knowledge in adjacent domains to contribute to big debates in IR. Doing so has produced some of the most important and enduring theoretical insights in the field—for example, how war and trade contributed to the rise of the modern state. We are doing the same thing. However, instead of looking to historians of Europe or the Americas, we look to historians of precolonial West Africa and anthropological studies of Southeast Asia. Crucially, we do this with a conceptual and theoretical framework that allows us to map this existing work onto concepts, theories, and methodological approaches more germane to traditional IR scholarship and to compare these regions to each other in novel ways.

In this book, we conduct a comparative analysis of non-Western states and state systems in the nineteenth century. With an original dataset of independent states during this period, we can answer simple but important questions, such as how many states there were, when they were born, and when they died. We then use these data as the basis to go deeper into the structure of four nineteenth-century state systems: East Asia, South Asia, maritime Southeast Asia, and West Africa. We provide a new angle on an old debate by testing whether prominent explanations for state centralization—specifically war, trade, and interaction capacity—can explain the choice between indirect and direct forms of rule in samples that are (mostly) different from those upon which these models were developed. We argue that a unified model can explain these choices across disparate historical regions and that the level of interaction capacity shapes not only the structure of states with respect to indirect and direct rule but also the systems they constituted.

Finally, it is important to position our contribution within the historical timeline. Our focus is on states around the world in the nineteenth century and the regional subsystems in East Asia, South Asia, maritime Southeast Asia, and West Africa. This is an interesting period in which the global system was drawing together, what William McNeill has flagged as the great merging of the ecumene.[10] It came before the final enclosure of the global international system around 1900, driven in large part by colonialism, in which all of the earth's landmass outside of Antarctica was formally claimed and became part of the sovereign state system—certainly by 1920 with the development of the League of Nations, all states were formally connected through diplomatic recognition. And it came after that period defining all human history in which the various regions of the world were unconnected in any diplomatic sense and quite often had no knowledge of one another. The nineteenth century is part of a larger era from the 1500s through the 1800s in which humanity became truly connected. It is the last point at which we can conduct true comparative analysis of concurrent regional systems.

STATES AND STATE SYSTEMS IN THE NINETEENTH CENTURY

We make three core contributions in the book. First, we catalog the number of independent states since 1816, and we detail the regional patterns in state birth and state death. We document the large number of states that were extinguished by European colonialism. Second, we develop a theoretical and conceptual framework for comparing state systems and show variation across four regions during the nineteenth century: East Asia, South Asia, maritime Southeast Asia, and West Africa. Third, we examine the effects that war, trade, and interaction capacity have on the structure of states and systems. We summarize these contributions in the subsequent sections.

Cataloging States

Our empirical contribution is a dataset on states and their international relations since 1816: the International System(s) Dataset (ISD), version 2.[11] The states in our dataset are known to historians and anthropologists as well as to historically minded IR scholars and political scientists. We synthesize this scattered scholarship into a more complete picture of world politics over time. By moving away from definitions of the state that pin recognition and statehood to European diplomatic ties, we can construct a more systematic portrait of the development of the international system over the past two hundred years and a more thorough understanding of precolonial, non-Western state systems that have hitherto been neglected. Like other scholars working in this area, we see abundant and diverse sociopolitical systems across the world in the early-modern period.[12] By shifting the focus from Europe, we investigate these systems on their own terms and explore them in a comparative format.

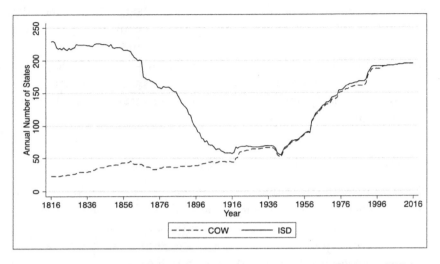

FIGURE 1.1. Annual number of states in the world per COW and ISD data, 1816–2016. *Source*: COW data sourced from Correlates of War Project, "State System Membership List, v2016."

Let us return to the question of how many states there were in 1820. We think that there were 219, more states than in the current international system and nearly ten times the number noted by COW. That is a dramatic difference with substantial implications. Most quantitative studies of war, diplomacy, and trade that include the nineteenth century are trained on a small and skewed sample of only about a tenth of the states that actually existed. Yet the world was filled with hundreds of states in the early 1800s, most of them in Africa and Asia, but these states largely disappeared by the beginning of the twentieth century in what may be the largest state-extinction event in history. Far from statelessness, there were complex state systems.

Figure 1.1 graphs the number of states over the past two hundred years according to both COW and the ISD. If one looks only at the COW trend line, one would conclude that the international system has expanded in terms of the number of states. The COW line shows that after a slow and uneven increase between 1816 and 1918, there was a steep uptick after World War I, a culling of states during World War II, and a sharp proliferation after 1945.

However, our data show a very different pattern, one that was concave over the past two hundred years. From a high of 230 states in 1816, the number decreased sharply throughout the late 1800s and reached a historical low in the first half of the twentieth century.[13] The ISD is roughly consistent with COW from the early twentieth century onward—both show a similar interwar trend and a post-1945 proliferation (see chapter 2 for details on coding differences). But for the first one hundred years after 1816, the two lines are strikingly different. Not only do our data show an altogether different trend in the number of states over time, but they also illustrate the consequences of the Eurocentrism in COW and the IR quantitative scholarship more broadly. Whereas COW identifies 23 states in 1816, the ISD lists 230. Whereas COW catalogs 46 states in 1860, we code 215. The average annual difference between the datasets during the 1816–1900 period is 153 states. All of these states were invisible to COW, and the vast majority of them existed in non-European regions stretching from West Africa through South Asia and over to East and Southeast Asia. These states composed vibrant state systems that were contemporaneous with the Concert of Europe, yet they are largely ignored in the COW list and in the IR scholarship.

Accounting for these states and bringing them back into the analysis reveal the mass state-extinction event that was consonant with colonialism and the closure of the ecumene. At least 270 states expired during the 1816–1920 period, with the bulk of state deaths occurring in the late 1800s. Some 219 state deaths occurred in Africa and Asia, and, of these states, only 27 were later reborn during the decolonization period after World War II. That means that 192 states, nearly the same number that exists today, were erased from the global map. Where were these states located, and what were their names? This is the subject of chapter 2.

Comparative Framework

Our theoretical framework is designed to make diverse systems legible and comparable. Borrowing from Charles Tilly, we anchor our framework with a focal but acultural definition of the state as a "coercion-wielding organization[] that" "exercise[s] clear priority in some respects" "over all other organizations within" a territory and has control over its external relations.[14] This definition helps us to identify statelike units across diverse contexts and categorize forms of the state depending on how they are internally organized. It does not require that states have clearly defined borders, only that they have authority over space and control their relations with other states. We contend that our definition enables an analysis of the variation in political order both within and above the state, a crucial move when attempting to understand state systems.

Notably, our approach to the comparative analysis of systems differs from the existing research. Take, for example, Andrew Phillips's and Hendrick Spruyt's works that compare international orders and societies across time and space.[15] Both offer fascinating comparisons of orders during the early-modern period, such as the Sinocentric system, the Islamicate, the system in Southeast Asia, and Latin Christendom. Their approach was to define international orders (or societies), determine their boundaries, and assess their similarities and differences. That is pattern matching at a high level of aggregation. In contrast, we start at the lower level of the state. We build from a culturally neutral definition of the state and then use that definition to construct a dataset of states across time and space. For us, states, not orders, are the primary unit of analysis and the basis of the comparison. With this approach, we can identify systems of states and compare them. We contend that ours is a more rigorous and data-driven approach that complements the higher-level analyses in the literature and picks up the numerous states and their structural patterns that are missed in the existing work.

We should stress that our use of the term *state* should not be taken to mean that having a state is somehow better than other forms of governance. As should be abundantly clear from the chapters that follow, we do not see states as arising in any teleological fashion but as the outcome of contingent decision-making processes by rulers embedded in concrete material, institutional, and cultural environments that shape the outcomes of those decisions. Whether states (or some types of states) are better at providing for general human well-being is outside the scope of this book.

As we discuss in chapter 2, our framework incorporates several additional concepts. The first is the *state system*, which arises when states interact and significantly affect one another's fate.[16] This is a general definition, once again taken from Tilly, and it is designed to capture variation in the thickness and density of systems. The second concept is *political centralization*, a measure of political order within the state capturing the extent to which state leaders concentrate decision-making power or delegate key prerogatives to substate actors and polities.[17] This concept captures not only the degree to which states are centralized or decentralized but also how states rule over space and are connected to other states in their system. Third, set above that base are the norms, rules, and diplomatic practices that constitute an *international order*. As we discuss, there is a local element to any international order (e.g., the mandala system, the tribute system, etc.) that makes it unique. But international orders are also the product of these structural factors. We argue that this framework can be used as a sorting device for comparative analysis.

Our next step is to outline two distinct models of state systems. The first model consists of centralized states able to project power over long distances, familiar to most IR audiences. We call it the *billiard ball model*.[18] The second model comprises decentralized states that display limited state reach, high gradients of rule, and complex patterns of vassalage. We call it the *bull's-eye model*.[19] Boundaries between states in the billiard ball model tend to be linear, whereas boundaries in the bull's-eye model are better described as "frontiers." While the billiard ball model relies on a binary distinction between hierarchy and anarchy, the bull's-eye model exhibits more ambiguous relations of not just hierarchy and anarchy but also overlapping and crosscutting forms of authority (heteronomy). Both models are stylized and are used as a heuristic device, representing specific visions of political order that could be placed on a continuum. If the first model best represents a traditional understanding of the European system in IR, the second model shows what happens when we dispense with assumptions of linearity and discrete territoriality and with a dichotomous view of hierarchy and anarchy. The models' utility is that different systems can be identified, located, and compared along the continuum.

Applying this framework to our case studies reveals interesting patterns. The East Asian system best approximates the billiard ball model of highly centralized states, mostly linear borders, and clearer distinctions between states. In comparison, the South Asian system was a blend of billiard balls and bull's-eyes but was closer to the bull's-eye model of decentralized states. West Africa and maritime Southeast Asia corresponded most to the bull's-eye model. Here, we generally found decentralized states composed of centers of power and dissipating orbits of control. Although linear borders did exist, frontiers were far more common. Limited state reach and uncertain control over peripheral areas yielded patterns of heteronomy.

Let us now revisit the three received wisdoms that we noted toward the start of the chapter. Each wisdom is wrong insofar as it offers a limited and quite narrow understanding of political order around the world in the nineteenth century. Did non-Western states look and behave just like European states—or at least a highly stylized understanding of those states? No, we found considerable variation in the structures of states and systems. But some states, especially in East Asia, did hew closer to that model. Here, we hasten to point out that if a substantial portion of the scholarship that aims to move beyond the West to "bring in the rest" has focused only on East Asia, it may be missing some of the true diversity in historical IR.[20] Were these regions stateless, as the second wisdom holds? No, we found ample evidence of states as we define them. To be sure, there was variation in state structures, and sections of land appeared relatively stateless, but we found states in abundance.

Finally, was political order elsewhere fundamentally different from political order in Europe? No, we found striking similarities across these systems as well as between them and the European system. Indeed, we show that a unified framework can capture both the similarities and differences between and within systems. States in maritime Southeast Asia, South Asia, and West Africa ruled, on average, in a similar, decentralized manner, even if they varied in other ways. Language used to describe the so-called mandala state of Southeast Asia could just as easily describe the bull's-eye state of West Africa. Importantly, these similarities obtained across diverse cultural contexts. Tokolor was an Islamic state in West Africa but ruled in a way very similar to Aceh in Southeast Asia. The Oyo Empire established tributary and subordinate relations with its neighbors (Dahomey and Nupe) on a smaller scale but not in fundamentally different ways from China and its neighbors or from the Mughal, Durrani, or Ottoman Empires and the states on their peripheries. These patterns across state systems are made legible with a theoretical framework that emphasizes the common challenges that rulers face across different economic, social, and environmental contexts. Chapters 8 and 9 provide a detailed exploration of these commonalities.

BILLIARD BALLS AND BULL'S-EYES

Patterns in State Centralization

The two models identified in the previous section help us see where systems sit on a spectrum and in relation to one another. They help us describe some aspects of what these systems were like. But we also want to explain differences between systems and within systems over time and space. These states and systems were not static or uniform places. States in South India were more like states in the centralized model than were states in North India, for example. East Asia sat between the centralized and decentralized models around 1800 but was more like the centralized model by 1900. What variables help to explain differences across these regions and within them?

A core proposition of the book is that the structure of state systems is shaped by the extent to which states govern in a centralized or decentralized manner. Much of the analytical part of the book is designed to answer this question—What causes bull's-eyes to become billiard balls? Political centralization is the main outcome we wish to explain (the dependent variable) and can be defined as the degree to which rulers control functions such as taxation, justice, external relations, and leadership appointment throughout their territory or delegate them to substate actors. Do rulers, for example, take taxes for themselves with bureaucrats appointed by the state, or do they allow locals to collect taxes and then pass them on to the state? Are court cases adjudicated by judges in the employ of rulers, or do they allow local law to prevail, overseen by local judicial mechanisms? Are local authorities vassal lords who can appoint their own children as successors to their realms, or are local authorities appointed by the state? The answers to these questions and the factors that shape these outcomes help explain how states and state systems are structured.

Through the book, we use many terms to refer to players in the building and shaping of states and state systems. Kings and queens are called rajas, sultans, obas, nawabs, caliphs, kings, and emirs, for example. However, we try to use some standardized language to refer to these different players where possible and appropriate, not to diminish the importance of local contexts and labels but to facilitate clearer comparisons across the diverse regions covered in this book.

Our argument—following others before us—is that political centralization is the outcome of a tussle between rulers who want to take more revenues and resources from their territories and subordinate vassals who want to keep those resources for themselves.[21] Whether states are centralized or decentralized—and therefore whether state systems are closer to billiard balls or bull's-eyes—is the outcome of conflict and bargaining between rulers and vassals. Rulers are individuals who control the state, sitting atop the hierarchy as the sovereign. Vassals often control their own territories, appoint their own successors, keep their own military forces, collect their own taxes, and appoint their own officials but are constrained in their ability to make war and contract with other states and may send resources to the ruler as tribute. Rulers want to control their vassals and take their resources by appointing their own governors and bureaucrats (as well as to make sure their governors do not turn into vassals or even rulers of independent states), and vassals want to appoint their own children as successors and govern their own territories, giving as little as possible away to the ruler. Rulers will sometimes use their generals and the army to force vassals to accept governors and bureaucrats, and vassals will sometimes use their armies or become elites to prevent this from happening. We will broadly differentiate between strategies of direct/centralized rule and indirect/decentralized rule.[22]

Let us work through a short example to make this struggle more concrete. Modern-day Benin is one sovereign state in West Africa, neighbored by Togo to the west and Nigeria to the east. In 1720, there were at least three independent states in Benin. On the coast was the kingdom of Hueda, which controlled the slave-trading beach at Ouidah. Farther inland was the kingdom of Allada, a sometimes suzerain of Hueda. Still farther inland on the Abomey Plateau was the kingdom of Dahomey. In the 1720s, Dahomeian armies swept down the plateau and conquered Allada and Hueda, also taking control of the slaving port of Ouidah. Allada and Hueda were now subject to Dahomey.

But what was the ruler of Dahomey, King Agaja, to do with these conquered territories? He could abolish their old rulers and send in the army and the bureaucrats to collect taxes and keep order, or he could keep the kings on their thrones and leave them to collect taxes (after all, they already knew how to do it), keep order with what was left of their armies, and make sure that they paid some of those taxes to Dahomey and refrained from consorting with other powers. Each of these options has its costs and benefits that we outline later here and in more detail in chapter 3. In short, sending in the governors and bureaucrats is more reliable and more expensive, whereas leaving the kings on their thrones as vassals is less expensive and less efficient. Which of these options prevails goes a long way to explaining the structure of states and systems. King Agaja chose a bit of both. First, he abolished the kings of Allada and Hueda. Eventually, however, Dahomey allowed the kings to return as vassals, but the slaving port of Ouidah was ruled by governors and some bureaucrats sent directly from Abomey (the capital).[23]

What makes it more likely that centralized (direct) rule is chosen over decentralized (indirect) rule and that states move from being bull's-eyes to being billiard balls? In this book, we explore three explanations and their interrelationship: interaction capacity, war, and trade. The first, interaction capacity, is a measure of the organizational potential within a system. Interaction capacity is the volume of exchanges and interactions between populations that a system can support.[24] As we discuss in chapter 3, it is a function of many technological, social, demographic, economic, and environmental factors. For example, it might take an hour for a modern worker to travel twenty-five kilometers to the office (in peak hour in Sydney). It would take a truck loaded with several tons of goods about the same time. But in the nineteenth century, the same journey could take a day by foot, assuming good weather and roads, and although a camel or ox could marginally increase the carrying capacity, it could not increase the speed of travel. A system where it takes less time to transport goods, people, and ideas has higher interaction capacity. Other factors will influence interaction capacity, such as the number and density of people because they raise or lower costs of trade. More people mean more potential consumers, which lowers the costs of transporting goods from one place to another and increases the potential for interactions between those locations. Language barriers, trade routes, mountains, and rivers may affect interaction capacity as well. Systems with high interaction capacity are those where interactions are dense and frequent among a large number of actors. Systems with low interaction capacity are those where interactions are sparse, local, slow, and relatively infrequent.

Systems with higher interaction capacity should, all else equal, be composed of centralized states because interaction capacity shapes the degree to which they can project power and rule over space. Most rulers want to extract money and resources from the areas they control, which helps them survive against internal and external rivals. We might think that the best way to do this, as most states do today, is to send bureaucrats to take those resources and compel subjects to hand over their money, their produce, or their children in the service of the state. But this way is risky and dangerous because people rebel when these demands are too onerous, and local rulers may bristle when direct rule reduces their share of revenue. Rebellions cost money to suppress and can spiral into dynasty-ending wars. Sending governors to peripheral and outlying regions can get expensive, and they don't always do what the ruler wants. Put simply, interaction capacity affects the cost and therefore the strategy of rule. We argue that rulers in low-density systems are more likely to employ indirect forms of rule, whereby vassals (chiefs, rajas, nobles, etc.) are permitted to extract resources from their territories in the manner of their choosing provided they pay tribute/tax to the ruler. As interaction capacity increases, direct rule becomes less expensive and more common.[25] Overall, systems with low interaction capacity should be composed of states that are more decentralized, and high-density systems should see the rise of more centralized states.

The second factor is war or, more abstractly, military competition. This is a measure of the potential for armed conflict between states in a system. It is essentially the level of the threat of war and conquest. Where states are threatened regularly by other states, international competition is high. Where wars of conquest are rare and rulers generally do not fear being invaded and conquered by other states, international competition is low. War has been given great causal weight in explaining the rise of the centralized state, summarized by the famous Tillian claim that "war made the state and the state made war."[26] The general proposition is that changes in military technology around the fifteenth century in Europe made warfare more expensive, requiring states to extract more revenue from their populations, resulting in larger, more penetrative bureaucracies. Those states that could extract more revenue survived, and those that could not were eliminated. If this bellicist argument for European state formation is widely known, it is not universally accepted. As we discuss in chapter 3, there is a wide-ranging debate on the importance of war in relation to other factors. Our contribution is to apply the argument to other state systems: Did war make the state in non-European locales?

The third independent variable is trade. Scholars such as Spruyt emphasize the importance of increasing trade levels across western Europe in the latter Middle Ages.[27] The commercial revolution incentivized elites to push for property rights, standardization, and political institutions that could protect their business interests. From this push was born an alliance between monarchs and merchants that empowered the state while marginalizing landed vassals. Other scholars, such as Victor Lieberman in his *Strange Parallels* series, also see a role for trade as it provides rulers with access to taxes, guns, and luxury items that are useful for conquering or co-opting rivals.[28] In all, it is argued that trade led to centralization. Like the bellicist argument, however, the importance of trade for European state formation is not universally accepted. Indeed, many theorists (including Spruyt) contend that its weight is conditional on other factors, such as (but not limited to) war. In the chapters to come, we examine the relationship between trade and centralization in other state systems.

Our findings reveal a complicated set of dynamics. Of the three explanations, interaction capacity matters most. Most of the states examined in this book were decentralized, and their systems more like bull's-eyes. Rulers who wished to extend the reach of the state were constrained by low levels of interaction capacity. In some limited instances, such as Mysore in South Asia, rulers centralized their power despite low capacity, which points to the importance of other cultural and institutional factors. But in general we observed that rulers had to settle for indirect rule. War and trade did not lead to centralization in most cases. We argue instead that the effects of war and trade on centralization are conditional on the level of interaction capacity. That is, war and trade have different effects on centralization depending on whether the underlying level of interaction capacity is high or low. In low-density systems, competition and war can empower subordinates as they increase the dependency of rulers on their vassals for military resources. Even if rulers want more from their populations, competition in low-density systems might weaken the rulers' grip on power in favor of elites and vassals, causing decentralization rather than centralization. It is only as interaction capacity rises and rulers can better project power and draw upon protonationalist ideas or when outside states threaten centralization that war weakens the exit options of vassals vis-à-vis their rulers and causes centralization. When the fates of vassals and rulers are tied together, war is more likely to produce centralization. Trade can also have different effects depending on the level of interaction capacity. Increases in trade might provide new resources to rulers, but they can also provide resources to vassals. When rulers have the potential to monopolize trade—or at least dominate it—vis-à-vis their vassals, trade can have centralizing effects. When rulers are less able to project power, trade can diffuse across the system, fragmenting states and causing decentralization. Again, we contend that interaction capacity helps explain why trade has different associations in different contexts as it shapes the ability of rulers to monopolize markets. Chapter 8 provides a summary of these findings.

These basic realities of indirect rule produce system-level effects. We find that systems of decentralized (bull's-eye) states share common characteristics across historical settings, including patterns of radial rule, fuzzy frontier regions instead of linear borders, and interstitial heteronomy. From this finding, we sketch a theory of international change at the end of chapter 9. We argue that states have struggled historically to project power and impose direct rule because the distances involved create information, principal–agent, and credible-commitment problems between ruler and vassal. Although it is difficult for rulers to break out of this equilibrium trap, increased interaction capacity or the spread of shared norms and institutions or both can help not only states but also the systems they constitute make the transition from being bull's-eyes to being billiard balls. The result is a change of system.

METHODOLOGY

We took a varied methodological approach when conducting our research.[29] The backbone of the book is the great effort put into the ISD, version 2.[30] As we detail in chapter 2, the ISD is the product of a multiyear research project funded by the Australian Research Council. With these data, we were able to identify the key units (states) in our study; examine patterns in a quantitative way with respect to political development, state birth, and state death; and then group the units into systems.

The middle portion of the book consists of four qualitative case study chapters on specific historical regional state systems: East Asia, South Asia, maritime Southeast Asia, and West Africa. For these chapters, we followed the standard guidelines for qualitative research specified by

Alexander George and Andrew Bennett.[31] Why did we choose these four systems over others? Could there be smaller or larger groupings of states that could be studied as a system? Our answer is threefold. First, these four systems constituted regional clusters of states. Although the states in them were often connected to states elsewhere, and one could imagine a continuum of connectedness from Japan to West Africa, these clusters have a density to them. Surrounding areas were often sparsely populated on account of geographic features such as the Sahara, the dense rainforests of the tropics, or the mountains of Central Asia. Geographic realities within each system also help connect the states in them—such as the Sahel, the Gangetic Plain, and the sea. Moreover, there is precedence in the literature to think of these regions as zones of interaction. The fact that we found clusters of states in these zones further shaped our thinking.

Second, these regions are understudied in IR research. We begin with East Asia because it is better covered in existing research and more familiar to readers, and it allows us to illustrate centralization mechanics at work. But there is very little work examining and comparing eighteenth- and nineteenth-century state systems in South Asia,[32] West Africa,[33] and Southeast Asia.[34] In fact, the neglect of Africa in IR research was the subject of a recent article by Jason Sharman.[35] Each of these systems is well studied in the modern period, but little work has been done synthesizing the vast stock of knowledge about the early-modern period accumulated by scholars in adjacent fields such as history and anthropology and relating it to theories and concepts more central to IR. We draw heavily on these secondary materials in the case studies.

Third, these regional systems present variation in the level of interaction capacity. A section in each chapter is committed to gauging that level in a context-specific way, and the cases proceed in roughly descending order of interaction capacity from East Asia through to South Asia, Southeast Asia, and West Africa. Sequencing the cases in this manner not only allows us to examine the effects of interaction capacity on centralization but also enables us to explore how it interacts with war and trade. Furthermore, each of these cases has intraregion variation in interaction capacity, war, and trade, perhaps best illustrated by the densely populated, war-prone, slave coast of West Africa and the sparse savannah and cities of the Sahel.

However, there are several caveats. First, none of these systems is completely self-contained and cut off from the world around it. They are not discrete in the same way that the contemporary international system includes and is bounded by the earth. They are not completely disconnected from one another in the manner that states in Africa and Eurasia were from states in the Americas before 1492. These systems are better envisaged as regional subsystems in the early-modern period, just before the global enclosure. They were relatively self-contained and certainly worthy of study.

There were other dynamic systems during the nineteenth century. The Great Lakes district of East Africa is one, and mainland Southeast Asia could easily have been connected to the maritime Southeast Asian case study. Although our set of case studies is not exhaustive, we chose the four clusters that effectively stood out. Furthermore, our clusters could be subdivided into smaller systems. As we discuss in the chapters that follow, we regularly ran across subsystems, such as the Balinese states or the states of the Yoruba zone. Similarly, we could expand the boundaries of systems to include larger areas. Nevertheless, we stand by our clusters as useful systems of study. We felt that smaller groupings would elide important connections, just as larger groupings would yield thinner and less coherent systems. Further research can explore these pathways.

PLAN OF THE BOOK

This book follows a narrative arc from the general to the specific and back to the general. In part I, "Theoretical Framework and Beginnings," chapters 2 and 3 start at a fairly high level of abstraction. In chapter 2, we define states, systems, and other key concepts, introduce the ISD, and show quantitative patterns across not only the four regions in the case studies but also the entire globe with respect to state birth and state death. Finally, we name the states that expired during the colonial enclosure. In chapter 3, we elaborate our theoretical framework for billiard ball and bull's-eye state systems and develop the theories linking war, trade, and interaction capacity to state centralization.

In part 2, "Regional State Systems," we zoom in to focus on four historical case studies. Chapter 4 focuses on East Asia, a historical system that has become increasingly familiar to contemporary IR scholars because of the rise of China and the desire to understand its past. Relative to the other systems, East Asia survived the colonial experience the most intact, for the states under observation here are essentially the same as their contemporary descendants. In contrast, most states described in the next three chapters no longer exist. In chapter 5, we turn to South Asia, the dense system that eventually came under British control. Chapter 6 focuses on maritime Southeast Asia, a dazzling state system that existed across the island chain that is now modern-day Malaysia and Indonesia. Chapter 7 centers on West Africa, a fascinating state system that until now has only been loosely covered in IR studies.

In part III, "Synthesis," we zoom out once more to discuss general patterns. Part of our goal is to explore foundational questions in IR that have thus far not been explored in a true comparative intersystem format. Our hope is to shed light on these questions, conduct a form of reconnaissance, and, ideally, open new paths for research. Chapter 8 provides a summary of the findings across the case studies, organized around five lessons: (1) most historical states were decentralized; (2) rulers were aware of the perils of decentralization; (3) rulers were constrained by low interaction capacity; (4) war did not lead to state centralization in most cases; and (5) trade promoted state formation but inhibited centralization in most cases. In chapter 9, we take the lessons learned to explore the dynamics of systems of decentralized states. These dynamics include patterns of radial rule, fuzzy frontiers, and heteronomy. We wrap up the chapter by outlining a theory of political rule and international change. In the conclusion, we summarize the main findings and speculate on where future research might make productive inroads, using the example of the decline-of-war debate.

PART I
Theoretical Framework and Beginnings

Chapter Two

THE BIRTH AND DEATH OF STATES BEFORE THE LEAGUE OF NATIONS

How many independent states were there in the nineteenth and early twentieth centuries before the colonial enclosure and the establishment of the League of Nations, and what were the patterns in state birth and state death? In this book, we use a concept of statehood that travels across regions and identifies fundamentally similar units, even though they may differ on other dimensions, such as the degree of political centralization. This chapter describes that concept and how we used it to identify and collect information on the features of states across the globe from 1816 to 2016, with a focus on the pre-1920 period. The product of our efforts is the International System(s) Dataset (ISD), version 2.[1] Using the ISD, we can identify and name the states that existed and provide answers to the questions asked at the beginning of this chapter.

The remainder of this chapter proceeds as follows. We first define the state, the state system, and a set of corollary concepts. We then discuss the purpose behind the ISD, how it was constructed, and the general findings that came from it. We next detail patterns in state birth and state death globally and regionally. And then, crucially, we list the states that expired during the global enclosure.

DEFINITIONS AND CONCEPTS

The *state* is the central concept in this book. It is an old word used in many ways, but we utilize a prominent, general definition offered by Charles Tilly: states "are coercion-wielding organizations that are distinct from households and kinship groups and exercise clear priority in some respects over all other organizations within substantial territories." Positing that "states have been the world's largest and most powerful organizations for more than five thousand years," Tilly is using the concept broadly to include "city-states, empires, theocracies, and many other forms of government."[2] For him, the latter were specific forms of the state.

Before we develop this definition further, let us pause to address two possible concerns. The first is the need to establish an appropriate basis of comparison. Whether we are comparing states or systems or some other organizing concept for human sociopolitical interaction, we need to define those terms in a way that travels across areas that may have had no connection to one another. Some readers will question whether disparate social phenomena can be compared in this way. According to Ludwig Wittgenstein, one's vocabulary is not context free; it depends on the language game in which they are involved.[3] A state or state system in the twentieth century is part of a different context than a state or state system in the Chinese Warring States Period.[4] In a similar, albeit more culture-focused way, Yaqing Qin argues that all social theory—and by implication the terms and premises on which theories are constructed—bear their cultural birthmark. Nothing starts from a temporospatial null.[5] Qin is correct, and so is Wittgenstein. But does that mean that all comparisons are invalid and that we are condemned to a form of solipsism?

We take a weakly positivist position and claim that diverse states and systems can be compared. No theory is created in a temporospatial null, our vocabulary is not context free, and concepts, to the extent that they travel at all, do not travel perfectly. Nevertheless, we submit that big comparisons are valuable, provided that care is given to the choice of what is to be compared and that the choice is explicit.[6] Rulers throughout history have faced common dilemmas related to political survival that, broadly speaking, can produce similar institutional solutions across disconnected contexts. This broader connection does not invalidate local cultural factors that can play a decisive role under some circumstances but rather shows that there is a logic of political survival that allows us to understand commonalities across diverse state systems independent of the language we use to describe them.[7]

A second concern pertains to our word choice. By positing his definition of the state, Tilly took a word with Latin roots and applied it to contexts that in many cases existed before and were independent of the establishment of Rome and the spread of Latin. He used a word derived from the Western experience to describe a phenomenon that has existed across time and space. Some readers may object on the grounds that the concept is thus fixed to a particular cultural milieu and a Western one at that. Laterally, they may challenge our claim to be using an acultural concept. Although we defend our conceptual choice in several ways in the paragraphs that follow, let us offer a practical reason here. A word must be chosen to describe a concept that is necessarily prior to the word. That is, there is no word or term that existed prior—and was applied—to each of Tilly's instantiations of the state because he is referencing regions over a 5,000-year history that had no political, let alone lexical, connection. If we used a word from the Chinese Warring States Period or from ancient India, we would encounter the same problem. The word *state* is the most commonly used word to describe a political form that has existed across time and space. We can either abandon the analysis because there is no word that truly began from a temporospatial null, or we can choose the best term on offer and strip it down to a stable concept that travels.[8] Doing the latter does not require that we embrace a kind of neo-Kantian formalism, where the state as a concept is prior to all experience.[9] Rather, we can conceive of the state as a pattern of human activity common to disparate cultures.

We extend Tilly's definition to require that the state controls its external relations—that is, it has external sovereignty. We use the term *sovereignty* in a general sense that is not exclusive to European political history. Here, it implies political authority, territoriality, and external recognition.[10] Although Tilly is unclear about the degree to which a state must exercise priority in this external sense, we maintain that this extension is critical because it permits a stable measurement of variation above and below the state, which we see as fundamental to comparing systems and states. This extension also combines and allows us to clearly differentiate between two traditional facets of the state, the internal and the external or, as Gianfranco

Poggi put it, "politics as allocation" and "politics as us against the other."[11] When we say "external relations," we are referring to the management of relations with units outside the state's realm of authority, particularly in regard to war making and alliance formation. These units can participate freely in the politics of the system.[12]

Consider the following illustration to help clarify our definition of the state, one that we return to later in the chapter. We can think of state systems as being composed of polities, which are coercion-wielding and hierarchical organizations that control a distinct territory or set of places. These polities have the capacity to exercise sovereign rights across various domains. But to simplify the illustration, let us imagine that polities control three functions: the right to extract military and economic resources (extraction), the right to administer justice (justice), and the right to engage in war and diplomacy with other polities (external relations). Let us also imagine that polities can bargain with other polities and share these functions. Finally, polities can transfer some of the resources they extract to other polities without ceding control of the right to extract those resources.[13] States are the subset of polities that retain control over their external relations. Consider a system with just three polities—*a*, *b*, and *c*—all of which start with control over extraction, justice, and external relations. There are three states in this system. All three entities have an administrative hierarchy to extract resources from their populations and can freely bargain with one another. If *a* takes over the external relations of *b*, then *b* ceases to be a state and becomes a part of *a*. Note, however, that *b* still retains extraction and justice rights, which becomes important when we define centralization. In our terms, however, *b* has become a vassal of *a*. States can control many functions, but to qualify as a state in our framework they must control the right to bargain and conduct diplomacy with other states. It is the threshold at which we differentiate between state and substate entities.

Control over external relations is a useful line to separate independent states from other polities (e.g., vassals, dependencies, protectorates) as it represents an authority claim in the interaction with other states. When other units recognize this claim, they are equals and units in the system. When polities recognize the claim of a state to represent them in the realm of international relations, they are nonequal polities and subordinate to another polity. According to Adam Watson, "The term independent states in a system indicates political entities that retain the ultimate ability to make external decisions as well as domestic ones."[14] This conception is consistent with the spirit of the Montevideo Declaration on the Rights and Duties of States of 1933. It is also consistent with most of the sovereign-state datasets, including the COW. It differs, however, from conceptions of the state that admit polities that possess internal but not external independence. Thus, the state in our framework needs to have both internal control and external independence, which excludes those federacies, protectorates, and various other types of vassalage that cannot enter into relations with other states as an equal.

To reiterate, we define the state as a coercion-wielding organization that exercises clear priority in some respects over all other organizations within a territory and has control over its external relations. We contend that this definition is transportable across time and space. States with internal control and the freedom to interact with other states are not a modern or Western phenomenon. Indeed, these characteristics are focal, differentiating the state from hunter-gatherer bands, roving bandits, and other nonstate actors.[15] It encompasses more specific concepts such as the national state, the nation-state, the territorial state, the city-state, and the composite state.[16] Our state is also different from subsovereign units such as federal jurisdictions, provinces, and protectorates because our definition requires that the polity in question has external sovereignty. We think of our units as "sovereign peaks" in political landscapes that resemble contour maps. Subordinate units such as federacies and protectorates are also peaks, but they are local maxima in the broader context because they have surrendered control over their external relations to a higher authority. Our definition does not require that states must be territorially contiguous and centralized or have clear borders. They could be decentralized, composite polities that control very few sovereign functions, have discontiguous territories and ill-defined frontiers, and still be classified as states.[17]

Two borderline cases can help illustrate how this definition works in practice. Tippu Tip was an (infamous) trader in slaves, ivory, and spices who operated in the late nineteenth century in parts of the region that are now the modern-day Democratic Republic of Congo and Tanzania. His trading missions were established by the sultan of Zanzibar like trading companies set up by European states. Tippu Tip would travel through East and Central Africa with caravans on journeys that could last years.[18] In

1887, a representative of the Belgian government offered him the position of governor of the Stanley Falls District in the Congo Free State, which he accepted.[19] Was the Tippu Tip empire a state? Under our definition, the answer is no. Stuart Laing claims that "there is little evidence of his having installed administration or justice or the machinery of government in any systematic way."[20] Tippu Tip also did not conduct his external relations independently of the sultan of Zanzibar. He marched under the sultan's flag, and even his decision to accept a Belgian governorship was taken only after obtaining the sultan's approval.[21] The territories that Tippu Tip controlled were not the territories of an independent state but a highly autonomous trading extension of the Sultanate of Zanzibar.

Rabih az-Zubayr was also a slave trader but part of an expedition sent by Egypt into the Sudan. In 1874, the leader of the slaving expedition was captured, and Rabih continued west with (perhaps) four hundred soldiers. By 1893, he had conquered the ancient Sultanates of Wadai and Bagirmi as well as the large and powerful Bornu Empire in modern-day Nigeria. Rabih established thin state structures as he went, appointing military governors to conquered provinces. He dealt directly with the British and French along with other indigenous rulers, even being recognized by the British as the true successor to the Kanem-Bornu Empire.[22] Was the area he conquered a state? Under our definition, the answer is yes because Rabih's administration exercised external relations independently. He never consulted his parent government in Cairo, and he forged an independent, decentralized empire in Central Africa.

Of course, most cases are simpler to classify than Tippu Tip's and Rabih's empires, but these fringe cases help illustrate where we draw the line for statehood, even in thin and decentralized systems where formal sovereignty-attributing institutions may be absent. Clearly, our definition pulls in many different types of states, including cases of decentralized rule, states without linear borders or developed bureaucracies, even states that admit a level of hierarchy in their relations to other states through tributary relations. These latter aspects become more important when we outline the dimensions upon which state systems can vary.

A potential criticism is that we are drawing a distinction between external and internal relations that was irrelevant or nonexistent outside of the European state system. This is the third received wisdom mentioned in chapter 1. Some scholars have argued that there was no clear distinction between internal and external in places such as Southeast Asia or precolonial Africa.[23] To the contrary, this is not the sense one obtains from the secondary historical material. Consider the following examples. The raja of Siak on Sumatra claimed the right to extract downriver resources and "affairs pertaining to external diplomacy and defence."[24] On the island of Sulawesi in modern-day Indonesia, otherwise autonomous polities deferred to the ruler (*datu*) "in matters of tribute and war only."[25] In nineteenth-century Nigeria, vassals of most Yoruba states had "no control over external affairs," something that characterized imperial rule in the Oyo and Ibadan Empires.[26] After conquering the Akin states of Ghana, the king (*asantehene*) of Asante forbade vassal kingdoms such as Akyem from going to war without permission and thus controlled "the foreign relations of the provinces."[27] In India, one of the goals of Safdar Jang, nawab of Awadh, was to secede from the Mughal Empire by "conduct[ing] an independent foreign policy." Richard Barnett lists seven features of successor states to the Mughal Empire that established the degree of their independence, one of which was to "engage in independent diplomatic and military activity."[28] In Japan, a key restraint on the autonomous daimyo, or regional lord, was that the daimyo could not engage in independent foreign policy.[29]

Rulers seem to have differentiated between relations with vassals and relations with outsiders across diverse contexts. Borders were often fuzzy and indeterminate, which made it difficult or impossible to draw a line demarcating what was inside (i.e., internal to) and what was outside (i.e., external to) the state. But that doesn't mean that there was no inside or outside, just that the boundaries were wide or not easily discernible. Siam was no less an independent state just because it had unclear boundaries in the nineteenth century.[30] Vague inside/outside distinctions matter more for peripheral polities with nominal relations of subordination to a state or states, as in the examples of Tippu Tip and Rabih az-Zubayr. In these cases, we defer to context-specific interpretations of what these hierarchies meant and the extent to which they constrained the freedom of polities to relate and contract with other states.

With a focal definition of the state, it is rather straightforward to develop a concept of the *state system*. Following Tilly once more, we contend that "states form systems to the extent that they interact, and to the degree that their interaction significantly affects each party's fate."[31] The basic idea here and in the literature more broadly is that state systems are composed of state units that interact and have effects on one another. This, of course, invites various questions regarding the intensity of the interaction as well as the scope and the degree to which states are influenced by the system. As Barry Buzan and Richard Little note, we could imagine different types of systems ranging from those that are only thinly connected along sociocultural lines to those that include dense institutional and economic linkages.[32] A different question pertains to the boundaries of a state system. After all, the early-modern period to some extent comprised several regional systems or subsystems that were loosely connected to a developing world system. Our approach in the book is to utilize a rather spare definition of the state system and put in abeyance the questions of scope and exactness. By doing so, we can then analyze a set of state systems and see how they varied.

Following Buzan and Little, we argue that to compare systems one needs to examine the extent to which a state shares sovereignty with entities below and above it (i.e., with other states), what they term "structural differentiation" and "functional differentiation."[33] Although we adopt these concepts, we prefer to use the less cumbersome and more recognizable terms *centralization* and *sovereign integration* in our analysis.[34] Centralization (structural differentiation) measures political order below the state, assessing the extent to which rulers delegate key prerogatives to substate actors and polities.[35] Sovereign integration (functional differentiation), or "integration" for short, is a measure of political order above the state, apprehending the degree to which rulers hand over authority functions to other states (i.e., to other entities with external sovereignty). Centralization and sovereign integration are concepts measured at the unit level that can then be aggregated to summarize features of a state system. A system with high levels of integration exists where many states hand over authority functions to other sovereign entities or institutions above the state. A system with high levels of decentralization exists where a large proportion of the states leave sovereign rights in the hands of vassals.

Let us return to our hypothetical state system with a, b, and c to illustrate these concepts. When we left the illustration, there were two states in the system, a and c, where a controlled the external relations of b but not its extraction rights. State a is (relatively speaking) decentralized because b still controls its extraction rights.[36] Now suppose that a takes control of

b's extraction rights by, for example, collecting taxes with governors and bureaucrats appointed by the ruler. State a is now more centralized because it has removed b's extraction prerogatives. Systems where states allocate decision-making powers to other substate entities—powerful families, regional kingdoms, and cities—exhibit high levels of decentralization.[37] We have kept the illustration simple, but these hierarchies might run several levels down if, for example, b has its own vassals.

Next, imagine that a also takes control of the extraction rights of c but not of its external relations. This is sovereign integration.[38] The United States, for example, controlled the Dominican Republic's revenue-collection infrastructure in the early twentieth century even though both were formally independent states.[39] The United Kingdom and France controlled Egypt's revenue collection for parts of the nineteenth century even though Egypt was an independent state.[40] The European Union is an institution that limits its member states' ability to formulate monetary and trade policy or policies related to human rights, the environment, and taxation. Systems where states pool aspects of their decision-making either through treaty or the creation of international organizations or both have high levels of sovereign integration. When few states share sovereign rights, there is a low level of sovereign integration.

Centralization is different from state formation.[41] State formation is when a state becomes a state. In our framework, this is when an otherwise autonomous polity gains control over its external relations (or when a vassal becomes a ruler). Levels of centralization vary within the sample of formed states. Few would deny that the Oyo Empire and Dahomey were states in West Africa (not the historians that we read, at least), but Dahomey was more centralized than Oyo. Vietnam (or, specifically, the Ngyuen Dynasty) was a state from 1802 (and before) through to French colonization in 1885, but its level of centralization increased through this period, especially in the 1830s and 1840s.

Centralization is also different from democracy, or the methods through which leaders are selected and institutions constrain executive decision-making. This is an important distinction because authors sometimes speak of centralization as autocracy, where the ruler removes elite constraints on decision-making. States can be centralized in the sense that there are few other autonomous centers of power but constrained in their decision-making by constitutions and electorates (such as modern-day

Norway). Similarly, rulers might be able to appoint their successors and dominate the court in the capital but control very little outside the city gates.[42]

Formulating a clear and operational definition of the state is critical for comparing state systems. Such a definition identifies the units for comparison and delineates political order inside and outside (or below and above) the state. Some critics may contend that our internal/external distinction is modern or Eurocentric, but as we have illustrated, the distinction regularly holds even across pre- and early-modern systems outside of Europe. Buzan and Little see elements of the inside/outside distinction emerging as early as the first chiefdoms and note that chiefs typically retained the sole "authority to engage in diplomatic relations with other chiefdoms."[43] Such distinctions were rarely as formalized as they are in the modern order, and, to be sure, we find considerable variation in the degree of autonomy inside and between states. But the inside/outside distinction is observable across historical locales. Our concept of the state does not require that it has the legal trappings and implications of contemporary sovereignty.[44] When we do use the term *sovereignty*, we are referring to the lighter sense in which an independent state controls its relations with other states.[45] There is, of course, variation with respect to how states compose themselves internally or vis-à-vis other states, but much of this variation is a matter of centralization and sovereign integration.[46] We discuss this variation in chapter 3.

THE INTERNATIONAL SYSTEM(S) DATASET (ISD)

Having established our concept of the state, we now need to explain how we operationalized that concept. We need to detail the criteria we used to identify states and to discuss the basic findings. That brings us to the ISD.

Our original purpose in developing the ISD was to correct a bias in existing IR datasets that excluded states in large portions of the world during the precolonial period. For example, figure 2.1 shows the number of states recorded in the COW State System Membership list for the pre–League of Nations period (1816–1920) and their approximate locations in relation to contemporary states.[47] The COW project has been the foundation of statistical work in IR and has provided the primary roster of states in the international system. Figure 2.1 gives the impression that the

THE BIRTH AND DEATH OF STATES BEFORE THE LEAGUE OF NATIONS

African continent was stateless, as was South Asia, Southeast Asia, and the Pacific. That impression is consistent with one of the received wisdoms we identified in chapter 1—that most of the non-European world was stateless in the nineteenth century. Yet historical sources point to numerous states and systems in these regions.[48] We know, for instance, that West Africa was amid a turbulent period of state birth and state death. Why are these states excluded from the COW list?

The regions appear empty of states because of the criteria used by the COW project to identify states in the pre-1920 era. The main criterion to qualify as a state in the COW register is that a polity needed to have diplomatic representation by both France and Britain at the level of charge d'affaires or higher.[49] This is a high threshold because it requires France and Britain to have sent formal diplomatic or ambassadorial staff to a receiver state with full powers to act on its own behalf. The purpose behind the criterion was to detect whether the polity in question was recognized as an independent state (external sovereignty). The architects of COW pinned international recognition in the pre-1920 era to Britain and France because those states maintained thorough records of diplomatic contact and because they were arguably the core of the expanding European state system. Moreover, there were no globe-spanning associations of sovereign states like the League of Nations or the UN prior to 1920—sovereignty clubs with rosters of membership. As such, the originators of COW chose Britain and France because they were the two key "legitimizers."[50]

The criteria used in dataset construction can have important downstream consequences. The state systems of the nineteenth century were not fully connected and are better envisaged as a set of regional systems that were gradually drawing together. Neither Britain nor France had sufficient presence to recognize many states at the required level. In Africa, for example, only two Europeans had even navigated the Niger River by 1831, the "young, impressionable, and barely educated" Richard Lander and his younger brother.[51] First contact between Europeans and the Bugandan Kingdom didn't occur until 1862. Europeans barely even knew these states existed by the mid–nineteenth century, let alone established formal diplomatic missions. France and Britain simply were not the relevant regional powers for many states. For the Luba Kingdom in Central Africa, the Lunda and the Belgians were important, not Britain or France. In Bali, the relevant powers were the competing local kingdoms and the

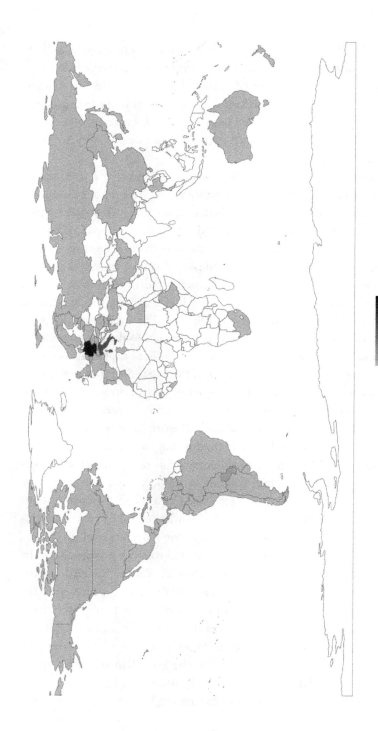

FIGURE 2.1. World map of states per COW data, 1816-1920. *Source:* COW data sourced from Correlates of War Project, "State System Membership List, v2016."

Dutch. The French were a small, distant, coastal trading enclave in the eyes of the massive Sokoto Caliphate in West Africa in 1816. At a basic level, Britain and France were simply more likely to recognize states that were geographically closer to them, which is perhaps one of the reasons why China and Japan did not join the European-based system, according to COW, until 1860. Importantly, diplomatic recognition is a strategic act,[52] and by conditioning statehood on the diplomatic practices of France and Britain, COW encoded the biases and selection processes of French and British diplomats into the DNA of its list. As a thought experiment, consider that the COW list and the family of datasets keyed to it have formed the backbone of quantitative research in IR. Would that research have derived substantially different conclusions on a range of topics if the designers had pinned diplomatic relations not to Britain and France but to China and the Ottoman Porte?

We are not the first to identify or attempt to redress these issues. Kristian Gleditsch and Michael Ward have created a list of states that relaxes the recognition criterion.[53] However, in their list there is no requirement that the political unit be externally sovereign, and, as a result, Gleditsch and Ward included entities even if their foreign policy was formally controlled by another, as Oman's was from 1891 to 1971.[54] In addition, Gleditsch and Ward missed a substantial number of states that have been picked up in the ISD. In her work on state death, Tanisha Fazal adds sixteen new states to the COW member list in the pre-1920 period and modifies the start date of another twenty-two by including states that had signed treaties of commerce, alliance, or navigation with either Britain or France even if they did not receive diplomatic missions.[55] In doing so, she demonstrates how quickly state membership expands by lowering the level of required diplomatic relations. Finally, the more recent historical V-DEM dataset records the features of eighty states from as early as 1789.[56] In contrast to the ISD, however, the historical V-DEM data are narrower because of the requirement that states must have a continuous existence into the twentieth century to be included. In Africa, for example, most states disappeared with colonialism by the end of the nineteenth century and are therefore not captured in the historical V-DEM. Other projects exist, such as GeaCron and Africamap, that have attempted to map historical statehood but are not based on a consistent definition of the state and tend to conflate states with ethnic groups and even small state systems. For example, the

GeaCron project treats Hausa in Nigeria as a state even though it was not a state in 1800 but rather a collection of independent states.

It must be acknowledged that these datasets and projects have made valuable contributions to IR scholarship. The COW project helped kick-start quantitative work in IR. Nevertheless, they present incomplete lists of independent states. We created the ISD to provide a more accurate list of states and a more comprehensive understanding of the development of the international system(s) since the early nineteenth century.

We used the following criteria in the ISD to identify states. A state must have: (1) a population of at least 10,000; (2) autonomy over a specific territory or set of places; and (3) sovereignty that is either uncontested or acknowledged by the relevant international actors. These criteria reflect the conception of statehood discussed earlier in the chapter. Sovereignty has an internal and external dimension. Internally, a state stands at the top of a hierarchy and is a force-wielding organization. In the ideal form, a state possesses a complete monopoly on the use of physical force within its borders, but few if any states possess such a monopoly.[57] Externally, a sovereign state has control over its external relations. By using criteria that stress the importance of internal and external control, we are taking the same general tack as COW and are consistent with the IR scholarship on sovereignty and the study of the international system(s).[58]

The first criterion, population size, has a practical purpose. A population floor is a scope condition for the unit of analysis, and its inclusion helps with data collection by filtering small entities about which it can be hard to gather information. Although any population threshold is in a sense arbitrary, we chose 10,000 because it is focal, is not too small to hinder our data-collection efforts, and provides consistency across the entire 1816–2016 period given that many UN member states have populations that barely exceed(ed) 10,000.[59]

The second criterion is about internal control; to count, a state must have autonomy over a specific territory or set of places. The government of the state must be superordinate to all other entities and government structures within that territory and have an identifiable elite and administrative infrastructure to extract resources from its territory. The state need not possess clearly defined borders; many states had fuzzy boundaries. Furthermore, it need not have control over *all* areas of governance, and, in practice, there is significant variation within states in terms of how decision-making powers are distributed.[60] For example, the Oyo Empire in nineteenth-century West Africa controlled little more than external relations, leadership succession, and judicial authority over capital crimes in relation to its vassals, while the vassals retained wide-ranging autonomy over decision-making in relation to taxation methods, policing, and local lawmaking.[61] These are variations in political centralization: the degree to which sovereigns delegate key prerogatives to substate actors and entities.[62] As we discussed earlier, a key element that defines a sovereign and that differentiates it from subordinate polities is its ability to formally manage its external relations.[63] As such, the second criterion is connected theoretically to the third.

The third criterion is meant to pick up external sovereignty that is either uncontested or acknowledged by the relevant international actors. Here, our purpose was to avoid the Eurocentric bias in COW and develop the concept of sufficient recognition.[64] For a period until the late 1800s, Japan existed in a relatively hermetic condition with few diplomatic linkages, but its sovereign independence was uncontested. Other states, such as Nicaragua, engaged in diplomatic relations, but just not with either Britain or France, and were regarded by their neighbors as sovereign. By taking a regionally sensitive approach, we can ascertain whether sufficient recognition was achieved by the polity. Accordingly, we define the relevant international actors as those states that, for all practical purposes, are the key legitimizers of the state in question. A regional approach also allows us to be sensitive to varying patterns of order and local systems of recognition. As we discuss in chapter 5, being a vassal of the Mughal Empire in the early nineteenth century was not a loss of sovereignty but recognition of independence.[65] Being a tributary of Karangasem, Borno, or Asante did not always imply the loss of external sovereignty. The general disconnectedness and gradual development of the international system(s) prior to 1920 render it problematic to make any one international state the key legitimizer. Although the key actors can vary depending on context, we argue (and have found) that they are identifiable.

Control over external relations is a key element for units in our dataset. It stresses the ability of states to interact with other states and be recognized by the relevant external actors as a state participating independently in an international system. We require that no other state has the formal right to determine the polity's external affairs. If we found evidence that neighboring states or major powers in the region recognized a state as independent, then we treated it as independent. Of course, this factor can be ambiguous in cases where other states gradually take control of another state's external affairs. In such cases, we recorded a state exit (death) when the larger state and other relevant actors began to treat the state in question as nonsovereign.[66] Altogether, these criteria constitute the conceptual foundation of the ISD. For a more detailed description, we invite readers to explore our article in *International Interactions*.[67]

The full dataset lists 439 states and 497 state episodes over the 1816–2016 period. The combined total represents a substantial increase over the totals for COW and other datasets, which identify roughly half that number. Most of the new cases were in Africa, South Asia, and maritime Southeast Asia during the 1816–1920 period. For example, COW identifies just 6 states on the African continent prior to decolonization: Ethiopia (1898–1936, from 1941), South Africa (from 1920), Morocco (1847–1912), Egypt (1855–1882, from 1937), Liberia (from 1920), and Tunisia (1825–1881). In contrast, the ISD identifies 118 state episodes during this time (116 unique states), which is also a substantial increase in relation to other projects that have aimed to identify states in Africa.[68] Likewise, whereas COW identifies only 2 states in South Asia prior to decolonization, Afghanistan (from 1919) and Nepal (from 1920), we identify 38. Figure 2.2 shows the number of ISD-identified states that existed within what are now the boundaries of a contemporary sovereign state. Standouts include Nigeria, India, and Indonesia—all outside Europe. These states were once the locations of regional state systems.

STATE BIRTH AND STATE DEATH

We have argued that the nineteenth century was composed of hundreds of independent states. However, previous research has neglected to study them comprehensively. That is unfortunate because the birth and death of states are of fundamental concern in international relations. How states are created, how they expire, and the frequency with which these processes occur are vital characteristics of regional systems. In this section, we discuss the patterns revealed in the ISD.

Fazal observes that state death was rare after 1945, a pattern supported in the ISD.[69] As figure 2.3 shows, state death was very common in the

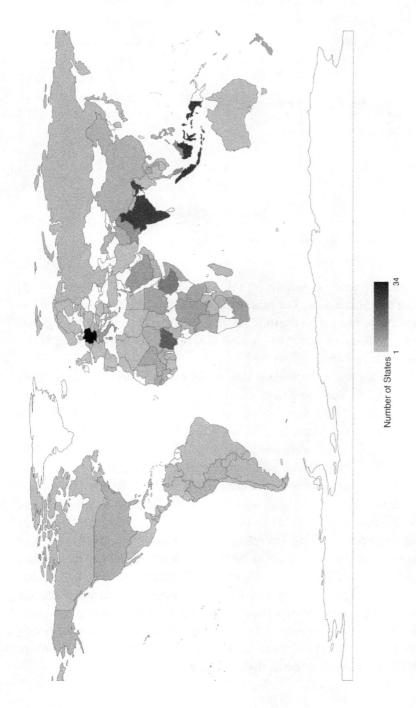

FIGURE 2.2. Number of states per the ISD, 1816–1920, within the borders of contemporary states.

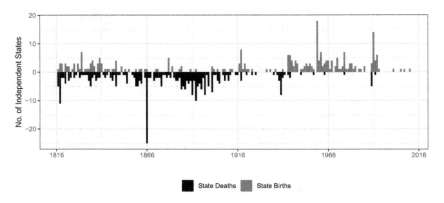

FIGURE 2.3. Global state births and deaths per the ISD, 1816-2016.

nineteenth century, especially with the acceleration of colonialism through Africa and South Asia. The nineteenth century is rightly characterized as a century of mass state death, reflecting the final enclosure of the global system.[70] However, state birth was also common at the beginning of the nineteenth century.

Figure 2.4 zooms in to show that in the early nineteenth century state birth in Africa and the Americas outstripped state death. Africa saw the rise of states such as Sokoto, Tokolor, the Wassulu Empire, the Gaza Empire, and the Zulu Kingdom. Nearly one-third of all state episodes in West Africa began in the nineteenth century, rising to nearly 45 percent in South Africa. In addition, nearly one-quarter of states in Southeast Asia were born in the nineteenth century, and almost all states in the Americas were born as the Spanish and Portuguese Empires collapsed. These were dynamic regions in terms of latecomer state formation.[71] The more accurate picture of the nineteenth century is of roughly equivalent levels of state creation and state death at the beginning of the century that by and large transitioned into state death. State birth dominated again in the post-1945 period, particularly because of decolonization.[72] Africa and Southeast Asia are unique in experiencing two waves of state birth in two centuries. Overall, these patterns are strongly suggestive that cycles of state birth, collapse, and reconstitution were a common feature of IR before the enclosure of the international system in the late nineteenth century.

THE BIRTH AND DEATH OF STATES BEFORE THE LEAGUE OF NATIONS

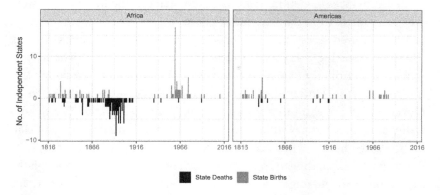

FIGURE 2.4. State births and deaths in Africa and the Americas per the ISD, 1816–2016.

State Birth

How were these states created? Did they emerge by conquering smaller polities and establishing new hierarchies, or did they secede from other states? Most states formed by breaking off from an existing state or emerging in the wake of a collapsing empire or larger state, with the highest rates of secession in the Americas, Central Asia, mainland and archipelagic Southeast Asia, and South Asia, along with Europe. For example, nearly nine in ten new states in Europe between 1816 and 1910 were formed by breaking off from a host state (see table 2.1). German states account for most of these secessions after the collapse of the Napoleonic Empire and the dissolution of the Rhine Confederation and the Kingdom of Westphalia, established under occupation by Napoleon.[73] Most states on the Indian subcontinent are successor states to the Mughal Empire, but we also find new states being formed over territory that was either stateless or ruled by smaller-scale polities in the rugged terrain of the Himalayas (Nepal, Sikkim, and Bhutan) or in the dense jungles of Southeast Asia (Sulu Sultanate). Southeast Asian states also emerged from the collapse of the Majapahit and Mataram Empires in Indonesia, along with numerous small states that seceded from the Gegel court on the Indonesian island of Bali. Most Central and South American states emerged as the Spanish Empire dissolved or from failed attempts at unification in the wake of Spanish decline, as in Gran-Colombia, the Peru-Bolivian Confederation, and the

United Provinces of Central America. New states in the Middle East were mostly splinters from the Ottoman Empire.

We measured secession in a broad way, including traditional secession, where a preexisting polity gains independence from another.[74] The separation of Ilorin from the Oyo Empire in 1796 is an example of secession in this traditional sense. However, secession also includes cases whereby states or movements form within existing states and rapidly expand. The Sokoto Caliphate is coded as having seceded from the Gobir Emirate as Usman Dan Fodio started his jihad from Gobir in 1804 capturing parts of his host state first and then expanding to encompass much of West Africa.[75] Although the expansion of Sokoto might be understood as territorial consolidation in this case, the original formation of an administrative structure occurred within another state that became independent and conquered other states.[76]

African regions, however, exhibit lower proportions of secession-type starts. Only one in two were secession births in West Africa, East-Central Africa, and southern Africa. More African states formed over territory without a clear state structure or over areas with small states and chiefdoms rather than by existing states voluntarily merging. One example is the Gaza Empire, which formed around 1821 in Mozambique. Gaza was formed after Nguini migrants moved north and conquered smaller-scale chiefdoms in southern Mozambique and northern Zimbabwe.[77] States forming over smaller-scale or more decentralized political areas in Africa likely reflects the difficulties of projecting power over space in precolonial Africa and the low population density, which left regions governed by small polities or decentralized kin networks. Such a structure, broadly speaking, characterized parts of Central and East Africa, along with parts of southern Africa. There are no clear-cut examples of states in Africa forming through the voluntary unification of smaller states.[78] Low rates of secession births may also reflect the lack of mega-empires like the Ottoman, Mughal, Spanish, and Napoleonic Empires from which large numbers of states could secede. In the Pacific, Tonga and the Maori states of New Zealand also formed by dominating zones of decentralized or small-scale rule.[79] Burma and Annam also formed by conquering and unifying smaller polities. Likewise, the Kathiri and Qu'aiti Sultanates in modern-day Yemen and Oman incorporated loosely organized family lineages and tribal formations under their rule.[80]

The line between secession and territorial consolidation is blurry in the African cases. Numerous states formed as elites or royal families fled military defeat and migrated from their home state to occupy parts of another state or tributary, from which a new state was created.[81] For example, after the collapse of the Oyo Empire in the 1830s, the *alafin* (king) moved his capital to "New Oyo," and Oyo survived there as a state in a much-reduced form.[82] Whether the territory of the new state is considered part of an older state is sometimes difficult to establish. Nonetheless, the ISD data capture the more fluid and dynamic processes of state formation in Africa, which were not clear-cut cases of secession (although such cases exist), as dominated in other parts of the world, or cases of preexisting states unifying, but complicated processes involving migration, religious revolution, secession, and the establishment of state authority over areas of decentralized rule.

There is also a trend toward secession over the 1816–1910 period. States that were already in existence in 1816 were born through secession in 67 percent of cases. Between 1816 and 1850, the number rose to 74 percent (62 cases) before rising again to 91 percent of state births in the 1850–1910 period (46 cases). As European states came to enclose more territory within their empires, building new states atop decentralized or small-scale societies—a common form of global state making in 1816—was largely extinct by 1920. Table 2.1 displays these patterns from 1816 to 1920.

State Death

The number of states collapsed over the nineteenth century. There were 230 independent states in 1816 but only 80 by 1900 and 65 in 1919—aggregate death rates of 65 percent and 72 percent, respectively. In 1916, there were only 57 states, the lowest number in the two-century period we cover. You would probably have to look back many centuries to find a similar global low. What processes account for this trend? Although the main picture of mass state death through European colonization is true, there are important nuances as indigenous processes of state death were more prominent earlier in the nineteenth century.

We differentiated between four different types of state death. *Colonization* occurs when the state is extinguished by a noncontiguous state, as characterized the wave of European dominance through South Asia, Southeast Asia, and Africa in the eighteenth and nineteenth centuries. *Conquest/annexation* occurs when the state is extinguished by a local power and absorbed into the territory of the occupying state. *Unification* occurs when

TABLE 2.1
Regional Patterns in State Formation and Death, 1816–1920

ISD region	Start by secession	Nineteenth-century birth	Borders	Violent end	Colonization death	Conquest death	Unification death	Ended before 1920
Americas	0.87	0.83	1.00	0.56	0.10	0.40	0.20	0.33
Western Europe	0.89	0.11	1.00	0.40	0.00	0.29	0.67	0.73
Eastern Europe	0.93	0.93	0.93	0.90	0.00	1.00	0.00	0.13
West Africa	0.50	0.29	0.10	0.85	0.69	0.29	0.02	0.96
East-Central Africa	0.53	0.23	0.18	0.76	0.51	0.37	0.03	0.94
South Africa	0.47	0.45	0.40	0.76	0.63	0.32	0.05	0.95
Middle East and North Africa	0.64	0.44	0.48	0.76	0.48	0.48	0.00	0.72
Central Asia	1.00	0.00	0.00	1.00	0.00	1.00	0.00	1.00
South Asia	0.78	0.05	0.18	0.59	0.95	0.05	0.00	0.95
East Asia	0.40	0.33	0.67	1.00	0.20	0.80	0.00	0.50
Mainland Southeast Asia	0.71	0.00	0.29	0.83	0.50	0.50	0.00	0.86
Southeast Asia	0.88	0.26	0.15	0.50	0.86	0.10	0.05	1.00
Oceania	0.22	0.56	0.50	0.00	0.43	0.00	0.57	0.78

Note: Figures are percentages in decimal form.

multiple states voluntarily agree to merge and form a larger state or confederation. Finally, *dissolution* occurs when a state collapses, and the "rump" or host state also disappears (the collapse of the Soviet Union is one example, the collapse of the Oyo Empire in West Africa is another).

As expected, most states died as they were colonized by noncontiguous (i.e., European) powers across South and Southeast Asia and the Pacific. Ninety-five percent of states in South Asia and 86 percent of states in Southeast Asia that existed before 1920 were extinguished by colonization.[83] East and South India were colonized by the beginning of the nineteenth century as the British swept west across the Indian subcontinent. Indonesian states were colonized by the Dutch, Malaysia by the British, Annam (Vietnam) by the French. In 1905, for example, Aceh was defeated by the Dutch and integrated into the colonial regime.[84]

But colonization is not the full story of state death. Colonization explains most but not all state deaths in Africa and the Middle East before 1920. Sixty-eight percent of state deaths before 1920 in West Africa, 63 percent in southern Africa, 59 percent in the Middle East, and 55 percent in East-Central Africa were by colonization. However, local powers also conquered and absorbed other local and often older states. For example, the Sokoto Caliphate conquered Nupe and played a hand in the defection of Ilorin from the Oyo Empire and the empire's subsequent dissolution in West Africa.[85] The Tukolor Empire absorbed the older Kaarta and Segu states and conquered Macina, while the Zulu Empire in the south absorbed the Ndwandwe and Mthetwa Kingdoms (local South African states). Ethiopia was its own state system in the nineteenth century, hosting more than a dozen states, all of which were eventually absorbed into the Ethiopian Empire. Had the ISD commenced with the earlier date of 1800, this picture would be even more dynamic because the Sokoto Caliphate conquered numerous independent Hausa states, such as Gobir and Zaria, between the 1790s and 1810.[86] Much of the Middle East was under Ottoman suzerainty or European rule by the beginning of our dataset, but of those states that emerged and survived in the 1816–1920 period, only 48 percent died by colonization (although there are a small number of cases). The remainder of deaths are accounted for by the struggle among Nejd (modern-day Saudi Arabia), the Ottoman Empire, and Jammal Shammar and the conquest of other local states by Nejd (Hejaz, Asir, and Jabal Shammar).[87] States in Central Asia were more commonly conquered by local powers, in this case Russia, which conquered and incorporated

Bukhara (1873), Khiva (1873), Kokand (1875), and Dagestan (1859).[88] China also conquered and absorbed Tibet in 1851.[89]

Nearly nine in ten state deaths in West Africa before 1920 were violent, compared to 59 percent in South Asia, around 50 percent in Southeast Asia, 30 percent in western Europe, and 56 percent in the Americas. More state deaths in Africa were by conquest/annexation, which were almost always violent. Nonetheless, violence associated with colonialism also varied across regions, where, again, it was most violent in Africa. Eighty percent of 71 state deaths by colonization in Africa were coded as violent in the ISD data, compared to 57 percent in South and Central Asia (35 deaths), and 51 percent in the Asia-Pacific (41 deaths). Anecdotally, the leaders of local states—especially in India—negotiated treaties of protection with advancing British forces, sometimes to bolster their position against other, local, internal, or external rivals. Udaipur, for example, concluded a protectorate treaty with the British in 1818 to shield it against Maratha attacks and taxes, as did Jodhpur, Jaipur, and Jaisalmer.[90] It is, nonetheless, unclear why colonization was so much more violent in Africa.[91]

Parts of the Americas were decolonized during the eighteenth and nineteenth century, and recolonization and conquest were uncommon there compared with Africa and Asia, accounting for just 10 percent of the outcomes of state episodes before 1920. Dissolution and unification were more common (e.g., unifying to form the United Provinces of Central America in 1823, only to dissolve again in 1840).[92] Unification in general was a rare form of state death outside of western Europe, where 67 percent of state episodes ended by unification. The formation of the North German Confederation in 1866 and then of the Confederation of German States in 1871 accounts for most state deaths by unification outside of the Americas.[93] The unification of Italy in 1860 and the creation of Aotearoa from the Maori states (Mataatua, Ngapuhi, Waikato, and Wanganui) in 1835 also are important examples of state death via unification.[94]

There are few clear global temporal trends in state death; the rate of colonization is steady over the 1816–1850 and 1851–1920 periods as Europeans moved across different continents at different points of the nineteenth century. For example, only 8 percent of the 13 state deaths in Africa from 1816 to 1850 were by colonization, whereas 69 percent were conquests by local states. The colonization rate rises to 69 percent between 1851 and 1920 (100 state deaths). This trend is flipped in South and Central Asia, where 96 percent of

THE BIRTH AND DEATH OF STATES BEFORE THE LEAGUE OF NATIONS

the 28 state deaths between 1816 and 1850 were by colonization, dropping to 57 percent between 1851 and 1920 (14 deaths). This transition marks the arrival of British colonization at the edge of the Russian sphere of influence, with Russia conquering Central Asian states in the late nineteenth century.

In summary, European colonialism explains the dramatic decline in independent states, but in the early nineteenth century, especially outside of South Asia, local processes of state death and state creation still prevailed. These systems give us a glimpse into how state formation and state death unfolded prior to the establishment of a single, global, international system.

DEAD STATES

There were several purposes in this chapter. The first was to specify core concepts such as the state and the state system. The second was to introduce the ISD—explain the reasons behind its creation, how it was coded, and what its basic findings are. The third was to chart patterns of state birth and death, which revealed a balance of state creation and destruction in the early nineteenth century, followed by a wave of mass state death. We now conclude by cataloging the independent states that expired during this period. Since the great majority of these states were not resurrected in the twentieth century, their names will be new to most readers, and it is therefore fitting to say them.

We identified a total of 270 states that expired during the 1816–1920 period. This period roughly corresponds to what has been called the long nineteenth century, and it was clearly a time of mass state death. Tables 2.2, 2.3, and 2.4 list all the states that died by sorting them into three regional groups: Africa, Asia, and the Americas and Europe. Note that some states that died were later resurrected (e.g., Korea), defined simply as a case where a former ISD state was reborn after 1920 and, with few exceptions (e.g., Zanzibar), exists today. Some states existed at several different temporal points in the nineteenth century (e.g., Gianyar). Not all states died violently—some expired through peaceful unifications—and not all died because of European colonization. Finally, although many states lost their external sovereignty, many retained aspects of their internal autonomy through forms of indirect rule and exist today as traditional kingdoms or regions in federal states.[95]

Here is a summary by region. Table 2.2 lists the 113 states that expired in Africa. Of the 14 states that would later be resurrected, 6 were in North

TABLE 2.2
State Deaths in Africa

State Name	Start Year	End Year	Resurrected?
Abuja Emirate	1828	1902	
Adamawa	1841	1893	
Algeria	1816	1847	Yes
Anjouan	1816	1886	
Ankole	1816	1898	
Aro Confederacy	1816	1902	
Ashanti	1816	1896	
Azanda	1816	1896	
Bagirmi	1816	1897	
Bamum	1816	1884	
Begemder	1816	1855	
Benin Empire	1816	1897	
Borgu	1816	1898	
Brakna	1816	1905	
Buganda	1816	1893	
Bunyoro	1816	1893	
Cayor	1816	1861	
Dahomey	1823	1894	Yes
Darfur	1816	1874	
Egba	1830	1893	
Egypt	1833	1882	Yes
Enarya (Limmu)	1816	1882	
Fouta Djallon	1816	1887	
Fouta Toro	1816	1891	
Fuladu	1872	1896	
Funj Sultanate	1816	1821	
Gaza Empire	1821	1895	
Geledi Sultanate	1816	1908	
Gera	1835	1896	
Gobir-Tibiri	1836	1898	
Gojjam	1816	1855	
Gomma	1816	1886	
Gonja	1816	1892	
Gumma	1816	1902	
Harrar	1816	1875	
Hiraab Emirate	1816	1900	
Hobyo (Obbia) Sultanate	1884	1889	
Ibadan Empire	1862	1893	
Igala Kingdom	1816	1886	
Ijaye	1832	1862	
Ijebu	1816	1892	
Ijesa	1816	1870	
Ile-Ife	1816	1849	
Illorin	1816	1824	
Jimma-Kakka	1830	1883	
Jolof (Djoloff or Wolof)	1816	1885	
Kaabu Empire	1816	1867	
Kaarta	1816	1854	
Kaffa	1816	1887	
Kanem-Bornu	1816	1893	

State Name	Start Year	End Year	Resurrected?
Kasanje	1816	1911	
Kazembe	1816	1872	
Ketu Kingdom	1816	1886	
Karagwe Kingdom	1816	1891	
Kong Empire	1816	1889	
Kongo Kingdom	1816	1888	
Kuba	1816	1900	
Lesotho	1823	1848	Yes
Lesotho	1852	1868	Yes
Libya	1816	1835	Yes
Loango Kingdom	1816	1834	
Luba	1816	1891	
Lunda Empire	1816	1885	
Madagascar	1816	1895	Yes
Majeerteen Sultanate	1816	1889	
Mandara	1816	1902	
Mandinka Empire	1878	1887	
Mangbetu Kingdom	1816	1873	
Maradi	1819	1898	
Massina	1816	1862	
Menabe	1816	1850	
Moheli	1830	1886	
Morocco	1816	1912	Yes
Mthetwa	1816	1817	
Ndebele Kingdom	1822	1893	
Ndwandwe Kingdom	1816	1820	
Nupe	1816	1832	
Nyungu Kingdom	1880	1894	
Oaugadougou	1816	1896	
Orange Free State	1854	1902	
Ovimbundu	1816	1902	
Owo	1816	1893	
Oyo Empire	1816	1833	
Rozvi Empire	1816	1834	
Ruanda	1816	1894	Yes
Saloum	1816	1865	
Segou	1816	1861	
Shilluk Kingdom	1816	1863	
Shoa	1816	1889	
Sikasso	1816	1898	
Sise Empire	1835	1881	
Sokoto Caliphate	1816	1903	
Sudan	1885	1898	Yes
Swazi Kingdom	1816	1894	Yes
Tegali Kingdom	1816	1884	
Teke Kingdom	1816	1883	
Tenkodogo	1816	1896	
Tigray	1816	1855	
Tokolor	1848	1893	
Toro	1830	1900	
Transvaal	1852	1877	
Trarza Emirate	1816	1904	

(continued)

TABLE 2.2
(continued)

State Name	Start Year	End Year	Resurrected?
Tunisia	1816	1881	Yes
Unyanyembe	1816	1892	
Urambo	1860	1890	
Urundi	1816	1890	Yes
Wadai	1816	1909	
Walo	1816	1855	
Yatenga	1816	1895	
Yeke Kingdom	1880	1891	
Zanzibar	1856	1890	Yes
Zinder (Damagaram)	1841	1899	
Zululand	1817	1879	

Africa.[96] Table 2.3 lists the 106 states that were extinguished in Asia, of which 13 would be resurrected in the post-1920 period.[97] To be sure, by grouping all these states into one "Asia" category, we obscure the stark regional differences. As we discussed earlier, state death in South Asia generally preceded state death in Southeast Asia. Finally, table 2.4 lists the states that died in the Americas and Europe, regions with different state-death patterns. Of the 10 states that died in the Americas, 6 would later be reborn. The four that were not resurrected include the Republic Texas, the United Provinces of Central America, the Peru-Bolivia Confederation, and Hawai'i. Strikingly, of the 41 states that died in Europe, only Montenegro would later be reborn. Aside from Montenegro and Austria-Hungary, all the state deaths occurred in the context of the German and Italian unification processes.

One can see that, when viewed broadly, the pre-1920 state-extinction event is led by Africa and Asia, a finding that is consonant with the central theme of this book. Africa accounts for the largest share of state death, at 42 percent. It was especially intense in the sub-Saharan regions of the continent, where only 4 percent of the states that existed in the nineteenth century were still independent in 1910. Asia accounts for some 39 percent of the state deaths during this period, leaving Europe and the Americas to account for the remainder. All in all, 219 states were erased from the maps of Asia and Africa, and only 27 of them would later be reconstructed. To put this in perspective, the difference between these figures is 192, almost exactly the number of current UN members.

TABLE 2.3
State Deaths in Asia

State Name	Start Year	End Year	Resurrected?
Aceh	1816	1874	
Afghanistan	1816	1879	Yes
Annam	1816	1885	Yes
Aotearoa (New Zealand)	1835	1840	Yes
Asahan	1816	1865	
Asir	1818	1872	
Assam	1816	1821	
Badung	1816	1906	
Bahawalpur	1816	1838	
Bangli	1837	1909	
Benjermassin	1816	1860	
Bharatpur	1816	1826	
Bhopal	1816	1817	
Bhutan	1816	1910	Yes
Bikaner	1816	1818	
Bohol	1816	1829	
Bone	1816	1905	
Brunei	1816	1888	Yes
Bukhara	1816	1868	
Buleleng	1816	1849	
Bulungan	1816	1885	
Cambodia	1816	1863	Yes
Chamba	1816	1843	
Champasak	1816	1829	
Chien Khouang	1816	1831	
Chitral	1816	1878	
Cutch	1816	1819	
Dagestan	1834	1859	
Deli Sultanate	1816	1862	
Dhar	1816	1819	
Dir	1816	1895	
Eastern Turkestan	1866	1877	
Fiji	1871	1874	Yes
Gianyar	1816	1842	
Gianyar	1849	1883	
Gianyar	1893	1900	
Gowa	1816	1911	
Gwalior	1816	1818	
Herat	1829	1863	
Hunza	1816	1891	
Indore	1816	1818	
Jaipur	1816	1818	
Jaisalmer	1816	1818	
Jambi	1816	1834	
Jembrana	1818	1821	
Jembrana	1849	1853	
Jodhpur	1816	1818	
Johore	1816	1885	
Kalat	1816	1839	
Kapurthala	1816	1826	
Karangasem	1816	1849	

(continued)

TABLE 2.3
(continued)

State Name	Start Year	End Year	Resurrected?
Kathiri Sultanate	1849	1918	
Kedah	1816	1821	
Kelantan	1816	1902	
Khaipur	1816	1838	
Khiva	1816	1873	
Kishangarh	1816	1818	
Klungkung	1816	1911	
Kokand	1816	1876	
Korea	1816	1905	Yes
Kotah	1816	1817	
Kunduz	1816	1859	
Kutai	1816	1844	
Lahej Sultanate	1816	1898	
Luang Phrabang	1816	1893	
Luwu	1816	1906	
Manipur	1816	1891	
Mataatua	1816	1835	
Mataram	1816	1830	
Mataram Lombok	1839	1894	
Mengwi	1816	1823	
Minangkabau	1816	1837	
Myanmar	1816	1885	Yes
Nagpur	1816	1818	
Negeri Sembilan	1816	1887	
Nejd (Saudi Arabia)	1816	1818	Yes
Nejd (Saudi Arabia)	1843	1891	Yes
Ngapuhi	1816	1835	
Oman	1816	1891	Yes
Pahang	1863	1887	
Palembang	1816	1823	
Perak	1826	1874	
Poona	1816	1818	
Punjab	1816	1846	
Quaiti Sultanate	1849	1882	
Riau	1819	1824	
Sampthar	1816	1817	
Sarawak	1841	1888	
Sawantvadi	1816	1838	
Selangor	1816	1874	
Siak	1816	1858	
Sikkim	1816	1861	
Sind	1816	1843	
Singhbhum	1816	1820	
Sirohi	1816	1823	
Sultanate of Maguindanao	1816	1861	
Sulu Sultanate	1816	1851	
Tabanan	1816	1906	
Tampin	1836	1887	
Terengganu	1816	1909	
Tonga	1845	1900	Yes
Tonk	1816	1817	
Udaipur	1816	1818	
Vientiane	1816	1827	
Waikato	1816	1835	
Wanganui	1816	1835	

TABLE 2.4
State Deaths in Europe and the Americas

State Name	Start Year	End Year	Resurrected?
Anhalt-Bernburg	1816	1863	
Anhalt-Dessau	1816	1866	
Anhalt-Kothen	1816	1847	
Austria-Hungary	1816	1918	
Baden	1816	1871	
Bavaria	1816	1871	
Bolivia	1825	1836	Yes
Bremen	1816	1866	
Brunswick	1816	1866	
Cuba	1902	1906	Yes
Dominican Republic	1844	1861	Yes
Dominican Republic	1865	1916	Yes
Frankfurt	1816	1866	
Haiti	1816	1915	Yes
Hamburg	1816	1866	
Hanover	1816	1866	
Hawai'i	1816	1898	
Hesse Electoral	1816	1866	
Hesse Grand Ducal	1816	1867	
Hesse-Homburg	1816	1866	
Hohenzollern-Hechingen	1816	1849	
Hohenzollern-Sigmaringen	1816	1849	
Lippe	1816	1866	
Lubeck	1816	1866	
Lucca	1816	1847	
Mecklenburg Schwerin	1816	1866	
Mecklenburg Strelitz	1816	1866	
Modena	1816	1860	
Montenegro	1878	1918	Yes
Nassau	1816	1866	
Oldenburg	1816	1866	
Papal States	1816	1870	
Parma	1816	1860	
Peru	1821	1836	
Peru-Bolivian Confederation	1836	1839	
Reuss-Greiz	1816	1866	
Reuss-Schleiz	1816	1866	
Saxe-Altenburg	1826	1866	
Saxe-Coburg-Gotha	1826	1866	
Saxe-Meiningen-Hidburghausen	1816	1866	
Saxe-Wiemar-Eisenach	1816	1866	
Saxony	1816	1866	
Schaumburg-Lippe	1816	1866	
Schwarzburg-Rudolstadt	1816	1866	
Schwarzburg-Sondershausen	1816	1866	
Texas	1837	1846	
Tuscany	1816	1860	
Two Sicilies	1816	1860	
United Provinces of Cen. America	1823	1840	
Waldeck	1816	1868	
Wuerttemburg	1816	1870	

Readers will likely be unfamiliar with most of these state names, yet they existed little more than a century ago and were contemporaneous with the Concert of Europe. They were for the most part extinguished by the colonial process, and surprisingly few of them were resurrected during decolonization.

Chapter Three

THE COMPARATIVE DYNAMICS OF STATES AND SYSTEMS

Scholarship in international relations has for the most part been the study of one system that began in Europe and then integrated with other regional systems to become the global system. Although there has been temporal variation—for example, the contrast between the Concert of Europe and the United Nations—historical IR scholars have worked mostly with the evolution of one case. But without examining other state systems, how can we know if conclusions regarding conflict and state building, to name just one area of research, are generalizable beyond the system from which they were drawn? IR scholarship needs to move beyond its traditional intrasystem focus to a broader intersystem perspective.

Our objective is to conduct a comparative analysis of different state systems during the nineteenth century. We want to know not only how many states there were but also how these states and the systems they composed were structured and what factors shaped that structure. Achieving this objective requires a theoretical framework that is portable across historical locales, and it is to the development of that framework that we now turn. In the previous chapter, we defined the state, the state system, and several related concepts. We now develop and contrast two models, one consisting of centralized states (the billiard ball model) and one composed of decentralized states (the bull's-eye model). Following that, we discuss existing explanations for transitions from decentralized to centralized rule. A rich tradition sees centralized states rising from the pressures of war or the opportunities provided by trade and urban growth or a combination of the two. However, we argue that although trade and war might help explain the rise of European states (which is debated), low levels of interaction capacity limit the extent to which states can centralize and moderate the effects of trade and war.

TWO MODELS OF THE STATE AND SYSTEM

In this section, we describe centralized and decentralized models of the state and system. Although states are the core unit in each model, the concept of the system is essential because it captures aspects of the relations between states. Both models are stylized, like ends on a spectrum. Taken together, they are useful for picturing the ways in which states and systems vary across historical settings.

The first model hews closely to the dominant vision of political order in IR, what we called the *billiard ball model* in chapter 1. It is perhaps most associated with Kenneth Waltz, who theorized that political systems are either hierarchic or anarchic. He argued that "domestic systems are centralized and hierarchic.... International systems are decentralized and anarchic."[1] In this binary vision, states are hierarchies; they are centralized and composed of a division of labor. In our terms, states do not share sovereignty with subordinate polities. Rulers take taxes directly from the population by means of bureaucrats, administer justice through courts of the state, and exclusively maintain an armed force. State systems, in contrast, are anarchies; they are decentralized and composed of like types with no division of labor. Moreover, the boundaries between states are envisaged as linear borders. An illustration of this kind of system could be cleanly rendered, something akin to a modern political map or a boardgame composed of tiles (see figure 3.1). In this model, states are centralized, and there is a sharp division between the inside and outside of the state.

Waltz's binary vision has received criticism over the years.[2] Critics charge that it is too parsimonious and too stylized and that we often see elements of hierarchy stretching across borders and between states. As David Lake argues, it is better to envisage order on a continuum between hierarchy and anarchy.[3] Even if Waltz's model accurately depicts aspects of

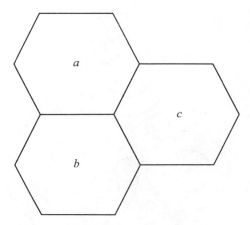

FIGURE 3.1. System of centralized states: the billiard ball model.

the modern international system, it is poorly suited to describe pre- and early-modern systems in Europe and elsewhere. We agree with this criticism but nevertheless use the model as a point of contrast.

The second model depicts a system of decentralized states, what we called the *bull's-eye model* in chapter 1. As figure 3.2 illustrates, decentralization creates a gradient of rule. State *a* might rule directly near the center, meaning that government authorities manage not just external relations but also extraction, justice, and other dimensions of governance. However, that rule dissipates the farther one travels from the center, and rulers increasingly share sovereignty and rely on local vassals in these outer areas to extract resources and provide public order.[4] Polity *y*, for instance, is a vassal that may enjoy local autonomy over issues such as taxation and justice, while its external relations are still managed by state *a*. Emirates in the Sokoto Caliphate, such as Kano and Zaria, were polities headed by emirs who were subordinate to the sultan in Sokoto, expected to transfer tribute, maintain order, and participate in foreign wars, but were otherwise independent. Vassalage contracts can be heterogenous, with some polities retaining more or less extensive rights or higher or lower tribute demands.[5] In this model, state reach is limited, and patterns of indirect rule through vassals are common.

In a bull's-eye system, networks of vassalage often produce frontiers rather than linear borders in decentralized systems.[6] As the authority of

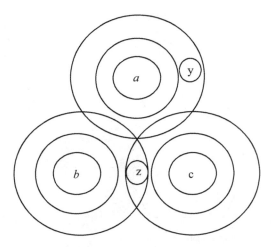

FIGURE 3.2. System of decentralized states: the bull's-eye model.

the state dissipates through heterogenous tributary relationships, pinpointing where one state ends and another begins can be difficult in frontier zones. Rulers may not have known where the boundaries were as delineation was sometimes a matter for local vassals to resolve.[7] For example, when the British asked the ruler of Siam in the nineteenth century where the boundary with Burma was located, his response was to ask the local chiefdoms.[8] Moreover, frontier zones can fall under the suzerainty of more than one power, creating indeterminate zones. In the eighteenth and nineteenth centuries, Cambodia paid tribute to Siam and Vietnam; the Kayah states in modern-day Burma were subject to Siam and Burma; small polities on the borders dividing China, Burma, and Siam were subject to all three; and the Laotian kingdoms of Luang Prabang and Vientiane were under "many overlords."[9] Finally, some independent states might sit astride the outer orbits of different states yet still pay homage or tribute to another state, as many successor states to the Mughal Empire did. States in the decentralized model are territorial in the sense that they control territory, but that territory is not always clearly delineated, at least not on the margins.[10]

Decentralized systems can contain elements of heteronomy. John Ruggie popularized this concept when describing the European medieval order as a "heteronomous institutional framework," a patchwork of overlapping, crosscutting, and entangled forms of political authority.[11] The medieval system was not anarchical, as Waltz imagined, but heteronomous, where states and kings sat at the top of hierarchical networks of vassalage relations but were themselves also crosscut and subordinate to other entities in some parts of their territories. Two entities could, for example, extract taxes from the same territory.[12] By approximately 1500 CE in Europe, heteronomy had been replaced by more hierarchical vassalage relations, where "the feudal nobility became subordinate to the central governments."[13] Elsewhere, we define heteronomy as a relationship in which a polity (or actor) is subordinate to at least two polities (or actors) that are not themselves engaged in a nested, hierarchical relationship.[14] In figure 3.2, polity z is a vassal to both b and c, and neither b nor c is engaged in a hierarchical relationship. This kind of crosscutting authority is an instance of heteronomy.[15] We postulate that heteronomy is possible in decentralized systems because of the ambiguity that arises on the frontiers between states. Decentralized systems contain elements of hierarchy, anarchy, and heteronomy.

Billiard balls and bull's-eyes are models representing two contrasting visions of states and systems. They are ideal types, points on a spectrum. Decentralized systems can fluctuate between periods when large states dominate and periods when small city-states are the norm. Mostly decentralized systems can contain centralized states, and state systems in the nineteenth century occupy positions between billiard balls and bull's-eyes. In that sense, the models present a framework for sorting and comparing the state systems in our case studies. Of course, they are simplifications designed to capture complex realities with few variables.[16] We expect that other factors matter, such as international order, defined generally as "stable patterns of behaviour and relations among states and other international associations."[17] International orders typically possess legal, ideological, and ritualistic features that resonate with local culture, and their features can have causal effects on the structural features of states and systems.[18] Although order is not central in these two models, we discuss it in the case studies and in chapters 8 and 9.

The models have inductive and deductive origins. Much of our early thinking formed inductively as we constructed the ISD and found recurring patterns in the structures of states and systems. From that we developed a deductive theoretical framework for comparative systems analysis that posited the central role of the state. We detailed this framework in our article "Between Eurocentrism and Babel: A Framework for the Analysis of States, State Systems, and International Orders" (2017). We argue that our two models—the billiard ball and the bull's-eye—can be used to compare any state system as long as there are states as we have defined them and they are interacting as a system. Although the models are timeless, they would not be useful for explaining human relations in the absence of states—where, for example, there are roving bands or loose tribal associations. Finally, the models are parsimonious; they are useful for controlled comparisons of key factors but necessarily elide other complexities of state systems.[19]

THEORIES OF CENTRALIZATION

The framework described in the previous section is useful for classifying and comparing states and systems, and we do this in the case study chapters for East Asia, South Asia, maritime Southeast Asia, and West Africa in the nineteenth century. Describing and comparing the structure of these systems with our framework are an important step forward, and we hope taking this step invites further explorations of the patterns we observe.[20] But state systems move dynamically along the spectrum of centralization. Studies of Europe, for example, trace a general transition over the past five hundred years from a system of decentralized states to the centralized states and linear borders of today.[21] Various factors, including war and trade, are thought to have driven these transitions—theories that we discuss later in this chapter. Most of these theories have been developed based on the European experience, and little is known about how well they travel to other regions. Here, we aim to move to dynamic analysis and establish hypotheses for the empirical chapters.[22] To this end, we discuss dominant theories of state centralization before outlining our preferred approach that emphasizes the conditional role of interaction capacity.

Centralization is our dependent variable, which we also call *state building* through the book. There is a rich literature on this subject, but as Lars-Erik Cederman and colleagues rightly note, the meaning of the term is deeply ambiguous.[23] We see centralization as the extent to which the state controls decision-making rather than allowing subordinate polities to make decisions autonomously. Conceptually, this transition is the same as from "indirect" to "direct" rule, although it is a continuous rather than a binary variable.[24] Removing the prerogatives of vassals and autonomous polities creates infrastructural power, or the ability of states to implement decisions through their societies.[25] A state that takes taxes with a salaried bureaucracy is more centralized than one that allows a vassal to tax and transfer some of the surplus to the center. For example, the fiefs of conquistadors in Spanish Mexico (the *encomienda*), who had their own militaries and tax systems, were gradually replaced with Crown-appointed tax collectors (the *corregimientos*).[26] When a ruler removes vassals' ability to decide succession in their fiefs, as the *kabaka* (king) of Buganda did in the nineteenth century, the state has become more centralized.[27] As should be clear from these examples, the mechanics of centralization involve taking away the powers of vassals, most often by replacing local officials with governors and bureaucrats appointed and paid for by the center. Instead of choosing their own successor, vassals have their successors nominated or appointed by the state. Instead of appointing their own tax collectors and gathering their own taxes, vassals must cede this power to bureaucrats from the center, who move in and collect the taxes. Instead of vassals maintaining law and order with their own armies, police and military forces salaried by the center (i.e., standing armies) perform this function. Instead of vassals choosing judges, crimes are tried in courts run by magistrates of the state. Centralization is the increasing encroachment of more bureaucrats and governors over the territory claimed by the ruler and the erosion of the vassals' privileges.

However, centralization involves a trade-off. First, leaving taxation, justice, and law and order to vassals is cost effective. Vassals have their own tax collectors, police forces, and judges, and they know the social and physical terrain better than distant rulers.[28] Piggybacking on preexisting institutions saves the ruler from paying, feeding, and moving the governors, bureaucrats, and soldiers who would be required for the ruler to rule directly. Moreover, if the governors, soldiers, and bureaucrats do move in, vassals might fight to keep their privileges or in other cases "exit" the state through secession or migration.[29] These rebellions can spiral out of control if other vassals think they can also secure their privileges or gain new ones by siding with the rebellion. Sometimes the ruler's generals do not obey, and then the ruler is really in trouble. In many ways, decentralized governance is safer and less costly.

Leaving the vassals mostly alone has its downsides, though. Revenue is lost because vassals will use their better networks and better information to lie about how much was produced that year (as just one example) and pay less tax, a tendency that is difficult for the ruler to monitor (a principal–agent problem). Allowing vassals autonomy, especially to keep their own military forces, also runs the risk that they will ally against the ruler at some point in the future and become rulers, even if giving them autonomy works in the short term.

These are the key trade-offs between centralized and decentralized forms of rule. We should also add that this is not a one-way street. Centralized states can decentralize. State-appointed governors can become vassals as they gradually appoint their own officials, keep their own garrisons, and collect and keep their own taxes. Vassals can become rulers if the center is weak and secession is a viable option.

Most states in the nineteenth century (and before then) began decentralized, and only some centralized to a significant degree.[30] Our aim in this book is to explain why some systems saw the rise of centralized states, especially the rise of moderate to large states, and others did not. City-states often had centralized tax administrations or judicial systems,[31] but the rise of medium-size states that displaced rivals as the source of sovereignty was a key development in the European system that many studies aim to explain.[32] What, then, explains the conditions under which states centralize? If most states begin with decentralized forms of rule, what differentiates those that successfully remove the privileges of autonomous polities from those that fail in the attempt? Most existing works have emphasized either war or trade or some combination of the two. We discuss these theories in the next section.

War and Trade

War and trade are thought to have driven centralization in Europe. These explanations are, of course, not the only ones, and others highlight the Catholic Church,[33] the Protestant Reformation,[34] exogenous shocks to institutions and demographics,[35] and the diffusion and emulation of political institutions.[36] Without minimizing the importance of these approaches, we focus on war and trade because they are dominant explanations in the field and are canonical in explaining state development. We are not able to test all explanations for state centralization in our case studies, but we hope this book is a first step enabling further theory testing in new historical samples. Chapter 8 also reflects briefly on the explanatory power of theories that emphasize emulation and ideology mechanisms, and we explore region-specific explanations in the case studies, including emulation, international order, and slavery. We first present war and trade as distinct approaches before discussing their interrelationship.

War is the engine of state centralization in perhaps the most well-known explanations.[37] Massed infantry, artillery, and sophisticated fortifications became necessary in Europe during the fifteenth and sixteenth centuries and increased the costs of war. Rulers needed to reach deeper into their societies for revenues or face being conquered and absorbed into more fiscally efficient states that could maintain larger, permanent armed forces. Feudal nobles, lords, or polities that controlled their own taxation systems and military forces were high on the hit list. Vassals often paid taxes to the king, but these taxes could be irregular and were inefficient because local intermediaries would take much of the local surplus for themselves.[38] States therefore embarked upon often violent projects to displace these local intermediaries and replace them with more direct forms of administration and taxation that were more valuable to the state and paid on a more predictable and regular basis.[39] These fiscal institutions were the foundations of the modern centralized state.[40]

There is considerable evidence to support the main tenets of this bellicist account in studies of Europe and East Asia.[41] Sebastian Mazzuca states that "it is safe to say that the bellicist approach is right." Cederman and colleagues conclude that "war did make states" in early-modern Europe, showing powerful statistical evidence that war was crucial to the territorial consolidation of European states.[42] Although the war-led path to centralization has faced criticism, a powerful line of thought links centralized states in Europe to the threat of conquest and incentives for rulers to replace inefficient and decentralized systems of rule with a more penetrative, rationalized bureaucracy.

A second approach emphasizes trade and urban development.[43] A commercial revolution in Europe around the tenth and eleventh centuries led to the rise of larger, more prosperous cities. Elites in these new cities wanted to avoid the unpredictable and exacting taxation demands of feudal lords (vassals) and had incentives to push for property rights and standardization. States were also willing to exchange standardization and predictability for revenues from merchants. Commercial development enabled states to go around powerful vassals by making alliances with city-based elites to exchange revenue for security, influence in commercial and fiscal policy, and some public goods. Cities provided kings with stable revenues that were used to build a centralized army and bureaucracy, which were eventually turned against the feudal lords.[44]

However, trade and urbanization do not always create centralized states. On the contrary, trade can create fragmentary pressures within state systems. In northern Europe during the fifteenth and sixteenth centuries, commerce created powerful cities that could demand independence from weak monarchs, a pattern that helped prevent centralization attempts by the Holy Roman Empire and that strengthened the Hanseatic League.[45] In Italy, trade in high-value products created strong city-states with little need to pool resources for protection, thus generating fragmentation. Trade yields centralization when it generates new classes and actors that provide states with allies for state-building projects rather than being captured by existing institutions in strengthened vassal kingdoms.[46] What matters is which groups trade empowers and by how much relative to the state.

Although there is a sense in which these theories are distinct, each tends to emphasize one factor more than the other rather than to exclude the other. Cities play an important role in generating national states according to Tilly's classic account in *Coercion, Capital, and European States* (1975), although the emphasis is on war as the main driver. Although Spruyt's account in *The Sovereign State and Its Competitors* (1994) emphasizes the commercial revolution in Europe, centuries of military competition weeded out inefficient institutional forms.

More recent work has explored the interrelationship between war and cities, suggesting that both may be necessary for centralization to occur.[47] For example, several studies show that commercial (i.e., trading) cities assisted the development of representative (i.e., democratic) institutions. As weak rulers needed more revenues to fund wars, they turned to merchant cities, which demanded representation and influence over public spending through councils and city parliaments.[48] Including cities in governance also allowed rulers to credibly commit to repay loans.[49] Over time, representative institutions allowed cities to hold rulers accountable by constraining executive power, thus overcoming the "commitment problem" whereby once rulers centralized their governments, vassals (and merchants) lost their bargaining leverage and ability to prevent future encroachments by the state. In turn, these representative institutions generated higher taxation revenues for kings and more penetrative states at the local level. War may also have forced people to seek refuge in fortified cities, which in turn became engines for representative institutions and fiscally penetrative states.[50] Such hybrid accounts emphasize that international competition and commercial cities were necessary to generate modern, fiscally efficient sovereign states.[51] Europe's fragmented geopolitics and rich cities were the crucible in which centralized (and eventually democratic) states were generated.[52] Theories emphasizing the interaction between war and cities (or representative institutions) are part of a growing movement suggesting that war affects state building only under certain conditions.[53]

In summary, to the question "Why did states in Europe centralize?" the dominant answer has been either that the relentless pressures of interstate competition meant only the most fiscally efficient states survived or that the growth of trade and cities provided new allies for predatory rulers or both—that centralized states are the marriage of rulers hard-pressed by the threat of war and wealthy cities demanding protection and representation.

Although these approaches were developed to explain state centralization in Europe from the medieval to the modern period, they make general claims that can be tested in other state systems. For example, if the bellicist theory is right, more centralized states should emerge in multistate systems where interstate wars were frequent, large, and expensive. If trade-led theories are right, we should observe centralization around trade hubs and cities as states strike deals with commercial classes to secure more revenue, especially where trade does not differentially strengthen vassals. Where trade can be captured by existing elites, it might cause fragmentation instead.[54] If hybrid theories are right, then centralized states should prevail where trading cities and states face the threat of war and incentives to pool their resources in the form of centralized, representative institutions.

What evidence is there that European-based explanations travel to other state systems? The record is mixed.[55] Victoria Tin-Bor Hui contends that war-based theories help explain state-building processes in China during the Warring States Period (656–221 BCE), while Chin-Hao Huang and David Kang argue that they provide a poor explanation for state centralization in Korea and Japan.[56] For Latin America, Miguel Centeno finds that only certain types of wars stimulated centralization, while Mazzuca argues that conditions of international hierarchy and free-trade capitalism (rather than autarky and international anarchy) caused weak, decentralized states in nineteenth-century South America.[57] In a similar vein, Jeffrey Herbst and Christopher Clapham suggest that the lack of international competition in Africa after decolonization helps explain why African states remain weak, although other studies find that precolonial warfare in Africa does not explain variations in modern state centralization.[58] Studies have also found evidence that states formed in areas of higher trade in Africa and that strong exogenous shocks—such as the Black Death and European diseases transmitted to the Americas—undermined the bargaining power of vassals and stimulated state centralization.[59] Victor Lieberman argues for a link between trade and state centralization in Siam, Myanmar, and Vietnam, where trade enabled rulers to obtain weapons, taxes, and other items that defrayed the costs and challenges of state building.[60] Others have questioned whether the war-based theory applies even to Europe, pointing out that centralized states emerged too early or too late in Europe for the bellicist theory to be a good explanation or that competition led to decentralization and collapse in key cases (e.g., eighteenth-century France).[61]

Most of this work aiming to understand non-Western state formation has focused on East Asia (China in particular) and Latin America. Very few studies have asked whether existing theories can explain the structure of political units in precolonial Africa, South Asia, or maritime Southeast Asia.[62] In the next section, we develop an alternative theory of centralization based on interaction capacity and explain why bellicist- and trade-based theories of centralization might not travel outside the high-capacity regions of Europe and East Asia.

Interaction Capacity

A different approach emphasizes how change (and stability) in the speed and cost of transporting goods, people, and information—which we, following Barry Buzan and Richard Little, call *interaction capacity*—places limits on the ability of states to project power.[63] We can think of interaction capacity as the latent potential for interactions between individuals in an area, which is largely a function of the costs in time and resources of interacting. Where transport and communications are slow and expensive, states maintain decentralized forms of rule. Where technological advances, favorable geography, or dense populations lower these costs, states begin to switch to more direct forms of rule. Rulers utilize indirect forms of rule (i.e., leaving vassals with substantial taxation and coercive autonomy) when slow and expensive interactions make direct forms of rule prohibitively expensive.[64] Direct rule is attractive to rulers because it cuts out intermediaries that may use superior local knowledge to shirk on payments and removes the bargaining power that vassals derive from maintaining military forces and better information.[65] But direct rule is expensive and risky because rulers must win, build, and maintain a new infrastructure of rule against local elites who often resist attempts to undermine their autonomy.[66] Indirect rule, in contrast, allows rulers to piggyback on existing institutions for extracting taxes and providing public order without having to move and pay their own personnel to complete the same tasks. Local elites can provide public order and generate taxes owing to superior information and shorter supply lines.

Moving the soldiers, bureaucrats, and supplies needed to maintain direct rule is more expensive where moving people and goods is slow and costly. In addition, the state's ability to implement more invasive taxation systems requires information on where people live, how much they produce, where they move, how old they are, and who they marry.[67] Land surveys, for example, are a key tool for centralizing regimes.[68] But obtaining information is not free, and where gathering information on populations is hard or expensive, more penetrative fiscal systems (and other institutions of state capacity) will also be expensive.[69] Where monitoring is more difficult, target populations or vassals may simply leave (i.e., exit). In this account, centralized states have tended to form where they are able to cheaply gather information on their populations and those populations are trapped, usually by geographical features.[70] Without good information, free riding and tax avoidance are easier, further reducing the utility of more direct forms of extraction.[71] As James Scott explains it, society must be legible to the state before centralization can occur.[72] Moreover, attempts to centralize often provoke rebellions as elites stand to lose short-term revenues and longer-term bargaining power. Even if elites do not rebel in the short term, centralization efforts can render the state more vulnerable to widespread rebellions and the defection of local potentates in the future.[73]

These barriers to centralization are high, and so states, in response, have often relied on decentralized forms of rule that leave wide-ranging decision-making power in the hands of local elites to avoid these communication and transportation costs, even if it means that local elites use their autonomy and local knowledge to challenge the state, shirk on commitments to transfer revenues, provoke local unrest, or rescind on commitment to provide soldiers in the case of war.[74] Decentralization is simply cheaper and less risky than more penetrative institutions. Instead of extracting resources directly, the state can outsource governance to local elites in exchange for a proportion of the locally generated tax revenue, usually under the threat of violence.

When interaction capacity rises and the costs of transport and communications decline, the costs of direct rule also decline. Transporting and supplying soldiers and bureaucrats over longer distances are cheaper and faster in relation to the available revenues, enabling the state to extend its governance infrastructure at lower cost. Moreover, it is cheaper and more efficient for states to gather information in the provinces (e.g., how productive the harvest was, how much trade occurred, how powerful the local military forces are), thus increasing the potential of the state to supply more direct forms of rule and reducing the bargaining power of vassals, a power that has arisen from advantages in gathering information locally.[75] Over time, as opportunities arise, states should progressively centralize their rule by displacing local potentates.[76] When states centralize also depends, however, on numerous other, often exogenous factors, such as war (which we discussed earlier) but also disease, changes in the international economy, changes in military technology, and religious shocks that undermine the ability of subordinate elites to resist the center's demands for direct forms of rule.[77] Otherwise capable states may at times choose indirect rule if it obviates the need to engage in sociopolitical projects that come with direct rule.[78] Nevertheless, we contend that, on balance, higher interaction capacity increases states' ability to supply centralized rule, and increasingly dense systems will over time accumulate more centralized forms of rule.[79]

THE COMPARATIVE DYNAMICS OF STATES AND SYSTEMS

What specific predictions would an interaction-capacity approach make about the structure of nineteenth-century state systems? Unlike war or trade approaches, an interaction-capacity approach would predict decentralized forms of governance when transport costs are high, despite local variation in the prevalence of war and the density of cities and trade. This approach, therefore, predicts similarities within and across systems rather than large variation as a function of war and trade.

For most parts of the world in the nineteenth century, land-based interaction capacity was constrained by the speed at which humans, pack animals, and horses could travel.[80] River and canal systems improved these speeds, but transporting goods, people, and information over land was expensive and slow and changed little over more than a millennia before the Industrial Revolution in Europe. Generally, long-distance land trade was limited to high-value but low-weight items such as salt, gold, ivory, and other precious items. It was only in the nineteenth century that these basic constraints were overcome by the development of the steam engine and subsequent developments in railways, ocean-going transport, and optical telecommunications (i.e., the telegraph). Such technological developments did not reach Africa, South Asia, or Southeast Asia until the late nineteenth century, and they generally came with and were enabled by colonial rule. Indeed, works in this tradition see the modern centralized state in Europe emerging only at the turn of the nineteenth century with the French Revolution and afterward.[81] Alexander Lee and Jack Paine note that the great "revenue divergence" between Europe and the rest of the world did not really occur until the early twentieth century.[82] Many states (including European states) did not establish censuses or statistical agencies until the late nineteenth and early twentieth centuries.[83] Elements of decentralized forms of rule persisted long into the eighteenth and early nineteenth century, even in Europe, such that "at the beginning of the nineteenth century, no Western state (with the possible exception of Britain) had a 'modern' bureaucracy."[84] From this perspective, centralized states should be an anomaly as state rulers face basic constraints on their ability to project power, which force them to cede autonomy to regional vassals and potentates. Systems should look much more like bull's-eyes than billiard balls.[85]

We derived these explanations for centralization—war, trade, and interaction capacity—mostly from existing work. One of our objectives is to retest these theories in samples that they were not trained on, a replication exercise of sorts. However, we also advance a positive argument. War and trade have positive effects on centralization when interaction capacity is high but negative effects (i.e., they cause or entrench decentralization) when it is low. This argument also implies that we accept the tenets of the interaction-capacity approach outlined earlier.[86]

Our conditional argument derives from a logical problem with war-based (and to a lesser extent trade-based) theories. To explain centralization, we should start with decentralized states. As we have defined them, they are states with autonomous vassals. Most decentralized states fought wars with levies of soldiers and weapons from their vassals. Wars are won by keeping vassals onside and assembling a sufficiently large force. More international competition might increase the ruler's need for revenues to pay for soldiers and guns to protect the state, but it also deepens the ruler's dependence on vassals to provide these resources. Put differently, for decentralized states, war empowers vassals vis-à-vis the ruler, not the other way around.

Vassals derive their bargaining power from autonomous capacities to tax their populace and mobilize their own armies. They are unlikely to relinquish this power when they are strong in relation to the ruler. On the contrary, vassals are likely to demand stronger guarantees of lower taxes or even more autonomy. If war empowers regional elites at the expense of rulers, they should demand more autonomy, not accept less, creating pressures toward decentralization rather than centralization.[87] Therefore, war only deepens the dilemma of decentralized rule; it does not alleviate that dilemma.

Exit is key to this dynamic. Where vassals have good "outside options" (i.e., other choices that are as good or better as the current situation), they can threaten to provide less than demanded, abstain from contributing, secede from the state, or even join the enemy. For example, shifting overlord relations had little practical local effect as most Balinese states ruled by co-opting local rulers. *Deshmukh*s—landholding elites in precolonial Maharashtra—would readily swap sides in war depending on the predicted victor or who could offer the best terms or both.[88] Rulers cannot take more from their vassals in these cases; they must compensate them.

However, where vassals' exit options are weak, the ruler has a stronger hand. If vassals believe they are worse off as independent states or under a new ruler, then rulers can demand more in terms of resources to maintain the security of the state and the vassal's place in the state. Where exit options are weak, increased competition might strengthen the ruler vis-à-vis their vassals, who might be better off accepting state pensions or positions in the bureaucracy rather than foreign rule.

Interaction capacity shapes whether exit options are good or bad. When interaction capacity is low, and the costs of extending state infrastructures are high, rulers pay higher costs to punish recalcitrant vassals and know less about their subordinates at a time when they desperately need resources and information. These conditions strengthen vassals' exit options because avoiding punishment is easier and the possibilities of independence are more promising. If interaction capacity also shapes longer-term processes of economic and cultural integration that tie vassals closer to their rulers, then the development of protonationalist ideas might reduce the value of exiting the state for vassal polities. Finally, in low-capacity settings, few rulers can even threaten to rule directly in locations far from the capital, and for some vassals warfare might be an opportunity to (re)negotiate tributary demands with a new player whose (indirect) rule might be better than that of the current ruler. As interaction capacity rises and direct forms of rule become cheaper, the prospects of losing autonomy under a foreign government might be worse than accepting a loss of autonomy and integration into a more centralized state. Where decentralized forms of rule are more efficient, international competition should select out states that attempt centralizing projects and face more frequent instability, rebellion, and collapse. We pick up these conjectures again in the case studies and in chapter 8 and speculate that war causes decentralization in low-capacity systems and centralization in higher-capacity systems.

A similar pattern could also be at work with trade. Trade might empower rulers with new weapons, more taxes, and luxury items that enable them to co-opt or overcome vassals. Trade might also create new social classes and powerful cities that could be allies in state-building projects. But trade could just as easily empower vassals, and as Spruyt points out, newly powerful cities could use their wealth to resist further state encroachments rather than accept them. What matters is whether rulers can capture and monopolize trade vis-à-vis their vassals. Where rulers can do these things, trade may cause centralization. Where rulers are unable to do them, the benefits of trade may diffuse, causing fragmentation rather than centralization.

If interaction capacity shapes rulers' ability to control their territories, then it also may affect their ability to monopolize and benefit from trade. As with war, we speculate that trade fragments states in low-capacity systems, making them more like bull's-eyes than billiard balls, but can drive centralization in higher-capacity systems.

Finally, let us discuss the origins of interaction capacity and its relationship to war, trade, and past state building. Interaction capacity in the nineteenth century (and earlier for some cases) was generated by factors that might be exogenous or endogenous to variables in our framework. Geographical and environmental conditions, including navigable rivers, rugged or mountainous terrain, and the presence of diseases (spread, for example, by the tsetse fly), have deep geotechnical and climatological roots and are probably not caused by past centralization, war, or trade.[89] Inferences drawn from variation in interaction capacity generated by these factors are stronger. Demographic factors such as population density, dispersion, and diversity are more mixed, being linked to migratory patterns over tens of thousands of years, religious conversion, trade patterns, past state building, as well as initial geographical conditions.[90] Technological developments and their adoption may be (but are not always) caused by local war, trade, and past centralization. China's road system and the Mughal trunk road increased interaction capacity but were caused by past state centralization projects (see chapters 4 and 5). Technological innovation and its adoption as indicators of interaction capacity require caution and case-specific interpretation.

With a case-based approach, we can provide context-based interpretations of where variations in interaction capacity, trade, and warfare came from instead of relying upon a single indicator. Linguistic differences might be caused by exogenous factors in one case but by past state-building projects in others. In West Africa and Southeast Asia, trade was generated by sea-going technological developments in Europe that did not revolutionize land-based interaction capacity and were not caused by centralized states in these regions.[91] High levels of trade in these cases were more plausibly exogenous to the main independent, conditioning, and dependent variables. Increases in competition across the regional cases were partially generated by the entry of Europeans or the diffusion of weapons, which, again, did not substantially change land-based interaction capacity.[92] We can be more confident in such cases that variation in trade and warfare are not caused by the (relatively stable) underlying interaction capacity. The main point is that a case-based approach allows us to condition the strength of our inferences on regionally specific drivers of the main variables.

CONCLUSION

Most theories of state centralization emphasize the outcome of struggles between the rulers of states and their vassals as the key dynamic explaining political (de)centralization. An important tradition argues that the fiscal demands of war drive states to absorb their vassals and replace them with a thicker, more efficient structure of revenue extraction. Economic theories point to changes in patterns of trade and productivity, suggesting that increases in development can sometimes create a confluence of interests and capabilities between urban elites and rulers that enables rulers first to go around their vassals and then through them when they are powerful enough. However, an interaction-capacity approach stresses that going either around or through vassals is expensive and risky, limited by constraints on the costs and speed of transporting goods, ideas, and people. Since these constraints continued to bite outside of Europe and the Americas into the twentieth century, state systems outside those regions should be very similar and characterized by decentralized states. Moreover, we argue that war and trade could have decentralizing effects in low-capacity systems and centralizing effects in the higher-capacity systems that have been the subject of most studies in the field (i.e., Europe and East Asia). All these theories make concrete predictions for the types of state systems that we should observe in nineteenth-century East Asia, South Asia, maritime Southeast Asia, and West Africa.

Naturally, we do not expect the story we discover to be the full story. We anticipate that there will be exceptions to our theory, but such findings could prove particularly instructive. Other factors likely help explain state centralization and the structures of systems. Perhaps issues related to culture or international order play a role. It may also be the case that relations between states, from sovereign integration to imperialism, help us understand the states and systems in the case studies. We will consider these possibilities in the chapters that follow.

PART II
Regional State Systems

Chapter Four

EAST ASIA

East Asia is an unusual case in relation to the chapters that follow because the four states we look at here—China, Korea, Japan, and Vietnam—survived the encounter with European colonialism and exist today. A contemporary map of East Asia looks like the map of East Asia in 1816. Moreover, China, Korea, Vietnam, and Japan were centralized states by the end of the nineteenth century and approximate the billiard ball model discussed in chapter 3. China and Korea centralized centuries before the period we examine, but Japan and Vietnam consolidated direct rule in the mid–nineteenth century.

This chapter is a hinge between the theoretical mechanisms developed in chapter 3 and the regional case study chapters to follow. East Asia is better studied in IR scholarship than are South Asia, Southeast Asia, and West Africa, and we have benefited from a rich and developing discourse that connects IR and political science with East Asian history. These cases provide a vehicle for illustrating and testing mechanisms thought to link interaction capacity, war, and trade to centralization by drawing upon this growing stock of knowledge on East Asian institutional development.

East Asia in the nineteenth century conforms to the main theoretical models discussed in chapter 3. It had high interaction capacity and trade, with increasing competition through the century. Centralization in China and Korea was plausibly the product of past competition, trade, and high levels of interaction capacity, while a case can be made that nineteenth-century centralization in Vietnam and Japan was connected to increased competition in a high-capacity system that generated protonationalist ideologies over many centuries. But there are hints that centralization was not a foregone conclusion. War sometimes empowered vassals over rulers, rulers were wary of the fissile impacts of trade, and centralization projects were often unsuccessful. These patterns hint at scope conditions for trade- and war-based theories. War and trade rent rather than unified states that we examine farther on in the book. Finally, we are cautious with our causal claims. Past centralization influenced trade, war, and interaction capacity, raising the possibility of reverse causality. Other unobserved factors may explain levels of interaction capacity, trade, war, and how rulers govern, for example, and the patterns observed in this chapter might be driven by such omitted variables.

This chapter uses a structure that we will follow in the subsequent case study chapters. We describe the states and the system they composed; we gauge the level of interaction capacity, the intensity of trade, and the frequency of war (i.e., we describe the independent variables); then we assess the degree of state centralization (the dependent variable) and draw conclusions about whether our key independent variables help explain the features of state centralization in the system.

STATES AND THE SYSTEM

Our notion of the East Asian system covers the littoral zone stretching from Vietnam to China and over to Korea and Japan (see figure 4.1). This shared cultural space was brought together by the sea and by the centuries-old influence of China, and the four states are commonly studied as a system.[1] The glue, it seems, is the central role of the Chinese state stretching back to the Tang Dynasty (618–907 CE), if not the Han (202 BCE–220 CE). Part of this influence is the legacy of Confucian law and ethics, which were spread to and adopted by Vietnam, Korea, and Japan. In an analogy to Europe, Alexander Woodside argues that Confucian practices influenced the region in the way that Roman law influenced western Europe.[2] But unlike the experience in Europe, where Rome was never reincarnated

FIGURE 4.1. States and population densities in East Asia per the ISD, 1816–1920 and 1800. *Note:* Shows population density in 1800. More opaque circles represent clearer borders noted in the ISD. Population density has been capped at a maximum of 120 people per square kilometer to facilitate comparison with the other three systems. *Source:* Population density data are from Klein Goldewijk et al., "The HYDE 3.1 Spatially Explicit Database of Human-Induced Global Land-Use Change Over the Past 12,000 Years."

in any enduring way despite a series of attempts, East Asia experienced a set of dynastic cycles that reinforced a Confucian and Sinocentric order. Built on these state practices was a pattern of interstate relations that is often referred to as the tribute system (which we discuss more fully later). Overall, our treatment of these states as a system is consonant with the literature.

There are four states in our analysis (note that we adopt the contemporary names as shorthand). The first is China, or more specifically the Qing Dynasty. It was a state in 1816, the start of our coverage period, and has remained an independent state into the twenty-first century. The second state is Korea, sometimes referred to as "Choson" in reference to the ruling dynasty.[3] Like China and the other states in this set, Korea was in existence in 1816. However, according to the ISD, it ceased to be an independent state from 1905 to 1945, when it was made a Japanese protectorate. The third state is Japan, independent over the entire period. Although there was a regime change during the Meiji Revolution in 1868, we record a continuous state. The final state is Vietnam, commonly called "Annam" during this period. It was an independent state in 1816 but ended in 1885 when it was made a French protectorate.[4]

We have focused on the traditional four states in the historical Sinocentric system and excluded the more distant states of Southeast Asia. Although states in Java, Malaya, Siam, and Burma were connected to China at points, they were less integrated with the Sinosphere than Vietnam. Indeed, in the 1800s these connections were quite thin. We also excluded the European powers that were gradually making inroads in the region. Although they were increasingly important actors, they were not constituent units in the system.

Similarly, we excluded various tribal groups along China's northern and western frontier as well as Central Asian states such as Eastern Turkistan, Kokand, Tibet, and Bukhara. In part, we did this because many of these tribal groups did not display the necessary statelike formations that we looked for in our data collection. Those that were more statelike were not traditionally part of the East Asian system. Much has been made of this difference in the literature. David Kang argues that China's relations with its eastern neighbors relied on a shared Confucian cultural foundation, while its relations with northern and western tribes were based more on hard power.[5] China's relations were bifurcated into a zone of peaceful relations based on soft power and hegemony and a zone in which China engaged in a more militant realist strategy that Alastair Johnston calls "Parabellum."[6] Overall, for the ISD we focused on the core units in the system.

Let us pause here to address an interesting feature of this system, which is that these four states exist today, unlike most of the states in the chapters to come. Although Vietnam and Korea expired at one point, they were reborn in the twentieth century.[7] However, these states are in a sense new to the IR literature, particularly in the quantitative literature, because they were excluded from the COW dataset for much of the period in question. According to COW, both China and Japan entered the international system in 1860, Korea entered in 1887, and Vietnam did not enter until 1954, when it won independence from France.[8] As we discussed in chapter 2, the reason for these late entries is that COW determined a state's recognition based on whether it had full diplomatic relations with both Britain and France. Although China was clearly a state long before 1860, it was not until then that it established formal diplomatic relations with these key European states, even if it had negotiated with European emissaries as early as the 1600s.[9] The same can be said of Japan. This is one consequence of the Eurocentrism in COW that our study is meant to remedy. These four states had existed and interacted for centuries. Long before they established diplomatic relations with Britain and France, they were sovereign states in the conventional sense of the term.[10]

East Asia was also a system with a small number of relatively large states. As a basis of comparison, our other case studies cover similarly large geographic areas but consist of smaller and more numerous states. States in East Asia were expansive and, as we will show, institutionally centralized. This was particularly the case with the Qing Dynasty, the largest and most centralized state in our study.

A final but crucial characteristic of the East Asian system was its international order. It was a hegemonic system with a clear order builder over the centuries: the Qing Dynasty and its predecessors. Although that order was the product of the system, it nevertheless had reciprocal effects on the states themselves in terms of how they interacted and how they were structured.

China played a central role in the recognition of the East Asian states through the tribute system. Here, it had two key functions. First, there was investiture, which, as Kang writes, "involved the explicit acceptance of subordinate tributary status and was a diplomatic protocol by which a state recognized the legitimate sovereignty of another political unit and the status of the king in that tributary state as the legitimate ruler."[11] The second complementary function was the sending of envoys by the subordinate state to the Qing court. These elaborate missions occurred at regular intervals. They reinforced the relationship between the two states and facilitated trading relationships as well as cultural and intellectual exchanges.[12] To imagine this practice in contemporary terms, it would be like the newly elected president of Mexico traveling to Washington, DC, to pay respects to a military-economic superior and perceived center of civilization and, in exchange, be formally invested by the U.S. president as the leader of Mexico. All this would be done in a highly elaborate manner that signifies the hierarchical relationship. Of course, as Ji-Young Lee points out, in East Asia part of the dynamic was a two-level game in which Korean, Japanese, and Vietnamese rulers used these diplomatic missions to consolidate their positions at home.[13]

The tributary model was the key structure of the system. It put one state at the apex and charged it with the role of recognizing and investing the peripheral states. The subordinate states delegated this key authority function to the Qing court. Whereas modern states depend on UN recognition, states in the East Asian system depended on China's blessing. To be sure, there was variation among the subordinate states' relationships with China. Whereas Korea was the model tributary, Japan often rejected the central role of China and, at points, tried to place itself at the civilizational center.[14] But, overall, the subordinate states were formally independent states embedded in an enduring hegemonic order. Lee describes the East Asian system using the following definition of hegemony: "A structure in which a single powerful state controls or dominates the lesser states in the system." Moreover, Lee differentiates the hegemonic relations of the East Asian system from an imperial structure by pointing out, following Michael Doyle, that empires exert control over the external and internal affairs of the peripheral units.[15] We agree with Lee that China's relationship with Korea, Japan, and Vietnam was not one of informal empire; it was hegemonic. The Qing Dynasty had imperial relations with other actors on its continental periphery, but this is not an apt characterization of its relationship with the other three states in the system.

EAST ASIA

The dynamics of the Sinocentric tribute system is a developing discourse. An earlier vision of the system is referred to as the "Fairbankian model" after the early work of John King Fairbank.[16] Seen through this lens, the tribute system was rooted in a nonegalitarian and Confucian sense of order that sorted surrounding peoples and states into three zones based on the extent to which they embraced Confucian culture. These zones were hierarchically arranged, and non-Chinese states tended to comply for material/trade-related reasons. However, critiques of the Fairbankian model include that it was too much of an Anglophone historiography, that it imagined an overly static tribute system, that it did not problematize how China and its neighbors changed over time, and that it did not take social interactions into account. Much of these critiques became grouped under a subsequent generation of scholarship called the "New Qing History."[17] Essentially, this later scholarship envisaged a more dynamic, protean, and complicated tribute system. Cutting across this evolving literature on the tribute system are more focused analyses on the frontier politics of the Qing Dynasty (and prior dynasties) with "barbarian" groups, the dynamics of investiture, the interstate economics of the system, and the more philosophical/cultural ideas that undergird the order (sometimes referred to as the Tianxia—All Under Heaven—approach).[18] Later in the book we argue against the uniqueness of China's investiture and tributary system, not by looking closer into East Asian sources but by comparing patterns of political order in China with other, less well-studied systems. Perhaps investiture was uncommon in relations between states in Europe by the nineteenth century, but it was a widespread practice in South Asia, Southeast Asia, and West Africa. This suggests that the Chinese tributary system was unusual not for its structure but in how institutionalized, expansive, and durable it was.

Overall, this order differed in various ways from the other international orders examined in this book. First, it was hegemonic, a feature that shaped the structure of both the states and the system. Yongjin Zhang and Barry Buzan refer to the system as an "ordered sovereign inequality," a term developed by Christian Reus-Smit.[19] The states were independent but existed in an unequal (hegemonic) arrangement. In terms of international order, this arrangement led to substantial deference to the central state, or what Lee calls "symbolic obeisance."[20] Second, the cultural content of the international order was unique. The Confucian tradition was, as Woodside describes, a kind of civic religion that connected the statesmen, intellectuals, and bureaucrats of the different states.[21] Moreover, the specifics of the investiture process and manner in which diplomats would kowtow to the Qing court were performative attributes of that specific order.[22]

Part of the success of the tribute system was the institutional legacy on which rulers could draw lessons as they forged relations across the system. Joseph MacKay unpacks how each Chinese dynasty chose various characteristics of previous dynasties, as though off a menu, when deciding how to order their system. Borrowing from Ann Swidler, MacKay calls these characteristics the "repertoires of international order." Thus, the Manchu (Qing) tried to adapt the successes and avoid the failures of the Ming, Yuan, Song, and so on. As Mackay and others have noted, these dynasties varied considerably.[23] James Millward argues that Chinese order builders, not unlike the realizers of the American myth of Manifest Destiny, regularly invoked (and still invoke) a concept he terms "manifest history," an unbroken line back into history connecting these dynasties and their eras of greatness.[24]

As discussed previously, a core component of the tribute system was the process of investiture and the regular sending of envoys to the Qing court. This symbolic obeisance has strong constitutive elements, as legitimacy for Korea, Annam, and Japan depended in part on Qing recognition.[25] Of course, rulers in the subordinate states had additional motives for seeking investiture, one of which was to shore up their domestic legitimacy. It is not clear that recognition from the Qing court was always paramount. And to be sure, Japanese rulers often took a more detached position on its importance. The Sinocentric system may not have possessed the same level of constitutive recognition as the modern UN system, but the importance of recognition for system membership was greater in this case than in the other state systems examined in the book.

INTERACTION CAPACITY, TRADE, AND WAR

Interaction Capacity

East Asia was a high-capacity system because of geographical and historical endowments. It encompasses several river basins and high-yield agricultural regions that have supported high population densities (see figure 4.1). China had a population of approximately 330 million in 1800, which rose to 430 million by 1850, more than a third of the global population.[26] As a point of contrast, in 1800 the British Isles had a population of 16 million, France 28 million, and Russia 37 million.[27] Meanwhile, Japan had a population of 30 million in 1800 and 33 million in 1850.[28] Korea's population during the early 1800s was about 10 million. Finally, Vietnam's population was estimated to be 7 million.[29] By the 1800s, all states hosted dense clusters of cities (see figure 4.2). Overall, these states had dense population clusters roughly on par with western Europe, slightly lower than parts of South Asia, and higher than Southeast Asia and West Africa.

In addition, as in Southeast Asia, in East Asia the sea permitted faster maritime transit, and major rivers connected many interior cities and populations with the sea. All else equal, larger and denser populations in East Asia increased the level of interaction capacity by lowering the marginal costs of transport, as did navigable river systems, especially for commercial transactions, and generated denser interpersonal and intergroup ties. These geographical drivers of interaction capacity are relatively exogenous to (i.e., not likely to be caused by) state centralization. The built infrastructure and cultural landscape also enhanced the states' ability to interact. We are more cautious here because these factors might be caused by state-building projects before the eighteenth and nineteenth centuries, raising the possibility of reverse causality. However, more exogenous factors that increase interaction capacity might also increase the probability of successful state-building projects in the past, which further increase interaction capacity in subsequent periods. That said, states benefited from a communications network of roads and canals and monitored border crossings.[30] Even though Japan was a decentralized state, it hosted "dense information networks" in addition to "dense commercial and urban networks" that created a "conscious membership in a cultural community."[31] Vietnam was divided into two main regions—the densely populated Red River Basin in the North and the Mekong Delta in the South—but previous administrative centralization from the North, cultural assimilation, and colonization had created a shared sense of Vietnamese identity among the elite by the late eighteenth century.[32] China was, of course, the central node in the network. Finally, the Confucian system of laws and norms provided a kind of administrative/diplomatic lingua franca that further facilitated communication.[33] Interaction capacity fell in the remote interior regions, where roads and shipping were absent. But

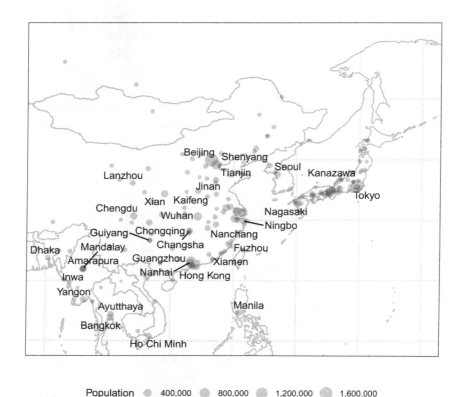

FIGURE 4.2. Cities in East Asia, 1750–1900. *Source*: Data are from Reba, Reitsma, and Seto, "Spatializing 6,000 Years of Global Urbanization from 3700 BC to AD 2000."

by the standards of the early nineteenth century, interaction capacity in this system was high.

Trade

East Asia was a trade hub for centuries. Historians have "estimated that three-fourths of all the silver produced in the New World from 1500–1800 found its way to China, because the Chinese economy was the most highly developed in the world and its products were better and cheaper than those of any other country."[34] Chinese trade junks reached as far as Indonesia and India and were important to the economy of Vietnam, Japan, Korea, as well as, farther afield, Myanmar and Thailand.[35] The nineteenth century was an inflection point in terms of global economic production and changing fortunes. Britain began to industrialize just as the Qing Dynasty showed signs of decline; the highwater mark of its three great emperors (Kangxi, Yongzheng, and Qianlong) ended in 1796.[36] The Chinese market and to a lesser extent the Japanese market were valued by expanding and frustrated European powers, whose policies led directly to the Opium Wars starting in 1839 and the opening of Japan in 1853.

Trade in East Asia was mostly a state-managed enterprise. The Chinese, Vietnamese, and Korean states not only promoted trade but also pursued a kind of laissez-faire approach that sought to eliminate substate tax farming.[37] Trade drove the expansion of major cities, especially in Vietnam, where modern-day Hanoi and Saigon were strategically placed on the coast to capture (and regulate) Chinese trade missions. An exception was Japan, a relatively decentralized state that before the Meiji Revolution was unable to prevent local daimyo (regional lords) from interfering with and taxing passing traders. This weak political control was visible to the other states in the system. As Kang writes, court officials in Korea were "acutely aware that the shogun and the Muromachi bakufu [the shogun's officials] could neither prevent piracy nor regulate trade, much less govern areas far from Kyoto."[38]

War

East Asian states entered the late eighteenth century and early nineteenth century having experienced relatively few interstate wars between the core states, best exemplified by Japan's long peace of 1603 to 1868. Competition increased, however, as Vietnam fought multifront wars from the late eighteenth century, European powers became increasingly assertive, and a resurgent Japan fought China and conquered Korea.

Scholars have noted the historical rarity of interstate conflict between East Asian states. Picking up on arguments made by Kang and others, Robert Kelly posits the existence of a Confucian Peace, one that bears a resemblance to the so-called Democratic Peace.[39] The four states experienced comparatively few interstate wars during the five centuries before the 1800s, as shown in figure 4.3, where battles were rare prior to a sharp jump in the mid-1800s. Although there may have been frequent wars on the frontiers and inside these states (i.e., intrastate war), there were few

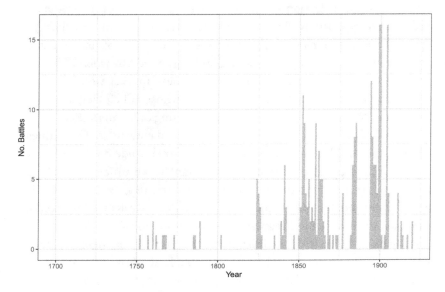

FIGURE 4.3. Battles in East Asia, 1700–1920. *Source*: Data are sourced from Miller and Bakar, "Conflict Events Worldwide Since 1468 BC."

conflicts between them, and far fewer than European states experienced during that period. In one empirical study, David Kang, Meredith Shaw, and Ronan Tse-Min Fu document the relative absence of interstate war in East Asia between 1368 and 1841.[40] To be sure, there were interstate wars, such as the great Imjin War (1592–1598) and the Chinese invasion of Vietnam in 1788. Moreover, wars involving East Asian armies, when they occurred, were larger and deadlier than wars in West Africa and Southeast Asia. Nearly all conventional wars in East Asia between 1800 and 1913 were fought by standing armies, averaging 6,000 deaths per war, with nearly 77,000 soldiers deployed per East Asian actor per conflict.[41] But such wars were relatively infrequent in the lead-up to the nineteenth century.

If the Confucian Peace theory holds, how can it be explained? This question is the subject of a fascinating and ongoing debate. Scholars working on this issue highlight at least four explanatory factors, all potentially interrelated and none mutually exclusive. First, Kelly, following Kang, stresses the importance of Confucian culture and its antiwar norms.[42] Much like one explanation for the Democratic Peace, it is argued that the Confucian Peace is built on a normative/cultural consensus regarding appropriate conduct. It is grounded in Confucian culture. A second factor, one favored by Kang, stresses the legitimacy baked into the Sinocentric tribute system.[43] The key states typically (though not always) accepted China's central role as legitimate. It was when states challenged China's legitimacy, as Japan did during the Imjin War, that the Confucian Peace broke down. Both factors, culture and legitimacy, are interrelated and point to the importance of international order, an issue we return to later.

A third factor is hegemony. China was the clear hegemon during most of the era under study, and it certainly existed during the standard period of the tribute system. In Kang's argument, hegemony intersects with culture and legitimacy to produce peace, but it is fundamentally about the peace-inducing effects of hard material power, in contrast to the ideological soft power of culture and legitimacy. The potential pacifying and stabilizing effects of hegemony and hierarchy have resonated with traditional arguments regarding hegemonic-stability theory.[44] That understanding, in turn, has given support to the position that hegemonic systems are more passive than those where power is balanced, and it has been a popular theme in the developing Chinese IR literature.

A fourth factor, identified by Andrew Phillips, centers on Qing imperial policies, which usually obviated the need for conflict. Arguing that most of the proponents of the Confucian Peace are unapologetically constructivist, Phillips points out that it took smart Qing policies to navigate diplomatic relations with its neighbors.[45] Some of these policies were coercive in nature, designed to win the allegiance of interlocuters. Furthermore, the Qing rulers played on the civilized-versus-barbarian distinction to drum loyalty among tributary states. Overall, Phillips is underscoring the importance of policy choices.

One caveat to the Confucian Peace is that conflict on the periphery was intense and violent, mostly for the Vietnamese and Chinese states that possessed open frontiers on the Asian continent.[46] As Johnston describes in his Parabellum paradigm of Chinese grand strategy, conflict on the frontier was frequent, a finding confirmed by Kang, Shaw, and Fu.[47] Kelly argues that Chinese policies vis-à-vis the Zunghar Mongols in the 1750s were genocidal.[48] Similarly, Peter Perdue describes how the gradual westward expansion of the Chinese state into the nineteenth century absorbed, removed, or annihilated non-Han populations.[49] China also fought several wars against its peripheral neighbors: Kokand (1825–1838,

1830–1831, and 1865), Tibet (1912–1913), and Eastern Turkistan (1866–1871 and 1876–1877).

Geopolitical competition, however, increased as the nineteenth century progressed. As Jason Sharman discusses, lead European states were practicing gunboat diplomacy during this time to open markets or acquire territory or both.[50] After sending two official missions to the Qing court in 1793 and 1816 to address the trade imbalance and accumulation of silver in China, the British government supported merchants in the developing opium trade. The influx of narcotics into China would result decades later in the First Opium War (1839–1842) and the Second Opium War (1856–1860). Both conflicts resulted in a weakened China, internal conflicts such as the catastrophic Taiping Rebellion (1850–1864), and territorial loss in Hong Kong and the treaty ports.[51] The Boxer Rebellion (1900) also involved the European powers and Japan.

Wars with European states heightened threat perceptions in China and Japan.[52] Tensions within the Tokugawa elite, for example, intensified as the U.S. admiral Matthew C. Perry forced Japan, which had maintained tight control of European interchange for centuries, to open its borders in 1853.[53] The shock of that encounter led to the downfall of the Tokugawa Shogunate, the Meiji Revolution, and eventually the industrialization of the country. It would be the newly formed and expansionist Japanese Empire that would seize control of Korea in 1905 after defeating Russia in the Russo-Japanese War of 1904–1905.

Conflict exposure had spatial variations in East Asia through the late eighteenth and early nineteenth century, with Vietnam being the most war exposed and Japan the least. In 1750, for example, Vietnam was divided into two hostile states (Dang Ngoai in the North and Dang Trong in the South). Both states collapsed in 1771 with the Tay Son Rebellion, which evolved into an interstate war engulfing the region from 1771 to 1802, drawing Chinese invasions from 1784 to 1789.[54] A restored Nguyen Dynasty from 1802 then fought in Cambodia (and against Siam) in 1812, 1831–1834, and 1841–1845 and fought the French in 1833–1839, 1847, 1858–1863, and 1873–1874. Of all the cases in East Asia, Vietnam appears to have experienced the most pressure from interstate war (see figure 4.4).

In contrast, both Korea and Japan had fixed land and sea borders.[55] Japan had seen a long (internal and external) peace from 1603 and the establishment of the Tokugawa Shogunate to the Perry incident in 1853

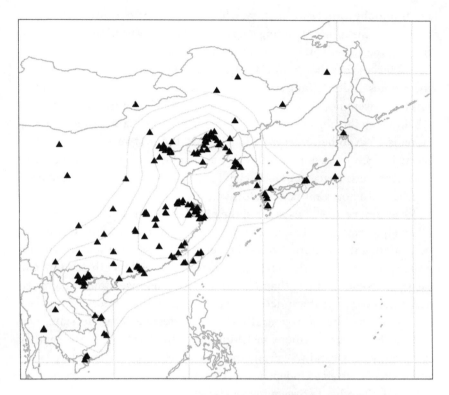

FIGURE 4.4. Battle locations in East Asia, 1750–1920. *Note*: Contour lines represent estimates of conflict-location density. *Source*: Data are from Miller and Bakar, "Conflict Events Worldwide Since 1468 BC."

and the Meiji Revolution in 1868, which involved widespread fighting across the islands. Japan then faced internal rebellions in 1877 and in Taiwan in 1895, and it invaded Korea in 1905, putting down rebellions there between 1907 and 1910. Japan also fought a war against China in 1894–1895.

Although interstate wars in East Asia were relatively rare, intrastate wars were frequent and intense. In their study, Kang, Shaw, and Fu found that whereas only 4 percent of China's conflict incidents between 1368 and 1841 were with one of the other core states, some 60 percent involved civil wars.[56] The remaining conflicts occurred with steppe peoples and pirates. Furthermore, for Korea and China, internal revolts were responsible for the largest number of conflict years over the same period, some 227 years compared with only 28 years of interstate war.[57] This pattern holds into the nineteenth century, with 64 percent of wars involving China occurring intrastate, including some of the most devastating wars, such as the Taiping Rebellion, costing hundreds of thousands of lives. This finding indicates that the Confucian Peace does not extend to conflict inside these states. Indeed, Kang suggests that one reason these state's substantial militaries were not fighting one another is that they were "putting down rebellions, guarding the central government, and maintaining essential systems."[58] Another interpretation is that the system created a set of inwardly facing Praetorian states that avoided war with one another. Like the Democratic Peace, the Confucian Peace is at best an in-group dynamic; conflict with non-Confucian actors was common.

In summary, East Asia entered the nineteenth century on the back of a relatively peaceful period, at least understood in terms of interstate conflicts among the four core states. There was, however, variation: Vietnam was exposed to more devastating warfare in the eighteenth century and early nineteenth century than the other states and over time as competition increased over the nineteenth century. European interventions and invasions, the rise of a centralized and aggressive Japanese state, and regime-shattering rebellions in China made the late nineteenth century more competitive and war prone than the previous centuries. Only Japan and China survived as independent states past the early twentieth century (although the other two were revived later).

POLITICAL CENTRALIZATION

Of all the state systems examined in this book, the East Asian system best approximates the billiard ball model. Governments typically possessed well-developed bureaucracies and commanded substantial political reach. Kang writes that the states in this system were states in the Weberian sense.[59] There were agreed-upon borders between the core states, and the writ of the monarch generally extended to those borders. This was not a particularly heteronomous system in which peripheral vassals could play rulers off one another and derive a form of dual vassalage.[60] Of course, Japan was an exception in terms of its decentralized governance.[61] This system also had a comparatively developed international order. Let us now expand on each of these points.

Much has been written on the institutional development of the East Asian states. For example, Woodside argues that China and Vietnam shared a neo-Confucian administrative system that generated strong patterns of top-down, bureaucratic, direct rule.[62] Public servants typically came through the examination system and were often appointed to various posts around the state. The resulting bureaucracy was designed to exercise territorial control in an efficient and centralized manner that, at its best, homogenized language and culture. Practices that are often associated with the development of the French state were, in many ways, preceded in the East Asian states by centuries if not millennia.[63] Chin-Hao Huang and David Kang claim that the basic template of government emerged during the Qin Dynasty in 221 BCE. Woodside writes that starting "no later than the fifteenth century, the rulers of all three societies [China, Korea, Vietnam] organized their central administrations around six specialized ministries, dividing government into matters of personnel and appointments; finance and taxes; rites and education; war; justice and punishment; and public works."[64] Scholars generally agree that the basic template for a strong centralized state took hold in China and was subsequently exported to Korea, Vietnam, and Japan.

To preview the following chapters, compared to West Africa, South Asia, and Southeast Asia at the time, the East Asian states (except Japan and Vietnam to an extent) delegated authority to vassals less often and governed directly. In fact, Kang argues that the decentralized mandala structures of Southeast Asian polities were absent in East Asia, where states had greater reach and institutional/bureaucratic development.[65] China, Korea, and Vietnam maintained sizeable and permanent military forces. Provincial rule was guided by bureaucrats who came through the examination system. Populations were counted through centrally run cadastral surveys, a practice that began in Vietnam as early as the eleventh century and even earlier in China.[66]

Combined with these practices of population and land measurement was the use of linear borders. Andy Hanlun Li contends that these states, in particular China, possessed a modern sense of territoriality long before similar Western notions were brought to the region.[67] That is, maps were used to claim and delineate territory. The resulting borders were clearest at the interior lines of the system between China and Korea and between China and Vietnam, borders that were established by the end of the eleventh century.[68] These two key borders were demarcated and managed by the state. Being an island nation, Japan had less need to determine its borders.

Governance on the western continental frontiers of both China and Vietnam was imperial, consisting of zones of control and forms of indirect rule. Woodside describes China's westward expansion into the interior by drawing a fascinating analogy with nineteenth-century U.S. westward expansion.[69] As the reach of the Chinese state expanded, the state absorbed and sometimes eliminated non-Han populations.[70] Similarly, according to Woodside, "in the early 1800s, one Vietnamese emperor combined the doctrine [of a centrally controlled state], as China had in the early 1700s, with a campaign to convert the hereditary leaders of Vietnam's hill-country minorities into appointed circulating bureaucrats with examination-system degrees, who might or might not share the ethnic identities of the minorities they ruled."[71] Vietnam also tolerated heteronomous governance in Cambodia and Laos. Cambodia was a tributary of Siam and Vietnam for parts of the nineteenth century, and Xiang Khouang was a vassal of Vientiane and Vietnam in the late eighteenth century.[72] This difference between the interior borders of the system and exterior frontiers corresponded with the institutions of the Chinese state. As MacKay notes, diplomatic relations with other Confucian states were handled by Confucian bureaucrats in the Libu (Board of Rites), whereas relations with frontier groups were managed by Manchu bannermen in the Lifan Yuan (Court of Colonial Affairs).[73]

Rulers in China and Korea governed centralized states for hundreds of years before the nineteenth century. Japan and Vietnam, however, began the nineteenth century as relatively decentralized states and transitioned to centralization during this period. Like Korea and Vietnam, Japan had embraced the civic religion of Confucianism. During the fifth and sixth centuries, it began to adopt Chinese notions of the relationship between the ruler and the rulers' subjects. The Taika Reforms of 645 centralized the state by appointing regional governors and implementing a "population census, a centralized tax system, a legal code, and a civil service examination, all based on the Tang [Dynasty] models."[74] Later reforms, such as the Taiho Code and the Yoro Code, sought to implement additional Chinese-style governance practices. Japan was essentially following the path of Korea and Vietnam, if on a different schedule.

However, the Japanese state experienced a long period of decentralization that continued into the nineteenth century with the Tokugawa Shogunate (1603–1868, also called the Edo Period).[75] Japan's emperor remained the de jure sovereign, but the shogun held de facto power, governing a core around Edo (Tokyo), with the remainder of Japan's territory divided into vassal domains called *han* that were governed by daimyo rulers.[76] By 1720, there were about 260 *han* of varying sizes and status. Mark Ravina defines the relationship between the regional lords (daimyo) and the central authority (shogun) as a compound state: the "daimyo maintained independent standing armies, wrote their own legal codes, set and collected their own taxes, controlled and policed their own borders. The shogunate maintained a monopoly on foreign policy, but the daimyo were entrusted with the management of their own domestic affairs."[77] The daimyo also appointed their own officials and patrolled their own borders.[78] Vassals were autonomous, but the shogun maintained a formal central position, even requiring that daimyo spend alternating years in Edo, dismissing daimyo for personal offenses, and even overseeing their marriages and adoptions. As Eiko Ikegami states, "The Tokugawa shoguns forbade the daimyo to declare war as well as to make independent alliances with other daimyo. Moreover, the daimyo were not allowed to erect new castles or to build large ships. Even a project to repair the stone walls of one's own castle required formal submission from the shogunate."[79]

While a bureaucracy governed core Tokugawa domains, shogunate presence in the daimyo territories was thin: the shogunate "never introduced direct institutions of government, such as a national bureaucracy, a standing army, national police, or a national taxation system, to enforce direct supervision of the citizenry and their possessions," states Ikegami.[80] There was an equilibrium; the Tokugawa Shogunate was the largest and most powerful of the Japanese domains, but the daimyo were strong enough to resist centralization so that "the bakufu was forced, even from the beginning, to placate and cosset them wherever possible."[81] This relationship has yielded various metaphors indicating decentralized rule, such as a "concentric ring," "neofeudal state," and "compound state."[82]

Japan's neofeudal shogunate rule was more centralized during the seventeenth century and weakened in the eighteenth.[83] Three daimyo per year were dismissed between 1616 and 1651, but over the next two hundred years this number declined to one. Information dried up, and the demands on the daimyo were reduced.[84] On the eve of the Meiji Revolution, larger vassals were behaving like independent states, with some, such as Satsuma, sending a separate delegation to the Paris Exposition of 1867 as it "tried to work out independent status as ruler of the Ryukyu Islands."[85] Japan shared similarities with other decentralized states discussed in this book, with the possible exception that a strong ideological and institutional glue held the Japanese state together.

The Meiji Revolution of 1868 was an inflection point in Japanese history. Attempts at centralization were made in the late Tokugawa era—for example, the Bunsei reforms and the Tempo reforms—but in each case regional lords were able to check the center's ambitions. Then the shock of Admiral Matthew Perry's visit in 1853 helped tip the scale by creating a "crisis of foreign policy."[86] Increased competition initially empowered the larger, more autonomous, and more distant vassals such as Chosu and Satsuma to assert their independence by backing a revitalization of the emperor's powers.[87] The shogun was caught between demands to curtail foreign interference, dependence on increasingly recalcitrant vassals, and demands to create a strong miliary and fiscal state. These tensions were "insoluble," and despite further decentralization with the Bunkuyu Reforms of 1862, Marius Jansen writes, "the negative aspects of the foreign presence had dealt mortal blows to some of the institutional aspects of Tokugawa power." "With central power diminishing, the future of Japan was to be decided by a contest among regional powers, and the chief contestants were the great domains of southwest Japan and the bakufu itself."[88] Fighting between the shogunate and rebel daimyo began in 1863–1864, and despite last-ditch attempts to centralize *bakufu* administration (in shogun-controlled territories), the shogunate was defeated in 1868. Domains were replaced with prefects in 1871; samurai were either repressed or bought off with government bonds or positions in the government; a state conscript army was created in 1873; a national bureaucracy (staffed at the senior levels by loyalists from the Satsuma, Chosu, Tosa, and Hinzen domains) was created; and central fiscal institutions were established.[89]

Japan possessed the right conditions for political centralization—urbanization, economic integration, shared institutional and cultural memory. The result of the transition was a more coherent central authority in the name of the emperor, "direct administration through a unified central bureaucracy[,] ... the establishment of a hierarchy of offices that linked the center to the localities without sharing power," as well as universal conscription.[90]

EAST ASIA

Vietnam also transitioned to direct rule in the nineteenth century. Vietnam (Dai Viet) was a centralized, neo-Confucian state from 1453 to 1516, but succession wars partitioned the country into Dang Ngoai (sometimes called "Tonkin" and dominated by the Trinh Dynasty), which ruled the North, and Dang Trong (sometimes called "Cochin China" under the Nguyen Dynasty), ruling in the South, with its capital in Hue. Both states ruled with hybridized models of direct rule and autonomous regional vassals, more pronounced in the South than in the North. For nearly two centuries, this stalemate prevailed until the Tay Son Rebellion (1771–1802), which started as a provincial rebellion against direct rule, ended the Trinh and Nguyen states, and replaced them with a brief period of Tay Son rule (1788–1802).[91] In 1802, however, the Tay Son were expelled by the only surviving nephew (Gia Long) of the Nguyen Dynasty, who unified the country and renamed it "Viet Nam."

At unification in 1802, Vietnamese rulers could look back to the centralized fifteenth-century Ly state (1463–1516).[92] However, Gia Long first resurrected the mixed decentralized/Confucian rule that the Nguyen state had previously employed.[93] Years of warfare in the North and the South had made Dang Ngoai and Dang Trong rulers dependent on warlords. In Saigon and Hanoi, autonomous military governors levied their own taxes, appointed their own subordinates, tried their own cases, and used their own seals in the populous North and the Mekong Delta. Victor Lieberman describes the Vietnamese state as a "solar polity" until the 1830s, invoking images of decentralized rule.[94]

It was only when Gia Long's son, Minh-mang (1820–1841), assumed power that "Gia long's decentralized solar polity" was replaced with "a Pattern D [highly centralized] system of 31 provinces from the Chinese border to the gulf of Siam."[95] Territory from Siam to China was reorganized into provinces, prefectures, and districts; tax collectors were salaried; a complex system of information gathering down to the district and village level was developed; the Confucian schools were expanded; and a large standing army was assembled. An important move toward centralization was removing the power of the Hanoi and Saigon warlords. In 1831, the northern military protectorate was folded into a "Chinese-style provincial system," and in 1832 the southern protectorate was abolished upon the death of its governor-general, Le Van Dyuet.[96] Dyuet's son and successor, however, launched a massive rebellion that drew in a Siamese invasion and was not suppressed until 1835. Dissolving the two "military viceroyalties . . . marked an important new phase in the Nguyen court's effort to assert political control and to transform the nature of its governance," states George Dutton.[97] Although centralization was still limited, especially at the village level, according to Lieberman, "Hue by 1840 had better control over the chief Vietnamese-speaking lowlands than any regime since the early Trinh, and possibly the early Ly." Hue attempted its centralization projects on the more remote Laotian and Cambodian regions that it conquered in the early 1800s. But these projects failed: in Laos, these reforms "bred bitter revolts," and in Cambodia they led to a Siamese-backed rebellion that crossed into southern Vietnam in 1840–1841. Resistance to centralizing policies was widespread, with more than three hundred revolts recorded between 1802 and 1841.[98]

EXPLAINING (DE)CENTRALIZATION

Much of the received wisdom from European political development is that war and perhaps trade made states. All core East Asian states governed with relatively direct forms of rule by the end of the nineteenth century. Do we find evidence that interaction capacity, war, and trade are responsible for that development? Did other factors play a role?

We begin with interaction capacity, which is a measure of a system's capabilities with respect to transportation, communication, and organization. High levels of interaction capacity should enable rulers to move from decentralized to centralized forms of governance. The East Asian case broadly supports this argument, although we are careful to note that states often created interaction capacity by building roads and infrastructure. Nonetheless, there is an extent to which some of East Asia's interaction capacity was caused by plausibly exogenous factors. China, Vietnam, Korea, and Japan had historically high population densities sustained by high-yield rice-producing basins aided by interior river systems, leading to the rise of large and proximate cities. More people lowered the costs of economic and social interactions, which in turn lowered the costs of centralization.

In Japan, for example, population growth in the eighteenth century in combination with the Tokugawa Shogunate's inability to regulate trade created an integrated national market: "By the early 1800s," states Lieberman, "two centuries of market expansion had eroded the barrier between city and countryside and had produced an unprecedented lifestyle convergence among townspeople, wealthy peasants, and lower and middle samurai."[99] Jansen notes that "literacy, travel, and a lively economic interchange between areas had transformed and joined together what had still been separated culture zones at the beginning of the Tokugawa years."[100] Japan's domestic economy had commercialized and integrated during the Tokugawa period, despite international isolation. Ikegami argues that a national market economy was facilitated by daimyo decentralization, vertical integration, peace, and infrastructure investments by the shogunate.[101]

A similar process was underway in Vietnam, aided by previous centralization projects in the fifteenth century but also driven by more exogenous population growth, commercialization, and economic growth in the North and around Hue. By the nineteenth century, despite nearly two centuries of divided and mixed rule, a distinct Vietnamese identity emerged in the core population basins, driven by economic and cultural change and state efforts at assimilation.[102]

East Asia's greater interaction capacity—driven by high population densities and favorable geographic conditions—probably did underpin processes of integration that drive state centralization. Lower transport and exchange costs also made extending state infrastructures cheaper, but they also stimulated processes that further lowered administrative costs that could be capitalized on when the conditions were right. A critical element seems to have been linguistic and cultural homogenization, especially at the elite level, which lowered the extent to which governance was perceived as alien and had to overcome the hurdles of language and cultural dissimilarity. Lieberman's centralization thesis—applied specifically to Vietnam—is that population growth, economic growth, and commercialization created circuits of interaction that not only deepened ethnic, cultural, and linguistic homogeneity but also reinforced the foundations for forms of direct rule. This is not yet a causal relationship, but rather an association that can be self-reinforcing (i.e., interaction capacity provides incentives for experiments in centralized rule that are more successful; these experiments create physical and cultural infrastructures that make future experiments more likely to be successful; and so on). However, the sources in this chapter provide reason to think that dense populations, easier communications, and trading links initially eased the burdens of direct rule and made centralization possible.

For example, centralization appeared first in the higher-density regions of East Asian states. Vietnam's fifteenth-century experience with centralized rule was concentrated on the "compact, easily monitored, and ethnically uniform" river basins in the North.[103] Gia Long ruled a unified Vietnam again by 1802, but initially only Hue and its surroundings were administered from the center. From the 1830s, centralization expanded but was most successful in regions where Vietnamese cultural and linguistic unity was highest, which was the product of longer processes of cultural change and assimilation. Centralization projects failed where interaction capacity was lower. Cambodia and Laos were ruled by Vietnam for parts of the nineteenth century, and rulers in Hue applied Chinese models of direct rule. Yet administrative reforms in these distant and non-Vietnamese kingdoms provoked rebellion by regional elites and Buddhist monks, drew in Siamese military support, and threatened southern Vietnamese territory. Vietnam lost control of its Cambodian territories as a result. Although Vietnam and Japan remained relatively decentralized states until the mid–nineteenth century, increases in interaction capacity through the preceding two centuries helped create the foundation for more centralized forms of government to (re)emerge when other factors (such as war or trade) triggered opportunities for institutional change.

Second, the trade-based argument regarding centralization is that commercial competition promotes the development of fiscally competent states. The higher the trade levels, the greater the need for centralized states to manage the potential income. Overall, the high trade levels in East Asia were consonant with the high level of state development. The pursuit and promotion of trade were one of the objectives of diplomatic missions between states. Kang is quite clear that trade was a prominent feature of the tribute system prior to Western encroachment.[104] There is thus a clear correlation between trade and state formation. Domestic and foreign trade probably played a positive role in Vietnam's centralization process. Saigon and the Mekong Delta (controlled by the Nguyen states throughout) emerged as commercial hubs, providing easy-to-control taxation revenues and access to European weaponry that enabled the southern state first to survive against northern encroachments and then to end the Tay Son Rebellion and unify the country. Southern trade provided the material and weaponry to construct a standing army, which was 115,000 strong under Minh-mang (r. 1820–1841) and was a crucial tool in the suppression of resistance to centralization. Domestic economic growth and internal trade also increased, and tolls on domestic trade accounted for a larger share of state revenues, providing the resources to create a salaried bureaucracy. As Lieberman states, commercial expansion "magnified the range of government income, facilitated extraction from the rural economy, simplified the transmissions of resources, and in the case of salaried officials, strengthened administrative discipline."[105] Although Japan was more isolated from international trade, domestic economic growth and trade increased the availability of taxable transactions there, which smoothed the centralization process.

The third hypothesis about centralization is the Tilly dictum that war makes the state. Did it make states in East Asia? Since China and Korea had centralized centuries prior to our window of analysis, this section focuses mostly on Vietnam and Japan. However, authors such as Hui have argued that China's early fiscal and bureaucratic centralization is well explained by bellicist theories, wherein China followed a similar process to that observed in Europe. On the face of it, the presence of centralized states in a zone of "Confucian Peace" might appear to contradict the bellicist argument. Low levels of war and high levels of centralization are the opposite of what the "war makes states" argument would predict. However, the lack of conflict among China, Korea, and Japan is probably in part explained by the presence of early-centralized states. As we will see in subsequent chapters, a common cause of warfare between states is decentralized rule that creates uncertain and fluctuating border zones and severe information and commitment problems between ruler and vassal. Early centralization may have enabled China, Korea, Japan, and Vietnam to bind themselves to an international order that limited uncertainties and lowered the probability of war. Low levels of war and high levels of centralization are not strong reasons to think that the bellicist theory is false in this case.

The evidence is more favorable if we look at Japan and Vietnam, the two cases that moved from semidecentralized to centralized forms of governance during our period. Japan's enduring decentralization could be attributed to the lack of international competition that reduced the shogunate's need to extract more revenues from the daimyo. The Matthew Perry incident in 1853 is often cited as the external shock that awakened the shogunate to the realities of new international competition, where Japan's weakness was attributed to its decentralized system of government.[106] This appears to be a textbook case of the "war makes states" thesis as a rising external threat triggers domestic reform.

Vietnam also provides reasonable evidence for the bellicist theory. Vietnam was probably the most war exposed of the four cases before the mid-nineteenth century, having been partitioned into two hostile and partially decentralized states from the sixteenth century to 1771, which was followed by the Tay Son Rebellion, invasions by China, war with Cambodia (often with Siamese intervention), and increasing hostilities with the French. War's initial impact, however, was to incentivize more decentralized forms of rule or at least to empower warlords, who were afforded autonomy in governance in return for loyalty to the new regime. After uniting Vietnam in 1802, Gia Long initially rewarded his generals with governorships in the North and South, a pattern reminiscent of the earlier Nguyen state's maintenance of a system of military governorships up to 1771.[107] In fact, for the Nguyen and Trinh states of the eighteenth century, more centralized forms of governance—although limited—only emerged later when the front between the two states had stabilized.[108] After unification, it was not just the threat of outside invasion that signaled the need for reform but internal rebellions in 1833 and 1835 (which were a reaction to centralization efforts). Warfare may also have contributed to the unification and centralization of Vietnam by destroying the entrenched Trinh and Nguyen Dynasties and reducing elite opposition to Minh-mang's centralization reforms. Under constant military pressure from inside and out, Vietnam transitioned to a centralized state in the mid-nineteenth century.

While interaction capacity, war, and trade may have played a positive role in driving more direct forms of governance in East Asia, studies of East Asian states are prominent for highlighting the role of administrative models, emulation, and institutional diffusion. In their recent work on the East Asian model of state formation, Huang and Kang argue that it was not war that forged East Asian states but rather the deliberate goal of emulating the Chinese model. They contend that China had devised a kind of ur-state as far back as the Qin Dynasty in 221 BCE, with gradual modifications over the centuries. They stress that the Qin state was not the product of war but rather "a result of unification and the needs to administer a massive territory and to consolidate political rule beyond the aristocracy in the state and royal court itself." In the centuries that followed, the neighboring states that took hold in Korea, Vietnam, and Japan observed the cultural and material power of the subsequent Chinese dynasties and sought to emulate that model of the state. Here, emulation is conceived as an active process of adopting ideas and policies thought to be appropriate for the cultural setting.[109] In this way, the emulating states came to adopt key institutions such as the civil service exam, the central administration, and the formal diplomatic processes of the tribute system, not to mention myriad distinctly Chinese cultural elements related to language, art, architecture, and so on. These states' purpose in making these adoptions was not to compete militarily but to reproduce in their own society what they saw as superior in China.

This is a fascinating thesis, one that is consistent with many related treatments on the historical influence of China on its neighbors.[110] Future work can explore the degree to which emulation mattered and whether military competition mattered at all. Hui, for example, maintains that the pressures of military competition are part of the explanation for state formation in ancient China.[111] But rather than dive into that debate, which would go beyond our purpose in this book, let us accept the general thrust of this argument and think about its implications in comparative terms. An important parallel with the bellicist thesis is the relationship between systems and states. Both theses posit that the attributes of a system can have downward effects on the structure of the units (states), a point emphasized by Huang and Kang.[112] In the bellicist vision, competitive military pressures in the system yield structural changes in the states. Similarly, the trade-related argument sees change at the state level following from competitive pressures at the system level. The emulation thesis is also an outside-in argument—that is, factors in the system have local effects—but here the aim is not to compete but to emulate.

Emulation as a mechanism for state centralization highlights the importance of international order. In chapter 2, we adopted Bentley Allan's definition of international order as "stable patterns of behavior and relations among states and other international associations" that give rise to "historical periods characterized by distinct combinations of political, military, and economic practices."[113] International order between states is essential for emulation because it provides the basis upon which ideas can be shared and made legible. Huang and Kang assert that the diplomatic missions of the tribute system were the key diffusion mechanism.[114] As we will see in the mandala concept in Southeast Asia, discussed in chapter 6, prevalent ideas in international order can have shaping effects on states. We contend that richer and more developed international orders ought to display stronger effects on state structures. That is, the system-shaping importance of international order rises as it becomes more robust.

Consider the investiture process, another core element of the tribute system. Ji-Young Lee argues that this was essentially a two-level game played by the leaders in secondary states.[115] For example, Korean leaders were socialized into an international order that assigned legitimacy—a largely unspoken but shared understanding—to the investiture rights of the Qing court. When Chinese ideological hegemony was resonant, as it usually was, then leaders would leverage the blessing of the Qing court to consolidate power at home. That recognition gave them legitimacy in the eyes of their domestic audience. Overall, international order conditioned how member actors thought about legitimate state recognition. The modern UN system effectively does the same thing by awarding sovereign recognition to aspiring members.[116]

We agree that emulation is an overlooked mechanism in state centralization. States such as Vietnam modeled their centralization projects (both successful and failed) on Chinese blueprints, up to and including the mid-nineteenth-century reforms.[117] The mechanism of emulation highlights the role of systems effects and the importance of international order for both constituting and diffusing the ideas and practices that are to be emulated. We suspect, like Huang and Kang, that these dynamics operated across other historical systems over time.[118] Although every international order over time has been unique, and some of the content of those orders may not travel well, the larger complex of order and emulation is modular. Orders create the possibility for emulation and learning across units, particularly if there is something like a Confucian Peace among the states. Indeed, those practices can outlive the core states that upheld the order, as we saw with the desire of the Vietnamese to emulate the Tang Dynasty even after it had expired and as we will see with the Mughal legacy in South Asia (chapter 5).[119]

In summary, the East Asian case provides some evidence for the theories of state centralization provided in chapter 3. By 1900, China, Korea, Japan, and Vietnam looked much more like billiard balls than bull's-eyes.

EAST ASIA

In Japan and Vietnam, conditions were right for experiments with centralized governance to succeed. Interaction capacity was high, lowering the costs of extending administrative infrastructure by providing more taxation revenues per distance traveled and stimulating a slow process of economic and cultural integration that produced more ethnically homogeneous populations by the opening of the nineteenth century. This interaction capacity was partially a product of geographic factors that produced denser populations, easier riverine communications, and the legacies of previous attempts at administrative centralization. Growth in foreign and domestic trade provided dynasties with greater taxation revenues and weapons that they used to fund bureaucracy and standing armies, and war provided either a stimulus to disempower autonomous regional lords or destroy them in dynasty-ending conflicts. Finally, all East Asian states had Chinese models of direct rule to draw upon that were often accepted as legitimate by elites embedded in a Sinocentric international order, further lowering the costs of direct rule. The East Asian case is, therefore, a useful illustration of the main centralization mechanisms at work.

However, some of the tensions that we pull apart in the following chapters were also present in East Asia. Trade was an important resource to state elites, but only if they could monopolize and control it. Japan was fearful of trade's destabilizing effects and sought isolation. Jansen states that "foreign trade ... had the effect of weakening the bakufu's ability to control domestic commerce and opened Japan to the ports as well as opening the ports to the foreigners."[120] Vietnam's coastal geography and partition into two rival states for more than two hundred years can be partially explained by competing access to commercial ports in the North and the South. Increasing competition provided the spur to Japanese centralization and probably paved the way for Vietnamese unification, but it sometimes empowered regional elites and warlords, who demanded autonomy and more decentralized forms of rule in exchange for agreeing to unify. Indeed, the initial impact of competition in Japan was first to empower regional vassals vis-à-vis the center, who eventually overthrew the regime. Chinese models of direct rule were available and considered legitimate, but centralization projects based on this model varied in their implementation over space and time. Japan was aware of Chinese models of direct rule for centuries but inconsistently applied them. Beasley states that Western models of centralized rule (especially Prussian models) were also more important for Japan.[121] Administrative models were a constant in Vietnam, but governance fluctuated between successful application of Confucian models to mixed forms that combined bureaucratic centralization with regional autonomy and independence. These variations are clues. War and trade might have been, on balance, centripetal forces in East Asia during the eighteenth and nineteenth centuries, but they also had the potential to unleash centrifugal pressures. Administrative models might have been available, but that does not explain why they were successfully deployed in only some, not all, circumstances. As we argue in the coming chapters, the impacts of war and trade are likely conditional on the underlying level of interaction capacity.

CONCLUSION

This case study provides a glimpse of a fascinating state system just before the global enclosure. Relative to South Asia, maritime Southeast Asia, and West Africa, the East Asian system is an anomaly. It consisted of only four states, and all four are well-known modern-day states. Although two of the states—Korea and Vietnam—died around the turn of the twentieth century, they were resurrected in the post-1945 period. In comparative terms, the East Asian system appears to have reached a high level of stability before the colonial encounter. Its states were strong, hierarchical states with enormous populations in a system that possessed borders and rich patterns of diplomacy. These cases point to a role for—and illustrate the operation of—all the mechanisms discussed in chapter 3, perhaps functioning in an interlocking and self-reinforcing way. It also highlights the role that international order plays in shaping both states and systems. But these cases also suggest that the forces driving centralization in East Asia could have very different effects elsewhere. In the following three chapters, we step outside of the well-trodden terrain of East Asian state building and into the less well-studied South Asian, maritime Southeast Asian, and West African systems.

Chapter Five

SOUTH ASIA

It is difficult to imagine how different a nineteenth-century map of South Asia might have looked compared to a map drawn today. Instead of six states, there were nearly forty, the majority in modern-day India. Instead of stable borders, the eighteenth and nineteenth centuries saw turbulent state creation and mass state death. Most of India was ruled by the Mughal Empire at the beginning of the eighteenth century, one of the largest land-based empires in history. Just fifty years later, though, it had collapsed, leaving dozens of new states competing for regional dominance. Farther east in Bengal and Madras, the British East India Company (EIC) was expanding and would envelop the subcontinent by the middle of the nineteenth century. South Asia was at that point a system between empires.

Although in some ways South Asia is an ideal-type case for bellicist theories of state formation,[1] we do not find much evidence that war-based or trade-based theories explain centralization there. State centralization was patchy. Most states—despite constant warfare, strong trade networks, and several attempts at centralization—governed through vassalage and indirect rule. Only the Mysore Kingdom emerged as a clear centralizer. Rather, to the contrary, some evidence suggests that warfare and competition generated decentralization as desperate rulers exchanged autonomy for military service and revenue. We suggest that similarities in governance across the subcontinent are better explained by relatively low levels of interaction capacity, despite conflict and high levels of trade.

This chapter utilizes the same structure as the previous chapter on East Asia. It first describes the state system. It then investigates the level of interaction capacity and the frequency of war and trade and assesses the degree of political centralization across the system before examining how well these key independent variables explain that variation. But unlike the East Asian chapter and more like the case studies on Southeast Asia and West Africa that follow, this chapter explores a mostly decentralized, bull's-eye system whose member states no longer exist.

STATES AND THE SYSTEM

A panoply of states governed South Asia, including the Rajput states in modern-day Rajasthan, the Maratha Confederacy and its successor kingdoms, newer states such as Khalistan across the modern Indian-Pakistan border, and the older mountain kingdoms of Nepal, Sikkim, Bhutan, and Assam (see figure 5.1). By 1816, the date when we start recording states in the ISD, the British had conquered many indigenous states in eastern India or placed them under protectorate status or both, which under our coding rules removed their external sovereignty, even if many retained varying degrees of internal autonomy. These protected states include the southern Indian states of Travancore, Mysore, and the Nizam, along with Bengal (in modern-day Bangladesh and India) and Awadh. All the Maratha states were under British protection by 1818, as were the Rajput states. It took the British longer to expand into the Punjab, and it was only after two wars with Ranjit Singh's state Khalistan that it was subdued in 1848.

State death is the dominant story in this system. Only 5 percent of state episodes started after 1816, in contrast to the case in Southeast Asia and West Africa (see chapters 6 and 7, respectively). Wind the clock back to 1750, however, and state formation was the norm in South Asia. In 1707, the Mughal Empire claimed much of India and Pakistan, east to Bengal and Bangladesh, and deep into southern India.[2] Delhi was sacked by Nadir Shah from Persia in 1739, raided by the Marathas and the Durrani Empire, and became a protectorate of Scindia (Gwalior/Ujjain) in the late eighteenth century and then of the British Empire in 1803.[3] New states rose

FIGURE 5.1. States and population densities in South Asia per the ISD, 1816–1920 and 1800. *Note:* Shows population density in 1800. More opaque circles represent clearer borders noted in the ISD. Population density has been capped at a maximum of 120 people per square kilometer to facilitate comparison with the other three systems. *Source:* Population density data are from Klein Goldewijk et al., "The HYDE 3.1 Spatially Explicit Database of Human-Induced Global Land-Use Change Over the Past 12,000 Years.".

from the receding tide of Mughal power, including the Maratha states of Pune, Indore, Gwalior, and Nagpur; the Rajput states such as Jaipur in Rajasthan; independent states in Awadh and Hyderabad carved out by former Mughal governors; and the south Indian kingdoms of Mysore and Travancore.[4] As we will see later, although the physical presence of the Mughal armies and administrators evaporated, they left behind a source of international order that structured the South Asian international system into the early nineteenth century and colonial period.[5] The Mughal Empire provided a language and grammar for rule that the newer regional states adopted to order their interactions.[6]

We extend the discussion back to the 1750s to include these important states. Because most South Asian states had been colonized by 1820, much of the source material describes the mid- to late 1700s, which remains relevant for understanding the structure and international relations of the early nineteenth-century states in South Asia. Of course, this period also encompasses the rise of the EIC as, first, a powerful regional player in the East and the South and eventually as hegemon of the subcontinent under the British Crown. As in the West African system in chapter 7, in South Asia the period we examine (from the 1750s) involved dynamic state creation followed by colonization.[7]

The South Asian system was fragmented, composed of at least 38 states from 1816 to 1900 (approximately 7.5 states per million square kilometers). States in South Asia governed larger populations (on average) than states in West Africa and Southeast Asia, with more than a million people per state and some states probably ruling more than 10 million people. Starting from modern-day Afghanistan, the South Asian states include the Durrani Empire (1816–1879), Chitral (1816–1878), Hunza (1816–1891), Dir (1816–1895), Kalat (1816–1839), Khaipur (1816–1838), Sind (1816–1843), and the Sikh state of Khalistan (1816–1846). Eastward, most states were successors to the Mughal Empire, including the Rajput states and their neighbors: Bahawalpur (1816–1838), Karputhala (1816–1826), Bikaner (1816–1818), Jaisalmer (1816–1818), Jodhpur (1816–1818), Sirohi (1816–1823), Cutch (1816–1819), Udaipur (1816–1818), Tonk (1816–1817), Jaipur (1816–1818), Kotah (1816–1817), Kishangarh (1816–1818), and Bharatpur (1816–1826). Central India was dominated by the core states of the Maratha Confederacy—Pune (1816–1818), Indore (1816–1818), Gwalior (1816–1818), and Nagpur (1816–1818)[8]—in addition to Bhopal (1816–1817), Dhar (1816–1819), Sampthar (1816–1817) and

Sawantvadi (1816–1838). Finally, there were the mountainous states on the border with China and Myanmar: Nepal (1816–present), Sikkim (1816–1861), Bhutan (1816–1910), Assam (1816–1821), and Manipur (1816–1891). Only Nepal avoided European colonization.

INTERACTION CAPACITY, TRADE, AND WAR

Interaction Capacity

Overland interaction capacity was low across South Asia, limited by the availability of navigable rivers and the speeds at which pack animals could travel. As Tirthankar Roy states, "In general, transportation overland was both costly and unreliable."[9] Tapan Raychaudhuri notes that the transport networks in eighteenth-century India were "not comparable" to those that had developed in Japan prior to the Meiji Revolution.[10] However, there were important regional variations, albeit small when compared to the changes in overland carrying capacity brought about by the railroad. Without access to navigable rivers and with the lowest population densities, western and southern India, including Maharashtra and Peninsular India, had the lowest interaction capacity. Stewart Gordon notes that "even in the best of times, Maharashtra had limited communications and transportation."[11] Dharma Kumar contends that roads in South India "were poor even by Indian standards."[12] Here, the movement of goods and information was capped at the speeds and capacity at which humans and pack animals could travel. Tirthankar Roy is worth quoting at length on the difficulties of overland transport in western and southern India: "The overland system's carrying capacity at the very peak of its development was a little over 10,000 tons, which was a tiny fraction (less than 1%) of the possible south Indian grain output of several hundred million tons. For comparison, in 1901, the main south Indian railway companies' cargo amounted to over five million tons. If we add the Great Indian Peninsular Railway, which connected Bombay with the western part of the Deccan plateau, the number will rise to eight million tons. This was an increase of 800 times."[13]

Interaction capacity was higher along the Ganges, Indus (i.e., Punjab), and Yamuna Rivers, where bulk commercial goods could be transported, although even in these cases the "undeveloped state of transport" made overland transport expensive.[14] Tom Kessinger notes of North India that over land "only goods with favorable value-to-weight ratios were traded, since without all-weather roads and bridges, carriage by horses and donkeys in the hills and pack-bullocks in the plains was very costly, often multiplying the original costs of goods several times."[15] Carrying capacity was probably highest at the delta of the Ganges in Bengal. Roy notes, for example, that "Bengal had advantages, such as the low price of food and cheap transportation along the deltaic rivers. The larger of the river systems could be used to move cargo to and from northern India at a relatively small cost."[16] Roads, however, were "dilapidated," and carts and oxen were used for overland transport in eastern India.[17] Bengal and the Ganges Basin were also the areas with the highest population densities that rivaled, if not exceeded, those in China and the other East Asian states, and South Asia was more densely populated than West Africa or Southeast Asia in general.[18] In 1700, there were approximately 29 inhabitants per square kilometer, compared with roughly 3 inhabitants per square kilometer in Africa.[19]

Most of these people were concentrated along the Ganges–Yamuna River Basin, running from Delhi to the delta in Bengal, which supported between 100 and 110 people per square kilometer and similar numbers in areas around Awadh and Benares.[20] Much of this high population density was the result of relatively high-yield agriculture "owing to the availability of very fertile land ... rather than to any technological excellence."[21] As we will see, Bengal was also a productive and trade-rich region.[22] Western, central, and southern India were more sparsely populated, and Afghanistan and western Pakistan were very sparsely populated.[23]

Cities and Trade

Cities were concentrated in a band along the Ganges Basin, which had an urbanization rate of 8–10 percent.[24] C. A. Bayly estimates that sixty cities in northern India had an approximate population of 10,000 people or more in 1770.[25] Figure 5.2 shows cities with more than 20,000 people between 1750 and 1900. The largest cities included Lahore, Delhi, and Agra, whose populations declined after the fall of the Mughal Empire, as well as the growing cities of successor states, such as Luknow, Benares (Varanasi), Madras, Calcutta, and Murshidabad.

SOUTH ASIA

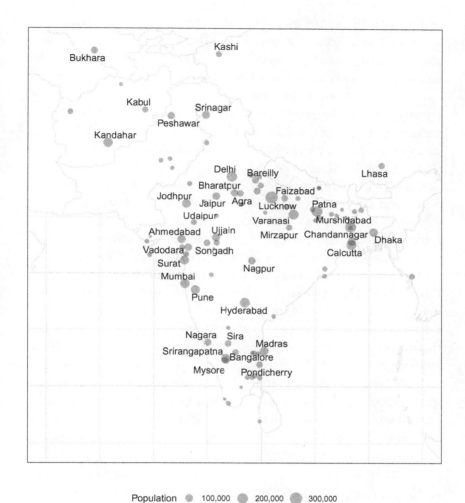

FIGURE 5.2. Cities in South Asia, 1750–1816. *Source*: Data are from Reba, Reitsma, and Seto, "Spatializing 6,000 Years of Global Urbanization from 3700 BC to AD 2000."

Historians identify two types of cities: state created and trade created. Most interior cities were state created, forming as rulers extracted tributes from the countryside, generating demand for goods and services.[26] Such cities rose and fell with the fortunes of states and tended to be larger than surrounding cities. Delhi, for example, was home to 400,000 people in 1680 but only 100,000 in 1800. Pune also grew from a small town to a major city with the fortunes of the Maratha Confederacy.[27] Farther east and along the Ganges, cities were more hybridized, with stronger links to trading networks and powerful merchant-banker families that jostled with regional dynasties, as in Lucknow (Awadh) and Benares (Varanasi).[28] South from the Ganges Basin, cities were smaller and more sparsely distributed. Pune and Hyderabad had around 100,000 people at the end of the eighteenth century, and Mysore about half that number.[29] These three examples were cities created by states, being linked closely to the Maratha Confederacy, the Nizam state, and Mysore, respectively.

Coastal cities thrived as some interior cities depopulated in the eighteenth and nineteenth century with the collapse of the Mughal Empire. Bombay, Calcutta, and Madras, for example, grew to be the largest cities in India by the nineteenth century because of their proximity to the Indian Ocean trade and the relative peace in areas of EIC rule.[30] Port cities grew on trade, with a large, relatively independent and diversified merchant class. Major trading and banking firms were in these cities, often after fleeing from unstable parts of northwestern India.[31] Banking and financial networks also existed in western and southern India but were more closely tied to the state. Port cities drew their resources from oceangoing trade and less from land taxes and tributes in comparison to the interior cities.

In the mid–seventeenth century, there were three major trading networks. The first ran down the Ganges and Yamuna Rivers and along the great Mughal trunk road from Lahore to Delhi and Agra, then on to Benares (Varanasi) and Calcutta. Transport costs were lower on these (mostly) navigable river systems, and bulky goods such as grain, sugar, salt, indigo, and cloth, in addition to higher-value items such as silk and spices, were exchanged along the river.[32] By the mid–eighteenth century, with Delhi in ruins and the northern Indian trade routes declining, Bengal and the East became the center of trade, population, and production on the subcontinent. Bengal was already the Mughal Empire's most profitable region, but trade with the EIC and local successor states propelled Bengal into the position of the economic fulcrum of South Asia. This belt along the Ganges, especially toward the east, hosted areas of stable, high-yield agricultural production that largely survived and even grew under the political instability of the mid- to late eighteenth century. These regions included not only Bengal but also core regions of the Awadh Kingdom (the Baiswara region, for example) and Benares.[33] Delhi and Lahore were also connected to the trans-Himalayan networks, largely trading in low-weight but high-value items.[34]

Trade routes ran north to south, but transport costs were higher because of the lack of navigable rivers and road networks. Bullock caravans (called *banjaras* or *lambadas*) departed from points along the Ganges, heading south, largely carrying grain but also cotton and salt demanded by the armies of the Deccan Plateau that could not source these commodities directly from the coast.[35]

Finally, ports on the Indian Ocean traded in textiles, with locally produced cloth being exchanged for silver or gold.[36] This Indian Ocean trade was concentrated in EIC-controlled ports but also (earlier) from Mughal ports such as Surat in the West or Hooghly in the East. Although accounting for a small proportion of India's precolonial gross domestic product, trading links with the Indian Ocean generated large cities, banking and financial institutions, as well as demand for education and public goods along the coast; as such, they were the staging post for the colonization of the entire subcontinent. For these coastal parts of India, the eighteenth century was a period of urbanization and expansion of monetary connections, with "increasingly broad networks of clients and . . . financial instruments that enabled them [bankers and financiers] to take up key roles in the political system."[37]

South Asia, then, was diverse in terms of its trade and cities. Trade along the Ganges and high-yield agriculture created large cities spread along the river, dense populations, and powerful independent merchant classes, especially toward Bengal and Awadh in the East. These new commercial classes were potential allies for state builders. Central and southern India were more sparsely populated, and communications were slower. Cities rose and fell as rulers extracted tributes from the countryside to the urban centers.

War

With the expiration of the Mughal Empire, South Asia was transformed within fifty years from a relatively stable hierarchy to an intense, uncertain, competitive, multistate system that pushed the successor states to their limits of revenue extraction. As we have seen, numerous states emerged from the Mughal Empire, roughly in the period from 1750 to 1850, when the last of the indigenous Indian states were conquered. The most important were the Maratha states (Pune, Indore, Gwalior, Nagpur, and Baroda), Hyderabad, Khalistan (Punjab), Awadh, Mysore, Travancore, and the Rajput states. Although not counted as a state after 1816 in the ISD, the EIC could also be considered as an independent state before the India Act of 1784, which gave the British government authority over the EIC.[38]

All these states faced intense military competition from each other and the EIC. The Maratha states were constantly at war, invading and extracting tribute north into Rajasthan, east into Orissa, and south into Mysore. From the 1750s, the Marathas defeated the remnants of the Mughal Empire and pushed as far north as the Punjab, where they were checked by the Durrani Empire at the Battle of Panipat in 1761.[39] They fought wars against Hyderabad (1795–1796), Mysore (1771, 1785–1787), the Rajput states, and the British (1775–1782, 1802–1805, 1817–1818). Khalistan fought the Durrani Empire from the west (1813, 1818–1819, 1822, 1837) and two wars with the British from the east (1845–1846, 1848–1849). Mysore fought the Marathas (1771, 1785–1787), Hyderabad (1799), and the British, the latter in a series of wars (1766–1769, 1781–1784, 1789–1792, 1799) that ended in the conquest of Mysore.[40] Smaller states also experienced constant war and competition. Wars between Rajput states were common; Bikaner fought wars with Bharatpur from 1746 to 1787 and with Jaipur in 1801 and was invaded by "five different armies" in 1808.[41] Chitral warred constantly with the neighboring Gilgit, Yasin, and Sikh states.[42] Sind attempted to invade and annex Cutch five times between 1762 and 1777.[43]

Figure 5.3 illustrates an increase in battles from the mid-1750s, which was sustained until the 1850s and the conquest of Khalistan and Afghanistan. Figure 5.4, focusing on the one hundred years from 1750 to 1850, shows a concentration of warfare around the core Maratha areas in northern and central-western India as well as in the South (a combination of the Seven Years War, the Carnatic Wars, and the Mysore Wars), with a third concentration on the eastern and western borders of Khalistan.[44]

Several scholars suggest that eighteenth-century South Asia experienced a "military revolution" with similarities to the military advances in Europe. Cavalry-based warfare was rivaled by larger, more professionalized warfare consisting of armies of massed infantry equipped with firearms and artillery.[45] As Jason Lyall records in *Divided Armies* (2020), indigenous Indian states (the Marathas, Khalistan, Sind, the Durrani Empire, and Bharatpur) averaged 56,000 soldiers, and all but one (Sind) had standing armies.[46]

SOUTH ASIA

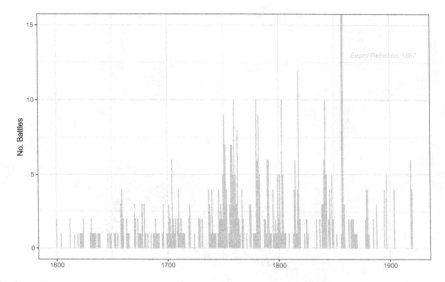

FIGURE 5.3. Battles in South Asia, 1600–1920. *Source*: Data sourced from Miller and Bakar, "Conflict Events Worldwide Since 1468 BC."

Between 1750 and 1850, states on the subcontinent increasingly experimented with semiprofessionalized standing armies. Khalistan had up to 50,000 westernized troops by 1840 in an army of 67,500 infantry, 27,575 cavalry, and 4,130 artillery personnel and was self-sufficient in the manufacture of guns and artillery. Mysore had 144,000 "disciplined troops" and a 180,000-strong militia in 1783. Awadh had a standing army of more than 50,000 in the 1750s.[47] Tipu Sultan combined numerous European military innovations (including the *trace italienne* fort) with indigenous techniques of warfare. Already in 1753, the Marathas could field 125,000 soldiers, and some Maratha states (especially Sindhia [Gwalior/Ujjain]) attempted to create a larger, disciplined, standing army.[48] The Battle of Panipat in northern India in 1761 was one of the largest land battles ever fought in South Asia. South India was a highly competitive, multistate system.

Historians argue that wars placed India's successor states under intense pressure to raise revenue. As Tirthankar Roy states, "Fragmentation of political power intensified conflict.... [M]any new states could not raise more taxes with their existing military and administrative means. Therefore, the drive to expand the revenue base employing extortion and conquest of

REGIONAL STATE SYSTEMS

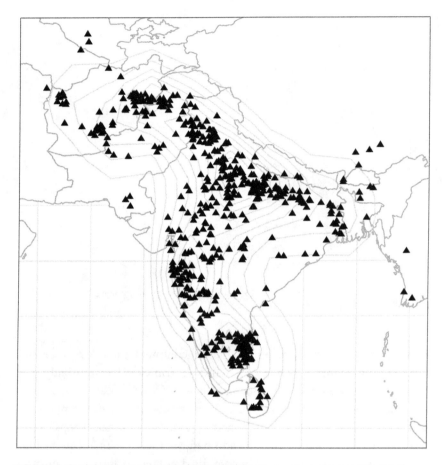

FIGURE 5.4. Battle locations in South Asia, 1750–1850. *Note*: Contour lines represent estimates of conflict-location density. *Source*: Data are from Miller and Bakar, "Conflict Events Worldwide Since 1468 BC."

weaker neighbors was always present."[49] Wars created the demand for more revenue, but how successful were the South Indian states in centralizing their administrations? We turn to this question in the next section.

POLITICAL CENTRALIZATION

South Asia exhibited features that should activate bellicist- and trade-led pathways to state centralization. In many ways, the end of the Mughal

Empire provided opportunities for institutional innovation.[50] Northern India was a densely populated, fertile, productive region subjected to threats from the south (the Marathas), the east (the EIC), and the west (Khalistan). War stretched the fiscal resources of states in the South and the Central West of India as well. Competition created demand for more revenue, and the population- and trade-dense parts of India had surpluses that could be tapped. Local states had indigenous institutions of direct rule to draw upon, and the EIC could utilize blueprints of centralized institutions from Britain.[51] All of the pieces seem to have been in place. But did states create centralized institutions to manage these new military threats? Did they displace powerful intermediaries, which in precolonial India were usually landlords, military governors, and tributary kingdoms? Did a system of billiard ball states form instead of a system of bull's-eye states?

Political centralization in South Asia during the late eighteenth and early nineteenth centuries was "patchy."[52] Some states, such as Mysore, did displace vassals and construct new, albeit short-lived centralized institutions. Other states, such as the Marathas, created centralized institutions over limited land areas. But the broader picture is that, despite variations in the prevalence of war, trade, and cities, states in South Asia converged on similar, decentralized institutional solutions, which "reflected the states' incapacity to erect a viable fiscal administration at the local level."[53] Local power brokers were generally co-opted, not displaced, by the new states, and as we discuss later in this chapter, despite patches of centralization across the subcontinent, war activated centrifugal (i.e., decentralizing) pressures by empowering regional warlords and landlords. This section discusses the political institutions of local South Asian states, moving roughly from north to south, with a separate section on the EIC at the end.[54]

The main states of North India were Awadh, the Maratha states, and Khalistan. Awadh was a former province of the Mughal Empire in the fertile, densely populated, and trade-rich area along the Ganges (including Lucknow and Varanasi, two of the largest cities in India at the time). Awadh (like Hyderabad) became increasingly autonomous from the Mughal Empire and was independent by 1754.[55] Awadh's nawab ruled a territory roughly the size of England, Scotland, and Wales combined, with perhaps 21 million people by 1774.[56] Awadh's "crown lands" included some of India's most productive agricultural regions, and the nawabs of Awadh benefited from the rise of Bengal as the commercial and financial center of the subcontinent.[57] The 1750s and 1760s were a turbulent period as Awadh came under pressure from the EIC from the east, Afghan armies from the north (Awadh was a participant in the Battle of Panipat in 1761), and Marathas from the south. Although Shuja's reign as nawab (1754–1775) saw increasing centralization of the military and the concentration of Mughal-held titles and rights in the newly independent dynasty, Awadh lost the Battle of Buksar in 1764 and signed a (vaguely defined) subsidiary alliance with the EIC entailing a large war indemnity and the stationing of an EIC garrison. From 1764 to 1775, Shuja continued to centralize the military, creating an army of approximately 100,000 soldiers.

However, there is little indication that Awadh underwent significant institutional centralization. Most revenues came from Mughal-era jagirs (land-based revenue-collection rights) and the granting of new jagirs over conquered territories in the mid–eighteenth century (as in Rohilkhand and Etawah).[58] By 1773, EIC troops were defending Awadh's borders from Maratha raids, for which the nawab paid an increasing fee to the EIC. By the late eighteenth century, the EIC demanded up to 50 percent of Awadh's annual revenue for the maintenance of EIC troops and payments in arrears. But these revenue demands caused further decentralization. Revenue collection was increasingly farmed to autonomous, armed, revenue farmers that constituted semiautonomous kingdoms within a kingdom.

Richard Barnett's study of Awadh between Mughal and British rule, including documentation of its full accounts for 1779–1780, provides an unusually detailed picture of the political economy of a precolonial Indian polity. His research outlines a decentralized revenue-collection system based on revenue farming and the granting of jagirs. This system was partly efficient in the fragmented landscape of armed zamindars (local-level landed elites), but it also involved hiding revenue from the EIC to avoid claims on the nawab's accounts. Frustrated, the EIC tried to extract revenues directly after being granted jagirs within Awadh. First, EIC agents threatened and then attacked the zamindars to compel payment but lacked local knowledge and legitimacy and succeeded mostly in provoking rebellions and causing cultivators to flee the depredations of increasingly pressed revenue collectors. Revenues fell in EIC-controlled areas. The EIC even occupied the government of Awadh in 1783–1784 and experimented with direct rule to extract taxes from what it saw as the rich yet inefficient and corrupt kingdom. Yet the EIC's experiment with direct rule achieved only "revenue skimming" and drove the kingdom to the brink of full-scale rebellion, causing the EIC to renegotiate the subsidiary alliance, including a greatly reduced debt payment.[59]

Only in the most productive regions was there evidence of deeper state encroachment. Bayly argues that the nawabs created centralized points of market exchange in the most productive areas, where trade was taxed (along with artisans in some cases). These new market officials operated alongside rather than over the top of local autonomous elites and were mutually beneficial as links to the broader trade network stimulated further trade, increasing the revenues of the local elites and the nawab. Tribute revenues were still collected autonomously through jagirs and revenue farmers. In summary, Awadh was a decentralized kingdom based on grants of revenue-collecting rights to armed, autonomous vassals, and it decentralized further under the EIC's crushing revenue demands.[60]

Let us now turn to the Maratha Confederacy of the Deccan Plateau. The Maratha polity blended monarchy, confederacy, and independent statehood through the eighteenth and early nineteenth centuries. The monarch and sovereign of the confederacy was the raja at Satara, but by the eighteenth century power lay with the peshwa, or prime minister, who commanded the army and administrative apparatus.[61] Five powerful families dominated the Maratha state: the Peshwa in Pune, the Bhonsoles in Nagpur, the Holkars in Indore, the Gaikwads in Baroda, and the Sindhia in Gwalior/Ujjain. They were the families of Maratha soldiers from the early to mid–eighteenth century.[62] Each ruled their territories autonomously, while providing revenue to the peshwa and being subordinate to the peshwa in matters of war and foreign affairs.[63] By the beginning of the nineteenth century, however, the Marathas had fragmented into at least five independent states that retained a symbolic tie to the Maratha peshwa (in the ISD these states are Pune, Indore, Nagpur, and Gwalior) but acted independently.[64]

Maratha states were at war from the 1750s to their demise in 1817–1818, creating severe fiscal shortfalls. Sovereignty in the Maratha Confederacy, however, was already mostly fragmented and decentralized. First, the Maratha Confederacy was a huge, decentralized polity. Although the peshwa in Poona was the sovereign, the states of the confederacy were autonomous. Nagpur, Gwalior, Indore, and Baroda began as military assignments made by the peshwa, with their own armies, revenue collection, judicial institutions, and rights to make land grants.[65] The Treaty of Bassein in 1803 separated Pune from Nagpur, Gwalior, and Indore, but these states had grown increasingly independent since the 1770s.[66] Nagpur and Gwalior/Ujjain, for example, conducted their own treaties, made their own alliances, and warred against other states.[67]

Sovereignty was also fragmented within these individual Maratha domains. All rulers held crown lands that were directly administered by bureaucrats appointed and salaried from the center.[68] But Maratha rulers governed largely by co-opting a class of landed elites, sometimes called *deshmukh*s or zamindars. André Wink calls these elites "co-sharers" of sovereignty and argues that Maratha governance was based on the notion of *fitna* (sedition), which was a pattern of shifting alliances and conflict that facilitated the expansion of Maratha institutions while limiting the extent to which states could penetrate to the village level.[69]

*Deshmukh*s (or zamindars) were semiautonomous rulers with local armed forces and the rights to extract revenue, administer local justice, receive income from tax-free lands and in-kind services, and call on support from the central government.[70] In exchange, they would send a proportion of their revenue to the state, join military campaigns, and put down rebellions.[71] Landed elites benefited from investiture of their rights by the sovereign, and the rulers benefited from the information, tax revenue, and enforcement capability of local actors. In core areas of Maratha governance, typically in the agricultural plains and lower hills, landed elites were subject to government oversight through land surveys, accountants, and reporting demands but still retained power over cultivators that was "irreducible by centralizing efforts of the sovereign."[72] The Maratha states did, therefore, maintain a bureaucratic staff, appointed and salaried by the center to monitor and oversee revenue collection in its territories, but local elites retained considerable autonomy.

Outside of core areas of governance (such as in the Rajput areas, Orissa, and peninsula regions to the south), the Marathas left local rulers (including Mughal rulers) in place, demanding tributary payments under the threat of conquest and violence. These outlying areas were, according to Wink, "vast regions over which the Marathas had only limited sovereign rights."[73] For example, in the harder-to-reach parts of Orissa, the raja of Kharda acknowledged the suzerainty of Nagpur and paid tribute while maintaining his own "segmentary state" of jagir holders.[74] Such tributary kingdoms were a common feature of Maratha rule. Taxes and tributary payments depended on a vassal's bargaining power and especially on their local strength and ability to rebel.[75] This was a thin state structure: "State officers collected what revenue they could from revenue farming arrangements and from tributary chiefs who stayed virtually independent."[76]

Maratha boundaries were often unclear. Gordon describes Maratha frontiers as follows: "We see that the concept of 'boundaries' of these polities is not very useful. The rights of the Nizam and the Marathas not only interpenetrate[d], but they often collected revenue from the same pargana or village."[77] In contested zones, the Marathas, the Mughals, and the Nizam (for example) could extract revenue from the same pargana (collection of twenty to one hundred villages).[78] As the Marathas and Mughals contested Malwa, *deshmukh*s in Malwa probably paid tribute to both.[79] Overlapping sovereignties were also produced by the receding Mughal Empire. Indore and Nagpur were formally vassals of the Mughals and the Maratha peshwa but were independent states. Gwalior and the Scindia family, too, were recognized as independent by the British, the nominal vassal of the peshwa, and the regent plenipotentiary of the Mughal Empire (the highest post in the Mughal government).[80] The nawab of Bengal's finances were controlled by the EIC in the eighteenth century, yet the nawab was a vassal of the Mughal Empire and an independent ruler in judicial affairs.[81] Awadh was formally subordinate to the Mughal Empire— even though the emperor controlled no Awadh territory through parts of the eighteenth century—and could award jagirs to the EIC but at the same time have its external relations controlled by the EIC.[82]

Even if the general pattern of governance was decentralized, there is evidence of deeper centralization and state encroachment. Maratha advances into North, East, and South India were rapid during the early to mid-eighteenth century. Conquests were sometimes followed by centralization. One example is the peshwa's rule in Malwa, based on Gordon's detailed analysis of original documents in the Pune archives. Malwa is a plateau in central India, where the cities of Ujjain, Bhopal, and Indore are located. Malwa was raided by the Marathas for tribute from the early 1720s but was conquered and became a part of Maratha domains with the Peshwa-Nizam treaty of 1738. Regions in Malwa under the peshwa's control then transitioned from "one-time, transitory" tribute payments that could be extracted only by force to "regularized" tribute backed up by the threat of force, but revenue collection remained in the hands of local intermediaries.[83] These tributary arrangements, although cheap, were irregular and unreliable and diverted military resources from other areas. The zamindars (local revenue collectors and landholders) were increasingly replaced by officials salaried by the peshwa, first in areas with little existing local administration (i.e., no authority above the headman) and eventually in areas where zamindars were unable to pay their tribute demands. The peshwa also created an urban and rural police force. From around 1745–1760, the quantity of information transmitted between the Malwa provinces and Pune accelerated. What began as yearly assessments of yields and accounting of tribute payments became semiannual, then monthly, and in some cases even weekly or daily information that flowed between Malwa and Pune.[84] By the 1750s, according to Gordon, this correspondence included records of salaries, tax payments, reasons for noncollection, expenditures on road repairs, and even the costs of producing the report. Remarkably, after high initial overheads for direct forms of rule, these costs declined as garrisons were removed and rule stabilized. Gordon concludes that this was a level of centralization unusual for the period and that "the main effect of this bigger and more differentiated bureaucracy was the regulation of a wide range of economic and social relationships, unregulated since the Mughal administration had been broken in the 1730s."[85] Sekhar Bandyopadhyay notes that it was only in Malwa, Khandesh, and Gujarat that the Marathas "tried to put in place some kind of an administration."[86]

It is unclear whether Pune maintained this centralization in Malwa after the Battle of Panipat (1761), which limited the northern expansion of the Marathas and their tribute-gathering abilities.[87] As Tirthankar Roy notes, the real fiscal crises began after imperial expansion was halted at Panipat, while other wars on multiple fronts continued.[88]

Madhav Rao's tenure as peshwa (1761–1772) stabilized governance in the core Maratha domains,[89] but after 1773 there is evidence that warfare contributed to decentralization in the Maratha domains and led rulers to abandon experiments in centralized rule. Fiscal problems were compounded by succession crises in Pune after the death of Madhav Rao in 1772.[90] By the 1770s and into the last decades of Pune's rule, under the pressure of increased warfare with the British, Mysore, the Nizam, and internal unrest, the peshwa resorted to handing over taxation powers to military commanders.[91] Michihiro Ogawa documents a steep rise in the number of villages that were converted from government administered (i.e., ruled directly) to jagir administered (i.e., assignments of land to military elites) from 1761, especially in the Indapur area (close to Pune) after 1768. Roy notes that Maratha rulers ceded powers "to the large holders of land grants inside western Maharashtra." Gordon notes a "serious" shift in power from the center (Pune) to the periphery after 1773. Wink documents a dramatic increase in revenue farming in the peshwa's domains under Baji Rao II from 1804 (and earlier in Nagpur). Revenue farms were appointed on short contracts, but in this context they denoted the extrication of the state from society and a response to crisis and uncertainty. An intricate system of checks and accounts was "almost entirely done away with."[92]

Demands for revenue and soldiers made Maratha rulers more dependent on the regional warlords and semiautonomous vassals who controlled these resources, which, in turn, made those groups' autonomy more rather than less secure. Moreover, in the search for more military resources, the Maratha rulers distributed land grants to military commanders in exchange for participation in wars. These land grants usually entailed autonomous taxation authority and obligations for military service and tribute. Roy states, "As the need for taxes increased, pressures from the top to the bottom layers increased. However, the top layer had little means to coerce the bottom layers. In most cases, the Maratha state system in Pune is a good example[;] the state negotiated with the local warlords, offered them incentives to encourage more cultivation, giving them more power instead of taking away their control. . . . Fiscal pressures at the top led to extensive revenue farming and dependence on anyone with the political means to collect taxes on behalf of the state."[93]

Centrifugal pressures were an endemic aspect of Maratha sovereignty. As Wink explains, rulers governed by "wedging" themselves into a system of conflictual, vested rights in land, "without which no state could survive." Landed elites, in turn, estimated "the chances of success of the conquering power against those of the established sovereign."[94] The system remained in balance so long as landed elites were persuaded or intimidated into siding with the ruler, but it could be disrupted by crisis or armed conflict. War led the Maratha states to become steadily poorer, more fractious, militarily weaker, and more indebted. There is also evidence that this condition characterized the region: "In most indigenous states, conquest empowered the military aristocracy who shared the fruits of the new acquisitions and thus weakened the center," states Roy.[95]

The Sikh state of Khalistan (in the modern-day Punjab regions of India and Pakistan) emerged in another productive, densely populated region that experienced intense warfare. The Punjab, a rich province under the Mughal Empire, was by the late eighteenth century raided by Marathas from the south and the Durrani Empire from the northwest. In 1799, Ranjit Singh created an independent Sikh state, Khalistan, with its capital at Lahore by conquering and uniting smaller chiefdoms. From inception, Khalistan was encircled by conflict, first with the Durrani Empire and then with the British, even while it was raiding Jammu and Kashmir to the north. We have seen that these wars were often large and fought with an increasingly modernized army. However, although Khalistan created a relatively centralized standing army, the administration only partially caught up. Some land revenues were collected by state officials called *kardars*, but 40 percent remained alienated through jagirs.[96] Khalistan utilized vassalage relations with smaller kingdoms and elites, who were required to provide revenue and troops to Ranjit Singh as well as to abstain from "political relationships with each other, or with another sovereign."[97] Ranjit Singh "failed to decimate completely the semi-independent landowning aristocracy."[98]

Other South Asian states were structured in a decentralized way. The Mughal successor state of Nizam (with Hyderabad as its capital) depended on local intermediaries to raise revenues and soldiers and was a composite kingdom of landed, autonomous elites and semi-independent, tribute-paying kingdoms. As Karen Leonard puts it, "The Hyderabad government was organized only to receive and disburse revenue, not to collect it."[99] The Rajput states of western India were linked by aristocratic and caste ties that created a common culture and nobility, but political authority was fragmented. First, there were many states, each ruled by an aristocratic clan. Second, the states were decentralized. Rajput kings were often the first among equals and sought symbols of external legitimacy, such as Mughal ranks and titles, to bolster their rule against strong and autonomous vassals.[100] Maharajas extracted revenues from Crown lands, but most administration was in the hands of land-holding nobles (jagirs), who collected revenues, mobilized military forces, and administered justice independently of the ruler. The maharaja did not tax these nobles aside from tributary payments on some occasions, and they remained a powerful counterweight to the center.[101] In 1828, Walter Hamilton noted of Bikaner, out toward the desert in Rajasthan, "Like all states in this waste of moving sand, its limits are difficult to settle, vast tracts being claimed and rejected by all parties as political circumstances happen to support or oppose their pretensions."[102]

States in Baluchistan were based on tributary payments from tribal chiefs. Nina Swidler notes that the boundaries of the states in Baluchistan (Kalat, Khaipur, and Sind) were also "unstable, defined by shifting political relations rather than territorial integration." As we will see in the chapter on West Africa, these nominal suzerain relations could span thousands of kilometers. The Durrani Empire's tributary relations reached as far as southern Pakistan, and over the state of Kalat, Swidler notes, the empire held "a minimal suzerainty that was rarely enforced."[103] The Durrani Empire (based in Qandahar) ruled in a largely decentralized way: "Provincial governors handled local administration," states Thomas Barfield, "and were practically independent of Qandahar in most nonmilitary matters. Such positions gave them so much autonomy they were virtual minikingdoms." At the beginning of the nineteenth century, the kingdom "was decentralized and fragmented, dependent largely on the feudal levies of troops and plagued by a shortage of resources." Using language that corresponds to our bull's-eye model, Barfield states that Central and South Asian states were like "swiss cheese," where administration ran from direct at the core through indirect at the margins to the purely theoretical or symbolic in the outlands. By the end of the nineteenth century, however, and after two wars with the British, the state was "a centralized government with a national bureaucracy that displaced formerly autonomous regional leaders and their feudal clients." Autonomous (and sometimes independent) polities such as Qandahar, Herat, and Turkistan were destroyed, and taxes were collected directly from landowners by state officials.[104] This centralization, however, was funded by the British and occurred during the period of British protection and is less relevant to the examples of indigenous centralization that we examine in this book.

Similar terms are used to describe the cluster of states in Northwest Pakistan (Dir, Chitral, and Hunza).[105] As far east as the Ahom Kingdom in modern-day Assam, we find similar decentralized structures, in this case based on "feudal" land fiefs given to military leaders and vassal kingdoms "agreeing to furnish quotas of men for rendering whatever service was demanded of them."[106] Exposure to wars in Assam also weakened the state.[107] In summary, most of the South Asian states in the period that we examined were decentralized, ruling through feudal levies, local kingdoms, or tribal formations that retained wide-ranging autonomy. These states were bull's-eye states.

It is in southern India—interestingly away from the population- and trade-dense northern corridor—that we find the clearest case of centralization. Mysore was a successor state to the Vijayanagara Empire and declared independence from the Mughal Empire in 1783 but was de facto independent before this point.[108] The area around Mysore was less densely populated than other parts of the subcontinent (roughly on par with Scotland at the same time), but Mysore faced threats on multiple fronts from the Marathas, the Nizam, and the British.[109] South Asia, Mysore in particular, may have experienced "proto-industrialization" through the development of local merchant capitalism that approached conditions seen in Europe before full industrialization.[110]

Mysore's centralization commenced under the rule of Haider Ali and then continued under his son, Tipu Sultan. When Ali came to power in 1761, he inherited a kingdom based largely on tributes. His main innovations were to centralize control of horses and cannon and to wrest military power from hereditary chiefs, replacing it with a large standing army.[111] The main economic innovations occurred during the reign of his son, Tipu Sultan, who ruled from 1782 until 1799, when he was defeated and killed by the British.

Mysore's rulers were aware of the limitations of decentralized rule. Tribute payments were "irregular and only realized by threats."[112] Tipu Sultan himself apparently believed that tax farming was inefficient because of revenue lost through corruption.[113] His reforms were designed to displace local tax farmers with "central fiscal institutions" and "directly extract surpluses from the productive level of society without the mediation of powerful intermediary groups."[114] Tipu, for example, created a civil bureaucracy charged with levying taxes, and it absorbed as much as 25 percent of revenues by the end of his reign, constituting a "veritable primitive public sector."[115] Before Tipu Sultan, tax farmers had been successful warriors and often members of the Brahman caste with wide-ranging authority, but the sultan pensioned off many of them. *Amidars* (local tax farmers) were, for example, banned from extracting more to make up shortfalls and were punished if villagers fled because of their depredations. Supplies required for administration were provided by the state, and the *amidar* was prohibited from receiving goods and services for free.[116]

After the Treaty of Seringapatam with the British in 1792, which nearly halved the territory of Mysore, the kingdom underwent further rationalization and reorganization. Administrative staff levied land taxes that made up, perhaps, 70 percent of the kingdom's revenue. Land was inspected and assessed by these staff, and taxes were to be paid directly to local officials. Tipu's bureaucrats assessed local production, and revenue collections were recorded by accountants who were in part salaried by the state and prohibited from cultivating lands.[117] State expansion was stimulated by Haider Ali's and Tipu Sultan's investments in roads, especially in the countryside, and to a lesser extent in canals, dams, and tanks.[118] As Burton Stein describes Mysore's expansion, Tipu established sandalwood and black pepper monopolies, provided agricultural loans, promoted irrigation with state funds, manipulated exchange rates, ordered the construction of gun foundries and saltpeter factories, and established a state-run mint. All of this represented the state's deeper encroachment into the domestic economy. Although it is unclear how deep Tipu Sultan's reforms were after just seven to ten years, there appears to be a consensus that Mysore was at least an example of a semicentralized, European-style state in South Asia by the time it was conquered by the EIC in 1799. Stein states that "until the time of Tipu Sultan, no military regime in the South, whether Muslim or Hindu, was able to shift most of its income from tribute . . . to the direct collections of state officials."[119]

Finally, there is the EIC. Scholars debate whether the EIC was a state.[120] It exercised statelike functions, including de facto independence in its dealings with indigenous Indian states, especially in the 1760s and through to the India Act of 1784.[121] The turning point for the EIC occurred when the nawab of Bengal captured Calcutta in 1756, and then Governor Robert Clive of the Bengal Presidency recaptured the city, defeating the nawab's forces at the Battle of Plassey in 1757. Clive placed a pliant nawab on the throne and in return received a jagir (military land grant) worth 28,000 pounds, thus involving the EIC in Mughal politics and revenue collection for the first time. This entanglement deepened in 1765 when the Mughal emperor appointed the company the dewan (revenue-collecting officer) in Bengal, Bihar, and Orissa, making the EIC a territorial administrator of the empire. The EIC initially supervised the system of tax collection based on the local zamindari system but in 1772 abolished the Mughal tributes and experimented with company-appointed European tax farmers.[122] Territorial and military expansion continued. The EIC's army grew to 154,000 soldiers in 1803, subjugating Mysore in 1799 and Awadh in 1801, capturing Delhi in 1803, and conquering the Maratha states in 1816–1818.[123] Costs also ballooned, though, and the EIC was bailed out in 1773 by the British Crown with the Regulating Act. Further fiscal and military crises resulted in the India Act of 1784, which subordinated the EIC to the English Crown.[124] From 1784, it is difficult to separate the EIC acting as a local state from the British Empire.

Nevertheless, in 1793 the Permanent Settlement Act came into power in Bengal and later extended to Madras and Varanasi. The act disarmed the zamindars, removing a source of their autonomous power. But the zamindars were granted hereditary rights to land and relative autonomy in revenue collection in exchange for a fixed sum of revenue.[125] As P. J. Marshall notes, the EIC created one of the most centralized fiscal-military states in South Asia, but the 1793 act demonstrated the limitations to state centralization, even for a polity that could call upon the financial and military power of the British Empire: "Twenty-five years of trial and error had proved that it was better to accept a fixed sum through the agency of the *zamindars*, for all their faults, than to go on experimenting."[126] In summary, over the twenty years of quasi-independent territorial administration, the EIC attempted to centralize its administration by replacing local tax collectors with state-appointed tax farmers, only to face financial crises and state intervention. The solution was a hybrid that left eastern India's intermediary layer of autonomous, landed aristocrats in place, albeit with reduced autonomy and power.

EXPLAINING (DE)CENTRALIZATION

Governance in South Asia was a collaborative project between state (usually military) elites wishing to extract resources and local actors who did much of the day-to-day governance (taxation and administration of justice, for example). The widespread use of tribute as a means of resource extraction, the level of autonomy enjoyed by vassals, the vague and unclear frontier zones, the tussle between the state and local elites over hereditary rights, and the thin level of central control are key similarities among the main indigenous South Asian states of the period. Mysore and the EIC were the clearest exceptions, although there were patchy areas of centralized control in the Maratha state of Pune.

War- and trade-based theories do not appear to explain these patterns well. War was widespread across the subcontinent, and historians are clear that the fall of the Mughals and the rise of regional states transformed South Asia into a competitive multistate system. This rupture between 1750 and 1850 created opportunities for institutional innovation and a "military revolution" that pressed rulers for more revenue to fight wars, just as bellicist theories would predict.[127] But did these new rulers centralize their administrations? Did they displace local elites and take taxes for themselves?

The answer is mostly no. Hard-pressed states such as Khalistan, Pune, Gwalior, Nagpur, and Indore attempted to create standing armies but ruled in largely—and for some cases even highly—decentralized ways. Some states tried to imitate the EIC and build disciplined standing armies, especially by employing European advisers, but the fiscal institutions rarely followed in their wake. The Maratha Confederacy was a fragile alliance of semi-independent states as it broke away from the Mughal Empire, and the member states ruled largely by granting jagirs (revenue-collection rights) to military commanders in exchange for revenue or by co-opting existing layers of landed elites and tributary kingdoms. When the tribute started to run out, the Marathas borrowed from banking families and courted mercenaries (the so-called Pindaris) to wage wars. There were examples of centralization—in Pune, for example—but they are offset by the apparently decentralizing effects of competition that took hold after the 1760s. Far from reducing the dependence of rulers on local elites who controlled military and economic resources, warfare increased this dependence and set in motion fragmentation processes and further decentralization. The demands of war did not allow states to go through or bypass their elites for more revenue (at least in most cases). Rulers needed these elites more than ever.

Trade-based theories also do not fare especially well in explaining this region's state system, although the picture is more complex. The Ganges

Basin was a highway of trade in bulk goods and high-value, low-weight items, and this trade produced strong merchant cities, especially in Bengal, which was the Mughal Empire's richest, most productive, and most populous region. The Ganges Basin hosted some of India's key cities of the era (Agra, Lucknow, Varanasi, Calcutta, Murshidabad). The rulers of successor states in these regions were weak, however, and governed through tributary relations with economically powerful elites. For example, increased economic productivity and trade had a complex effect on the state of Awadh. On one hand, productive regions produced stable states in the sense that they were less vulnerable to shocks produced by instability and war. On the other hand, rising productivity created new local dynasties that accepted Awadhi suzerainty but maintained local autonomy. Moreover, we have seen that after the Battle of Buxar in 1764 Awadhi rulers decentralized their governance structures. Trade, therefore, does not appear to have enabled indigenous states to go around vassals by making a new pact with merchant classes. If anything, it made them more dependent on the revenues from rich landlords and merchants.

Interestingly, the EIC did attempt to create a more centralized system of revenue extraction in Bengal—the most populous and commercial region of India by the late eighteenth century—by using company-appointed tax farmers. But the company's efforts at territorial administration were arguably a failure and were abandoned in 1793 with the Permanent Settlement Act. Without the intervention of the British Crown in 1773 and 1784, the EIC faced bankruptcy, suggesting direct rule was expensive and risky, even for an organization that could easily draw upon models of centralized rule. Administration and war produced financial crisis in the EIC, just as it did for Indian states, but the company did not need to offer tax grants to military commanders in exchange for more troops or money to pay soldiers because it could call upon the financial and military might of the British Empire. After 1784, the EIC simply did not face the same dilemmas of rule that indigenous South Asian states did.

For indigenous states, the options were more limited, and granting autonomy to warlords in exchange for cash and fighting power was a common choice. In fact, the EIC and British Crown's governance strategies after the India Act were remarkably like indigenous strategies of rule.[128] The Crown and the governor generally ruled over matters of diplomacy and war (i.e., external relations), while the EIC had autonomy over administration and trade, drawing on a form of decentralized tax collection.

Finally, the clear case of indigenous (semi)centralization did not emerge where these war-and trade-based theories would predict. Mysore rose in a trade- and population-poor part of South India, isolated from the commercial networks of the North and East and the population-dense Ganges Basin. And although Mysore experienced intense military pressure from the British and the Marathas, this pressure was not necessarily more intense than that faced by the Marathas or Khalistan, neither of which created strongly centralized states. Historians such as Frank Perlin see Mysore as an example of "fiscal-militarism," or the creation of a centralized revenue administration in response to the demands of war, but a wider aperture raises the question why other states exposed to similar military pressures did not take the same path.[129] If the pressures of war led Mysore to create a centralized state, why did warfare activate centripetal pressures in some cases but unleash centrifugal forces in others? Local states may not have had time to develop stable fiscal institutions, with some of the Maratha states lasting approximately a century and other states roughly only half that.[130] Centralization can happen quickly, however. The most dramatic example is Japan, as shown in the previous chapter, but Vietnam's centralization occurred over a thirty-year period, similar to Mysore.

Interaction capacity can help explain the general *absence* of centralized states, despite economic and political pressures pushing rulers in that direction. As we will see with West Africa, a common theme involved the difficulties of transporting people and goods over long distances. Roy points out that even in the population-dense area of Bengal, for example, the difficulties of overland transport increased the incentives to rely on tax farming and decentralized rule. Wink notes that indirect Maratha rule in Orissa (until 1803) is similarly thought to have been caused by low agricultural yields and the difficulties of overland transport.[131] Kaveh Yazdani also writes that transportation and administration infrastructures in southern India were "pre-modern" and acted as a limit on how far the center could expand its extraction infrastructure. Wink, however, notes that the "regulated" areas of the peshwa's domains tended to be the "agricultural plains" and lower hill regions, where populations were denser and more easily accessed.[132]

Even if we accept that low interaction capacity creates generally unfavorable conditions for centralization, it does not appear to explain within-case variations in South Asia. Carrying capacity was highest along the Ganges and especially in the delta region in Bengal, but centralized indigenous states did not form there. The exception is the EIC, which after the Permanent Settlement Act was able to limit the autonomy of zamindars, but as we discussed earlier, the company faced a different incentive structure than local states, which limits its relevance as an example of indigenous state building. The Kingdom of Kabul also centralized because the British financed administrative reforms there, obviating the dilemmas associated with the costs of direct rule. Moreover, the one clear example of state centralization, Mysore, emerged in Central-South India, where interaction capacity was low compared to northern and eastern India.

Part of the difficulty here is isolating changes in interaction capacity from changes in trade and the rise in cities. Natural variations in interaction capacity also tend to increase trade and economic productivity, which may drive fragmentation and decentralization, offsetting improvements in the ability to extend direct rule. Rivers (especially river deltas) stimulate trade, and there is evidence that high levels of trade create decentralized merchant-based orders.[133] Put differently, rivers and deltas are not pure increases in interaction capacity and tend to correlate with other changes that might drive decentralization. Furthermore, two of the examples of centralization in South Asia are "outsourced" centralization. The EIC was a similar story. The true exception is Mysore, which emerged in an area with relatively low interaction capacity.

Where does this leave us? For South Asia, war-based theories do not explain state centralization well because there was substantial war throughout the region but few centralized states. Indeed, there is evidence that war produced decentralization in some instances. Centralized states also did not form in the trade- and production-rich regions of India before or after the Mughal Empire. These areas also had the highest interaction capacity. Former governors of the Mughal Empire in Awadh and Bengal created independent states (although these states were often still tributaries of the empire) but retained indirect patterns of governance based on land grants. Finally, the clearest example of a centralized state forming in South Asia is the Mysore Kingdom, which formed not in the trade- and population-rich parts of India but in the more sparsely populated regions of Central-South India. None of the theories would have predicted state centralization in Mysore. We explore these anomalous cases in chapter 8, where we tie together the similarities across cases that can help us understand the multifaceted ways in which states might centralize.

CONCLUSION

South Asia was a system between two empires in the eighteenth and early nineteenth centuries. The end of the Mughal Empire created a competitive and uncertain state system, fueled by innovations in military tactics and weaponry that placed increasing pressures on rulers to extract resources from their populations. These new successor states were born throughout South Asia, traveling from the population-dense and productive regions of North India and Pakistan, along the trade corridor to the delta of the Ganges in Bengal, then south to the drier and poorer regions of Maharashtra and Peninsular India. In the East, the British (and to a lesser extent the French) enmeshed South Asia with the world economy, creating new economic opportunities, institutional models, and eventually the ruling elite of the entire region.

Despite these variations, however, modes of governance were similar. Military elites ruled through land grants to commanders in exchange for tribute. These military governors were in turn dependent on local landlords (and sometimes merchants) who did most of the on-the-ground administration, tax collection, and military mobilization. State agents often supervised and monitored these local elites. Although the South Asian vassal units were somewhat different from the Southeast Asian and West African ones (landed elites and military governors versus tributary kings and queens), the devolution of decision-making beyond basic demands of allegiance and tribute to lower levels of the hierarchy was similar. Rule was largely a game of alluring and holding the allegiance of local powerbrokers, preventing secession, and avoiding factional conflict. Shifting patterns of vassalage were common. Borders were often vague and frontierlike, with zones of heteronomy arising on the fringes of decentralized states. These patterns are common in other systems characterized by slow communications that place thresholds on the extent to which the center can rule directly. These systems are decentralized bull's-eye systems.

REGIONAL STATE SYSTEMS

Existing theories do not explain these patterns well. Indeed, we found evidence that war drove decentralization at least as often as it stimulated centralization. Centralization requires that rulers disempower vassals. But competition in South Asia empowered vassals, who held the means of military force. Of the more than forty states reviewed in this chapter, only two or three were clear centralizers by the end of the nineteenth century, and only one was a clear case of indigenous centralization. Mysore was an exception in this regard, something we return to in our discussion of the dilemmas of decentralized rule in chapter 8.

Chapter Six

MARITIME SOUTHEAST ASIA

We now move from remnants of the Mughal Empire to the islands, jungles, and sea-lanes of Southeast Asia. The islands of maritime Southeast Asia are ruled today by five states: Indonesia, Malaysia, Brunei, East Timor, and Singapore. Yet only Brunei existed as a state in 1816. Modern boundaries between Indonesia and Malaysia are the product of a treaty in 1824 separating Southeast Asia into British and Dutch spheres of influence. At the beginning of the nineteenth century, however, there was no natural division between Indonesia and Malaysia. In 1816, archipelagic Southeast Asia was a single and highly integrated state system of nearly forty states with a cultural history going back millennia.[1] Perhaps this contrast is best captured by the island of Bali. Today, with its sandy beaches, excellent surf, and yoga retreats, Bali's main export is tourism. But this small island was home to nine independent states in the early nineteenth century. Their main export? Slaves. Balinese states fought unremitting wars with each other and the Dutch, and they constituted a vibrant subsystem within a state system that has been relatively neglected in the IR scholarship.

The maritime Southeast Asian system allows us to explore the explanatory power of trade- and war-based theories of state centralization. Trade was central, and states rose and fell with fortunes in commerce. Trade also produced merchant groups that rulers tried to co-opt into their state-building projects. Warfare was common, especially on Bali, but also in Sumatra and Sulawesi. However, these trading networks and conflicts were undergirded by high sea-based interaction capacity, which produced shared cultural norms and an international order, but low land-based interaction capacity. Decentralized rule was the norm. Nearly all indigenous states governed by affording vassals autonomy, a system encapsulated by the concept of the mandala state and mandala system. They were bull's-eye states in a decentralized system. We conclude by suggesting that although trade did facilitate state formation, it could impede state centralization, and that warfare provided more of a stimulus to decentralization than to centralization. While these findings contrast with much of the existing literature, we suggest that the low level of land-based interaction capacity may condition whether trade and war have centralizing or decentralizing effects.

STATES AND THE SYSTEM

In this chapter, Southeast Asia encompasses Peninsular Malaysia and modern Indonesia from Sumatra to Maluku (see figure 6.1).[2] Where the Indus-Ganges River systems were the connective framework for South Asia, and the Saharan and Atlantic trades were for West Africa, here it was the ocean that linked the relevant political units. Southeast Asia was a trade cynosure because maritime routes from East Asia to South Asia had to pass through the Malacca Strait or, less commonly, the Sunda Strait. Moreover, the coveted spices of Maluku extended these trade routes into the eastern portion of the island chain. This trading network combined with the region's natural waterways to produce a dynamic cultural zone. As with the cultures of South Asia and the Mediterranean, the various island groups could point to empires of antiquity, such as Majapahit (1293~1517), as a cultural touchstone, a memory of greatness.[3] Indeed, Majapahit once encompassed and to varying degrees ruled over the entire region.

Mainland Southeast Asia north of Malaysia, including modern-day Thailand, Myanmar, and Indochina, are not covered in this chapter. We also exclude most of the Philippines. Although these regions are often included in greater Southeast Asia, we took a narrower focus. Outside of the Sulu Archipelago, the main islands of the Philippines are farther north, less connected to the island chain surrounding the straits, and more

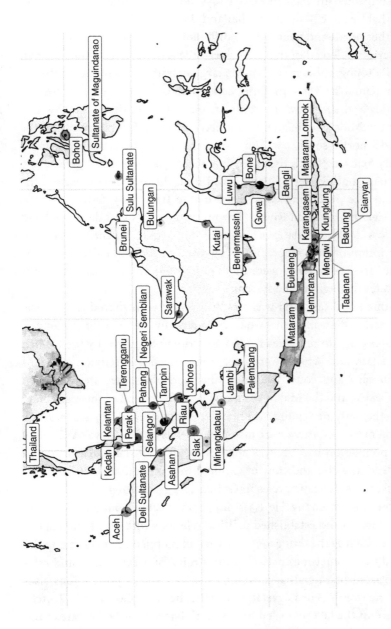

FIGURE 6.1. States and population densities in maritime Southeast Asia per the ISD, 1816–1920 and 1800. *Note:* Shows population density in 1800. More opaque circles represent clearer borders noted in the ISD. Population density has been capped at a maximum of 120 people per square kilometer to facilitate comparison with the other three systems. *Source:* Population density data are from Klein Goldewijk et al., "The HYDE 3.1 Spatially Explicit Database of Human-Induced Global Land-Use Change Over the Past 12,000 Years."

closely connected to the Sinocentric system. Meanwhile, the mainland regions that became Myanmar, Thailand, Laos, Cambodia, and Vietnam were farther north and qualitatively different. Geographically, these states and societies coalesced in the great river valleys of the mainland. One can see from a topographic map that the large massif of mainland Southeast Asia—or Zomia, as it is sometimes called—creates the conditions for riverine states and societies.[4] In contrast, maritime Southeast Asia, which includes the Malay Peninsula, was inherently more fragmented than the mainland's north–south corridors, and the maritime states were more outwardly focused.[5] With the exception of central and eastern Java and to a less extent southwestern Sulawesi and Bali, the archipelago lacked the substantial rice-producing capabilities of the Irrawaddy, Salween, Chao Phraya, Mekong, and Red Rivers. The maritime states that developed had smaller, less-dense populations and were more trade dependent. They fit the description of thalassocracies as opposed to the tellurocracies of the mainland. In general, they were more connected and exposed to neighboring states throughout the system.

Maritime Southeast Asia was a cultural zone with shared experience. Chinese and Indian influences had resonated in the area for millennia. Many states came to practice Hindu and write in Sanskrit. By the twelfth century, Islam and Arabic were becoming the courts' religion and language. Literary and court traditions that had blossomed in Java, Bali, South Sulawesi, and the Malay-speaking western portion of the region had spread to the outlying regions.[6] Although this cultural mixing was assisted by trading networks, there were also populations on the move. A Chinese migrant population had been established by at least the fourteenth century. Indeed, the ebb and flow of Chinese migration and political influence tracked the dynastic cycles in China. The great Ming Dynasty naval expeditions under Zheng He (1371–1433/1435) visited Southeast Asia on several occasions and established political relations with numerous states.[7] Sea peoples such as the *orang laut* consisted of mobile, waterborne populations, and they sometimes patrolled the straits for local sultans and rajas in a negotiated manner that is reminiscent of frontier populations elsewhere in the world.[8] The devastating conflict between Gowa and a Dutch-led alliance in the late 1660s led to a partial diaspora of Makassarese and Bugis, who, as M. C. Ricklefs puts it, "took to their ships like marauding Vikings in search of honour, wealth, and new homes." For generations to come, "these fierce warriors were the scourge of the archipelago."[9] Finally, European incursions and acquisitions under the Portuguese in the early 1500s and later by the British and the Dutch shaped the culture of the system irrevocably.

We now turn to an accounting of the states by region. Like South Asia, maritime Southeast Asia was a fragmented system consisting of thirty-nine unique states, more states per million square kilometer (approximately thirteen) than any of our other case studies. More than a quarter (26 percent) of state episodes began in the nineteenth century. Bali and Lombok were especially dynamic, with states forming, collapsing, and being reborn through the nineteenth century. Gianyar in southeastern Bali, for example, was separated from Klungkung (another Balinese state) after the Dutch–Bali war, becoming an independent state in 1849, only to be reconquered by Klungkung in 1883. The raja was deported, and the kingdom disintegrated into competing houses. The raja's son fled captivity, however, and restored the kingdom in 1885, eventually accepting Dutch protection and sovereignty in 1900.[10] The Dutch also played a hand in establishing Jembrana (also on Bali) as an independent kingdom in 1849 by restoring its dynastic line and separating it from Bueleng after the Dutch–Bali war.[11] Jembrana remained independent for only seven years, accepting Dutch protection in 1856, and was ruled directly in 1882. The microstate of Mataram (Lombok) conquered and absorbed other local polities on Lombok by 1839—in addition to expelling Karangasem, its nominal overlord on Bali—ultimately establishing itself as an independent state that expanded onto the island of Bali.[12] Other examples of state creation outside of Bali include the separation of the Johor-Riau Empire into the kingdom of Johor (in modern-day Malaysia) and Dutch-controlled Riau (in modern-day Indonesia) in 1819. This split also effected the independence of Pahang from Johor in 1823. In Malaysia, Perak seceded from Thai sovereignty with British assistance in 1826. On Borneo, James Brooke, the famous "White Raja," accepted the governorship of Sarawak from the sultan of Brunei in 1841, from which he proceeded to carve out an independent state by the mid-1800s.[13]

Most of these states were small; the median population size was less than 100,000 people. Starting west, we identified seven states on the island of Sumatra: Aceh (1816–1874), Deli (1816–1862), Asahan (1816–1865), Siak (1816–1858), Minangkabau (1816–1837), Jambi (1816–1834), and Palembang

(1816–1823). As was the case elsewhere in the system, these states were gradually taken under Dutch control via conquest or agreement or both. Across the strait in Peninsular Malaysia, we counted ten states: Kedah (1816–1821), Perak (1826–1874), Selangor (1816–1874), Pahang (1863–1887), Kelantan (1816–1902), Terengganu (1816–1909), Negeri Sembilan (1816–1887), Tampin (1836–1887), Johore (1816–1885), and Riau (1816–1824). Although most of these peninsular states ended with British acquisition, the northern states of Kedah and Kelantan were for a time brought under Siamese control. Moreover, the islands of Riau were acquired by the Dutch in 1824. Altogether, these states were connected down and across the strait through patterns of ethnic kinship—for example, the people of Negeri Sembilan had originally migrated from Minangkabau—and dynastic marriage.

The main islands of Java and Borneo possessed fewer independent states by 1816. Having founded Batavia in 1619, the Dutch had been in Java for nearly two hundred years before our research period and had defeated several older states and controlled much of the island. As the headquarters of the Vereenigde Oostindische Compagnie (VOC, Dutch East India Company), Batavia provided a central position along the east–west axis of the island chain that was in reach of the key entry points to the straits. From there, the Dutch expanded in fits and starts, at times barely surviving.[14] By 1816, the chief opposition was provided by Yogyakarta (1816–1830), an historic inland empire of South-Central Java that had been divided by the Treaty of Giyanti in 1755 into the Sultanate of Yogyakarta and the court of Surakarta. Although Yogyakarta was nominally subject to Batavia from the eighteenth century, Dutch residents in Yogyakarta functioned "more like ambassadors" in the early nineteenth century.[15] It was only after the Java War (1825–1830), in which at least 200,000 Javanese died, that Dutch control was consolidated.[16]

Borneo is an immense island at 748,168 square kilometers, one of the biggest islands in the world and the largest in Southeast Asia, apart from New Guinea. Those accustomed to Mercator projections are often surprised at the size of an equatorial region such as Indonesia, but to put sizes in perspective, Borneo is roughly three and one-half times the size of Great Britain and more than five times the size of Java, a surprising fact given the much greater population of Java and greater historical role of Javanese politics and culture. In part for geographic reasons, fewer states were created in Borneo. As we discuss in the section on political centralization, coastal states never penetrated far into the interior, and the area remained a frontier region well into the twentieth century.[17] We identified five states in Borneo and two in the islands to the northeast: Benjermassin (1816–1860), Kutai (1816–1844), Bulungan (1816–1885), Brunei (1816–1888), Sarawak (1841–1888), Maguindanao (1816–1861), and Sulu (1816–1851). The first three states—Benjermassin, Kutai, and Bulungan—were colonized by the Dutch. Brunei, on the north coast, came under British rule in 1888 and was reborn as a sovereign state in 1984. Sarawak was formed in 1841 by an Englishman named James Brooke, the so-called White Raja who was the inspiration for Joseph Conrad's character Lord Jim. Sarawak was brought under British control in 1888, along with Brunei. The Sulu Sultanate had been a powerful maritime state in the island chain connecting Borneo to the southern Philippines, but its last remaining territory was absorbed by the Spanish in 1851.[18] Finally, the Sultanate of Maguindanao on the southwest coast of Mindanao was connected to the system through culture and trade. It was brought under Spanish rule in 1861.[19]

We identified three states on the island of Sulawesi, including Bone (1816–1905), Gowa (1816–1911), and Luwu (1816–1906). The fertile region of southwestern Sulawesi was the center of the Makassarese and Bugis homelands, two closely related ethnic groups known for their martial skills and seafaring ability. They fought the Dutch for more than two hundred years, but in the early days of the twentieth century their power was finally broken.[20]

Most of the remaining states were on Bali, which had consisted of several warring states since the fall of Majapahit in the sixteenth century.[21] But here, unlike most of the states to the west, Islam had been held back, and the monarchs, or rajas, practiced a form of Hindu. Clifford Geertz maintains that Bali's relative isolation was in part the consequence of geography; its main ports were situated on the south side of the island, facing the Indian Ocean, and not on the north side, where it could interact with other islands via the more tranquil Java Sea.[22] The nine Balinese states are: Karangasem (1816–1849), Buleleng (1816–1849), Jembrana (1818–1821, 1849–1853), Badung (1816–1906), Gianyar (1816–1842, 1849–1883, and 1893–1900), Klungkung (1816–1911), Mengwi (1816–1823), Tabanan (1816–1906), and Bangli (1837–1909). To these we might add the Kingdom of Mataram (1839–1894) on the neighboring island of Lombok, given its high connectivity to the Balinese states.[23] The Dutch had traditionally avoided Bali because of the turbulent interstate politics. However, events altered these political dynamics and drew in foreign intervention. One event was the eruption of Mount Tambora in 1815, an ecological disaster that killed at least 25,000 people in Bali alone but transformed the domestic economy within twenty years because of the ash deposits and enhanced soil fertility. From an island that traditionally exported slaves, Bali became a key agricultural exporter in the region.[24] The Dutch, aiming to monopolize that trade as well as to tamp down on the constant threat of Balinese piracy, became embroiled in a series of intrigues and conflicts that lasted into the early twentieth century. By 1911, the Dutch had taken control of the island.

The final set of states, or political actors, in this system comprised the European colonial powers. The Portuguese retained control over eastern Timor throughout this period, a backwater in their dwindling empire. The British, in contrast, were a constant power in the region. Not only did British shipping and naval forces traverse the area to reach outposts in East Asia, Australia, and the Pacific, but the Crown took possession of Dutch territories for a time during the Napoleonic Wars. British presence was established in Singapore in 1819 and through fits and starts over the next one hundred years. The Anglo-Dutch Treaty of 1824 created spheres of influence for the two powers and a hardening frontier that became the border between modern Malaysia and Indonesia.[25] Finally, the Dutch arguably had the biggest colonial influence on the region. By 1800, the Dutch government had assumed control from the VOC and via its expansion into the maritime system formed the Dutch East Indies.

Not all Southeast Asia was controlled by states. Large tracts of land existed in the interior of the major islands and sometimes on the coast that were not claimed by states. In many cases, the land was inhabited; we just did not find evidence of statelike entities in some places. As in West Africa and, we daresay, much of the world prior to the twentieth century, it was not the case that all available land was demarcated and formally claimed.

Nevertheless, as we discussed in chapter 2, the states we have named were states by our definition. In his analysis of precolonial Southeast Asia, Amitav Acharya argues that Southeast Asian states meet Tilly's definition of "coercion-wielding organizations that . . . exercise clear priority . . . over all other organizations within substantial territories," which we adopted.[26] Although they may not have met the standards of the Weberian ideal-type state with clearly defined borders and a modern bureaucracy, they are states in the sense of possessing a strong degree of internal and external sovereignty.

INTERACTION CAPACITY, TRADE, AND WAR

Interaction Capacity

Despite the low population densities (discussed in the next section), Southeast Asia had high (seaborne) interaction capacity. An important consequence of interconnectivity in a maritime system is the increased ability of all, or nearly all, states to interact. Aceh could trade with Gowa, just as either could trade with Yogyakarta or Kutai. States on the Malaysian Peninsula were sometimes tributaries of Aceh in Sumatra, for example, and states on the Malaysian Peninsula were often vassals of the Riau-based Johor-Riau Empire. The raja of Pahang in Malaysia was the vice regent (*bendahara*) of Johore-Riau, and Pahang was simultaneously an independent kingdom in the late eighteenth century and early nineteenth century.[27] This weblike pattern was replicated diplomatically as states sent embassies to each other, recognized one another, and engaged in forms of diplomacy.[28] States were connected through an oceanic commons, unlike in West Africa, where land- and river-based connections meant that states traded primarily with their immediate neighbors.

Overland interaction capacity was limited, probably as slow as in West Africa or mainland South Asia. Southeast Asia's interior was covered by dense jungle and forest whose hostility was symbolized by the ever-present danger of tigers.[29] Although states were connected by the sea, land-based connections were slow, expensive, and risky. Population density may have been slightly higher in Southeast Asia than in West Africa but was many times lower than in East Asia, South Asia, or Europe.[30] As in West Africa, the relative abundance of land and scarcity of people made labor expensive, and slavery was common.[31] However, as in South Asia, there are important intraregional differences in Southeast Asia. Java (and, to an extent, Bali and South Sulawesi) supported high-yield rice production and had higher population densities than Sumatra, Borneo, or the Malaysian Peninsula. Some of these population densities approached those observed in Burma, Siam, and Vietnam.[32] As David Henley argues, these areas had historically high population density, perhaps because of the nutrient-rich volcanic soils.[33]

In summary, maritime Southeast Asia exhibited a higher level of interaction capacity in the early nineteenth century than West Africa. State leaders did face the same challenges of thin populations and frontier zones, but the system's waterways enhanced the states' interconnectivity.

Cities and Trade

There was a vibrant trading system throughout the archipelago. Anthony Reid writes that commerce was thriving across the islands from at least 1400, with increases in the 1511–1640 period and afterward.[34] Unlike in West Africa or even in South Asia before the dominance of the EIC, international trade probably accounted for a high proportion of economic activity within the core trading zone of Indonesia and Malaysia.[35] It was the desire to tap and eventually monopolize the spice trade that lured the Portuguese and the Dutch. Earlier states, such as Majapahit and the Malacca Sultanate, harnessed the trade routes, including the maritime Silk Road, as part of their economy.[36] Commerce gave the thalassocratic port cities a source of authority, a source of income, and the ability to endure.[37]

Seaborne trade promoted the rise of port cities along the coasts, inwardly fringed by a hostile and jungled interior, often lacking an agricultural hinterland, and dependent on imports of Javanese rice.[38] Maritime Southeast Asia may have been one of the most urbanized regions of the world in part because of a few large coastal cities but also because of these thin interior populations. Achin (modern-day Banda Aceh), Malacca, and Surabaya may have had 50,000–100,000 people by the seventeenth century (see figure 6.2).[39] Indeed, the Malay word for state, *negeri*, has its origins in the same word that also means city. Trade growth led to the emergence of an influential merchant aristocracy called the *orang kaya* in some port cities in the seventeenth and eighteenth century, which has been compared to the class of "patrician merchants" in Europe. The *orang kaya* often held positions at court solidified by dynastic marriages and created a common court culture.[40] The seaward, thalassocratic nature of most states oriented them toward other states in terms of trade, conflict, and political intrigue.[41]

Southeast Asia was sparsely populated outside of these cities. Hendrick Spruyt writes that the low-density population and large hinterland into

MARITIME SOUTHEAST ASIA

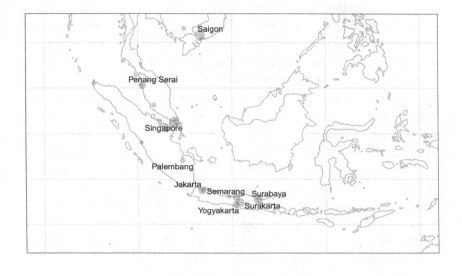

FIGURE 6.2. Cities in maritime Southeast Asia, 1750–1900. *Note*: Because of the relatively low number of cities in maritime Southeast Asia (just eight), all cities are labeled on this map, independent of their size. *Source*: Data are from Reba, Reitsma, and Seto, "Spatializing 6,000 Years of Global Urbanization from 3700 BC to AD 2000."

which populations could exit incentivized leaders to prioritize people over territory. Stanley Tambiah notes these patterns in his analysis of political order in Southeast Asia, as does James Scott in his examination of peripheral populations on the mainland.[42]

War

Maritime Southeast Asia exhibits the lowest levels of warfare across our case studies so far (see figure 6.3). The lack of conflicts between indigenous states is striking, but reporting bias may be an issue.[43] Scholarship on the region, for example, typically asserts that warfare was common among indigenous states.[44] Regular succession crises, polygamy, autonomous vassals, poor communications, and overlapping boundaries created the conditions for frequent wars within and between states (see figure 6.4). As Spruyt observes, one consequence of decentralized states without formal boundaries is the uncertainty of control.[45] Balinese states fought many wars in the eighteenth and nineteenth centuries, and other states fought each other (Johor fought the Aceh Sultanate, for example) and experienced numerous internal wars.[46] Whether utilizing land-based or naval forces, states periodically raided other states and their outlying regions to secure resources (usually slaves) or to plunder or both. Doing so was a way to project power, weaken adversaries, and bolster the ruler-conqueror's legitimacy. Perhaps poor documentation has resulted in the exclusion of these Southeast Asian wars in the scholarship.

However, lower levels of observed warfare may reflect more frequent but less severe conflicts. Reid, for example, argues that warfare in seventeenth-century Southeast Asia saw few direct casualties because defeated groups could move and settle elsewhere or agree to establish tributary relations.[47] Wars of annihilation may also have been counterproductive because the purpose of conflict was often to capture slaves or generate tribute, neither of which was facilitated by destroying subject groups.[48]

We think that wars in maritime Southeast Asia are underreported in conflict datasets, even for the nineteenth century. Contrary to the datasets, Ricklefs describes Bali as a "vast battlefield" for much of the nineteenth century, and Anthony Day describes the violence of the Balinese wars, but scarce documentation makes the details difficult to verify.[49] However, the number of severe wars was probably lower than in West Africa or South Asia over the same period. The Dutch and English were established (albeit peripherally) in Southeast Asia by the eighteenth century, whereas Europeans did not navigate the lower Niger River until 1830. Source biases should be worse for West Africa (and for South Asia), yet more wars were recorded in both regions during the nineteenth century, which leads us to think that the number of large wars, especially between indigenous states, was comparatively low in Southeast Asia. Moreover, Javanese states with the capacity to mobilize large armies, such as Yogyakarta and Surakarta, experienced a long peace between the Treaty of Giyanti in 1755 and the Java War of 1825, with the VOC playing a balancing role on Java.[50]

Between 1816 and 1920, most major wars involved the Netherlands, which fought the Java War (1825–1830) against elements of the Yogyakarta Sultanate,[51] two wars against the Balinese states (1848 and 1894), a war against Bone (1859–1860), and the Aceh War (1873–1878).[52] Of these conflicts, the Java War was perhaps the most significant. It brought Java firmly under Dutch control and cost up to 200,000 Javanese lives.[53] Similar but

MARITIME SOUTHEAST ASIA

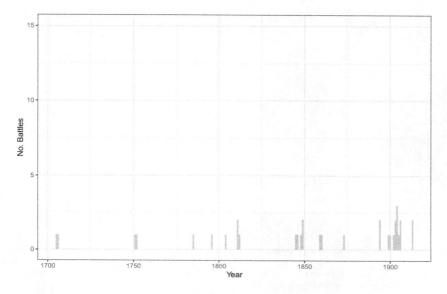

FIGURE 6.3. Wars in maritime Southeast Asia, 1700–1920. *Source:* Data are from Miller and Bakar, "Conflict Events Worldwide Since 1468 BC."

smaller conquests occurred on other islands throughout the nineteenth century and into the early years of the twentieth. Dutch colonialism extinguished the independence of most states in the region.

Three additional wars of colonial suppression occurred during the period we examined: the second Dutch–Aceh War between 1904 and 1907 after the sultanate had capitulated; the Spanish-Philippines War (1896–1898); and the war between the United States and nationalist rebels in the Philippines. Competition in Southeast Asia may have increased as the nineteenth century approached, but this increase occurred as one state (the Netherlands) dominated the system more and more.

In summary, warfare was probably less intense in maritime Southeast Asia than in the other case studies during roughly the same period. Several large and brutal wars were fought in the nineteenth century, but nearly all of the wars recorded in the main conflict datasets involve the Dutch and a local indigenous power. We do not observe the same large, indigenous armies arrayed against each other as in the Maratha–Mysore wars in South Asia and in the Dahomey–Oyo or Yoruba wars in West Africa. However, this does not mean that competition between indigenous states was

REGIONAL STATE SYSTEMS

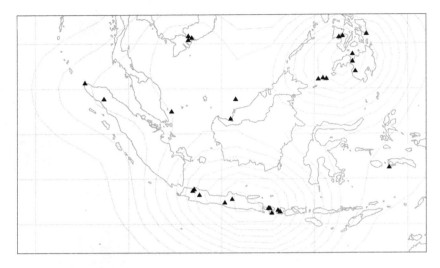

FIGURE 6.4. War locations in maritime Southeast Asia, 1750–1910. *Source*: Data are from Miller and Bakar, "Conflict Events Worldwide Since 1468 BC."

low. Conflict and violence were frequent, often precipitated by competing claims to succession or incentives to capture people, territory, and tribute. Bali stands out as a conflict-prone and competitive region during the nineteenth century through a combination of intense warfare between local states and the periodic intervention of the Dutch, who did not effectively subdue the island until the beginning of the twentieth century.

POLITICAL CENTRALIZATION

Few existing theories would predict centralized states in maritime Southeast Asia. Population densities were low; cities were scattered along the coast; and although states could interact easily over sea and some rivers, transport and communications were slow over land. However, a vibrant trading network generated resources that could be used in state-building projects and new commercial elites who might be co-opted by rulers to displace their vassal lords. Moreover, population densities were high in Java and Bali, where interaction capacity may have been higher, and Bali stands out as a high-competition region where centralized states could potentially have formed.

Kings (or queens), sultans, or rajahs claimed sovereignty, backed by a royal court and officials appointed by the sultan, who were often titled *orang besar* or *orang kaya*. Beyond the court, however, decentralized forms of rule were common. Indeed, the mandala, denoting the orbitlike form of decentralized rule that we see recurring across multiple regions, is most closely associated with Southeast Asia. The Sanskrit term *mandala* translates roughly to "circle" and has been used to describe authority that radiates outward from the ruler, dissipating as a function of distance from the center.[54] At the center of each circle was a city-state, sometimes called *negeri* in Malay.[55] The concept is invested with cosmological significance regarding a spiritual core—or an "exemplary center," as Geertz puts it—and its surrounding space.[56] It is traced to the Arthasastra, a third-century BCE Sanskrit text usually credited to Kautilya, a statesman, scholar, and thinker during the Maurya Empire.[57] The Arthasastra, or "Science of Polity," was essentially a political treatise that has been compared with *The Art of War* and *The Prince*.[58] In his recent treatment of this topic, one that we return to later in the chapter, Spruyt discusses the many ways in which the mandala design was used not just administratively but also spiritually and architecturally.[59]

O. W. Wolters describes Southeast Asia as a system of pulsating and overlapping mandala states.[60] In the absence of permanent borders between states,[61] the authority of one state dissipated across a vaguely defined area and intersected with the outer rings of another center of power. Similar metaphors are used in the literature, such as Tambiah's "galactic" polity, Victor Lieberman's notion of the solar polity—"decentralized state structures in which provincial planets revolved around an imperial sun whose gravitational pull ebbed rapidly with distance"—and the description of power as the light radiating from the center of a torch or candle, diminishing in intensity with distance from the source.[62] This sort of orbital imagery runs through the literature.[63]

At a basic level, mandalas are a depiction of decentralized governance. Rings of the circle denote areas where subordinates have greater autonomy. Rule tended to be direct in the capital, which often was a trading port. Farther inland, however, governance became more indirect as governors or chiefs were afforded autonomy in their commercial and judicial affairs in exchange for a proportion of the tax revenue (tribute) and military levies. Farther inland (or across the sea), kingdoms with their own sultans or rajas might exercise de facto independence but be nominally subordinate and tributary to more distant powers. Balinese states, for example, were symbolically subordinate to Klungkung, the successor state to the Gelgel Empire, which ruled the island of Bali until the mid-seventeenth century, when Gelgel fragmented into nine competing, independent kingdoms.[64] Klungkung retained a symbolic and ceremonial superiority in relation to other Balinese kingdoms, creating a thin layer of hierarchy or order above the state, and Gelgel is another example of older empires leaving legacies that order patterns of recognition and hierarchy between states.[65] Even the Dutch employed these loose forms of sovereignty, especially in their dealings with the Javanese sultanates and Balinese states.[66] But, importantly, the mandala refers to a collection of ideas or international norms about how governance should be structured—norms that may or may not have played a causal role in shaping how these states were structured in practice, a question we return to later in this chapter.

A survey of governance across states during the nineteenth century shows that descriptions of decentralized rule are common. As in previous chapters, we also draw upon descriptions of states from the eighteenth century because the majority of these Southeast Asian states existed before our 1816 start point in the ISD. We move roughly from Sumatra to the Malaysian Peninsula to Java, Bali, and Lombok, then to Sulawesi, Borneo, and the neighboring Philippine Islands.

On Sumatra, Minangkabau governance was divided between the nucleus (the *darat*) and more autonomous territories in the periphery that were "obliged to pay homage and tribute."[67] Aceh was a "polyglot port state" with unclear frontier zones, governed through "a system of territorial vassal lords, or uleebalang, [that] ruled their territories in the interior with much latitude."[68] The raja of Siak claimed control of external affairs but left taxation and trade matters in the hands of sixteen "petty chiefs" and was the nominal sovereign of sometimes independent rajas, such as the raja of Deli.[69]

Kedah, in what is now modern-day Malaysia, was a feudal-like state where semiautonomous state agents would pay tributes to the ruler.[70] Borders in Kedah and Kelantan were of "no significance" and "creations of the 20th century."[71] Although Kedah was an independent state for periods, it was also a tributary to Siam. Whether Kedah was in or out of Siam was impossible to say. Even the sultan of Kedah and the king of Siam disputed the meaning of the tributary relationship.[72] Other Malay states ruled through the appointment of fiefs to trusted chiefs who retained autonomy but were responsible for local order and the collection of revenues, often from mining areas.[73] The Minangkabau kingdom of Negri Sembilan was so decentralized that the sultan (*yam-tuan*) exercised control only in matters of foreign affairs, while the nine confederated kingdoms retained landownership, taxation rights, and judicial autonomy.[74] At points, even the sultan's claim to control foreign affairs was contested and nominal, as substates such as Tampin and Rembau seceded or acted increasingly independently of the *yam-tuan*.[75]

Javanese states (or Yogyakarta in our study) governed through autonomous vassals. Ricklefs writes in his extensive study of the Yogyakarta Sultanate in the mid- to late eighteenth century that the king's "administrative power was limited" and that the ideal king "refrained from interfering in the day-to-day administration of the countryside, which was in the hands of largely autonomous officials and dignitaries."[76] We will see later in the chapter that centralization attempts on Java were severely punished.

Scholars describe the Balinese kingdoms as mandalas or theater states where "the realm was composed of shifting concentric circles of lesser rulers, each a lord in his own right, around the royal center." Shifting alliances between vassals and rulers created vague border areas.[77] Hans Hägerdal states simply that "the demarcated borderlines between realms that are found in Western history simply did not exist in Southeast Asia until modern times." Jembrana, one of these Balinese kingdoms was so loosely structured that there was "nothing in the pre-colonial 'state' that was reminiscent of bureaucracy, standard regulations, or monopoly of power[;] ... the Jembrana court was situated in the circle of subordinated lords around the center."[78]

On Sulawesi, the Kingdom of Luwu was "composed of sixteen autonomous principalities, each of which was answerable to the ruler, or *datu*, in matters of tribute and war only," and they were "nested like increasingly diminutive Russian dolls within dolls." Specifically, these subordinate kingdoms were expected to "pay a nominal annual tribute, to provide buffalo for all court celebrations against only nominal payment[,] ... to request permission before they changed their *adat* (traditions), and to wage war against enemies of the *datu*."[79] Similar descriptions characterize states on Borneo and the southern islands of the Philippines, especially Sulu and Mindanao. In Bulungan, for example, sparse population densities in the interior of Borneo gave rise to nebulous frontier zones.[80]

In sum, maritime Southeast Asia was governed by city-states that employed decentralized rule in their hinterlands and tributary relations (sometimes overlapping) farther afield. We will see this same pointillist pattern of governance in West Africa, where bull's-eye states and radial states dominated the landscape. What is unique about Southeast Asia is the lack of exceptions to decentralized rule. There was no Mysore (chapter 5) or Dahomey (chapter 7) where rulers removed autonomous decision-making powers from vassals or tributaries.

EXPLAINING (DE)CENTRALIZATION

Maritime Southeast Asia was a fragmented system of small, decentralized states—a bull's-eye system. Overland interaction capacity was low, but oceangoing interaction high, creating a shared international order. Most cities hugged the coast, but the largest cities were in the interior of Java—in particular Surakarta and Yogyakarta. The level of international competition is harder to establish but was probably lower than at comparable points in West Africa or South Asia and increasing with European encroachment. To what extent do these patterns fit existing theories of state formation and centralization? We deal first with trade, then war and interaction capacity. The section concludes with a discussion of how cultural concepts, such as the mandala, may have affected state forms.

Trade appears to have facilitated state formation but inhibited state centralization. Trade meant taxes and revenues to purchase elite support and weapons, and it enabled the diffusion of new ideas of political authority. Rulers who could control trade could dominate the affairs of their neighbors and build states in the process. For example, Acharya argues that "in Southeast Asia, trade created states in many ways. It provided new resources such as arms and weapons and luxury goods for redistribution. Just as importantly, it gave rulers new ideas of political organization and legitimacy, which they used to expand their authority and control. Control over trade routes was a crucial basis of political organization."[81]

However, trade impeded state centralization because fluctuations in supply and demand, especially from China, South Asia, and Europe, made trade-based revenues difficult for rulers to monopolize and regulate. Trade could empower rulers but also empower rivals and elites as markets changed and new resources were discovered.[82] For example, pepper "defied monopoly" and created dozens of semiautonomous "pepper-rajas" along the coast of northern Sumatra, fragmenting the Sultanate of Aceh. Ricklefs notes that the "spread of pepper production meant independent sources of wealth for many lords of small ports who were nominally vassals of Aceh. As Europeans and Americans competed for access to this pepper, the northern part of Sumatra became a centre of political disintegration."[83] Pepper revenues also facilitated the independence of sultanates such as Deli, Langkat, and Asahan from Siak in the early nineteenth century.[84] Acharya notes that growing international trade allowed a "multitude" of landfalls to thrive, and Lieberman cites trade as one of the reasons why archipelagic Southeast Asia never consolidated into a smaller number of larger states. Jeyamalar Kathirithamby-Wells writes that in Siak "unprecedented growth [in the late eighteenth and early nineteenth century] brought improved wealth and influence among the lesser chiefs and aristocracy, prejudicial to internal cohesion."[85]

Perhaps the most extreme example is the formation of Chinese trading republics (*kongsi*) on Borneo (and elsewhere in Indonesia). Although we do not include these republics as states in the ISD, Chinese communities initially migrated to Kalimantan as gold miners and formed autonomous communities with governments, judicial systems, currency, taxation, schools, and religious centers. These communities became increasingly independent of their nominal sultans on Borneo as they expanded into trade in opium, salt, and gunpowder and were only suppressed by the Dutch in the Kongsi Wars (1822–1824, 1850–1854, 1884–1885).[86]

Highly independent mining princes were also a force on the Malaysian Peninsula in the eighteenth and nineteenth centuries. Selangor's ruler was challenged in the mid-nineteenth century by the rise of new "enterprising" elites who gained control of trade along the river, benefited from Chinese-worked tin mines, and effectively divided Selangor into five rival territories.[87] Moreover, the maritime nature of trade made attracting skilled seafarers an essential part of state building, but these seafaring groups were often fiercely autonomous and difficult to control.[88]

Therefore, trade may contrarily help explain why Southeast Asia was a fragmented system with many independent, competing states that did not coalesce into a single empire before the final expansion of the Dutch in the nineteenth century. Trade facilitated the formation of many states but placed them on shifting sands, making expansion and centralization precarious and risky. Moreover, as we discuss more fully later, trade was hard to regulate because of the low level of land-based interaction capacity, which exacerbated centrifugal effects and created incentives to rule by granting autonomy to vassals.

What about bellicist theories? Did the "lack" of war depress centralization? Initially, this might appear to be the case. Competition was relatively low, and without outside pressures to construct more penetrative fiscal institutions, vassals retained considerable autonomy. Yet there are several reasons to think that war or the threat of conquest did exist but did not play the role expected by bellicist theories of state centralization. First, although the data suggest that there were lower levels of war, there is little doubt that levels of competition and violence were high, and this combination of competition and violence provided rulers with constant incentives to innovate and consolidate their rule.[89] Rulers had to contend with the possibility of external invasion and the constant threat of rebellion from vassal kingdoms that could cascade into dynasty-ending wars.

Moreover, low levels of war in Southeast Asia are debatable. Ricklefs, for example, sees war on Java becoming more intense, bloodier, and European-like by the early 1700s as states adopted European weapons and tactics. By 1765, the Yogyakarta Sultanate could mobilize perhaps 100,000 soldiers. Mataram experienced several bloody succession wars during the eighteenth century (1704–1708, 1719–1723, 1746–1757), resulting in a split dynasty—the partition of Mataram into the Yogyakarta and Surakarta Sultanates—and the increasing interference of the VOC in Javanese affairs.[90] The VOC actually became a court of arbitration between the rival sultanates with the reaffirmation of the Treaty of Giyanti (1755) in 1790, which coincided with the longest period of peace on Java since the sixteenth century (approximately 1757–1825). Furthermore, these wars resulted in greater decentralization as the Sultanate of Surakarta was forced to accommodate the semisovereign (even dual-sovereign) territories of Mangkunegara I, leader of one of the main rebel armies.

Some scholars, such as Anthony Day, point out that Southeast Asian states did not centralize even though they still fought "massive" wars, especially in Bali and on the mainland.[91] Although the VOC and British were important players in the Southeast Asian system at the beginning of the nineteenth century, they were hardly hegemonic, and the system remained multicentric and competitive until the mid–nineteenth century, when the Dutch took closer control of Java and eventually of the outer islands and the British increasingly controlled the Malaysian Peninsula. The nineteenth century can then be seen as a period of increasing competition as more assertive European powers expanded.

It is difficult to imagine that the same incentives that pushed European rulers to centralize their rule were not also present for insecure Southeast Asian rulers. Indeed, even if we accept that the intensity of warfare was lower, rulers did attempt reforms that would have centralized these states, only to face backlash from disaffected vassals. As in South Asia, we see evidence that war empowered rather than disempowered vassal polities, upon whom rulers in Southeast Asia were dependent to wage wars in the first place. Vassals could easily switch sides and negotiate for tributary relations rather than annihilation, and populations could relocate in response to external threats.[92] Since most armies were not standing armies in Southeast Asia but were mobilized with contributions from vassals, warfare increased rather than decreased the dependence of the center on its subordinates. Defecting subordinates were common as "vassals and tributary rulers shifted their loyalties from ruler to ruler as opportunity presented itself."[93] Spruyt notes that "contrary to the expectation that such violence would lead to greater centralization—the well-known 'war made the state' thesis—the reverse was true. Since any king, or usurper, could be challenged by his vassals or family members, attempts at centralization were frequently doomed from the outset. Galactic polities contained multiple gravitation fields that could pull the center apart. Charismatic challenges, arising from many corners, could demonstrate merit by winning their struggles against the center."[94]

Ricklefs notes in his study of the Yogyakarta Sultanate that centralization was risky because "dissident dignitaries could decide to change allegiance to another king without risking their fates in rebellion."[95] Although examples are scarce, two of the largest wars in Java (the wars of succession described earlier) and the Java War (1825–1830) resulted in weaker, decentralized kingdoms forced to accommodate large semisovereign territories within their realms (the Java War resulted in the creation of the Disangana enclave within Surakarta). Dutch entry into Java and Bali increased the level of competition on these islands but fragmented states by providing an outside ally who could aggravate secessionist tensions. On Java, the Dutch forced Surakarta to accept new, powerful subordinate vassals, which the

British later did to Yogyakarta in 1816. On Bali, the VOC peeled vassals in the North from Karangasem and Klungkung and reestablished new independent dynasties (such as Jembrana) that further fragmented the system.

Southeast Asian wars were probably less intense because of the low underlying level of interaction capacity. Defection was common because conquering rulers could not credibly commit to directly ruling new acquisitions owing to the challenges of extending state administration. Autonomy in exchange for loyalty and tribute was a common solution to this problem that left vassals intact and the conquered with an increased flow of resources until the next potential conqueror came along. Wars of annihilation were probably rare because they were counterproductive and costly. People were also probably able to move in response to conquest, again because of low population densities and conquering armies' weak ability to administer the territories they conquered. This pattern is strongly suggestive that the nature of war and decentralization have deeper underlying causes. In the case of Southeast Asia, the low level of overland interaction capacity is an oft-cited cause of decentralization. Put differently, less intense warfare was not a cause of decentralized states, nor were decentralized states necessarily a cause of low levels of warfare. Rather, both reflected the incredible difficulty, risk, and costs of extending state infrastructures over territory.

The two most common explanations for Southeast Asia's decentralized states and fragmented international system are the low level of interaction capacity and the prevalence of cultural concepts that favored decentralized rule. Numerous historians point to how limitations on the movement of people and goods overland checked ambitions to centralize the state. Speaking of the Majapahit Empire, Lieberman states, "Wretched transport meant that to retain outlying dependencies, the center had to combine marriage alliances, spies, supernatural sanctions, and military threats with acceptance of extensive autonomy." He further notes that "far-flung population clusters mandated decentralized state structures in which provincial planets revolved around an imperial sun whose gravitational pull ebbed rapidly with distance."[96] Ricklefs writes that on Java "geographic fragmentation and local traditions" necessitated the accommodation of vassal princes and aristocrats and that "armies of occupation far from the court were a physical impossibility."[97] Discussing the indigenous states of

Malaysia, Barbara Watson Andaya and Leonard Andaya write that tensions between center and periphery were endemic because "local revenues, frequently considerable, made it possible for an ambitious chief to acquire a fair degree of independence, and geographical distance enabled him to virtually ignore the existence of his suzerain."[98] In reference to Perak, Kathirithamby-Wells notes that "the difficulty of communication over rough terrain and the isolation of the *hulu* (up-river) from the *Mir* (downriver) worked against the effective maintenance of centralized control by the ruler. The tin mines which were the main source of wealth were widely scattered and lay in the hands of the *orang besar* [vassal rulers] so that the ruler could not easily control and centralize outlets for produce."[99]

Yogyakarta and Aceh attempted centralization projects but failed. Yogyakarta under Susuhunan Amangkurat I (r. 1646–1677), for example, murdered the old elite, established new, directly appointed administrative posts to govern vassal kingdoms, demanded a census, removed freedom of movement, and proclaimed a monopoly of trade—all classic centralizing moves. The result, however, was massive rebellion and the collapse of the empire, which was rescued only by the intervention of the VOC. As Ricklefs points out, "By his tyrannical rule, his murders, his attempts to destroy regional autonomy and his inability to exercise military power, Amangkurat I had destroyed the consensus of notables which was essential to legitimacy and effective rule." Centralization risked the legitimacy and military foundations that bound the kingdom together: "If the king attempted too much, perhaps actually trying to govern and administer daily affairs throughout his kingdom, he would rapidly alienate those upon who[se] support he depended, and, again, the fragile state structure was likely to fall." According to Ricklefs, Susuhunan Amangkurat I's mid-seventeenth-century centralization bid was "doomed to failure; the facts of geography, communications, and population, which determined that administrative authority in Java must be decentralized, could not be changed by royal fiat. As a result of his policies, Amangkurat I alienated powerful people and important regions and, in the end, produced the greatest rebellion of the 17th century; this brought about the collapse of the dynasty and the intervention of the VOC."[100]

Aceh under Sultan Iskandar Muda (r. 1607–1636) tried to centralize rule by assigning key ports to governors, who on three-year cycles were tasked with enforcing trade monopolies. As Kathirithamby-Wells explains, these governors were supervised by agents from the capital (*panglima*s) and displaced the old royal aristocracy by co-opting a newer mercantile aristocracy (the *orang kaya*, or "rich men") to fill these new posts, which Lieberman sees as a move toward centralization similar (albeit on a much smaller scale) to that on Burma and Siam. However, Kathirithamby-Wells notes that this reorganization quickly succumbed to the pressures of decentralization: "Any success he [Iskandar Muda] had in [centralizing] was short-lived. Under the mild rule of Sultan Iskandar Thani and the sixty years of female rule which followed, Aceh witnessed the gradual erosion of royal power and the resurgence of the orang kaya as a powerful force. The trend climaxed in the emergence of the *panglima* as powerful territorial heads."[101]

Southeast Asian rulers were therefore willing and even looked to reduce or consolidate their concentric circles of power when they believed it was possible. If we look farther north to mainland Southeast Asia, other mandala states such as Siam also attempted major centralization projects in the late nineteenth century, eroding the power of older tributary states such as Lanna (Chiang Mai) and integrating them into a centralized bureaucracy.[102] Decentralized rule was inefficient and dangerous; taxes were lost, subordinates could rebel and defect, and it was difficult to monitor and govern the kingdom. But centralization was more dangerous. To alienate the elite was to undermine the economic and military foundations of rule. Low interaction capacity created strong incentives to rule through decentralized contracts, and deviations from this strategy were punished.

Finally, Southeast Asia is notable for its set of cultural blueprints for the way that states should be ruled. The mandala was a polity where power radiated in concentric circles, wherein state presence became weaker with each transition to the next circle. Several scholars place causal weight on these elements of international order, arguing that states in Southeast Asia were decentralized because that's how it was believed rulers *ought* to rule. Spruyt argues that "collective belief systems with religious views informed material political realities—not the other way around." Tambiah makes similar albeit weaker claims when he posits that ordering patterns undergirding galactic polities could not be fully explained by "vulgar utilitarianism or pragmatism."[103] In the case of Southeast Asia, this meant that cosmological ideas regarding the mandala yielded decentralized forms of rule that diminished in an orbital pattern. Here, international order is not simply epiphenomena; it shapes structure.

However, as we elaborate in the chapters to come, the mandala-like pattern of rule was also common outside of Southeast Asia, which suggests that similar forms of governance emerged from varied cultural contexts. The terms used for this pattern may be different—*bull's-eye state* versus *galactic polity*—but the resulting radial pattern is largely the same. Indeed, the literature on empire identifies radial structures as a common pattern whereby metropoles pragmatically project power over distance, a connection that Hermann Kulke made with the mandala.[104] Moreover, rulers in Southeast Asia attempted to centralize their administrations when the opportunity arose. Rulers were willing to reduce the number of their concentric circles of power when they believed it was possible. Perhaps Southeast Asian states constructed mandalas not because they believed it was the right form of government but because decentralizing governance was the safest path given other constraints. After all, if it was the cosmological idea, not everyday matters of control and interstate competition, that drove outcomes, then the system would have been more static rather than the pulsing and shifting political landscape that Wolters describes.[105] This issue of the relationship between international order and state structure is a vital one, and we return to it in chapter 9.

CONCLUSION

Before maritime Southeast Asia was folded into the Dutch and British Empires, it was a competitive, dynamic, interstate system composed of nearly forty unique states, almost none of which exists today. Swift ocean-borne trade and communication routes helped create dense interactions between states, a shared sense of political order, some levels of linguistic unity, and early exposure to foreign ideas, migrants, and political influences. However, movement over land remained painfully slow, and we have argued in this chapter that this put a brake on the extent to which states could centralize their rule. Indeed, the wealth generated by Southeast Asia's central trading position and slow communications over land may have combined to raise the barriers to centralized rule even higher. Not only were vassals hard to control because moving and supplying governors and bureaucrats were expensive and slow, but those unregulated vassals also could benefit from fluctuations in international markets that either weakened the center or strengthened their own internal sources of revenue. These factors created a hostile environment to centralizing rulers, leaving behind a fragmented system of trade-based city-states. From the seventeenth century on, no single power dominated the system, and nearly all the constituent states ruled by decentralizing their governing institutions. The concentric, radiating form of rule was so widespread that it may have generated collective understandings of governance—the mandala—a concept with cosmological importance and structural implications. Although the content of that order pervaded the system, we have provided reasons in this chapter that the mandala approach, understood as a form of decentralized rule (a bull's-eye state), was a response to material limitations on projecting power rather than a conceptual causal factor that strongly prevented rulers from overcoming and superseding their vassals.

Chapter Seven

WEST AFRICA

Today's West Africa consists of eighteen countries, from Senegal to Chad. They are the same eighteen states formed with decolonization, and their borders have hardly changed since then. There were twice as many states two hundred years ago, though, a number that grew by the mid–nineteenth century as new empires rose and others fragmented. Europeans were minor political players in 1816—although important economic actors—and the dynamics of the state system were shaped largely by indigenous rulers. In fact, if West African states died before 1850, they were more likely conquered by a local power than by Europeans. Yet in 1910 there was only one state left (Liberia) after Europeans swept across the continent in a short span of about fifteen years.

This chapter describes the system of West African states that ruled throughout the nineteenth century. Although these states varied from loose confederations to trading leagues to universalist empires to clusters of city-states and relatively centralized kingdoms, they formed a system of decentralized states: a bull's-eye system. The patterns we observe in West Africa challenge war- and trade-based theories of state centralization. Warfare was intense and increased in scale, severity, and frequency from the late eighteenth century through to the colonization of the last West African states. Most states were connected, either directly or indirectly, to the brutal Atlantic slave trade. The "slave coast" in modern Benin and

Nigeria became a crucible of war, trade in human beings, and state experimentation. But few centralized states formed in West Africa. Most rulers governed by allowing vassals autonomy and extracted revenues through tributary networks, which often extended beyond their borders. We suggest instead that the low level of interaction capacity limited the extent to which direct forms of rule were feasible, despite the high levels of warfare and economic incentives to directly control trade routes.

The West African system completes the path that we began with East Asia and then followed to South Asia and Southeast Asia. The order of that path was determined by decreasing levels of interaction capacity. Thus, West Africa is the lowest-capacity system. This chapter utilizes the same structure as the three preceding chapters. We begin with an accounting of the states in the system before moving on to discuss interaction capacity, war and trade, political centralization, and the main findings. We take a special look at the role of slavery in state building later in the chapter.

STATES AND THE SYSTEM

West Africa was a fragmented system, divided into (at different times) between thirty-seven and forty-five states (fifty-two unique states in total). Bounded by the Sahara to the north and the rainforests of Central Africa to the south, the system encompassed 8.5 million square kilometers and 40 million people.[1] Most states were small, with a mean population of around 832,000.[2] Although large empires emerged (the Sokoto and Oyo Empires, for example), and the western Sahel had supported empires in the past (the Ghana and Mali Empires), there was no legacy of a system-wide empire or state, in contrast to South Asia.[3] Not all areas were ruled by states. Mobile, nomadic polities traversed the fringes of the Sahara, and acephalous societies (i.e., those lacking hierarchical governance above the village level) were common from modern-day Senegal and Guinea-Bissau to the Igbo regions of the southeastern coast of Nigeria.[4]

Slavery was widespread. Although the Atlantic slave trade was outlawed by the British in 1807, it continued throughout the nineteenth century. The number of slaves taken from Africa (and West Africa) peaked in the forty years from the 1750s to the 1790s but remained steady from 1800 to 1840 before plummeting after the 1850s.[5] States were also linked by a north–south trade network running from the Sahara to the forest zones of the

WEST AFRICA

coast. A. G. Hopkins concludes that these trading networks gave West Africa a "tenuous economic unity."[6] Islamic culture and religion were also important unifying factors—nearly all states in the North were formally Islamic and linked by networks of religious scholars and pilgrimage.

Altogether we recorded fifty-two states in West Africa (see figure 7.1), starting with the Senegalese states of Cayor (1816–1861), Waalo (1816–1855), Saloum (1816–1865), Jolof (1816–1885), and Futa Toro (1816–1891), from which the jihad of Usman Dan Fodio spread across West Africa from the beginning of the nineteenth century. On the northern fringes of the Senegalese states and the Sahara were the more mobile Brakna (1816–1905) and Trarza (1816–1904) Emirates in modern-day Mauritania. On the southern fringe was the slave-based Kaabu Empire (1816–1867) and its successor state Fuladu (1872–1896). These Senegalese states were often in conflict with their larger eastern neighbors, especially Futa Djallon (1816–1887), Kaarta (1816–1854), and Segou (1816–1861). Kaarta and Segou were conquered and incorporated into the Islamist Tokolor Empire (1848–1893), which also defeated and incorporated the newly formed Islamic state of Macina (1816–1862). Along the forest belt and coastal regions of Liberia, Guinea, and Cote d'Ivoire were the Wassulu (1878–1887), Sise (1835–1881), and Kong (1816–1889) Empires, along with the state of Sikasso (1816–1898). Liberia (1847–present) was established as an independent state for freed American slaves and was the only West African state to avoid colonization (although it was created as a colony).

Farther east and south were the complex of states in modern-day Burkina Faso—Yatenga (1816–1895), Ougadougou (1816–1896), and Tengodgu (1816–1896)—and the Asante Empire in modern-day Ghana (1816–1896). Yet farther east were states under the Oyo Empire (1816–1833) before its collapse in 1833, including Dahomey (1816–1894), Ketu (1816–1886), Abeokuta (1830–1893), Ijaye (1832–1862), Ibadan (1828–1893), Ijebu (1816–1892), Ijesa (1816–1870), Ile-Ife (1816–1849), Owo (1816–1893), Benin (1816–1897), Aro (1816–1902), and Abuja (1828–1902).

On the northern fringes of Oyo were the occasional tributary polities of Nupe (1816–1832) and the "dual" Borgu Kingdom (1816–1898).[7] The formation of the Sokoto Caliphate (1816–1903)—one of the largest and most populous West African states in history—was probably the most significant political event in West Africa during the early to mid-nineteenth century. The caliphate displaced and supplanted the older Hausa city-states, two of

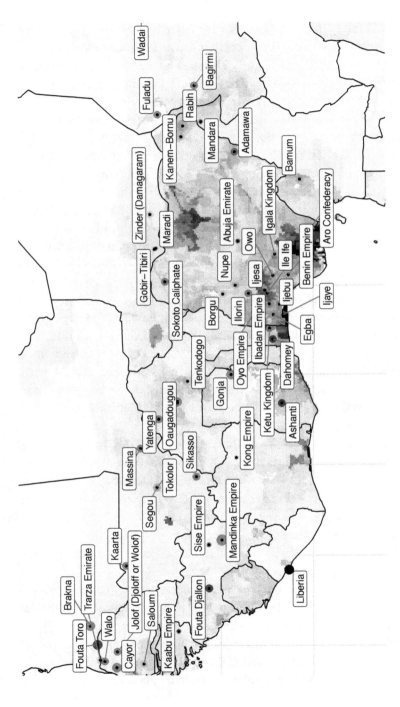

FIGURE 7.1. States and population densities in West Africa, 1816–1920. *Note:* Shows population density in 1800. More opaque circles represent clearer borders noted in the ISD. Population density has been capped at a maximum of 120 people per square kilometer to facilitate comparison with the other three systems. *Source:* Population density data are from Klein Goldewijk et al., "The HYDE 3.1 Spatially Explicit Database of Human-Induced Global Land-Use Change Over the Past 12,000 Years."

which survived on the northern frontiers of the caliphate, Gobir-Tibiri (1830–1898) and Maradi (1819–1898). Although originally part of Sokoto, Adamawa (1841–1893) became independent in the mid-1900s. States clustered around and were tributary to the centuries-old Bornu Empire (1816–1893), including Zinder (1841–1899), Mandara (1816–1902), Bagirmi (1816–1897), and Wadai (1816–1909). Finally, late in the nineteenth century the slave trader turned empire builder Rabih az-Zubayr swept from the east to establish an empire (1878–1900) atop Bornu.[8]

If this seems like a complex picture, it was. West Africa was a dynamic system of states, shaken by economic change, state creation, consolidation, and collapse. One-third of states in West Africa were born *after* 1816, compared to just 5 percent for South Asia and none of the four states in East Asia. Yet only Liberia survived to 1920, and none was resurrected later in the twentieth century. Europeans extinguished the sovereignty of most states and incorporated them into their imperial domains, but many died at the hands of other West African states.

These changes were rapid and far-reaching. For example, northern Nigeria was ruled by Hausa city-states in 1800 but unified under a single Islamic empire– the Sokoto Caliphate—a decade later. The jihad spread— first south into Yoruba country, sparking the collapse of the centuries-old Oyo Empire into warring successor states, then west, creating the Tokolor Empire, which conquered the Niger River states of Kaarta and Segou along with the Macina Caliphate.[9] Other military empires rose, including the Wassulu Empire in modern-day Guinea, the Mahdist state in the Sudan, and Rabih's state in central Sudan, which started as a Egyptian-sanctioned slaving expedition and ended with the conquest of Darfur, Kordofan, and parts of Borno.[10] Europeans were confined to coastal trading enclaves in 1816 but then extinguished nearly all of the indigenous states south of the Sahara between 1880 and 1903.[11]

New types of governance also emerged. Some rulers in Dahomey and Asante were able to concentrate power, create standing armies, and build bureaucracies that could monitor and tax populations to an extent not hitherto seen in the region.[12] The Macina Caliphate also attempted tax reforms, expanding its state infrastructures in the process.[13] Ibadan experimented with new hybrid forms of traditional and military governance, while neighboring Ijaye became a military autocracy. We explore the drivers of these patterns in the next sections.

INTERACTION CAPACITY, TRADE, AND WAR

Interaction Capacity

Interaction capacity was low in West Africa. Transport was slow and expensive, and communications by land were based "entirely on human and animal power."[14] For example, in the Oyo Empire "the costs of transport were high and precluded the possibility of substantial trade over long distances of basic foodstuffs and other commodities of great bulk and low value."[15] Across the desert and the dry savannah to the north, camels were used to transport bulk goods. Farther south, carriage was by foot or by donkey. Camels could travel twenty to twenty-five kilometers per day with relatively heavy loads,[16] while donkeys and humans could travel about twenty kilometers with lighter loads. Up to twenty-five to thirty tons could be transported along the Niger River, which provided one of the main transport corridors but was also prone to flooding and difficult to navigate.[17] Although transport was slow, it was well adapted to the environment. Transport times were not strikingly different from those of South Asia or East Asia or even Europe before the Industrial Revolution. As Hopkins concludes, "Freight charges per ton were no more expensive in Africa than they were in other parts of the world."[18]

Ivor Wilks's study of Asante is one of the most comprehensive analyses of interaction capacity in precolonial West Africa. Even toward the end of the nineteenth century, with improved road systems and bridge building, travel between Kumasi and the Dutch post of Elmina on the coast was a three-week round trip, with similar distances to the Cape Coast. What Wilks calls "message-delay," or the time taken for a message to be sent and returned, was between five to seven weeks from Kumasi to the northern parts of greater Asante. Goods-carrying caravans traveled at slower paces. Wilks concludes that there was no "revolution" in transport and communications in the Asante regions of West Africa before British colonization and the first rail link from the coast to Kumasi.[19]

Although interaction capacity was low everywhere in West Africa, disease vulnerability and terrain created regional variations. The tsetse fly carries a parasite that is harmful to domesticated animals, especially livestock and horses, and has for a long time been common along the West African coast from Sierra Leone to Nigeria and Cameroon.[20] Transport was limited to human foot speeds in the tsetse belt, while horses could be used farther north.[21] Intensive plow-based agriculture was also limited, as was the use of livestock to transport larger loads. As Marcella Alsan states, "Messages, carrying goods or military transport over land would have been hampered by the lack of large, domesticated animals."[22] However, these regional differences were relatively minor. Even in the North, horses were not widely utilized for transport because of the high costs of purchasing, maintaining, and replacing them.[23]

Trade and Cities

Population density in West Africa was low compared with the population densities of South Asia, East Asia, and Southeast Asia, and land was relatively abundant.[24] Greater distances had to be traveled between locations where economic exchange could take place, and migration was common. Several states were migratory, either in the sense that they were established by refugees (Abeokuta and Ibadan, for example) or because capital cities moved regularly. Segou is thought to have changed its capital six times, for example.[25]

However, the Hausa regions of northern Nigeria as well as the Yoruba and Igbo areas of southern Nigeria had higher population densities, levels of urbanization, and economic production.[26] These clusters are visible in figure 7.2, which shows cities in West Africa with a population greater than 20,000 between 1750 and 1900. Perhaps half of the population in the Hausa region lived in towns before 1900.[27] Kano, in northern Nigeria, had a population of about 30,000 at the beginning of the nineteenth century and was described as the "Manchester of West Africa."[28] Textile manufacturing in Kano probably clothed more than half the inhabitants of western Sudan. Kano grew to 100,000 people by the end of the nineteenth century.[29] The Yoruba regions of southwestern Nigeria and Benin also had higher population densities, with about a dozen towns of more than 20,000 people, including Ibadan, with a population of 70,000.[30] Of the thirty-six main cities in Yorubaland, six had populations greater than 40,000 (Ibadan, Ilorin, Iwo, Abeokuta, Oshogbo, and Ede), six had 10,000–20,000 inhabitants, and five had 5,000–10,000. As Catherine Coquery-Vidrovitch states, "Even though travelers may have exaggerated, the [population] numbers are large for premodern times. They are at least comparable to those of medium sized cities in Europe at about the same

REGIONAL STATE SYSTEMS

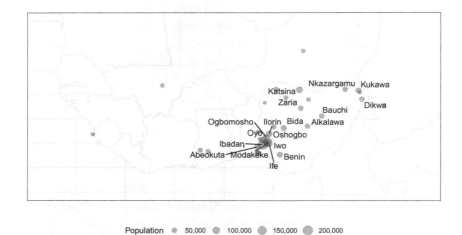

FIGURE 7.2. Cities in West Africa, 1750–1900. *Source*: Data are from Reba, Reitsma, and Seto, "Spatializing 6,000 Years of Global Urbanization from 3700 BC to AD 2000."

period." She notes that "the Yoruba were the most urbanized people in West Africa[;] ... they were unique in that their urban revolution had occurred without any direct European influence."[31] Moreover, these Yoruba cities were generated by a similar process of war and refugee flows as some versions of the bellicist theory outlined in chapter 3 suggest. The Igbo regions of southeastern Nigeria were also very densely populated, although without the same concentrations in cities.

Most production was for subsistence and exchange at nearby markets. Three important trade networks crossed the region: a domestic trade network, the trans-Saharan network, and the Atlantic slave trade. First, locally produced and imported goods, especially gold, kola nuts, salt, cowries, and cloth, in addition to slaves for domestic use, were traded within the region. Trade was more intense where ecological zones met, and most of these networks ran, therefore, north to south.[32] Much of the trade occurred in caravans and was conducted using currencies with accepted values, and there was a credit market that enabled merchants to obtain the capital for establishing long and risky trading caravans. For example, a trading expedition from Sokoto to Asante could take between six and twelve months.[33] However, expensive travel costs meant that trade was limited to high value-to-weight goods and serviced a thin layer of political and economic elites who could afford expensive commodities.[34] The city of Kano was a central hub, and Hausa traders linked the region through this trade network.

Second, there was the trans-Saharan trade in slaves, gold, salt, and kola nuts. Timbuktu and the northern Nigerian cities were central nodes in this network. Finally, there was the Atlantic slave trade, which peaked in the eighteenth century but continued "unabated" through the early and mid-nineteenth century despite being banned in the United Kingdom (the largest trader in slaves) in 1807.[35] Slaves were abducted from the interior by indigenous state monopolies, merchant slave traders, and smaller-scale conglomerates and taken to coastal ports such as Ouidah (in modern-day Benin) or Old Calabar (in Nigeria) to be sold as slave labor in the Americas and the Caribbean. Approximately 55 percent of all slaves were sold at ports in West Africa, especially ports in Benin and Nigeria. The slave trade had profound, devastating, and long-lasting effects on Africa and the Americas.[36] We discuss the implications of the Atlantic slave trade for state formation and centralization further in this chapter, as it has become a topic of some debate in IR. Toward the end of the nineteenth century, the Atlantic slave trade was replaced with trade in palm-oil products, ground nuts, rubber, and cocoa, which favored smaller-scale farmers and was a high-volume trade.[37]

Islamic mosques and schools also linked peoples across the Sahel and were crucial in the jihadist revolutions of the nineteenth century.[38] The Sokoto Caliphate co-opted these networks of religious scholars to hold the massive, sprawling empire together, to the extent that, as Allen Howard claims, Sokoto "created a territory" with commensurate changes in identity, especially with a deepening of Islamic belief and practice.[39] Movements such as the Sanusi brotherhood—part state, part trading guild, and part religious sect—traversed the Sahara from Fezzan in Libya to Borno in Chad. The marabouts (descendants of the Prophet Mohammed, religious leaders and teachers) in modern-day Senegal also cut across the borders of the Senegalese states.[40] Kinship and "ethnic" networks transcended borders, but some historians note that ethnicity played only a small role in ordering relations between groups in precolonial Africa; rather, states and economic changes more often provided the bases for ethnic claims in the postcolonial period.[41]

In summary, interaction capacity in West Africa was low compared with the other systems described in this book. The system was based on a sparse and largely self-sufficient population that produced little economic surplus above what was required for local consumption and trade. However, southwestern Nigeria hosted a dense population, urban centers, and trade networks, while entrepôt cities in northern Nigeria were linked by networks of longer-distance trade in gold, kola nuts, salt, textile manufactures, cowries, and slaves. Slave trading was widespread across the Sahara and in greater numbers south at the Atlantic ports.

War

War and competition were intense in nineteenth-century West Africa. Because of source biases, we cannot know with current data whether West Africa had more or less war than Europe during the same period (or earlier periods).[42] But qualitative and quantitative sources agree that international competition intensified during the nineteenth century. Figures 7.3 and 7.4 show the number of active war years in West Africa as recorded by Peter Brecke and the locations of wars as later georeferenced by James Fenske.[43] War years became more frequent from the beginning of the nineteenth century, and the wars were concentrated in the Asante-Dahomey-Yoruba zone of modern Nigeria, Togo, Benin, and Ghana.

European colonialism explains part of this increase. The British fought Asante four times (1806–1807, 1823–1826, 1873–1874, 1900) and ended the Sokoto Caliphate in a series of wars (1897, 1901–1903).[44] The French conquered what are modern-day Niger, Senegal, Mali, Burkina Faso, Guinea, and Chad by incorporating Senegalese states as well as the Tokolor (1893), Wassulu (1898), and Dahomey (1894) Empires.

The number, length, and severity of wars between indigenous African states also increased in the late eighteenth and early nineteenth centuries.[45] Much of this competition was triggered by the rise of the Sokoto Caliphate. Between 1790 and 1804, Usman Dan Fodio overthrew the Hausa city-states, creating a powerful empire in northern Nigeria. By 1810, the war had spread to Borno, which collapsed and then was restored under the (current) al-Kanemi Dynasty.[46] The Islamic revolution exacerbated secessionist tensions in the Oyo Empire, leading to the split of the city Ilorin from Oyo in 1817, several wars between the Oyo Empire and the new Sokoto emirates, and eventually the collapse of Oyo and its fragmentation into at least six city-states by about 1830—the most important of which were Ibadan,

WEST AFRICA

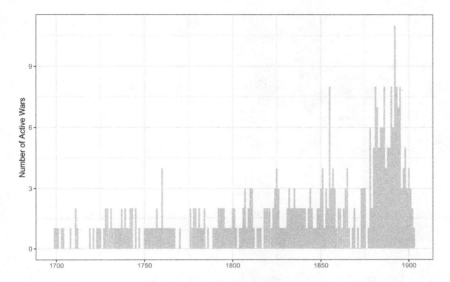

FIGURE 7.3. Numbers of active war years in West Africa, 1700–1900. *Source:* Conflict data are from Fenske and Kala, "1807: Economic Shocks, Conflict, and the Slave Trade."

Abeokuta, and Ijaye—and the full independence of the Dahomey Kingdom.[47] This fragmentation created an "intense" cycle of warfare and slave raiding that endured through much of the nineteenth century, including a sixteen-year conflict between Ibadan and its neighbors starting in 1886 (known as the Ekiti Wars).[48] Dahomey threw off a tributary relationship with the Oyo Empire in 1823 and invaded the Yoruba heartland by twice (unsuccessfully) attacking the Abeokuta Kingdom in 1851 and 1864.[49] Hemmed in by Dahomey to the west, Sokoto to the north, and the British to the south, western Nigeria became a crucible of "unremitting" geopolitical competition and war in the nineteenth century.[50]

From Sokoto, the revolution also spread west (rather, it started from the far west in Senegal), leading to the rise of the Macina Caliphate (1810) and the Tokolor Empire (1848), triggering a series of regional wars. The ancient kingdoms of Segou and Kaarta were conquered and absorbed by the Tokolor Empire, as was Macina. States in modern-day Senegal and Guinea-Bissau also fought more frequent and larger-scale wars in the nineteenth century, occasioning the collapse of older empires (Kaabu), the rise of new empires (Fuladu), and the expansion of indigenous states (for example,

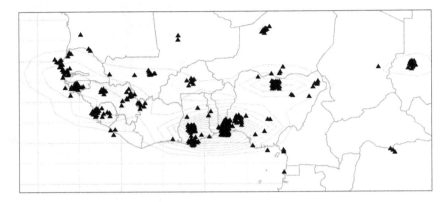

FIGURE 7.4. War locations in West Africa, 1700–1900. *Note*: Contour lines represent estimates of conflict-location density. *Source*: Data are from Fenske and Kala, "1807: Economic Shocks, Conflict, and the Slave Trade."

Futa Djallon).[51] In modern-day Ghana, Asante conquered the Akan states and established a regional hegemony that took the British three wars to break. These "widening indigenous conflicts in the nineteenth century" reflected changing dynamics between indigenous African states rather than direct conflicts with Europeans.[52]

Some might contend that the nature of warfare in Africa was different from warfare in the other systems studied, more like raiding than war. Most historians reject this view, though, especially for the nineteenth century.[53] In that century, war was an instrument of statecraft that would be familiar to twenty-first-century audiences.[54] For Fola Fagbule and Feyi Fawehinmi, the Yoruba powers were "focused on maximizing [their] relative geographical and political advantages, for economic success, measured by trade flows and customs rights. They were also determined as ever to remain independent from domination and enslavement."[55] Toyin Falola and Dare Oguntomisin state that Ibadan's foreign policy was "guided by rational calculations, self-interest, and the pursuit of an imperialist agenda."[56] Asante had a dedicated external-affairs staff, and the *asantehene* (king), Osei Bonsu (r. 1804–1824), is said to have espoused the proverb "Never appeal to the sword while the path lay open to negotiations."[57] Standing armies were more common in the nineteenth century, and firearms were employed by infantry armies by the late eighteenth century.[58] States such as Ibadan, Ijaye, Sokoto, Abeokuta, Asante, Sokoto, Segou, Kaarta, Bornu, and Tukolor had standing armies and fielded tens of thousands of troops in battle. States such as Asante could field 80,000 soldiers, Ibadan up to 60,000, Abeokuta up to 20,000, and Ijaye 40,000.[59] According to data from Jason Lyall, states in precolonial West Africa fought wars with 20,000 troops per side, on average, and nearly three-quarters of them had standing armies. Richard Reid characterizes the nineteenth century as a "military revolution" in Africa.[60] Moreover, wars in nineteenth century West Africa became what are called "total wars," resulting in the destruction of states such Owu and Ijaye, which were never resurrected, and the expulsion of reigning dynasties, which never again took power.

We think it is safe to say West Africa was a high-competition system through the late eighteenth and early nineteenth centuries, not only because European states were encroaching as the nineteenth century progressed but also because wars between indigenous African states increased in number and intensity. In particular, the Yoruba region of western Nigeria emerged as a dense subsystem and the locus of warfare. Whether this competition was as high as it was in Europe during the early-modern period is hard to say, but historical accounts and quantitative sources agree that the nineteenth century was an unstable and violent period in West African history.

POLITICAL CENTRALIZATION

The West African system approximates the decentralized system of bull's-eye states we presented in chapter 3, although mutually agreed-upon borders were common, and some states were centralizing, as we discuss later in this section. Capital cities were usually controlled directly, where taxes were levied at markets, at city gates, and from towns or farms in the immediate vicinity. Even within capital cities, however, governance could be divided between different wards with different levels of autonomy, as was the case for Abeokuta and Oyo Ile (the capital of the Oyo Empire). State boundaries did not extend far beyond city limits for smaller states, but for those states with more extensive territories, governance became more decentralized the farther from the capital one traveled. Rulers did not claim sovereignty over all aspects of governance in their vassal territories. Rather, they demanded tributes in slaves, kola nuts, cowries, and gold; the rights to approve new rulers in vassal kingdoms, demand military levies, and decide capital crimes; and that their vassals refrain from engaging in an independent foreign policy. Otherwise, independent but tribute-paying kingdoms were common at the fringes of West African states. For example, nearly all historians treat Dahomey as an independent state from the mid–eighteenth century after it conquered Allada and Hueda in modern-day Benin from 1724 to 1727, but it was a tributary of the Oyo Empire until 1823. Towns, villages, or even kingdoms might pay tribute to two or more states at the same time. Lagos had three sovereigns when it became a British colony in 1861 and continued to pay tributes to the Benin Kingdom and simultaneously acknowledged the spiritual sovereignty of Ile-Ife.[61] Sprawling tributary relations sometimes produced fuzzy borders where it was difficult to ascertain where one state ended and the authority of another began.[62] But demarcated and mutually recognized borders were common in (at least) Sokoto, Borno, the Yoruba states, and Dahomey.[63] Historians describe these states as bull's-eye states or radial states, signifying a small core surrounded by areas of increasing autonomy.

Despite the incredible variety of ecological conditions, population densities, trading networks, languages, religious affiliation, and cultural backgrounds, governance was remarkably similar. To illustrate this, we will take a representative tour of how historians have described West African states, moving from Senegal eastward to the fringes of the Borno Empire in modern-day Chad. We discuss Asante, Dahomey, and the Oyo Empire later in this section. In Senegal, the *damel* (ruler/king) in Cayor governed through village chiefs, whose primary role was to gather tribute for the king.[64] Kaabu in Guinea-Bissau was "defined to a large extent by the federated character of its political structure, rather than by a hierarchical central control over the empire's provinces."[65] The Segou Kingdom in Niger was a "series of subordinate but relatively independent provinces [that] were acknowledged in exchange for tribute."[66] Kevin MacDonald and Seydou Camara write that, "geographically, Segou exhibits the 'bulls-eye' [*sic*] structure typical of many historic West African states. There was a consciously defined and well-protected core (in this case approximately 120 × 60 km diameter, referred to as the *Toeda*) with rings of diminishing political domination and tribute beyond it, giving way to peripheral areas exploited by raiding."[67]

In the four Mossi kingdoms in Burkina Faso, the king was the "hub of the political system," but "the Mossi state was a decentralized one."[68] Most

Yoruba states in modern-day Nigeria and Benin (Oyo, Ibadan, Abeokuta, Ijesa, Ilesha, Ketu, Porto-Novo) were decentralized, constitutional monarchies where local town obas (kings) and *bale* (nonroyal heads) retained autonomy vis-à-vis their sovereigns. Successor states to the Oyo Empire, such as Ibadan and Abeokuta, replicated much of this governance model.[69] The Sokoto Caliphate was "a loose confederation of like-minded ruling groups[;] ... there was no central bureaucracy and no imperial army."[70] Emirs within the caliphate owed allegiance to the caliph in Sokoto and were required to seek investiture in the capital, collect taxes for the caliph, raise a military force, administer justice, and further the spread of Islam, but they had wide latitude in how they realized these objectives, including whom they appointed as officials in their administrations.[71] Tribute-paying but independent states, such as Adamawa on the borders of today's Nigeria and Cameroon, fringed the periphery. On Sokoto's eastern border was the centuries-old Borno Empire, which consisted of a core zone around Kukawa (the capital), then vassal polities with wide-ranging autonomy, then buffer states and tributaries (such as Zinder, Bagirmi, or Mandara) on the edges.[72] At times, Bagirmi paid tribute to Borno and neighboring Wadai.[73] Finally, R. S. O'Fahey argues that the Darfur Sultanate "may be seen structurally as a series of zones radiating out from the center, in each of which the nature and strength of the ruler's authority varied."[74]

Although decentralized rule was the norm, centralization projects were attempted in Dahomey, Asante, and Oyo. Dahomey was a minor player at the beginning of the eighteenth century but became one of the few West African states to replace autonomous vassal kingdoms with a form of direct rule. It was also one of the last states to be colonized by Europeans, defeated by the French in 1894. Dahomey emerged on Benin's Abomey Plateau as a tributary of the Allada Kingdom, a competitor to the coastal and slave-trading Hueda Kingdom (which controlled the key port of Ouidah). Dahomey capitalized on succession crises in Allada and conquered Allada in 1724 and Hueda in 1727, sending both monarchs into exile and occupying the port of Ouidah. By the 1760s, Dahomey had implemented a form of direct rule in Ouidah, led by the *yovogan*, or "Chief of the Whites." Provincial administrators in Ouidah were appointed directly by the king, collected taxes, and administrated Dahomeian law.[75] Monarchs in Allada were restored in 1742, but with reduced and symbolic powers.[76] Most administrative functions in Allada were in the hands of the regional governor, the *akplogan*. These direct forms of administration survived until the French conquest.

This provincial administration was complemented by a growing bureaucracy in the capital region that spread to neighboring towns and villages through the construction of palace complexes.[77] Archaeological evidence shows that from the 1700s Dahomey expanded palace building from outside of the capital (Abomey) first to economically valuable areas and then into the periphery in an increasingly uniform way.[78] As palm-oil production replaced the declining slave trade, the state increasingly controlled and regulated the palm-oil trade, a trend that accelerated in the nineteenth century under the rule of King Ghezo (1818–1859), who created a bureaucracy of state-appointed, revenue-gathering officials across the kingdom.[79]

Asante began as a confederation of autonomous, hereditary, military chieftains (*amanhene*) around Kumasi in the late seventeenth century but expanded to rule much of modern-day Ghana at its apogee in the early nineteenth century.[80] *Amanhene* in what Wilks calls "metropolitan" (or core) Asante retained their own taxation systems, rights of military mobilization, and legal systems but submitted to the king in matters of war and peace and were subject to direct levies and taxation from Kumasi. Some of these polities in the core, metropolitan Asante confederation even maintained their own subimperial systems into the early nineteenth century. Dwaben, a premier confederate state of Asante, for example, took tributes from as far as Gonja to the north. Thomas Bowditch described Dwaben in 1817 as an "independent ally" of Asante until it was destroyed and depopulated in 1831.[81] Provincial chiefs also constrained the *asantehene* (king) through the Asante National Assembly (Asantemanhyiamu), which included representatives of the main metropolitan chiefdoms and (sometimes) other vassals.[82] New kings were nominated by the queen mother and then elected by the Asantemanhyiamu, and important legislation was debated within the assembly. *Asantehene* were often constrained by the assembly's advice and recommendations.

Grades of indirect rule characterized Asante administration outside of this core. Kingdoms close to Kumasi (the capital), such as Adansi and Denkyira, were supervised by provincial chiefs and maintained a limited autonomy.[83] In what Wilks has described as the "inner provinces," Asante ruled through a network of "resident commissioners," or governors appointed from Kumasi, who maintained a small staff of district or junior commissioners.[84] Provinces south of Kumasi, such as Akyem, Akwapim, Wassa, Accra, and Assin, maintained internal autonomy so long as they refrained from engaging in independent foreign policy, contributed to Asante wars, and provided economic resources.[85] Farther from Kumasi, especially to the north, kingdoms such as Gonja and Dagomba paid occasional tribute to Asante but were de facto independent states. Toward the middle of the nineteenth century, these northern states also hosted resident commissioners in some key trading towns.[86] Taxation was the key difference among the metropolitan region, the inner provinces, and "greater" Asante. Tributes characterized taxation for peripheral vassals such as Dagomba and Gonja, whereas direct taxes and military levies, administered by bureaucrats from Kumasi, characterized taxation in the metropolitan area and some inner provinces.

Starting in the late eighteenth century under Osei Kwadwo (1764–1777) and continuing under the governments of Osei Kwame (1777—1801) and Osei Bonsu (1801–1824), however, the *asantehene* created a class of bureaucrats (*asomfo*) salaried by the king to enforce and implement laws emanating from Kumasi, so that, as Wilks asserts, "there can be little hesitation in characterizing the Kwadwoan revolution in government as a bureaucratic one."[87] Kwaku Dua I (1834–1867) reduced the influence of the provincial council by replacing it with the smaller Council of Kumasi, and Mensa Bonsu (1874–1883) increased taxation in metropolitan Asante and constructed a professional "new model army."[88] T. C. McCaskie notes that "the principal feature of the history of Asante society was the victory of centripetal control (central government) over the centrifugal tendencies."[89] Wilks concludes that before the British conquest in 1896, "the high degree of control established over the patterns of social, economic, and ideological organization produced in Asante was a combination of institutional features of a kind unusual in West Africa.... The Asante state in the nineteenth century was far removed from the 'feudalities,' to which many scholars ... have inclined to assimilate it."[90] Centralization projects under Mensu Bonsu culminated in a decade-long constitutional crisis and civil war from 1883 to 1894 as well as the restored autonomy and influence of the provincial rulers. For the moment, however, we note that Asante was an unusually centralized state in West Africa.

Oyo ruled an area in southwestern Nigeria about the size of modern Denmark (46,620 square kilometers) at its greatest extent in the late eighteenth century. Oyo was governed in a way typical of other decentralized West African states. Towns within core Oyo were subject to the *alafin* (ruler) but often had their own hereditary rulers.[91] In these towns, the *alafin* claimed authority over foreign policy, the investiture of new rulers, the adjudication of capital crimes and disputes that could not be resolved locally, and an annual tribute. Representatives of the Crown were stationed in most towns (the *ajele*), aided and monitored by messengers (the *ilari*).[92] Late in the eighteenth century, Oyo attempted to create a corridor from the interior to the slave-trading ports of Badgary and Little Adra by colonizing the depopulated Egbado lands. As trade flowed along this corridor, officials in Oyo attempted to centralize control of the area around the 1820s. The post of *onisare* (governor) was created at Ijanna to directly collect taxes and tolls, with the assistance of a staff of palace slaves, at the nodes of a complex system of turnpikes established along this trade corridor. Taxes and tributes in Egbado province were collected directly under the supervision of the *onisare* and transmitted to the *alafin*. The *onisare* was also of non-Yoruba origin, and this position could be rotated by the king.[93] This centralization experiment, however, did not last longer than a few years to a decade. By 1817, the vassal state of Ilorin had seceded from the empire and pledged allegiance to the Sokoto Caliphate, eventually triggering the implosion of the empire by 1836. Law sees the collapse of the Oyo Empire as a response to the *alafin*'s centralization attempts, which threatened the interests of the powerful Council of Military Chiefs, the Oyo Mesi, in the capital. This is a classic example of how centralization projects generate commitment problems between rulers and vassals. Rulers might want to govern through governors and bureaucrats whom they appoint, but doing so removes the bargaining power of vassals in the present and the future. Rulers cannot credibly commit to not removing more of their vassals' power in the future once they take some of it in the present. Vassals therefore tenaciously resist centralization projects that differentially benefit the ruler.

Dahomey, Asante, and Oyo were not centralized states, but they also deviated from the pattern of decentralized rule with partially successful centralization attempts. In the next section, we aim to understand why states in West Africa were decentralized and why these cases may have been different.

EXPLAINING (DE)CENTRALIZATION

Which theoretical frameworks best explain these patterns in West Africa? Do concentrations of war, people, and cities correlate with areas of more centralized rule, and to what extent did the slow and expensive pace of communications limit states' ability to centralize?[94]

War-based theories do not fare well. Southwestern Nigeria was the locus of interstate competition. This densely populated region with Africa's highest concentration of cities was subject to nearly a century of intense, multistate, geopolitical competition following the decline and collapse of the Oyo Empire (1833/1836–1893/1894). Wars were fought regularly with large, standing armies that increasingly consisted of massed infantry with firearms. Wars could end states and dynasties. These factors should have activated bellicist mechanisms of state centralization.[95]

For example, as the Oyo Empire fell, refugees spread across Yoruba territory, establishing new towns and new states. Ibadan, Ijaye, and Abeokuta were three of these new states.[96] This was a period of institutional innovation, but Ibadan and Abeokuta created decentralized states. Abeokuta was founded by a diverse group of warrior chiefs with strong roots in traditional authority. Even within Abeokuta town itself, different obas (kings) controlled internal matters within their quarters, under the supervision and control of a general state council. Abeokuta and its capital Egba maintained a "federated" state, despite being constantly at war and threatened from the north by Ibadan and from the west by Dahomey.[97]

Ibadan was formed by a diverse group of warlords with weaker ties to traditional institutions. Here, the warlords had a stronger hand in the state council, but provincial administration remained decentralized, combining traditional and military authority through the *ajele*, a class of warlord bureaucrats who collected tribute, supervised local law and order, and ensured that towns did not engage in independent foreign policy. Internal matters such as judicial and taxation powers remained with hereditary chiefs. More warfare made the *basorun* (prime minister) of Ibadan more, not less, dependent on these warlords.[98]

Ijaye was also formed after the fall of the Oyo Empire and its ruler, Kurunmi (r. ~1836–1862), created a relatively centralized administration around Ijaye and the surrounding towns. However, Ijaye was conquered and destroyed by Ibadan in 1862. Falola and Oguntomisin argue that centralization contributed to Ijaye's failure to survive in nineteenth-century Yorubaland. First, Kurunmi's centralization killed off or exiled capable war leaders, which limited military effectiveness. Second, his refusal to govern in the traditional way by acknowledging the (nominal) supremacy of Oyo and allowing his vassals to do the same alienated towns within his territory, depriving Ijaye of resources and allies. Most vassal towns on the upper Ogun River where Ijaye governed supported Ibadan in the war, and Kurunmi struggled to gain the support of local towns throughout his rule.[99] In other words, when Kurunmi went against the grain of decentralized forms of rule, war and competition selected out the more centralized Ijaye kingdom. Other parts of southwestern Nigeria, such as the Ekiti regions, Ilorin to the north, and the Igbo areas farther east, ruled in even more decentralized ways.[100] War did not seem to produce centralization.

More centralized states emerged where existing theories would not predict. Dahomey was on the periphery of the population-dense and urbanized region of West Africa, not at its core. Dahomey's rise occurred under the suzerainty of the Oyo Empire, not under intense, multistate geopolitical competition and not in a way that easily differentiates Dahomey from other states that had a tributary relationship with Oyo (such as Nupe or Ilorin, for example). Moreover, Dahomey is better seen as a cause of rising international competition than a consequence of it.[101] After defeating the Allada and Hueda in 1724 and 1727, respectively, Dahomey began a period of territorial expansion, invading the Yoruba states in the late eighteenth and early nineteenth centuries.

Asante's rise is even more problematic for the application of war- and trade-based theories. Parts of Asante's centralization occurred during a period of regional dominance, where, as Wilks puts it, there were no other states that could seriously threaten Asante. Rather, periods of peace in Asante are linked to successful centralization. Kwaku Dua I, for example, ruled for thirty-four years, to 1867, when, Wilks points out, "the power of the *amanhene* (provincial rulers) was drastically curtailed." These changes were possible because "the nation engaged in few other wars in the period thus lessening the Asantehene's dependence upon manpower resources of the *amanhene*." Competition produced later attempts at centralization, but they were unsuccessful. The 1873–1874 war increased the taxation and conscription demands on the provincial chiefs, who dethroned and exiled the king (Kofi Kakari) after 1874 and the sack of Kumasi. According to Wilks, the war exposed Asante's relative weakness vis-à-vis the United Kingdom, and in 1879 Kakari's successor, Mensa Bonsu, implemented reforms, including the creation of a new professional army equipped with modern repeater rifles and salaried by the state. To finance these reforms, Bonsu increased taxation in metropolitan Asante, especially after 1882, through a 50 percent tax on gold mining and the increased use of fines targeting the wealthier classes for the "shallowest pretexts."[102] By February 1883, provincial Asante was in rebellion with some regions demanding independence. In the same month, Kumasi was occupied by the "young men of the town" (*nkwanwaa*)—a class of people belonging to privileged families but blocked from paths of upward mobility—who exiled Mensa Bonsu and established a republican government in Kumasi. Several provinces then declared independence and resolved to restore Kofi Kakari (the previous king) to the throne.[103] What followed was a protracted war between supporters of rival claimants to the throne that took the form of a provincial (pro-monarchy) versus capital (centralizing and modernizing) conflict until Agyeman Prempe I was installed in 1888. Prempe's regime was characterized not by a return to centralized rule but by a government where "individual district heads, for a time at least, were permitted a higher degree of independence of action even in the field of foreign relations."[104] Competition and centralization attempts contrarily appear to have driven *decentralization* in Asante.

Rising competition also fragmented Asante by providing vassals with exit options. Increased British presence from the 1870s onward enabled Asante's northern vassals to pursue secessionist policies, and so Asante lost control of provinces such as Dagomba, Gonja, and Gyaman after the 1874 war.[105] A representative of Dwaben in 1874 is reported to have informed Asante that although the Asante were more powerful in the past, "it was quite obvious now that there was one still more powerful, and that was the English white man, so that the Brunfo [a neighboring group] did not see why they should not prefer the white man to Asante."[106] Mensa Bonsu himself noted that one region of Asante responded to his increased taxation demands by stating that "they intended going to live under the

British, for they had to pay too many taxes and fines under Mensah."[107] The subkingdom of Dadiase also stated that it intended on joining the British because the fines under Mensa were too high. Increased British military competition and centralization attempts fragmented the Asante state by providing tributary and vassal polities opportunities to pursue independence or to defect.

There is further evidence that war caused fragmentation and decentralization. We have already encountered the example of Ibadan, where the *basorun*, prime minister, was compelled to rule in a decentralized way to reward his war chiefs. The nearby polity of Ilorin was similar. Because of incessant warfare, the emir became increasingly beholden to his war chiefs. These warlords gained more power in the competition of nineteenth-century Yoruba politics, rendering the emir a "weak king."[108] In the early 1800s, the Sokoto Caliphate supplanted the older, fragmented Hausa city-states and directly threatened the Oyo Empire to the south. Oyo buckled under this new competition as tributaries and vassal kingdoms either defected and were peeled off, triggering cycles of further defection, warfare, and collapse.

At best, we think that war-based theories of state centralization have low explanatory power in West Africa. There are no clear cases of war-led centralization and several examples where war caused decentralization and collapse.

How do trade-based theories fare? Again, we think the evidence is weak. There are clearly cases where trade contributed to state centralization, but in looking at the system more broadly, it is hard to conclude that trade had a general centralizing impact across the region. Dahomey and Asante's centralization were linked to trade and economic production. Dahomey sent its governors and bureaucrats to the main slave-trading port (Ouidah). Asante taxed and controlled gold mining and ensured that the profits from north–south trade flowed to the state or to state-appointed traders. Asante's "great roads" were patrolled and monitored by a centrally appointed highway police to facilitate and profit from trade.

But Dahomey and Asante were not the only centers of trade in West Africa. Northern and southwestern Nigeria were regions of relatively high population density and urbanization, with denser trade networks than other parts of the system. Neither of these regions saw centralized states emerge, however. Northern Nigeria was governed by Hausa city-states before the Fulani revolutions and a decentralized empire afterward. The Yoruba heartland was governed by the Oyo Empire until the 1830s and then by a series of competing city-states afterward. These trade-heavy regions saw oscillations between rule by decentralized empires and fragmented city-states, but not the emergence of more centralized states.

Perhaps this was the "wrong" type of trade, and these were the "wrong" types of cities to fit trade-based theories. Much of the trade that flowed across West Africa was in human beings, and, as we saw earlier, slaves who crossed the Atlantic were often kidnapped from the West African interior and shipped from West African ports. There is a rich tradition of scholarship examining how the slave trade affected political institutions in precolonial West Africa, some of which suggests that the Atlantic slave trade drove state centralization. Very recently, this debate has been reinvigorated by Jason Sharman and Ayşe Zarakol, who argue that the Atlantic slave trade was a crucial engine of state formation and centralization in West Africa.[109] Dahomey and Asante, for example, may have centralized because they were well placed at the crossroads between the interior, where slaves could be captured, and the slave ports of the coast.[110] In this account, slaving provided both windfall revenues that rulers could use to purchase loyalty, weapons, and luxury goods as well as labor for plantation agriculture and staff for the military and bureaucracy. Displaced from their homes, slaves were used by rulers as more loyal and dependable servants. States that could capture more slaves could have bigger armies and bigger bureaucracies, which tipped the balance of power in favor of the center against the normal provincial checks on power that existed in numerous African states.[111]

However, there are reasons to be skeptical of a general link between slavery and centralization. First, states such as Oyo were well placed to capitalize on the slave trade, but trading in slaves contrarily empowered regional warlords, provincial military actors, and the *alafin* because the Oyo Empire did not have a monopoly on trade.[112] Provincial military leaders and the military chiefs in the capital destabilized and eventually dissolved the empire.[113] Second, while the slave trade was intense in the Bight of Benin, where the centralized kingdom of Dahomey formed, it was also intense in the Bight of Biafra, where few large, centralized states formed. In fact, southeastern Nigeria was ruled by a diverse set of political forms, from the coastal city-states of Bonny and Lagos to the shadowy Aro

Confederacy to little hierarchy above the village or chiefdom level in some regions. Slave trading, therefore, either stimulated or could support a variety of state forms.

In other cases, the chronology is the wrong way around. In Asante, for example, slave trading was most intense during the 1750s to the 1780s, but most of Asante's centralizing reforms occurred in the nineteenth century. Other states on the Senegalese coast, such as the Kaabu Empire, also rose on the Atlantic slave trade but remained highly decentralized. As David Laitin points out, exposure to the slave trade on the Nigerian coast caused some states to centralize and stay centralized, some to centralize and collapse, and others that were weak to stay weak.[114] Although the slave trade may be a good explanation for state formation (i.e., the birth of new states), it may be a weaker explanation for whether rulers were able to overpower their vassals and centralize or were instead rendered more dependent on their vassals. We pick up these themes up in chapter 8 when summarizing the findings from the case study.

Slave trading was gradually replaced by palm-oil products by the mid- and late nineteenth century. Palm oil could be produced by small-scale farmers and then sent to the coastal ports and shipped (mostly) to Europe, although it was also produced by slaves on state-run farms in places such as Dahomey and Ibadan. Palm oil transformed West Africa's economic geography. Areas of subsistence production and local trade became integrated with the international commodity market and generated surpluses that could be extracted by state rulers. J. Cameron Monroe suggests, for example, that Dahomey's centralization accelerated after palm-oil production spread and stimulated local-level, market-based economic growth. Local market taxes and head taxes were introduced, and tolls on trading routes were extended—all collected by state-appointed officials.[115]

But, once again, there are reasons to question whether the palm-oil trade contributed strongly to the rise of centralized states such as Dahomey. Palm oil was produced along the West African coast from Sierra Leone to eastern Nigeria. Neither Dahomey nor Asante was unique in its exposure to the palm-oil trade.[116] Other states such as Abeokuta, Ibadan, and the Aro Confederacy were deeply connected with the palm-oil trade and yet maintained decentralized forms of rule. Decentralized states prevailed in regions of high and low trade, and the more centralized states did not emerge in the areas with the highest exposure to trade and urbanization.

WEST AFRICA

If anything, trade contributed to political fragmentation where small city-states prevailed, perhaps by diffusing economic and military power and making state centralization projects risky and expensive. This is precisely what rulers of Asante feared. They knew that trade could bring money and weapons that were useful for state-building projects, but they also knew that trade could funnel money and weapons into their vassal kingdoms and could "break the spell of their conquests and undermine their power," as a British adviser noted in 1817.[117] This is a pattern we observed in the chapters on Southeast Asia and East Asia (Japan).

We think the simplest and strongest explanation for the widespread deployment of decentralized rule across West Africa is low interaction capacity. Moving people and goods required for direct administration was too slow and expensive. Low returns for extending state administration and providing public goods made states rely on indirect forms of rule. Several authors make precisely this point when describing the structure of states.[118] Jack Goody writes of Gonja that "owing to limitations in communications, the control of the paramount was inversely proportional to the distance from the capital." Of northern Nigeria, Roland Adeleye asserts that "long distances from the centre of supreme authority coupled with the heterogeneous ethnic groups with their disparate and often competing economic interests further rendered administration precarious and the evolution of a common ethos elusive."[119] Again, Ibadan is an instructive example. Centered in the population- and trade-rich Yoruba region, Ibadan and its rulers were faced with building a new state, which involved making real institutional choices.[120] As we have seen, Ibadan employed the *ajele* system of regional governors that left much control in the hands of local chiefs. Bolanle Awe writes that the *ajele* system was a direct response to constraints on interaction capacity: "Control of such a large area, however, raised its own problems; communications were poor and slow; Ibadan had not enough resources to maintain a standing army in each of these towns to ward off Fulani attacks or indeed occasionally to ensure that these towns remained loyal. Ibadan's method of dealing with the situation is embodied in the system of administration through the Ajele, the resident representative of Ibadan in a subject town. It was Ibadan's answer to the problem of controlling a gradually expanding empire in Yoruba country."[121]

Wilks's thesis is that the speed of communications, or "message-delay," helps explain the structure of Asante. He states that "the degree of political control exercised by the central government over the territory will be positively correlated with the rapidity with which instructions, that is, 'messages' can be transmitted." Wilks presents ample evidence for this proposition. Asante centralization occurred close to the city Kumasi and in the metropolitan and inner regions. Governance was too costly and ineffective in areas beyond these spheres, where indirect forms of rule were deployed, especially in taxation.[122]

Even in cases where rulers had opportunities to centralize because previous dynasties had been expelled, they sometimes still preferred indirect forms of rule. Although before our main period, as Dahomey expanded in the 1720s and 1730s, it defeated the rulers of Allada and Hueda. The ruling family of Hueda fled west. Rather than rule the areas directly, however, King Agaja of Dahomey pursued the Hueda royal family, attempting on several occasions from 1728 to 1733 to strike a deal with the son of the former Huedan king to return to Savi (the capital), repopulate the region, and become a tributary to Dahomey.[123] We suggest the difficulties of establishing state administration created strong preferences for rulers to govern through autonomous vassals, even in cases where sending in the governors and bureaucrats to rule directly might appear to be the easiest strategy. In sum, low interaction capacity put basic limits on the ability of states to project power, even in more urbanized, developed, and geopolitically active regions.

Critics might contend that although this approach helps explain why West African states were mostly decentralized, it does not explain why Asante and Dahomey were more centralized. To an extent, this is true, and the anomalously strong states in Dahomey and Asante can likely shed further light on non-Western paths of state development. However, an advantage of our approach in this book is the application of a consistent set of concepts across diverse regions. Historians and political scientists sometimes use the term *centralization* to describe Dahomey and Asante, but with different meanings. Centralization can mean autocracy. Kings in Dahomey and Asante, for some periods of their existence, were more unconstrained in their decision-making than other West African states. But this is not what we mean by centralization. Rather, our concept of centralization is the extent to which sovereign powers are in the hands of the state or are shared with subordinate polities. On this score, the land areas over which Dahomey and Asante centralized remained relatively limited.

Dahomey was unusual in West Africa, but its area of direct rule was small. On the Abomey Plateau and through a corridor moving down to Allada and then to the coast, state administration was conducted by royally appointed officials with widespread, political, economic, military, and judicial powers. Outside of these core areas, however, rule was more indirect, especially in the Mahi zones to the north and Yoruba areas to the east, where local chiefs retained more autonomy.[124] Although this area was (probably) the most extensive one of centralized rule in precolonial West Africa, it was still only about the size of modern-day Lesotho or Belgium.

Asante was a large empire, but the area of direct rule was likely limited to "metropolitan" regions around Kumasi, roughly 25,000 square kilometers, or the land area of modern-day Burundi.[125] Although governors and bureaucrats were present farther afield, there were few of them, and they played a supervisory role rather than directly governing vassal kingdoms. The land area over which the Asante state ruled directly, therefore, was likely limited to Kumasi and its environs, the great road system, and pockets of intensive gold mining.

West Africa's most centralized states, therefore, controlled only small territories directly before employing indirect forms of rule. Dahomey and Asante directly administered similar-size land areas (although Asante was larger overall), roughly the size of Africa's smallest modern states. The broader picture is of widespread decentralized rule, which we argue reflects constraints on the ability of rulers to project power.

Finally, interaction capacity helps us see why war and trade might have had only limited or even reverse effects on centralization (something we expand upon in chapter 8). War did not produce centralization because it did not change underlying constraints to state building. West African rulers were always seeking revenue and protection from internal and external threats. Presented with an opportunity to replace local vassals with agents loyal to the state, surely West African rulers would have taken it. Larger, more frequent, more threatening, or more expensive wars do not change the basic infrastructural constraints on extending power. Moreover, periods of intense military competition increase dependency on warlords, provincial rulers, and military entrepreneurs. Wars may place rulers in a weaker bargaining position vis-à-vis their vassal states, which can demand more autonomy in exchange for military resources—not less, as versions of the war-led theory of centralization would suggest. We can see that increased international competition can just as easily trigger decentralization and collapse as it can centralization. Along similar lines of argument, an increase in trade or urbanization also does not alter infrastructural constraints on state building, even if it creates new surpluses that can be extracted or new allies for would-be state builders. Without the ability to monopolize exchange, trade can empower rulers, but it might also empower their rivals, leading to decentralization rather than centralization.

CONCLUSION

West Africa was a dynamic state system in the eighteenth and nineteenth century. Old empires collapsed, new empires formed, and rulers experimented with new methods of government. Much of this system was intact as late as the 1880s, making it the one of the longest-living state systems in our study. Nearly all states were eventually colonized by Europeans, however, and only one survives as an independent state today (Liberia). Although most of the region was sparsely populated, southwestern Nigeria and Benin were a densely populated and urban region that was exposed to intense interstate competition through the nineteenth century. Despite these variations in trade, cities, and war, however, most states were decentralized. There were variations in size, how rulers were selected, the extent to which they were constrained in their decision-making by councils and other institutions, and what ideologies legitimized rule. Some empires (typically in the North) were huge, covering an area the size of modern-day France and the United Kingdom, while others were small city-states. Some rulers were elected by councils, some were military regimes, and others hereditary monarchies. Some rulers were unconstrained in the decisions they could make, while others deferred to powerful guilds and councils. Finally, there were Islamic states and a panoply of indigenous ideologies of rule, often involving divine ancestry.

But most of these varied rulers built similar institutions to administer their territories. The rulers might have different names—*emir*, *ajele*, *yaravon*, *akwanmofohene*, and *ilari*, for example—but states typically stood at the top of a hierarchy that demanded tribute, military service, loyalty (especially the right to determine external affairs), and a level of judicial sovereignty (a kind of supreme court) from vassals who otherwise retained the autonomy to tax how they wanted, maintain their own militaries, and make their own criminal laws. Even the most centralized states were able to extend their rule only over small land areas. We argue that low interaction capacity best explains these variations. Centralized states did not emerge where war and trade-based theories might predict, and more centralized institutions emerged where these theories would not predict. All rulers in West Africa were constrained by basic limits on the ability to transport information, people, and goods. Decentralized rule was an efficient solution to these constraints.

PART III

Synthesis

Chapter Eight

LESSONS FROM THE CASE STUDIES

This chapter assembles the core findings from our case study chapters. What have we learned about governance by studying state systems that are typically overlooked by international relations scholars? What have we learned about the impacts of trade, war, and the speed and fluidity of interactions on institutions by looking outside of Europe? This chapter is organized into five lessons. Some of these lessons are descriptive in nature, highlighting patterns across the case studies, while others are more analytical, speculating on the explanatory power of war-, trade-, and interaction-capacity-based theories. We hope these lessons provide a foundation for future studies on states and state systems and how they vary.

LESSON 1: MOST STATES WERE DECENTRALIZED

If we just studied Europe and East Asia, as much of the existing historical IR literature has done, we might conclude that centralized states were common across the world. This is the first received wisdom we flagged in chapter 1, but it is not the case. Centralized states comparable to France, China, or Korea were rare. We examined 135 states in the case study chapters, and 131 of them were outside of East Asia. Interpreting centralization generously, probably just 5 states outside East Asia centralized aspects of their rule. In West Africa, they were Asante and Dahomey, and in South

Asia they were Mysore, Pune, and Khalistan.[1] There were no clear examples in maritime Southeast Asia. Only Mysore potentially approached western European states in terms of its size and level of centralization. If we extended the case studies to central, eastern, and southern Africa, this number would not rise by much more. Overall, bull's-eye systems were far more common than billiard ball systems.

Rulers governed a small core. Taxes were collected at gates and markets in the capital, often by slaves or eunuchs, stored in the treasury, and used to support the elite court. Journeying farther from the capital, however, you could see that rule became more indirect. Just outside the capital, local (state-appointed) governors or princes of the court might ensure that subordinates paid their taxes (tributes) on time, did not plot against the center, participated in wars when the ruler demanded, kept local rebellions under control, and perhaps from time to time adjudicated serious crimes or referred them to the king or queen.[2] Journey farther afield, you would note that local elites had even more power and freedom. Representatives of the ruler might be present, but the demands would be lighter, perhaps as simple as paying tribute and homage to the center, sending soldiers on the ruler's military campaigns, and refraining from allying with other enemy powers. At the margins of the kingdom, local elites might be so autonomous that it would be difficult to determine whether you had exited the kingdom. Beyond these limits, vassals could be kingdoms paying tribute to the ruler only in word (and perhaps occasionally in deed), but otherwise free to rule their domains and interact with other states. Sometimes these tributary networks created hierarchies that embedded states in broader international orders. This structure was so common that we need not rehash the examples, except to say that rulers separated by space, culture, and language employed similar models of governance from Ibadan in Nigeria to Luwu on the island of Sulawesi to Sind in Pakistan to Pahang in Malaysia to Hyderabad in India and Karangasem in Bali.

These similarities should not obscure enormous differences on other dimensions. Rulers were selected in myriad ways. In West Africa, rulers in Senegal were elected by a powerful oligarchy; Yoruba kingdoms were constitutional monarchies, often hemmed in by powerful councils and guilds; the Sokoto Caliphate appealed to common Islamic law to hold its empire together; while kings in Benin invoked divine ancestry to legitimize their rule. In South Asia, the Mughal Empire played a lasting role after its decline as new states looked back to Mughal titles and glory to shore up their claims to sovereignty in an increasingly competitive world; Balinese kingdoms referenced their Hindu ancestry; Javanese kingdoms looked to past empires and an increasing Islamic influence; while Malay kingdoms drew inspiration and legitimacy from shared concepts of city-based statehood and the mandala system. Land was more important to sovereignty in South Asia than it was in Southeast Asia or Africa. Explaining these differences was not the purpose of this book, but contrasting the similarities in governance with the differences along so many other institutional and cultural aspects highlights how striking these similarities are.

It also leads us to suggest that, at least when it comes to explaining strategies of centralizing or devolving governance, claiming or sharing sovereignty, these variations are not powerful explanations. We expand on this observation later in this chapter and in the next chapter, but it is hard to sustain the idea that Southeast Asian states were decentralized because of pro-mandala norms or that rulers in Ibadan adopted the *illari* system because it was culturally appropriate when we find such similar state structures across vastly different cultural contexts.

This point should also not obscure the fact that there were subtle differences in how centralized some of these states were. Pune's centralization project in Malwa, for example, probably exceeded anything that the kings of Dahomey or Asante were able to achieve in terms of the thickness of bureaucracy and the fluency of information flow. Some states, such as Khalistan, were able to build standing armies, which is an important first step toward centralization. But we think these differences are small in comparison to the vast changes that occurred in Vietnam or Japan in the late eighteenth and nineteenth centuries. We have not here developed a clear quantitative index upon which to rank how centralized states were, but these subtle differences matter and are an important area for future research.

LESSON 2: RULERS KNEW THE PERILS OF DECENTRALIZATION

Devolving governance was inefficient and risky, and rulers knew it. From Tipu Sultan in Mysore to the *alafin* of Oyo to the rajas of Bali, rulers were aware that autonomous vassals would avoid paying tributes, shirk from military obligations, try to build up their own power bases, and seek

SYNTHESIS

further independence; they would also be hard to monitor and control and might even one day seek to overthrow or secede from the center.[3] Decentralizing governance meant less revenue, more conflict, more uncertainty, and more instability for the center.

Perhaps even though rulers were aware that giving their vassals autonomy was dangerous, they did not have any institutional solutions to the problem. Perhaps rulers were stuck in worldviews that declared that mandalas, jagirs, and *illari* were the *right* way to rule where there were few other options. Perhaps cosmological beliefs deeply shaped governance structures. In West Africa, supplanting vassals was not just hard but wrong if chiefs could claim descent from Ile-Ife. In Bali, perhaps the mandala concept was so embedded in discourses on governance that conceiving of centralization was impossible. Perhaps it was the lack of alternatives that drove decentralized rule.

We do not think this was the case. Many rulers were aware of the limits of decentralized rule and the potential benefits of basic administrative models of more direct rule. States attempted centralization projects across all case studies. Dahomean kings created administrative posts to directly rule Ouida and tried to supplant the old Allada royals. The Asante Empire placed governors, supplied and resourced by the state, in subordinate Akan kingdoms to monitor and govern its provinces more closely. Oyo tried centralization in Egbado province, seemingly as a last-ditch attempt to preserve the empire from imploding. The Sokoto Caliphate was very decentralized but mixed more and less direct forms of rule—more direct closer to Gwandu and Sokoto and less direct to the east (Adamawa) and to the south (in the Nupe areas). Sultans of Java and Aceh attempted to replace local elites with state-appointed and loyal bureaucrats, which backfired. Tipu Tip of Mysore believed that replacing local tax farmers with state-appointed agents would overcome some of the problems of decentralized rule.

At the very least, many rulers in West Africa, South Asia, and Southeast Asia knew that one solution to the problem of decentralized rule was to deprive vassals of autonomy and appoint agents employed by and more loyal to the state to rule those provinces. They also knew that doing so would demand increases in bureaucratic capacity and agents loyal to the patronage of the ruler over their vassals. Rulers across our case studies tried to co-opt new groups from slaves and traders to Europeans as well as eunuchs to serve as governors and supervisors of the state. Thus, a dearth of alternative institutional options does not seem to explain the lack of centralization.

LESSON 3: RULERS WERE CONSTRAINED BY LOW INTERACTION CAPACITY

Why was centralized rule so rare, then? If rulers knew the problems associated with decentralization and had alternative models, why did they not simply implement them? The simple reason is that centralized rule is expensive and risky because of the slow pace at which goods and people can be moved and the resulting obstacles to projecting power over distance.

Rulers could conquer. The caliph in Sokoto won lands in the area from modern-day Burkina Faso to Cameroon. But rulers could not administer all the territories they conquered. Doing so required tax collectors, police officers, administrators, and governors. Bureaucrats would need to be paid by the ruler rather than by a vassal, who might use the opportunity to build up their own power base. Bureaucrats would then have to be sent out to conquered territories, enough of them so that local powerholders were not able to expel and conquer them, along with additional staff to monitor the local bureaucrats and make sure that they were following the center's orders. A local garrison might also help, at least at first, but these soldiers needed to be paid by the state, not by a potentially rogue fief holder. Communication would also be crucial. Production would need to be assessed, yields and taxes calculated, people counted, expenses recorded, salaries paid, dissidents monitored, and governors supervised. All this information needed to be regularly transmitted between the center and the conquered areas. It would be even better if bureaucrats could be rotated between different provinces so that they would not build up their own tax bases.

All this moving about costs time and money. And the slower that goods travel, the more expensive it is to create this kind of centralized administration. This system of governance also creates something of a self-reinforcing cycle. To pay soldiers and bureaucrats, the state needs more money, more taxes, but the best way to get more taxes would be to centralize the administration. In other words, the state needs money to centralize, but getting that money requires centralization.

Interaction capacity puts basic limits on the ability of rulers to centralize. When information and goods move slowly, it is hard for rulers to monitor what their subordinate military commanders or governors are doing. It is more expensive to send out military expeditions to punish recalcitrant rulers. It is also more expensive to send, rotate, and maintain a staff that can monitor provincial rulers. Subordinates know this and that they can exploit their better local information to build up their own power bases and avoid taxation. With their stronger bargaining power, they demand more autonomy—the ability to tax what they want, to recruit and maintain their own armed forces, and even in some cases to decide who their successors will be. Rulers in low interaction-capacity systems are stuck in a dilemma. They need soldiers and taxes, but the most efficient way of getting taxes and soldiers is to exchange obedience for autonomy, which places a ceiling on the taxes and soldiers that the ruler can depend on. The consequence is that decentralized forms of rule were widespread across the globe for much of the eighteenth and nineteenth centuries and for presumably most of history.

Let us work through a short, semifictional example. Say you are the *alafin* (king) of Oyo in 1800. You can command a large army and conquer distant territories. Your empire is large, but your standing army is small. To fight wars and punish noncompliant tributaries, you need the cooperation of powerful military leaders in the capital and provincial lords who control their own troops. Most important is the Oyo Mesi, Council of Military Chiefs, in the capital, which raises and leads the army, but you also depend on levies from vassals in the provinces to whom you are just the first among equals.[4] The *basorun* is the most important member of the Oyo Mesi, who even has the power to compel you to commit suicide if your rule is disagreeable with their interests. The *are ona kakamfo* is the most important leader of the provincial armies. To make matters worse, to get taxes you depend on local provincial rulers with their own dynasties and governance structures who would prefer to keep taxes for themselves and throw off your rule. The loyalty of these provincial vassals is questionable, and you suspect that if offered a better deal, they would defect to another kingdom rather than defend your realm. You would like to change this situation and take the tax revenue that you know the vassal rulers are taking for themselves. What are your options?

LESSONS FROM THE CASE STUDIES

One solution might be to create a standing army. These soldiers would be paid directly by you and appointed directly by you, not by warlords whose loyalty is more questionable. With a standing army, you can have more freedom in the battles that you fight, have more confidence that your commands will be followed, and even send your army out to collect more taxes, knowing that they will be more loyal. All these moves would centralize the army in your hands.

But the Oyo Mesi and *are ona kakamfo* will not like this at all. They like their autonomy, and they like to be able to collect their own taxes and enjoy the spoils of war themselves. And they especially like that they can command you to commit suicide if they feel your rule has gone astray (technically, the *basorun* could command the *alafin* to commit suicide, and the *alafin* could compel the *are ona kakamfo* to commit suicide). The Oyo Mesi will resist any attempt you make to increase your military power.

Perhaps you could fight them and break their hold on the state. Once you have your standing army in place, you could reduce the power and privileges of the military chiefs. But to build a standing army, you need people, and you need more taxes to pay your soldiers. How will you get those taxes? Most of your tax-paying regions have their own local rulers that say you are the king and collect their own taxes with their own armies and give your tribute every year, but you know that much more could be collected and that those local rulers sometimes keep more for themselves. You also suspect that one day they could use those armies and cooperate with some of the other vassal states to create their own kingdoms and throw off your rule. You now might have a great opportunity to reduce the privileges of these vassals and take in more taxes by sending in the army and recruiting your own group of tax collectors who would send taxes directly to the capital.

But what will the army want in return? Surely, the Oyo Mesi will support the idea of more money and power. But since the military chiefs will do most of the conquering, they will want something in return, and probably they will want to govern these new vassal kingdoms—with autonomy—and send tribute back to the capital. This will further strengthen the Oyo Mesi and *are ona kakamfo*, which would make it more difficult to break their power and create a standing army.

This dilemma played out within the Oyo Empire. In the late eighteenth century, Alafin Awole tried to break the power of the *are ona kakamfo* by sending him on a suicide mission to attack an "impregnable" town. Anticipating that the provincial armies would lose and the *are ona kakamfo* would be compelled to commit suicide, Awole figured this ploy would reduce the power of the autonomous vassals. But the *basorun* (the most important member of the Oyo Mesi) got wind of the plot, and so, instead of attacking the town, the *are ona kakamfo* attacked Oyo Ile, the capital, and the *alafin* committed suicide. After being shunned for the position of *alafin*, the *are ona kakamfo* then moved north to Ilorin, where he carved out an independent kingdom that would play a key role in the collapse of the Oyo Empire.[5] Upsetting the delicate balance between rulers and vassals could have devastating consequences.

Herein is the heart of the dilemma of decentralized rule. Because transport and communications are slow, monitoring and enforcement from the center are expensive and risky. This means rulers cannot credibly commit to enforcing full control on their provinces, and vassal rulers and elites know they can't. To collect taxes (often in the form of tributes), the center exchanges autonomy for material resources and a limited circumscription of the vassals' power. Vassals might accept that their rulers are invested by the king, they might refrain from allying with other powers or going to war without the permission of the king, and they might send some of the local resources as taxes, so long as they are free to collect taxes as they want, enforce justice as they want, maintain their own armies, and appoint their own subordinates.

Historians and anthropologists across all the case studies in this book note that this basic dilemma shaped governance across West Africa, South Asia, and Southeast Asia in the eighteenth and nineteenth centuries. Slow communications and logistics necessitated decentralized rule. Rulers bargained with their vassals and ruled based on what they could get away with, but they regularly lost control of their vassals. Slaving and trading missions sent from Egypt and Zanzibar resulted in new empires. Secession was common. Centralization attempts were rarely successful and often punished severely, as in Oyo, Mataram, and Aceh.

Because centralization was so risky, it also makes sense that it was attempted only in areas closer to the capital, where the logistical dilemmas of monitoring and enforcement were lower, and in areas that were very valuable and thus worth taking the risk on. Outside of the core Abomey Plateau (the capital region), for example, the Dahomey Kingdom sent its governors to Ouidah, the main slave-trading port; rulers in Aceh sent governors to the pepper ports; the *alafin* in Oyo sent tax collectors to trade junctions connecting the capital to slaving ports; the nawab of Oudh posted his tax collectors in the markets of the most agriculturally rich regions; and the sultan of Mataram tried to crush the power of the northern port elites.

In addition, centralization projects were often attempted where vassals were weak, fragmented, or nonexistent. Oyo tried centralization by repopulating the Egbado province, with its relatively weak obas; Pune centralized first in areas of Malwa that were not administered above the level of the headman.[6]

The key question, then, is what enables rulers to overcome this dilemma? In the following sections, we argue that factors such as trade and war, thought to have stimulated centralization in Europe, do not appear to have had the same impacts at least in three of our regions we studied. But if low levels of interaction capacity limited the ability to centralize, were increases in interaction capacity associated with increases in centralization?

Before railroads and steam power, increases in interaction capacity were driven mostly by geographical features that increased the potential for dense settlements or enabled waterborne transport through rivers and deltas. Dense populations and viable waterborne transport often occurred together, as they did along the Niger Delta, the Ganges Delta and river system, the Red River and Mekong Deltas, ocean passages in Southeast Asia, and the river valleys of East Asia. Other increases in interaction capacity were caused by the legacies of older states, such as the great trunk road created by the Mughal Empire or the roads system created by previous Chinese rulers. Interaction capacity could also be increased by shared language, cultural affinity, and interpersonal trust, along with other administrative technologies such as shared scripts, although these factors often had their legacies in past experiences of centralized rule.

Increases in waterborne interaction capacity did not seem to be enough to break the decentralization cycle, though. Water made it easier to transport bulk goods and stimulated trade, which, we argue, had ambiguous associations with centralization and sometimes stimulated decentralization. Water-based increases in interaction capacity provided by the ocean also did not overcome problems with communications and transport over land, which remained severe. We saw this in maritime Southeast Asia, which had high seaborne interaction capacity but was a fragmented system of (mostly) city-states. Communications were fluid enough to diffuse and institutionalize an international order and shared concepts of rule and governance, often based in Malay conceptions of statehood, but the ocean did not enable rulers to extend their rule over land. Although evidence from the case studies, especially in the form of observations by historians, was clear that low interaction capacity creates the limitations that drive decentralized forms of rule, it was also clear that exogenous increases in waterborne interaction capacity did not necessarily solve this dilemma. The most centralized states in our study (China, Korea, Vietnam) did emerge in the region with the highest endogenous interaction capacity in the form of roads, past experiences with centralization, a common court script and language, but these processes are difficult to separate from state building and centralization itself. Nevertheless, a key lesson is that decentralized rule was necessitated by the difficulties of transport and communications over land and that waterborne increases in interaction capacity did not generally overcome this problem.

Across the case studies, there were five regions where interaction capacity was plausibly higher, driven by higher population densities and inland river systems: the Niger Delta and Bight of Benin, the Ganges River Basin and Bay of Bengal, the Mekong and Red River Deltas, the Japanese islands, and the rice-producing regions of Java and Bali. Of course, the river valleys of China and Korea are also important areas of higher interaction capacity, but we limit the discussion here to regions that started the nineteenth century with more decentralized forms of rule.[7]

Of these high-capacity regions, centralized states formed only in the East Asian cases (Vietnam and Japan), which should immediately indicate that increases in interaction capacity do not deterministically lead to successful centralization projects. In Vietnam and Japan, we saw that interaction capacity likely activated long-term processes of cultural and economic integration, combined with previous experiences with centralization, to lay the foundations for fast-moving institutional reform in the nineteenth century. But why did these same processes not occur in regions of South Asia, Southeast Asia, or West Africa that had higher population densities and access to delta river systems? Most puzzling is the Ganges Basin and the Bay of Bengal. In the late eighteenth and early nineteenth century, this was one of the most heavily populated parts of the globe, with a navigable inland river system, extensive manufacturing industries, and high agricultural productivity. It was home to some of Asia's (and even the world's) richest commercial families and the competition of "the anarchy" that accompanied the fall of the Mughal Empire. Why were rulers such as the nawab of Awadh or Bengal not able to overcome their vassals?

We can offer only speculations here, but foreign rule may have played an important role.[8] Northern India did not emerge into the nineteenth century on the back of centuries of competition and rule from locally competing states, which might have helped develop protonationalisms (as was, perhaps, the case in Burma, Siam, and Vietnam). The states of northern India also did not emerge from isolation, as Japan did. They emerged from Mughal rule in Delhi. The nawabs who governed regions of northern and eastern India were appointed by the emperor in Delhi and were often relatives or high-ranking military officers in the Mughal regime. These foreign rulers may have had stronger incentives to perpetuate decentralized forms of governance at the local level to avoid local resistance. They may also have been weak vis-à-vis their local vassals and especially dependent on them. When these nawabs became the rulers of de facto independent states in the eighteenth century, their territories had not undergone a process of assimilation between rulers and vassals but faced a fragmented landscape of powerful, armed zamindars, whose loyalty to the nawab in Lucknow or Murshidabad was questionable. The EIC exacerbated these fragmentary pressures by gradually peeling off territories and vassals from the East and North Indian states.

Perhaps the presence of foreign states and rule helps explain why other regions with high capacity did not centralize. A centralized Javanese state in the nineteenth century may have been possible. Java could look back to empires (Majapahit, for example) toward the end of the seventeenth century, and Mataram looked to be taking up the mantle of a unified Javanese state. But a failed centralization attempt, succession disputes, and war in the early eighteenth century drew in the VOC, which first took control of the coast and then organized the partition of Java into the Yogyakarta Sultanate and Surakarta in 1755, also including the autonomous region of Mangkunegaran. While the VOC could not conquer and absorb the Javanese states, it could play the role of spoiler, threatening to side with the ruler who best promised to realize the company's interests of stable but not too strong Javanese states.[9]

Vietnam and Japan (and, if we were to extend the analysis, Siam and Burma) stand in contrast to North India and Java, having been relatively isolated from European and other foreign influences and rule prior to the nineteenth century.[10] Japan was never ruled from Peking, and Vietnam had a long history of reasonably unified governance in its core areas of the Red River Basin. The Ava Empire (in Burma) was not ruled by the Mughals, and Siam was not governed by Burma or Vietnam (although was often in conflict with these states). In areas of historically high interaction capacity and population density, this relative isolation may have enabled interaction capacity to play out as longer-term processes of administrative and cultural assimilation that prefaced successful state-building projects in the nineteenth century.

This does not help us explain why more centralized states did not form in the more densely populated parts of West Africa, especially along the coast. Europeans were minor political players here until the mid–nineteenth century. Dahomey did centralize on the fringes of this zone, but the most densely populated parts of the Niger Delta hosted small city-states on the coast and highly decentralized kingdoms (and sometimes even more decentralized regions) inland. Perhaps the Atlantic slave trade exacerbated this fragmentation by enabling the rise of multiple small states along the coast and provoking a cycle of war, raiding, and mistrust that was the precise opposite of the more integrative processes in East Asia and mainland Southeast Asia.[11] We remind the reader that the preceding discussion is speculative and intended to identify puzzles to be explored in future work rather than to draw strong conclusions in the book.

Moreover, the previous examples should not obscure the fact that we think that low levels of interaction capacity were a primary reason why decentralized rule was so widespread across the case studies. There are two key pieces of evidence for this claim. First, low levels of (land-based) interaction capacity were one of the few constants across the case studies where most states were decentralized.[12] The lack of a system analogous to that of East Asia is striking. All four states in East Asia were centralized at some point in the nineteenth century. Less than 10 percent of cases in South Asia, West Africa, and Southeast Asia were centralized and, on this measure, were more like each other than like East Asia. In a sense, these three systems were different case studies where we observed similarities in governance that are hard to explain with factors that vary across the cases.[13]

In addition, broad variations in interaction capacity across the regions tracked with the adoption of direct rule. If we accept the basic premise that more people lower the marginal costs of economic and political interactions, as some do,[14] then East and South Asia had the highest population densities and the highest capacity for interactions and extensive adoption of direct rule. According to Roberto Foa, a significant proportion of western and southern India was governed by more centralized states in the mid- to late eighteenth century.[15] The depth of centralization was also higher in these regions. For example, Mysore and Pune probably employed more governors and bureaucrats over wider land areas than Asante did. This should not obscure the fact that within both South Asia and West Africa the more centralized states did not emerge in the subregions with the highest population densities. There is perhaps an analogy here to Germany, where even though population density was high across Europe, sovereignty was fragmented in the denser German regions until the nineteenth century.[16]

The second piece of evidence is that historians across the case studies point to dispersed populations, poor communications, and slow and expensive transport as factors that necessitated governance through autonomous vassals, often in direct contrast to a more direct "governors and bureaucrats" strategy. These are observations of the mechanisms at work or evidence of the causal process linking low interaction capacity to decentralization. However, high-capacity regions seem to produce centralized states only under some conditions, in the same way that a weak immune system might increase the underlying risk of severe illness but only under certain conditions (i.e., the contraction of a certain pathogen).

LESSON 4: WAR DID NOT CAUSE CENTRALIZATION (IN MOST CASES)

We saw in chapter 3 that European states are thought to have centralized because of the relentless pressure from warfare and international competition. This pressure created new incentives to build extractive fiscal institutions and standing armies that could compete and survive. Is this the pattern we see outside of Europe?

SYNTHESIS

Our conclusion is no—or, at least, not most of the time. There was no shortage of war and competition across the cases and no shortage of the "right" wars. West Africa experienced an intense cycle of warfare with the rise of Dahomey and Sokoto and the collapse of Oyo. Wars were fought with large armies, firearms, and more modern tactics and resulted in the destruction of both older and newer polities. These wars were, by most historical accounts, intense and spanned nearly a century. The epicenter of the Yoruba wars in southeastern Nigeria was also one of the most densely populated and urban areas of the region. Warfare in South Asia from about 1750 to 1850 was also intense, sometimes described as "the anarchy" as the Mughal Empire collapsed, leaving a competitive, multistate system in its wake.[17] States such as the Maratha Confederacy and its successor states (Pune, Gwalior, Nagpur, Indore, and Baroda), Khalistan, and Mysore fought each other and the rising EIC for supremacy of the subcontinent. Competition was also likely intense in parts of Southeast Asia, especially the island of Bali but probably also in parts of South Sulawesi and Java if we look back farther into the eighteenth century.

Despite these pressures, none of these systems transformed into one of medium-size, centralized states, like the billiard ball model we presented in chapter 3. The successor states of the Oyo Empire continued practices of decentralized rule from the "old" empire. The Maratha states practiced forms of vassalage and tributary relations to maintain a decentralized empire across much of the subcontinent. The Balinese states remained a collection of small, fragmented mandalas. Rather, it was the lowest-competition region of East Asia that most resembled a system of centralized states (although we accept that this system could have been the result of warfare in the more distant past). Moreover, there was considerable evidence that the pressures of warfare caused increased decentralization. After losing the Battle of Panipat in 1761, the Maratha Empire fragmented, and states such as Pune rolled back centralization reforms by offering warlords greater autonomy in exchange for services in battle. We saw a similar dynamic in Southeast Asia, where the pressures of war led to new autonomous enclaves maintained by powerful, autonomous warlords.

Only in a handful of cases did we see centralization, but it is hard to attribute the centralization in these cases to increased warfare. Dahomey's centralization is better seen as causing an increase in competition rather than the other way around, but this connection does not explain why other states in the same region that were less exposed to competition (e.g., Asante) centralized or why others that were potentially more exposed to competition (e.g., Ibadan) did not. Pune centralized its administration on the Malwa Plateau, but largely when the times were good, and the Marathas were on the ascendancy, taking increasing tributary revenues from an ever-expanding empire. When their expansion was checked and revenue pressures started to bite, they turned to more decentralized forms of rule to attract military commanders and soldiers.

Historians identify Mysore as a potential case of "military fiscalism," where the pressures of war led the sultan to create a standing army and displace unreliable vassals with agents appointed by the state.[18] Although there is some uncertainty as to how successful Mysore was in its centralization projects before being conquered by the EIC, even if we accept that Mysore was an unusually centralized state, it is unclear why other states exposed to similar pressures (such as Khalistan and the Rajput states) were not successful in centralizing their administration. Perhaps the most compelling example of increased competition causing centralization is Japan (and, to an extent, Vietnam in the late eighteenth and early nineteenth centuries). Relatively hermetic and closed to the outside world before the nineteenth century, Japan experienced a competition shock in 1853 when Admiral Matthew Perry forced the Tokugawa Shogunate to open its borders. The weakness of the shogunate was attributed to Japan's decentralized form of rule, and the Meiji Revolution from 1868 created a new, highly centralized Japanese state.

We think the best explanation for these patterns is that increases in competition can produce centralization, *but only in some circumstances*, while in other circumstances increased competition can cause decentralization. To understand why this might be the case, we need to return to our discussion of the "decentralization trap" described earlier. Recall that in our example, the *alafin* has a dilemma. He would like to reduce the power and autonomy of the military elite, upon whom the *alafin* depends to wage war, and to reduce the power of tributary kingdoms and vassals. However, these goals are hard because to reduce the power of the Oyo Mesi (the military elite in the capital) or the *are ona kakamfo* (leader of the provincial armies) the *alafin* needs a more loyal army. To build a more loyal army, he needs more money, and to get that money he needs to subdue vassal kingdoms and displace their elites. But to do the latter he needs the Oyo Mesi or the *are one kakamfo*, who will demand more autonomy in return. We are back to the original problem.

Would an external shock—a new competitor or competitors—change this equation? Other things being equal, no. Rulers might want more money to build bigger armies and defend their territory (although they should already want as much money as they can get away with),[19] but that desire does not change subordinates' willingness to submit to direct rule. The Oyo Empire faced just this situation in the early nineteenth century. A new empire rose on Oyo's northern border in the early nineteenth century, raiding, invading, and causing the defection of vassal towns in the north. Especially concerning was the fall of the city Ilorin in 1817, whose vassal ruler was the leader of the provincial Oyo armies.

Such an external shock does not enable our *alafin* to overcome his basic dilemma; rather, it exacerbates that dilemma. The main problem is that he needs the Oyo Mesi more than ever. The survival of the kingdom depends on it. He might want more revenue to build that standing army, but he has become more, not less, dependent on his military elite to survive, and, in turn, they are likely to demand more autonomy or at least to retain their current privileges. Moreover, the *alafin* probably now needs soldiers from the provinces and his vassal kingdoms, but he has no way of compelling his vassals to contribute their forces to defend the kingdom, aside from his own threats of punishment and the promise that provincial vassals can maintain their autonomy or even expand the size of their fiefs by conquering new territories and extracting new tributes. The basic problem is that centralization requires the center to be strong and the vassals to be weak. But competition in our example empowers the vassals against the center.

A crucial aspect of this dilemma is that vassals could switch sides. So long as vassals can credibly threaten to join the enemy, they can use competition to play off one suzerain against the other. Defecting vassals were extremely common in our case studies and clearly one of the major dilemmas of war. In the nonfiction case of the Oyo Empire, its vassals did defect, first Ilorin in the North, and the defections spread farther south, resulting in the collapse of the empire. But this was also very common elsewhere. Defecting vassals was a major concern to the Asante Empire.[20] In South Asia, *deshmukh*s or zamindars would readily defect to the sovereign offering the greatest benefits. Richard Barnett notes that in northern India bribing vassals was a good way to win wars, something the EIC were especially

LESSONS FROM THE CASE STUDIES

effective at, and something that Kaushik Roy notes was a feature of South Asian warfare in general.[21] Likewise, in Southeast Asia we saw that vassal kingdoms and states were only too willing to throw off central rule when the opportunity presented itself. Hendrick Spruyt notes that "lords [in Southeast Asia] in frontier zones could easily switch sides."[22] Defecting princes were central to the fall and split of the Mataram Empire.[23] So long as vassals could credibly switch sides, competition increased rather than decreased the bargaining power of subordinate elites. Put slightly differently, studies of state centralization in Europe sometimes claim that changes in warfare created new incentives to pool resources to face external threats. But this approach assumes that elites have no other outside options and assumes that they would prefer to band together with the center rather than potentially retaining their autonomy and joining with someone else.

For competition to produce centralization, then, it must strengthen the bargaining hand of the center or weaken the bargaining hand of the periphery. Under what conditions might competition cause this to happen? We outline two possibilities. First, vassals might relinquish some autonomy if they expect to be worse off under a new suzerain. This can happen when a new ruler (the potential conqueror) can credibly threaten to take away the autonomy of a potential vassal in the future. If, for example, the conquering state is a centralized state that can extend direct rule further, then a vassal may be better off relinquishing some autonomy to their current suzerain rather than siding with a new ruler who will likely take away more autonomy. We speculate that this is why warfare does not generally produce centralization in systems with low interaction capacity. States—conquerors and suzerains—cannot credibly commit to centralizing reforms because the costs are too high, making promises of autonomy credible from new potential suzerains. Warfare in low interaction-capacity systems probably exacerbates the decentralization trap, entrenching the devolution of power. One way in which rising, land-based, interaction capacity might cause centralization is by making direct forms of rule more viable and vassals more willing to give up some autonomy in exchange for other concessions (pensions or more limited autonomy).[24] Competition in higher-capacity systems may activate a cycle of centralization rather than decentralization.

A second possibility leans more on the role of collective beliefs, especially nationalism, or linguistic and cultural homogeneity. Yuval Feinstein and Andreas Wimmer find, for example, that centralization in Europe was more common where war was combined with nationalism.[25] Where vassals are more closely tied to the state through cultural and linguistic similarities or even through a sense of legitimacy derived from seeing the "state" as the rightful ruler of a certain "people," then competition from an outsider and the prospects of alien rule might mean that vassals are willing to sacrifice some short-term autonomy and survive within the current political arrangements. If the state is seen as legitimately representing the interests of a defined community, and rallying around that state is considered the best chance for the state to survive as an entity, then competition may weaken the bargaining hand of vassals that would be significantly worse off under alien rule. This could explain, for example, why a competition shock produced centralization in culturally and linguistically homogenous Japan, but not in more diverse India, Southeast Asia, and West Africa. In Japan, increased competition at first empowered the large autonomous daimyo of Satsuma and Chosu, who then overthrew the shogun. In the wake of their victory, however, there was no other game in town for weaker vassals, and many accepted initial offers of pensions and inclusion in a centralized regime.

Before moving on to discuss trade, we make a couple of additional but more speculative points. First, the "right" wars to produce centralization come from somewhere. Mobilizing tens or hundreds of thousands of soldiers, equipping them, and maintaining them in battle require enormous logistical effort. Larger armies that stimulated other states to attempt the same process were probably, at least in part, the effects of state centralization, raising the question of what comes before the large armies. Second, linguistic or cultural unity also has prior causes that relate to states' ability to rule consistently across territory, such that languages and rituals are standardized, and the state comes to be seen as legitimate. To the extent that interaction capacity creates states that generate a level of linguistic or cultural unity, autonomous subordinates may feel culturally bound to the state and accept less autonomy to increase the chances of fending off foreign rule.[26] In other words, aspects that might contribute *to* centralization are also probably caused *by* centralization. What we are suggesting here is that changes in warfare, changes in state administration, and changes in the norms around rule are dependent to an extent on the costs and ability of political entities to move people, goods, and information. Decentralized systems might be very

LESSONS FROM THE CASE STUDIES

similar in their political dynamics because low levels of interaction capacity meant most rulers faced the same dilemmas, and outside changes in war and trade did not change these deeper structural constraints.

LESSON 5: TRADE PROMOTES STATE FORMATION BUT INHIBITS CENTRALIZATION (IN MOST CASES)

What about trade? Did increases in trade provide rulers with new allies for their centralization projects that allowed them to go around and eventually through vassals to obtain more taxes and soldiers? We think trade contributed to state *formation* without driving state *centralization*.

Trade hubs were valuable territories. They offered taxes and access to valuable goods, whether they be luxury items or weapons from abroad, in addition to new ideas. Rulers could use these resources to build nascent bureaucracies, arm their militaries, and co-opt allies among the elite. Examples of trade-led state formation occurred across our case studies, from the states of archipelagic Southeast Asia—such as Aceh and Johor-Riau—to states in West Africa that rose on the Atlantic slave trade—such as Dahomey and the Oyo Empire—to the EIC itself in South Asia.

However, trade in fact inhibited centralization except under specific circumstances. Rarely were trade-dense regions also areas dominated by centralized states. The Hausa regions of northern Nigeria maintained a system of city-states for centuries before the Sokoto Caliphate. As we discuss later, the Atlantic slave trade on balance probably created a system of decentralized city-states and empires, and the trade-soaked sea-lanes of Southeast Asia produced a system of small city-states. Trade along the Ganges also did not necessarily lead to the rise of centralized states. For example, C. A. Bayly describes Awadh and Benares as "decentralized precolonial polities."[27]

Rulers knew the value of controlling trade-rich areas. Centralization projects were attempted most often in such trade-rich areas—the slaving ports of West Africa, the pepper ports of Sumatra, the textiles trade in Oudh. Dahomey sent its governors first to Ouidah; Aceh sent its governors to the pepper ports; and Mataram's great centralization drive was aimed at controlling the ports of northern Java. Awadh appointed the most "energetic and trusted" officials to the rich agricultural lands and markets of Baiswara and the banks of the Ganges.[28]

But successes were rare and short-lived, more often destabilizing states that attempted centralization and leading to new competitors. Despite its allure, trade was hard to monopolize and control, especially, as we argue later, in systems where transportation and communications were poor. Unless trade was concentrated, it tended to elude state control. A trade boom might empower one ruler but also that ruler's vassals and rivals. Moreover, trade patterns fluctuated, and a valuable region in one decade might be poor in another, disempowering some rulers and empowering others.

Trade created a shifting economic foundation for rulers that tended toward the fragmentation rather than the consolidation of states. We saw several examples of trade-led fragmentation. Siak in Southeast Asia thrived on the pepper trade, but in the late eighteenth and early nineteenth century it was unable to prevent the rise and de facto independence of "pepper rajas" in Deli, Langkat, Asahan, and Serdang along the Sumatran coast that rose faster on the same trade. Acehnese sultans attempted to co-opt the new mercantile class, the *orang laut*, by appointing them as governors and supervisors of pepper ports, displacing the old elite. But the sultans in Banda Aceh found it difficult to monitor and control their governors, and the ports soon became autonomous fiefs, again evading state control and extraction. On Borneo and the Malaysian Peninsula, mining and trade in metals—sometimes dominated by Chinese traders—led to the rise of new autonomous regions and quasi-states that existing rulers struggled to control.

A similar dynamic characterized eighteenth- and nineteenth-century West Africa, and here we discuss recent work in IR on the role of slavery in state formation and state building. Historians of West Africa have debated the relationship between slavery and state building for some time, but this discussion was revitalized by the recent work of Jason Sharman and Ayşe Zarakol in the field of international relations.[29] Sharman argues that the massive increase in external demand for slaves drove the formation of new, militarized slaving states in West Africa. Slaves made states, and the state made slaves, as the twist on Tilly's famous phrase goes. Rulers trading in slaves at Atlantic Ocean ports along the West African coast or selling slaves by using interior middlemen (and states) connected to the coast could access revenues, weapons, and goods that enabled them to dominate their rivals and capture more slaves. Because slaving was a violent and militarized enterprise, and because slaves were also used as soldiers and bureaucrats, this incentivized the rise of "slaving states" and created a violent, competitive, international order.

This story fits the one of trade-creating states, and the evidence in our case studies supports the idea that slave trading created states in the sense that many new states were formed. Examples of links between the slave trade and state creation abound. Dahomey is a paradigmatic example. But other cases such as Oyo, the Tokolor Empire, and the Sokoto Caliphate are also raised as examples of the "slaves made states" story.

However, we did not find strong evidence that slave trading facilitated state centralization. To be clear, Sharman's argument is about state formation (i.e., creation), but it is worth distinguishing between state formation and state centralization. Many states were born on the slave trade, but most of them were decentralized states. As we demonstrated in the chapter on West Africa, Dahomey was an outlier, an unusually centralized state in a system of bull's-eye states. On the contrary, several examples suggest that trade fragmented states, empowered regional warlords, exacerbated intercommunal tensions, undermined trust, and made governance more difficult, creating rather than removing barriers to state centralization. As Sharman points out, the slave trade had a dual effect: it provided resources useful for state-creation projects, and it increased violent competition between states over those resources. Because slaving was an inherently violent and militarized activity, the link between trade and war was pernicious in West Africa.

Examples abound where slave trading created decentralized states. Ouidah was the key slave-trading port that accompanied the rise of Dahomey, but the nearby slaving ports of Porto-Novo, Badagry, Lagos, and Little-Popo did not produce highly centralized states, but rather only small city-states. Farther along the slaving coast, the ports of Bonny and Old Calabar were also the center of city-states, not centralized kingdoms. Although the populous Igbo region of Nigeria was devastated by slave raiding, it did not produce centralized states; rather, the region remained relatively acephalous with smaller city-states along the coast. The Aro Confederacy was another state that rose on trade in slaves with Europeans. But the Aro state was not a centralized monarchy; it was part state, part guild, part secret society centered on the oracle at Arochukwu, which dominated parts of southwestern Nigeria despite few central state structures for administration.[30] These examples show that the Atlantic slave trade had, at best, a conditional impact on state centralization, sometimes facilitating it but at other times producing different or even novel, hybridized (although otherwise decentralized) state structures.

Moreover, there are examples of states that fragmented and even collapsed because of the Atlantic slave trade.[31] The Oyo Empire is an oft-cited example of a state created by the slave trade. This is of course true; the Oyo Empire rose because it capitalized on the growing trade with Europeans on the coast, selling slaves in the South and buying horses in the North for its calvary armies.[32] The slave trade also provided resources and bureaucrats (in the form of slaves) that began to tip the balance of power between the *alafin* and the Oyo Mesi in favor of the center.[33] But governance in the Oyo Empire was still decentralized: the *alafin* maintained a thin presence outside of the capital, was hemmed in by the powerful military elite, and was dependent on the *are ona kakamfo* (leader of the provincial armies). Robin Law sees the slave trade as contributing to both the centralization and the *collapse* of the Oyo Empire. One reason was that in Oyo there was "nothing approaching a royal monopoly of the external trade," which limited the extent to which trade contributed to centralization (especially in contrast to Dahomey and Ashanti). Slave trading likely empowered warlords as well as rulers in the capital.[34] In addition, the Oyo Empire's attempt to colonize the trade corridor between the capital and slaving ports on the coast to collect taxes directly may have alerted warlords in the capital and provinces to the risks of centralization, contributing to instability at the center and the eventual collapse of the empire. The collapse of the Oyo Empire then created many *new* states—Ijaye, Ibadan, Abeokuta—and further fragmented the West African political landscape. Slave trading no doubt contributed to the rise of Oyo, but it did not allow Oyo to overcome the dilemmas of decentralized rule, which were the eventual cause of its collapse.[35]

Our framework can help explain why trade assisted state formation but not state centralization, especially in low-capacity systems. The Atlantic slave trade did not create centralized states for similar reasons that the Indian Ocean spice trade did not create centralized states. Fluctuations in trade can empower either rulers or vassals. Where rulers were able to dominate or monopolize slave trading, this may have contributed to centralization in Dahomey or Asante. For Southeast Asia, Victor Lieberman argues that the ability of rulers in Burma and Vietnam to dominate coastal

LESSONS FROM THE CASE STUDIES

trading links contributed to the growing power of the center vis-à-vis its vassals.[36] But in other areas of West Africa, the ability to trade slaves on the coast potentially led to the rise of many small, decentralized city-states, as it did on the coasts of Sumatra and Malaysia. In the context of the slave trade, centrifugal pressures might have been exacerbated because to kidnap human beings, rulers depended on warlords, who grew more powerful militarily, economically, and politically because of the trade. As elsewhere, these warlords demanded autonomy in return for their military services. Moreover, as we have argued in this chapter and in previous chapters, in low-density systems war and competition can fuel centrifugal pressures by increasing the dependence of rulers on autonomous military elites to win wars. The Atlantic slave trade probably infused the region with state-building resources that allowed rulers to create many new states but simultaneously activated pressures that ensured these states would remain weak and decentralized.

In summary, we agree with recent work suggesting that the Atlantic slave trade created or formed states in West Africa, but in only isolated cases can we see evidence that it facilitated state centralization. Quite to the contrary, when seen from a regional perspective (and a broader comparative perspective), the Atlantic slave trade was associated with the creation of a fragmented system of highly decentralized empires and coastal city-states. We see little evidence for the theory of trade-led centralization in our case studies. Rulers attempted this path of co-opting commercial elites, but it was rarely successful. Centralized states did not emerge in trade-rich regions, but rather in areas more isolated from the main trading channels, and there was evidence that trade contributed to the fragmentation of systems and the decentralization of states. Trade simply did not enable rulers to overcome the dilemmas of decentralization. Most of the time, it seemed to exacerbate them. As often as trade provided rulers with new sources of revenue for state-building projects or created new potential allies for these projects, it empowered rivals with new resources to challenge those state-building projects or start their own. And new commercial allies soon turned into rivals when they discovered that they could keep most of the profits for themselves without having to tolerate state agents taking their local revenues. As much as rulers wanted to, most of the time they simply did not have the means to monopolize trade. Sending and resourcing state agents, soldiers, administrators, and accountants to enforce state monopolies were expensive and difficult. As such, the resources that inhere in trade were rarely captured by state elites but instead diffused beyond the reach of state, diffusing political power with them. Finally, trade tended to evade state control. Once trade in one area was controlled by a state, it tended to shift elsewhere, empowering other states and elites as it moved. There seems to be an interaction here again: trade may promote state centralization but needs to be the right type of trade, as argued by Spruyt, and the state needs the logistical capacity to control how trade revenues are appropriated.

CONCLUSION

Collectively, these lessons provide an image of the structure of states and how they governed before the final enclosure of the global system. We utilized comparisons across and within four regions to assess how war and trade—two commonly given explanations for political centralization in Europe—were associated with centralization in the nineteenth century. Although each system displayed unique characteristics, we found that the three decentralized bull's-eye systems—South Asia, maritime Southeast Asia, and West Africa—shared common features that were relatively absent in the more centralized billiard ball system of East Asia. Low levels of interaction capacity were key, and we found evidence that the impact of war and trade might be conditioned by levels of interaction capacity. War and trade seemed to spur centralization in East Asia but not in the lower-capacity regions of South Asia, Southeast Asia, and West Africa. But the systems that arose from these interacting states possessed other corollary features. These system-level characteristics are the subject of the next chapter.

Chapter Nine

SYSTEMS OF DECENTRALIZED STATES

One of the great dilemmas for rulers throughout history has been how to project power over distance. How does a ruler—be they a rajah, a queen, a sultan, or an empress—govern people and territory that they cannot see and experience directly, at least not without taking a journey of days, weeks, or even months? The development of electronic communication and motorized transportation enhanced power-projection capabilities and thus modified rulers' calculations, leading to profound changes in the global system. But before those technological leaps and before the global enclosure that occurred not uncoincidentally at the same time, rulers faced a timeless dilemma: to rule directly using loyal personnel sent from the center or to rule indirectly by relying on local vassals who maintained a modicum of autonomy. In the previous chapter, we examined how war, trade, and interaction capacity helped explain patterns of state centralization and decentralization across different historical systems. We found that decentralized states were the norm. In this chapter, we continue the conversation by zooming out to outline the system-level effects of decentralized states. What do systems of bull's-eye states look like, and how are they different from systems of billiard ball states? We believe that the answer to those questions will illuminate not only the system dynamics of South Asia, Southeast Asia, and West Africa during the nineteenth century but also arguably the dynamics of most premodern state systems.

The remainder of the chapter proceeds as follows. We begin by revisiting our broad definition of the state, which includes various manifestations of decentralized rule. Mindful of that definition, we then catalog recurring governance patterns in the case study chapters. Our contention is that mandalas, bull's-eye states, and empires represent common albeit regionally contextualized solutions to the dilemma of projecting power over distance. We then consider the relationship between international order and the structure of state systems. Overall, we maintain that systems of decentralized states exhibit noticeable characteristics such as patterns of radial rule, frontiers instead of borders, and relations of heteronomy. We conclude the chapter by considering the dynamics of decentralized rule and outlining a theory of international change.

DIFFERENT NAMES FOR THE SAME PHENOMENON

States are the core unit of analysis in this book. They are the ground upon which we identify systems and consider their internal dynamics. We defined states as hierarchical, coercion-wielding organizations that subordinate all other organizations within a defined territory and have control over their external relations. This is a broad definition that builds from Tilly, and it encompasses a range of subforms, including "city-states, empires, theocracies, and many other forms of government."[1] We clarified in chapter 2 that for a polity to count as a state in our dataset there must be a political apparatus that is territorially stable, but it need not be a particularly complex and thickly institutionalized organization, and the territory over which it rules does not have to be contiguous or delimited by linear borders. As such, the set of states includes the big and the small, the centralized and decentralized, those that possess discrete borders and those whose boundaries are characterized by frontiers.

As we discussed in the previous chapter, a core takeaway from our research is that most of the states we examined were decentralized. The state systems in West Africa, Southeast Asia, and South Asia best approximate the bull's-eye system we described in chapter 3. Although states may have varied within each system in terms of their level of centralization, the norm was decentralization amid frontier zones of uncertain rule. We have argued that low levels of interaction capacity help explain these patterns.

SYSTEMS OF DECENTRALIZED STATES

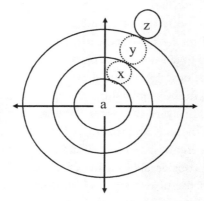

FIGURE 9.1. Diagram of a bull's-eye state.

There is a striking and repeating configuration across diverse historical locales whereby states tend to rule in a radial pattern of decreasing control. In plain terms, there is a political center surrounded by orbits of dissipating state reach. As one moves farther from the center across those orbits, the relative autonomy of local political actors increases, and the state becomes increasingly decentralized. Scholars of West Africa called this the "bull's-eye state," composed of a well-defined political core (the Toeda) surrounded by dissipating rings of domination.[2] Figure 9.1 provides an illustration of this pattern, where the smaller circles x, y, and z denote smaller polities that stand in relation to a, the core state. Here, polity y is situated on an outer orbit of control and has more autonomy than polity x, which is closer to the core. Meanwhile, polity z is sufficiently distant from the center to control its external relations and count as an independent state. State z is truly on the frontier. It may be subordinated to the much larger and more hegemonic state a, but it is still independent, unlike x and y.

Terms such as *galactic polity*, *solar polity*, and *mandala* are common descriptors for states in Southeast Asia.[3] As we discussed in chapter 6, the mandala concept is traced to the Arthasastra, an ancient Indian text credited to Kautilya that, among other things, advances arguments for how to project power over distance.[4] The same radial patterns of control were found in the South Asian case but were less common in the centralized states of East Asia, with the exception of Japan and parts of Vietnam. In sum, scholars have described the same pattern of rule across diverse and, in many cases, unconnected settings and have offered a common practical explanation related to the challenges of power projection over distance and the related need to develop forms of vassalage.

Notably, the same descriptions used for mandalas and bull's-eye states have also been used in the scholarship on empires.[5] To be sure, *empire* is a contested term used in a variety of ways. Some scholars argue that empires are merely forms of the state and that there is no clear distinction.[6] Others see them as fundamentally different types, but the reported nature of the difference(s) varies considerably.[7] And some are content to treat *empire* and *imperialism* as useful descriptors.[8] However, given our theoretical framework and set of definitional choices, we say that empires can be understood as a type of state. This was one advantage of Tilly's broad definition, which includes empires as a subset. Had we instead selected a narrower definition of the state, it is possible that we would have excluded empires. For example, Tilly's concept of the national state, a more specific form of the state, is thought to be different from empires because it is more centralized and nationally homogenous.[9] But our definition of the state does not take a position on ethnonational composition. Furthermore, it treats the issue of centralization as a variable. Empires are states that typically exhibit high levels of decentralization.

There is a clear relationship between empires and other decentralized political forms. Empires are often described using language such as *bull's-eye state*, *solar polity*, and *mandala*. For example, Karen Barkey describes the Ottoman Empire "as a solar system, with planets circling the central sun, pulled in and held by the center's gravitational force."[10] Likewise, Michael Doyle's analysis of empires highlights the degrees (and zones) of control that existed across both ancient and modern empires.[11] Notably, many of the states in our analysis were described, at least by historians, as empires (e.g., Oyo Empire). This begs the question: Are not empires just a state with a mandala configuration, where expansion may be common, vassals are numerous, and frontiers are frequent? Hermann Kulke makes the same connection between imperial and mandala structures.[12] Mandala states and bull's-eye states are just empires by other names.

In sum, our analysis of these states and systems leads us to conclude that decentralized rule exhibits common patterns across time and space. One cause of these patterns is the need to project power with limited capacity.

One consequence of limited capacity is a noticeable configuration of radial rule. The names for these political forms as well as their scale vary, but they are the same phenomenon.

THE RELATIONSHIP BETWEEN STRUCTURE AND ORDER

Some readers may wonder if our conclusion is too materialist in character. We argued that there are regular structural patterns to state systems over time because state leaders face common trade-offs with respect to the form of rule. These choices are usually manifest as patterns of decentralized rule. But what about the effects of culture, norms, and ideas? What about international order?[13] International orders typically possess legal, ideological, and ritualistic features that resonate with local culture, and they can have causal effects on the structural features of states and systems.[14] What is the relationship between structure and order? Does order arise in a somewhat derivative manner from the structural realities of a system? Or does the content of the order have causal effects on how systems are structured? These are vital questions in comparative systems analysis, questions that highlight the potential causal importance of ideas, norms, and culture.

An order-driving-structure approach might see the outcomes differently. For example, if one begins with the religious, spiritual, and ideological content of a system—that is, if one begins with order—and then looks at the structural relations between the units, then one might conclude that order plays the more determinative role. This is the outlook many scholars have, particularly and perhaps naturally those who do thick history and conduct deep anthropological studies of specific cultures. Clifford Geertz explained the court rituals and theater of the Balinese states as behavior that shaped power relations; "power served pomp, not pomp power."[15] More generally, Hendrick Spruyt conducted a comparative analysis of international orders (societies) and argues that collective belief systems (order) shape structure, "not the other way around."[16] As we discussed in the chapter on Southeast Asia, many argue that the cosmological ideas regarding the mandala determined the resulting pattern of rule. These patterns were not the product of vulgar pragmatic calculations, according to Stanley Tambiah; they were baked into the cosmology of the culture.[17] Thus, order shapes structure.

An advantage of comparative analysis is that it gives researchers leverage to separate the common from the truly unique. Although we cannot know the exact relationship, we speculate that there are feedback effects between structure and order. For example, it matters that those scholars who study Southeast Asia have assigned substantial causal weight to cosmological order—ideas did shape some political outcomes.[18] However, given that their approach is deeply ethnographic and case specific rather than comparative and multicase, it makes sense that they would prize the distinctiveness of cosmological order. We conjecture that the ideas resonant in the mandala concept, stretching back to Kautilya, are a unique narrative for a common solution that other disconnected cultures have arrived at using different language and narratives. After all, Kautilya's objective was an insightful and pragmatic political treatise. Would not a winning treatise succeed and be adopted down the line, while ill-advised and weakly strategized treatises are dropped? In addition, practical considerations played a role, for it is not as though polities possessed perfect circles of control. Like in West Africa, Balinese states controlled pie-shaped river valleys that conformed to the topography and the resulting obstacles to power projection.[19] The Mandala concept was an ideal grounded in religion that both legitimated and motivated an otherwise common approach to political order.

That is not to say that order is simply an expression of structure; the causal arrow does move in the other direction. In terms of the mandala concept, there are probably cases where rulers chose to organize their realms in a particular configuration not simply on account of power relations but because of belief. They might have granted greater autonomy to a political actor than was warranted or insisted on more control than they could enforce or both. Alternatively, order might invest vassals with the notion that their autonomy was in line with cosmological blueprints, leading them to work harder to hold that autonomy than might otherwise be warranted. We came across such arguments regarding West Africa (especially the Yoruba states) and Southeast Asia, where decentralization was in part explained by belief systems that legitimated autonomy.

We conjecture that increasing interaction capacity ought to shift the causal weight in the direction of order. That is, international order has greater effects on structure in high-density systems. For example, sovereign recognition in the contemporary international system depends on full UN membership.[20] Although Somaliland and Northern Cyprus are functional states and may have been recognized as such in earlier periods with different recognition criteria, they are currently denied full recognition because they cannot join the UN. In the absence of the international legal personality that comes with full legal membership in the community of states, they cannot access formal financial aid, utilize international post, conduct commerce with foreign banks, and join international organizations that are reserved for sovereign states. The degree of their sovereign integration is reduced by the norms, principles, and membership criteria of international order. Clearly, order can affect structure.

Our review of the case studies shows two areas in which high interaction capacity increases the potential effects of order on structure. First, it can play a role in determining who is a recognized state in the system. The East Asian system was the most developed and high-capacity system in our set, and accreditation by the Qing court was important for state leaders. We found milder forms of investiture in other systems—a matter we return to later—but they were less developed there than in East Asia. Second, we found that in cultural zones with a legacy of former imperial control, state leaders were more likely to structure their states and seek recognition using the concepts and political grammar of the former order. That is, norms of legitimacy are one legacy of empire that continues to have ordering effects on the structures of subsequent state systems. We suspect that these legacies might have been enduring where rulers were domestically weak and faced powerful vassals. C. A. Bayly, for example, notes that Mughal titles continued to play a powerful role in post-Mughal India.[21] Even the English EIC adopted Mughal titles to shore up its weak domestic legitimacy. On Java, descent from the line of Mataram was a prerequisite for rule in the partitioned successor states (Yogyakarta and Surakarta). The successor states to the Oyo Empire, Ibadan and Ijaye, adopted titles bestowed from the receding Oyo. In a way reminiscent of analyses of the postcolonial African state, international legitimacy may be a powerful resource for internally weak rulers.[22]

FRONTIERS INSTEAD OF LINEAR BORDERS

How were border regions structured across historical regions? The picture in much of the existing literature is of fuzzy frontiers in non-Western systems where demarcating the authority of one polity from another was difficult.[23] Speaking of the inside and outside of states might even be meaningless if the authority of states overlaps and interpenetrates that of other states. Only with the cartographic revolution and changing technological capabilities that enabled states to represent and imagine territory in two dimensions did linear borders proliferate. But to what extent is this picture accurate? Is there evidence of border formation outside of the core European and American regions? And what is the relationship between borders and systems of decentralized states?

Let us first describe what we mean by these phenomena. Many states had fuzzy borders where it was difficult to pin down where one state ended and another one began. Put simply, linear borders as we experience them today were rare. For example, if one were to travel the seventy kilometers from Trondheim, Norway, to Sweden today, they would know when they entered Sweden because there is a big sign on the road saying, "You are now entering the kingdom of Sweden." The markings on the road change, the signs change color, and, not least of all, the language changes. Most states in our book were not like this. Such a journey would be more like traveling east from Trondheim, where you know you are in the Kingdom of Norway, toward the Kingdom of Sweden but are not quite sure when you have left one kingdom and entered the other. You might even travel through frontier zones where people claimed to be part of neither the Kingdom of Norway nor the Kingdom of Sweden. Rather than linear borders, you have a fuzzy frontier.

Our discussion begins with a variable in the ISD designed to capture basic information about borders. Research assistants were asked whether the state in question had clear, agreed upon borders and to code that variable based on how much of the perimeter of that state was characterized accordingly. Although experimental, this variable provides a general picture of boundaries across regions. We found that nearly all states in Europe and the Americas had clearly defined borders. East Asia also scored highly where linear borders were concerned. Most borders in Europe by the nineteenth century were mutually agreed upon and defined by treaty, although often contested.[24] For example, the many German states that emerged after the Napoleonic Wars were usually small, discontinuous territories with borders defined at the Congress of Vienna.[25] Anhalt-Dessau, Anhalt-Dessau-Kothen, and Anhalt had precise borders and discontinuous

SYSTEMS OF DECENTRALIZED STATES

territories. The borders of many other European states were clearly defined and agreed upon by treaty. The borders of Belgium were agreed upon in the London Conference of 1830.[26] Borders in the Central and South American states were also relatively clearly defined. By 1858, for example, Nicaragua's borders with Costa Rica and Honduras were demarcated.[27]

Clearly demarcated borders were rarer outside of Europe and the Americas in the nineteenth century. Only about 10 percent of states in West and East-Central Africa and 15 percent of states in Southeast Asia and South Asia had precisely defined borders, rising to nearly 33 percent on mainland Southeast Asia and Oceania and about 45 percent in the Middle East. A surprising 42 percent of southern African states had clear borders, perhaps reflecting the impact of British negotiation of border treaties with many local states, including Lesotho and the Boer states. African states with clearer borders tended to be states with European connections, such as Liberia, Orange Free State, Transvaal, South Africa, and Lesotho, although there were a handful of states with clearer borders in the non-European-connected Ethiopian highlands (Kaffa, Gomma).

Outside of Europe and Latin America, then, most states had fuzzy boundaries or frontiers in the nineteenth century. There were areas of clear control by the state, but they graded off into zones where local rulers had more autonomy. The capital might not even know where its boundaries were, which was largely a matter for local rulers under the suzerainty of the center to resolve. Moreover, frontier zones could be under the suzerainty of more than one power, thus creating genuinely indeterminate zones of heteronomy (as discussed later). Indeed, as we have discussed, the descriptions of boundary zones are remarkably similar across regions. The corollary of radial patterns of rule is that boundaries were graded and frontierlike.

However, there is variation within regions. Although states in Southeast and South Asia had mostly fuzzy boundaries, many states had parts that were more clearly defined. One example is the Durrani Empire (Afghanistan), which had clear borders with the British Raj in the East and formalized its borders with Bukhara in the eighteenth century after several wars, while the empire's remaining boundaries were imprecisely defined. Another is the Sokoto Caliphate, a sprawling and decentralized empire in modern-day northern Nigeria, Mali, Cameroon, and Niger. To the north, where Sokoto faced continued war and resistance from the remnants of Hausa city-states, Gobir and Madari in particular, frontier posts, or *ribat*s, were established with relative density. These *ribat*s were an explicit policy, accelerated under the rule of Muhammad Bello and designed to "close the frontier" against neighboring states. Rather than being loosely monitored and controlled areas, the *ribat*s were led by close relatives of the ruler. Sokoto's border to the east with the Borno Emirate was a combination of demarcated border points and areas with buffer states. Parts of the border with Borno were probably mutually agreed upon by the two states.[28] Sokoto's southern and southeastern boundaries were more fluid, however, and the *ribat*s were sparse and not always ruled by close relatives of the caliph but were marked by existing frontier towns rather than state-established posts.

Buganda was one of the most centralized states in precolonial Africa, but it emerged into a competitive international environment, surrounded by other states, especially the previous regional power, Bunyoro, but also Ankole and Busogu.[29] Buganda's boundaries were clearly marked: "The Ganda state had, as it were, sharp edges: one was either in it or outside it."[30] Especially clear was the border with Bunyoro, which was ritually maintained: "Human and animal victims, called *byonzire*, were taken across the border to Bunyoro and Busoga and sacrificed, both to rid Buganda of dangerous diseases and to 'cleanse' Buganda's armies when they returned from military expeditions."[31]

In North Africa, the borders among Morocco, Algeria, and Tunisia were "gradually drawn" over the eighteenth and nineteenth centuries through repeated interactions, while borders to the south faded gradually into the Sahara. Morocco's control over the Rif Valley and Libya's control over the Fezzan, for example, were fluctuating and thin.[32]

In Southeast Asia, Siam's borders were fuzzy and characterized by overlapping sovereignty, except for the border with Burma (then the Ava Empire), where the boundary line was drawn by the path of an oxen through the jungles and hills. Although this line was not precisely demarcated and monitored, it represents an attempt to establish clearer boundaries between two polities.[33]

In sum, there is a relationship between systems of decentralized states and the frontierlike boundaries between them. Linear borders were most common in East Asia, Europe, and the Americas. They were less common in other regions of the world, as shown by our particular attention on West

SYSTEMS OF DECENTRALIZED STATES

Africa, Southeast Asia, and South Asia. As noted, there are plenty of exceptions. Decentralized states sometimes formed more precisely demarcated and enforced borders, and centralized states such as China possessed fuzzy boundaries on their western frontier. Nevertheless, frontiers and fuzzy borders are more common with decentralized states.

Borders were fuzzy because rulers had different leverage and bargaining power over different vassals and formed different agreements with them about how the area would be governed. Stronger vassals usually had more autonomy, and because the state's ability to send and sustain soldiers and administration deteriorated with geographical distance (on average), so did their bargaining power. More outlying vassals had more autonomy as a result. Vassals close to the capital were clearly "in" the state. But what about vassals that maintained their own military forces, chose their own successors, levied their own taxes, and made their own laws? To what extent could a vassal be under the sovereignty of another if only a handful of agents from the center were resident? Were they administrators, governors, or just ambassadors? Were these vassals "inside" or "outside" the state? And what about provinces even farther out, which might do all of the things listed as well as make war with other states freely and have their own vassals, even if they acknowledged that the center was the source of all sovereignty? Gonja or Dagomba existed in such a position vis-à-vis the Ashanti Empire (in modern Ghana); Zinder was in this position vis-à-vis Borno (in Niger and Nigeria today), and the Rajput states were so vis-à-vis the Maratha Empire in India. As rulers gradually lost sovereignty with distance and vassals gradually gained sovereignty, there was rarely a one-dimensional line that someone could step over and transition from the territory of one state to the territory of another (although these lines did sometimes exist).

Borders were even fuzzier because a vassal's de facto sovereignty might change as the center's inability to monitor and compel its outlying vassals shifted with its political fortunes. Ivor Wilks points out that one reason for the indeterminacy of the borders of greater Asante was the frequency with which peripheral villages could change to the "protection" of other rulers.[34] And the meaning of suzerainty, vassalage, and sovereignty was contested at the margins. A tributary relationship might be important to some vassals but require little more than gifts from the nominal subordinate. Where these forms of fading, decentralized governance prevailed, drawing a geographic line to separate states was arbitrary and more a matter of how one defined the state rather than the group's realities. Rather than states as billiard balls or state systems as chessboards, metaphors such as the light from a candle, solar systems, galaxies, and bull's-eyes describe states across most of our systems. These metaphors capture wider transitions between sovereignty than one-dimensional lines permit.

To be clear, lacking an inside/outside boundary does not mean that the polities we examined were not states, nor does it mean that our definition of the state and identification strategy for states are invalid. Making such a concession would be the equivalent of saying that Dahomey was not a state because its northern borders with the Mahi were fuzzy or that Asante was not a state because it was difficult to tell if Dagomba and Gonja were independent tributaries or more tightly controlled vassals. Some regions were clearly inside the state, and some regions were clearly outside it. Whereas the zone that separates Norway from Sweden today is very thin (a line), the zone that separated the Asante Empire from its neighbors was wider.

Finally, we think that decentralized governance and fuzzy borders are not only related but also driven by severe limits on the ability to project power because of low interaction capacity. Low interaction capacity in the systems we have studied meant that the ability to chart borders, to monitor outlying vassals, and to interact with other states and create shared and mutually agreed upon borders was limited. Fading sovereignties combined with limits on monitoring produced fuzzy borders.

Heteronomy

We have found that systems of decentralized states are more likely to produce patterns of heteronomy. To a large extent, this outcome goes hand in hand with the scarcity of linear borders and frequency of frontiers. Elsewhere, we define heteronomy as a relationship in which a polity (or actor) is subordinate to at least two polities (or actors) that are not themselves engaged in a nested, hierarchical relationship.[35] In a sense, one actor (or state) has two masters.

Figure 9.2 illustrates a scenario with three political units: a, b, and z. Whereas both a and b are independent (bull's-eye) states that display the same patterns of decentralized rule discussed earlier, polity z is a vassal of both. Here, a and b were not engaged in a hierarchical relationship. This kind of crosscutting authority is heteronomy.[36]

SYSTEMS OF DECENTRALIZED STATES

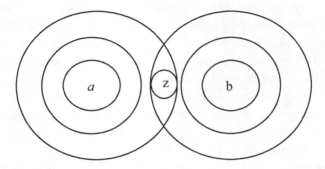

FIGURE 9.2. Heteronomy.

The case studies revealed substantial evidence of heteronomy. The West African system has been described as a "vast pointillist landscape" of scattered independent states, where the authority of the ruler tended to dissipate as a function of distance from the center and then to intersect with the orbits of other states.[37] Kenneth Little wrote in 1967 that it was "possible for a given people to pay homage to more than one high chief at the same time."[38] Smaller vassal units on the intersecting obits of two larger states, such as Sokoto and Katsina, often paid tribute to both.[39] Bagirmi was a state nestled between the Kanem-Bornu Empire and Wadai. Catherine Coquery-Vidrovitch and Mary Baker write that "[around 1886], Bagirmi was a sultanate in full decline, sometimes under Wadai control, sometimes under Bornu control and sometimes even paying tribute [mainly in slaves] to both."[40] Meanwhile, trading towns in eastern Gonja were subject to both the Asante Empire and the Gonja Kingdom.[41] Although perhaps less common, we found similar patterns in the South Asian system, where two greater powers such as the Marathas and the Nizam would claim the same smaller unit, such as Khandesh, as a vassal.[42] Finally, heteronomy was common in Southeast Asia. Here, the image of the two-headed bird captured the political relationship of a political unit oriented toward two heads of power.[43]

Heteronomy arises because of the uncertainty regarding political control on the outer and intersecting rings of two or more bull's-eye states. Local groups on the edge of these dissipating orbits of power often find themselves in a tug-of-war between two states, and they can exploit the distance to create a form of dual sovereignty. This form of heteronomy is often characterized by vague relations of vassalage or suzerainty and obligations for resource transfers that do not clearly define the sovereign functions over which the dominant states claim authority. Figure 9.2 illustrates the sort of two-headed bird that straddles the outer orbits of control between the larger polities *a* and *b*. This is a crosscutting form of heteronomy, one that is informally derived because *a* and *b* have not agreed on the terms with respect to *z*.[44]

This form of heteronomy exists where boundaries are vague and disputed. It existed historically in regions and systems that emphasized centers of power more than the boundaries between states. These regions were characterized by frontiers instead of by sovereign borders as we know them today, especially when there existed wilderness into which dissatisfied populations could retire.[45] This was a common pattern from the desert frontier of the northern Sahara to the hill tracts of Southeast Asia.[46] It quite often occurred on the edge of empire.[47] Notably, we did not find evidence for this form of heteronomy in the East Asian system, except on the outer edges, in particular the western frontiers of both China and Vietnam. Meanwhile, the borders between the core East Asian states were clearer and more linearized. Instead of frontiers, there were borders.

Let us pause to summarize several observations. Heteronomous relationships blur the lines between states. Heteronomy tended to occur in low-density systems where open land existed; where frontiers were common, perhaps more than linear borders; and where states faced challenges in power projection. We found ample evidence of this in our case studies. From this evidence, we conjecture that this form of heteronomy was common historically. However, its frequency appears to have waned as interaction capacity increased. We did not find evidence for it in the core of the East Asian system, the case that most resembles the modern international system.

DECENTRALIZED RULE AND INTERNATIONAL CHANGE

Political science and international relations are replete with models of how centralized states behave that help explain war, economic development, and democratization, to name a few social phenomena.[48] Yet all these models are premised on the notion of a centralized state—that is, a state led by a ruler who can implement decisions over the full gamut of policy decisions across their territory. However, for most rulers in this book and, we wager, throughout history, this assumption does not hold. The reality was messier, far more like *Game of Thrones* than *The West Wing*. Low levels of interaction capacity hindered rulers' ability to extend their political reach. In small states, doing so was not as much of a problem. But once rulers aimed to expand their rule, the problem arose. It strikes us that most theories of the rise of centralized states are not theoretically embedded in a model of decentralized rule or at least a model that captures a dynamic of strategic bargaining between rulers and vassals. One exception is Spruyt's theory, which argues that the microfoundations and mechanisms of the bellicist theory of state formation need to factor in the winners and losers of centralization projects.[49] Given the findings in this book, we can contribute to this literature by outlining the causes and consequences of decentralized rule and developing a theory of international change.

Here is a summary of the theory. Decentralized forms of rule emerge because states can conquer farther than they can rule. Although there are limits to how far a typical ruler can raid and conquer, such limits usually extend beyond the range of what they can rule directly. We have already outlined the general reasons for this problem but let us identify three specific mechanisms here: (1) information problems because the quality of information degrades as a function of distance from the capital;[50] (2) principal–agent problems because it is difficult to ensure that the vassal does what the ruler expects them to do;[51] and (3) weak credible commitments because distant vassals can renege on deals and defect to other rulers, and rulers cannot commit to not exploiting vassals further if they remove their autonomy. Taken together, this means that conquered territories, kingdoms, lords, and elites (i.e., vassals) have bargaining power and exit options. The centrifugal pressures of the resulting system yield patterns of radial rule, fuzzy frontiers, and heteronomy—that is, bull's-eye state systems. We contend that increased interaction capacity can help states and systems to centralize their rule and transition into systems of billiard balls, thus changing the system.

We specify three mechanisms for why rulers struggle to centralize their rule. The first is information asymmetry.[52] Vassals have more information about their populations and territories than rulers do. They know more about local production and who can be taxed, more about local power dynamics and how to keep order, more about local geography and how to fight on their territories, and more about their own military strength and mobilization capabilities. Conversely, it is typically harder and more expensive for the ruler to gather this information. Information asymmetries matter because they make rulers more dependent on their vassals.[53] Rulers need their vassal's local expertise, and, in exchange, vassals demand to keep their autonomy (and try to enhance it). These information asymmetries also mean that vassals can get away with misinforming rulers about population and taxes and can hide information about their local strength and intentions. Information asymmetries keep rulers in a weak bargaining position vis-à-vis their vassals. All else equal, information asymmetries are greater in low interaction-capacity settings because of the slow speed of information over distance.

Because it is hard for rulers to learn about their vassals, decentralized governance is characterized by principal–agent problems (the second mechanism). The crux of this idea is that rulers (principals) can demand that their agents (vassals) do something (i.e., collect a certain amount of tax or raise a certain number of troops), but vassals may or may not follow through on their promises. If it is expensive for the principal to monitor and enforce compliance with the agent, these principal–agent problems are severe. Decentralized states are characterized by weak enforcement mechanisms between the center and the periphery. From the rulers' perspective, these principal–agent problems are the cause of lost tax through corruption, uncertainty over their vassals' intentions and behaviors, and the ever-present threat of rebellion. Centralization projects were often motivated by a desire to reduce the number of resources lost to local corruption and the risk of vassals defecting. Vassals are strong in decentralized states because of these information asymmetries and principle–agent problems. Once again, the lower the level of interaction capacity, the greater the principle–agent problem, all else equal.

Monitoring and information problems can help explain why tributary relations were so common across the case studies. Demanding tributes, however irregularly paid, was one way of extracting resources in distant territories where monitoring costs were low. Tributaries might also have benefited from these arrangements if they could tap into symbols of legitimacy that shored up their rule vis-à-vis their own vassals who were hard to monitor and control or could buy "protection" from a threatening rival. Investiture relations—often combined with tributary systems—may have their roots in decentralized rule and the information problems it entails.[54]

The third mechanism is the commitment problem. We have discussed how rulers in many low-capacity systems could not commit to centralizing their rule because it was too risky and expensive, but there is a deeper commitment problem that makes centralizing bargains hard to strike between rulers and vassals. The core of this problem is that even if rulers have the resources to remove some of their vassals' autonomy, and even if the vassals might be better off in the short term by accepting a loss of autonomy, rulers cannot commit to *not* exploiting their new, weaker vassals in the future. Vassals are strong today because of their autonomy. Autonomy is the source of the vassals' bargaining power. Vassals derive power from keeping their own militias, creaming off their own taxes, and keeping rulers in the dark about the goings-on in their territories. Centralization involves the loss of that autonomy. If rulers take some autonomy from their vassals today, they cannot credibly promise not to take more tomorrow or in a year's time when the vassals are weakened in relation to the ruler. Centralization is a slippery slope.

In most decentralized states, rulers cannot commit to centralizing reforms because the costs are too high. But if things change and rulers have incentives to centralize, to reduce the autonomy of their vassals, those vassals are likely to fight hard to avoid any loss of their autonomy, however incremental that loss might be. Even small losses of autonomy can cascade into great losses of autonomy in the future. If vassals know this, then they should be highly sensitive to centralizing moves by rulers and have strong incentives to fight hard early on to avoid them. These commitment problems make centralizing bargains difficult to reach.

These three mechanisms create an exit problem wherein outlying vassals in decentralized states can switch allegiance to another ruler, become independent, or simply migrate away from the territory. Exit increases the bargaining power of vassals by providing them with alternative offers.[55] Just like having a job offer from another employer might make your current employer offer a higher salary, the threat that a vassal will defect to another state increases the vassal's bargaining power. Across our case studies, exit was a crucial component of centralized versus decentralized rule. Historians, anthropologists, and area specialists write that defecting vassals were common in West Africa, Southeast Asia, and South Asia and that the threat of defection is a key explanation for why states were decentralized. For example, M. C. Ricklefs discusses how the partition of Java into two states and three major polities in the mid-seventeenth century limited the extent to which rulers could centralize because their vassals might exit to a rival polity.[56] We saw how winning wars in South Asia was as much a game of attracting vassals as of winning battles. And simply moving the kingdom was a viable option in parts of West Africa. Conversely, centralization projects were more successful where exit was more difficult, as in nineteenth-century Vietnam and Japan.

Other researchers have noted the importance of exit to decentralized rule, but it helps us explain why factors such as war might have differential effects on centralization, contrary to the standard assumption.[57] Where exit is easy, wars increase the market of credible suzerains, like getting multiple job offers. Here rulers have to offer more to keep their vassals onside, and one of their main currencies is autonomy. When exit is hard (or less credible), rulers must give away less to keep their vassals onside, and when vassals would be better off staying with the ruler than defecting to another vassal (like getting a bad job offer), this can be an opportunity to offer vassals less (i.e., take away their autonomy). War seems to have had centrifugal effects where exit was easier (West Africa and Southeast Asia) and more centripetal effects where it was hard (Japan being the paradigmatic example).

These dynamics of decentralized governance produce several system-level characteristics that are commonly found in bull's-eye systems but not in billiard ball state systems, all of which were discussed earlier in the chapter. First, rulers tended to rule in radial patterns that reflected their political reach—for example, mandalas, bull's-eyes, solar polities. Second, the regions between states took on fuzzy frontierlike characteristics instead of linear borders. Third, instances of heteronomy often arose on the interstices between bull's-eye states. These are common features of decentralized states and the systems they compose. Although their occurrence may be explained in given locales by referencing local norms and ideology—for example, the mandala system—their occurrence is nevertheless common.

It is difficult to overcome these basic obstacles to the projection of rule and thus transition from a bull's-eye to a billiard ball. The bellicist position regarding war and state making does not hold for much of the non-Western world.[58] A key reason for this is that war or the threat of war does not produce centralized states in low-capacity regions, which most historical systems typically were. In high-capacity scenarios, the specter of war can enable a ruler to outmaneuver or marginalize vassals and shore up power in the center. But this is harder to do in low-capacity systems where outlying vassals are highly autonomous, boundaries are fuzzy, and heteronomy exists. Here, a vassal can easily switch sides or join a different power when a given ruler is offering protection in exchange for continued indirect rule. Warfare in low-capacity settings essentially creates fragmentary pressures among states, placing outlying vassals in what amounts to an iterated auction in which rulers try to offer the best terms. It is only when the system becomes sufficiently centralized that the bellicist centralizing mechanisms may kick in.

In a similar way, increasing trade levels will not on their own help forge centralized states. In the case studies, we found that although commerce does incentivize rulers to establish revenue-taking institutions, it does not promote centralization because vassals can create these same institutions and reap the benefits while maintaining high levels of autonomy. Meanwhile, the central state will struggle to take control of these institutions as long as the challenges of projecting rule still hold. To centralize rule effectively, rulers need to mitigate the principle–agent problem and the problems related to poor information and credible commitments. Increased war and trade do not on their own help rulers in these regards. In fact, they can just as easily exacerbate these problems.

Increased interaction capacity is one common way to overcome these obstacles. Low levels of interaction capacity are a key reason why information asymmetries are severe. Increasing the speed of transit over distance increases the speed of information flow and makes it easier for rulers to monitor vassals, which reduces the principle–agent problem. Likewise, the threat of exit is reduced because, all else equal, if it is easier for rulers to reach their vassals with governors and bureaucrats, then it is harder for those vassals to defect because the threat of punishment is higher. If decentralized rule is an equilibrium outcome in low-capacity settings, then increased interaction capacity can shift the equilibrium in the direction of the billiard ball state.

To illustrate, imagine a premodern ruler who attempts to govern her vast realm by relying on communications that do not exceed the speed and carrying capacity of human labor and draft animals. At some radial distance, she would have to rule indirectly. Now imagine that she and her agents were given cell phones and the ability to teleport instantaneously.

These capabilities would result in the annihilation of distance, and she could now speak with any individual across her land and send troops instantly to even the most distant outpost. The results of that radically increased interaction capacity would be (1) a dramatic improvement in the quality of information; (2) a reduction in the principle–agent problem because agents (vassals) can be much more closely monitored and disciplined; and (3) an enhanced ability both to credibly commit to distant rule and to demand credible commitments from vassals. Of course, this example is exaggerated, but the point holds: increases in interaction capacity will, all else equal, help rulers to overcome these basic obstacles to rule.

To be sure, interaction capacity is not the only factor that matters for centralization. Norms, institutions, and cultural identities can make exit harder by connecting the fates of ruler and vassal.[59] Admittedly, this is a broad category that requires more research. If, for example, an outlying vassal comes to identify culturally and ethnically with the ruler far more than with any other proximate rules, then the vassal is less likely to defect. This is one of the reasons why rulers would grant distant fiefdoms to their kin and eventually create a Gellnerian setting wherein lords could more easily identify and communicate with their monarch than with their own subjects.[60] Such bonds are even stronger once national consciousness develops and connects the provinces to the center. Increased competition and outside threats should have a stronger centralizing effect when exit is harder. One of the lessons from the East Asian chapter is that the Chinese model of the state generated norms and institutions of rule that reduced the problem of distance. Relative to the other three systems, East Asia was a high interaction-capacity region. But that alone cannot explain the remarkably centralized state institutions as well as the patterns of order between the states. Credit must also be given to the Confucian bureaucratic mode of governance that not only helped China to centralize its rule over a vast territory but also inspired neighboring states to emulate the same policies and institutions.

The collective effect of each ruler centralizing power is the transformation of the system. Radial rule is flattened as rule moves from indirect to direct, borders become formalized and linear, frontiers fade, and heteronomy ends. In a sense, the system is rationalized as it transitions from a system of bull's-eye states to a system of billiard balls. In Robert Gilpin's terminology, there would be a "systems change," a change in the nature of the actors and the character of the system.[61] Our theory explains the same systems change that Spruyt writes about in his work on the rise of the sovereign state system in Europe,[62] but it emphasizes a different dynamic: the projection of power over distance. Rather than war and trade, it stresses the causal importance of interaction capacity. Finally, it provides a modular explanation that can be applied across diverse state systems and is not tied to a particular cultural setting.

CONCLUSION

Decentralized states were common historically. Although rulers knew the benefits of centralization, they struggled to project power over distance and overcome the information, principle–agent, and credible-commitment problems with vassals that could threaten exit. The macro-consequence was systems of decentralized states characterized by radial patterns of rule, frontiers instead of borders, and heteronomy. Any transition from decentralized to centralized rule and the corresponding transition from bull's-eye systems to billiard ball systems were not, on their own, the result of increased war or trade. The transition out of the decentralized equilibrium required an increase in interaction capacity or an infusion of norms and institutions to bring rulers closer to their vassals or both.

CONCLUSION

We began this book by declaring that international relations has a problem. It is a field that mines the historical experience to identify general and even timeless patterns across a range of topic areas such as how states fight and how they are formed. But for the most part IR has focused on only one case: the contemporary international system that developed from the nineteenth-century European state system. By excluding other historical systems, in particular those that were contemporaneous with nineteenth-century Europe, it has raised the issue of external validity because what happened elsewhere may be different from what happened in Europe. Indeed, before conducting this research, we were not even sure what "elsewhere" consisted of. Was the rest of the world stateless? If not, how many states were there, and what was their fate? How did the structures of those states vary? Did the systems they compose share common features?

Our answers to these questions were organized around three contributions. First, we built a comprehensive register of all independent states since 1816, detailed the regional patterns in state birth and state death, and documented the large number of states that were extinguished by European colonialism. Second, we developed a theoretical framework for comparing state systems and applied it to four regions during the nineteenth century: East Asia, South Asia, maritime Southeast Asia, and West Africa. Third, we examined the effects that war, trade, and interaction capacity had on state structure. In this chapter, we summarize what we have learned. Along the way we discuss broader questions: Can we understand diverse and disconnected state systems with a unified framework? Or, put another way, does our study of nineteenth-century systems point to new theoretical insights that can help us understand big issues, such as the rise of the centralized state and the transition to the modern international system? Our response is yes, and although our stance might be controversial, we think important differences across state systems and changes within them can be understood with a framework that highlights the logics and dilemmas of ruling over space. In the final section, we reflect on how our comparative, data-driven approach can contribute to other important questions in the field, with an illustration using the decline-of-war debate.

IDENTIFYING STATES AND COMPARING STATE SYSTEMS

We set out to provide tools to help identify states and state systems in a way that highlights the most important similarities and differences across them. States are the bedrock of this framework. How they share sovereignty above and below themselves—with vassals and with other states and institutions—are two key contours of state systems. These choices determine the extent to which units in the system are centralized and the extent to which their relations with each other are regulated and ordered by institutions and orders above the state. As others have argued, we think of state systems as networks where sovereignty-controlling polities are the nodes.[1] The ties these polities form with other polities to make states, hierarchies, institutions, and orders create the texture of state systems.

Importantly, statehood is untied from any cultural moment, so we can identify statelike entities across state systems that might not even have been aware of each other or were characterized by different beliefs about how politics should be ordered and structured. If we can consistently identify the foundational political units of systems, then we can work up to understand their similarities and differences in a systematic way. The alternative, we think, has been to begin with a typology of qualitatively different state (or substate) forms that often lack demarcation points or are embedded in larger normative debates. Simply looking for empires, city-states, and national states, for example, creates problems because scholars might disagree on what an empire or a modern state is. We start with a

CONCLUSION

thin and inclusive definition of the state and treat the features that separate empires from modern states as variables rather than as the constitutive features of the state (or empire or city-state) itself.[2]

One of the core contributions of the book is using our definition of the state to create a true global register of states in the nineteenth century. The backbone of that endeavor was the International System(s) Dataset, the core topic in chapter 2.[3] We discovered that the world was thickly populated with states during this time. There were 230 states in 1816, a high that has not been reached since. As figure 1.1 illustrates, our data-collection efforts reveal a striking concave trend in the number of states over the past two hundred years. That pattern is invisible in more Eurocentric state member lists such as the one produced by the Correlates of War project. What is also invisible in those lists is the mass state-extinction event that occurred with the colonial global enclosure by the end of the nineteenth century. We show that a total of 270 states expired during the 1816–1920 period, with the bulk of the state deaths occurring in the late 1800s. The great majority of these states were not reborn during the decolonization era. Simply naming these dead states was part of our project.

Let us pause here and respond to possible objections. Perhaps we are not using a culturally neutral definition of the state divorced from the beliefs of a specific historical locale. Perhaps what we have done instead is take a fundamentally European concept—the state—with roots in European political practice and thought, strip it of the most obviously Eurocentric and modern features, and then look back into history. Furthermore, at the heart of our definition of statehood is the notion of an inside-outside distinction that reeks of Westphalian sovereignty.[4] According to this assessment, rather than letting political forms emerge inductively with sensitivity to shared beliefs, understandings, and discourses about those political forms,[5] we see only the most European-like forms of organization or, worse, see nonstate forms of organization as states. Such a critique thus might conclude that our framework is still fundamentally Eurocentric.

We do not think this objection is valid, at least not in a way that is fatal to the project. The objection is true in the trivial sense that, as we discussed in chapter 2, no concept starts from a cultural null. But if we are using a Eurocentric view of the state that is not fit to illuminate non-Western systems (or that illuminates the wrong or least interesting parts), then it is odd that we find so many entities that fit the definition and odd

CONCLUSION

that we find historians emphasizing the same basic political structures and dilemmas that rulers faced. Rulers in Mysore were concerned with local elites shirking on their tribute payments in almost the same way as the *alafin* of Oyo or the king of Dahomey were concerned, even though these two regions were quite disconnected from each other in the early nineteenth century. In a very similar way to the peshwa at Pune, the caliph of Sokoto aimed to deter his subordinate emirates from defecting to rival kingdoms and to secure his frontier. Rulers seemed concerned with similar problems across diverse cultural contexts, which led them to come up with similar institutional solutions. To some, our concept of external-relations-controlling states will be too radical to accept, while others may well wonder why we have spent so long belaboring the point.

A related criticism might be that our focus on states has produced a distorted view of state systems. We might start from the ground up, but if the ground is wrong, our conclusions will also be wrong (or, at least, less important than we suggest). Perhaps state systems were composed of more mobile units or networks of authority relations that were horizontal, not hierarchical, or complicated crosscutting forms of sovereignty that left states as bit players in larger regional dynamics. Indeed, the existing literature might very well give this impression.[6] However, we think our approach has an advantage. By applying the same concept of the state to different regions and being sensitive to forms that escape our framework, we can provide initial answers to such questions. As we set about our research, a possible outcome was that states were not important or common actors in non-Western international systems. This is not what we found, however, at least for the nineteenth century. Historians and anthropologists speak of states as the most important actors (and often call them states) in places such as Africa and South Asia.[7] These systems were not fully enclosed by states, but we think we have established strong empirical grounds to claim that states were important, if not the most important, political actors in the non-Western state systems of the nineteenth century. We remain open to the idea that in systems composed of highly decentralized states, substate actors—provincial lords, military governors, vassal kingdoms, and village-level chiefs and councils—are equally important actors. In addition, perhaps the institution of statehood had already diffused globally by the nineteenth century, and if we were to look farther back in time, we would see that states were less important. We cannot answer that question, but

CONCLUSION

our framework can help. If in the future a new study finds that states were not an important unit of state systems in the fourteenth or eighteenth centuries but donned this mantle in the nineteenth, that would be a fascinating discovery.

Finally, we defend the project on empirical grounds. The starting point was to get beyond the West—to address a problem of Eurocentrism at the heart of IR. This project takes an important step in this direction. IR's *global* maps were blank but are now filled with hundreds of independent states. At least in this sense, our definition of the state is useful.

With states as the core unit, we then looked to the features of systems that they formed. How did states structure relations with subordinates and other states? After developing our core concepts of the state and state system, we then identified a set of additional variables: centralization, sovereign integration, and interaction capacity. We outlined two models of state systems: a centralized billiard ball model and a decentralized bull's-eye model.

In chapters 4–7, we applied this framework to four non-Western systems during the nineteenth century: East Asia, South Asia, maritime Southeast Asia, and West Africa. We began with East Asia both because it was the most familiar to the average reader and because it possessed the highest level of interaction capacity; we finished with West Africa because it was the lowest-capacity system. In East Asia, we found a small number of centralized states (billiard balls) embedded in a relatively developed international order. Crucially, East Asia was unlike the other three regions and is probably unrepresentative of other premodern state systems. This is an important point given that much of the current move in IR to get beyond the West is focused on East Asia. In contrast, the other three systems approximate the bull's-eye states that we theorized in chapter 3. To be sure, there was variation within and among all four systems, but the identified patterns held broadly.

Our final contribution was to test several theories for why states were or were not able to centralize their rule. What were our findings? First, there were many similarities in governance across systems in the nineteenth century, despite differences in culture, religion, geography, and history. Systems were more like bull's-eyes than billiard balls, with the exception of East Asia. Many rulers governed by allowing their vassals autonomy to collect their own taxes, maintain their own armies, and arbitrate their own disputes so long as they paid tributes and refrained from consorting with other powers. The autonomy that vassals held typically varied with distance from the center because the extension of state power was expensive and risky. The mandala in Southeast Asia could just as easily describe the bull's-eye or radial state in West Africa. These similarities even extend to tributary networks and hierarchies beyond the boundaries of states, most developed and institutionalized in East Asia but clearly present in South Asia, Southeast Asia, and West Africa. Even the legacies of old empires were similar, providing a grammar to order relations between states and providing legitimacy to administratively weak rulers. This finding is important because it hints at the idea that rulers across diverse and mostly disconnected regions faced similar dilemmas of governance and came up with broadly similar solutions.

Second, low levels of interaction capacity created strong incentives to rule in decentralized ways. There are two key pieces of evidence for this proposition. For one thing, the similarities in methods of rule point to factors that are reasonably constant across the cases, and we suggest that rather than variations in the cultural content of international orders or available administrative models, limited interaction capacity helps explain the predominance of bull's-eyes states. For another, historians across the case studies note how geography, population densities, and poor communications created incentives to rule through autonomous vassals. Decentralized rule was held in place by powerful self-reinforcing mechanisms that made centralization projects risky and expensive when rulers depended on their vassals for economic and military resources. Vassals jealously guarded this autonomy and would often fight to keep it. This "decentralization trap" was also reinforced by severe commitment problems. Rulers proposing to remove some autonomy from vassals could not commit to not taking more autonomy in the future because the source of a vassal's bargaining power was their autonomy. Low interaction capacity exacerbated all these problems by making it hard for rulers to monitor their vassals and ensure that they paid the right tribute or did not build up their own local power to challenge the center (the information and principal–agent problems).

Third, decentralized rule helps us to account for other system-level features. Fuzzy borders, heteronomy, and the widespread presence of

CONCLUSION

interstate hierarchies and tributary systems can be explained by focusing on decentralized rule. Although there has been a tendency to see these features as anomalous, unique, disconnected features of state systems, we suggest that they for the most part arose from a common source. Fuzzy borders arose because vassals tended to acquire more autonomy with distance from the ruler's capital. Some forms of heteronomy arose when two decentralized states overlapped. Tributary systems were an efficient form of resources extraction for rulers who could conquer farther than they could administer and where the rulers of weak, decentralized states were looking for sources of legitimacy to bolster their rule. Investiture was so common because it benefited stronger powers who wanted influence over their vassals and weaker powers facing jealous and powerful vassals at home.

Fourth, war and trade had variable effects on whether systems were billiard balls or bull's-eyes. Once we stepped outside of East Asia, war and trade tended to reinforce centrifugal forces, fragmenting and decentralizing states. The logic is simple. In most cases, war and trade empowered vassals vis-à-vis their rulers, not the other way around. This was especially the case in low-capacity systems where rulers lacked the ability to monopolize trade and depended heavily on autonomous vassals to fight wars. War may have contributed to state centralization in Europe, East Asia, and parts of mainland Southeast Asia, but it had few—and even contrary—effects in the other regions in our study. We conjecture that war might trigger centralization only after long-term processes that tie the fates of rulers and vassals, reducing the credibility of vassals' threat to defect to another ruler.

Finally, these four findings lead us to conclude that to better understand international change we need to understand the logic of decentralized rule. What were the key dilemmas that rulers and vassals faced, what were their options, and what were the forces that held decentralized states together? We suggest that principal–agent problems, information problems, and commitment problems shaped the preferences of rulers and vassals for decentralized rule in dynamic, interpolity bargaining environments. Such models of decentralized rule can help us understand the conditions under which the dilemmas of decentralized rule were eased, the varying impacts of triggers such as trade and war, and ultimately why some systems moved from being bull's-eyes to being billiard balls.

CONCLUSION

REVISITING THE DECLINE-OF-WAR DEBATE

Where do we go from here? Can we make theoretical advances based on our findings? Can we contribute to prominent ongoing debates in the field? We believe that combining the ISD with a framework for comparative analysis opens numerous directions for research. In this final section, we highlight an area of particular interest to us: whether war has declined over time.

We need comprehensive historical data if we want to understand long-term patterns in conflict. Consider the debate on whether war has declined. On one side is a set of scholars who argue that warfare has declined over time for reasons pertaining to technological change, great-power dynamics, and civilizing processes, among others.[8] Other scholars have challenged this claim by finding contrary evidence and by identifying methodological weaknesses in how the decline-in-war studies were conducted.[9] The question animating this debate is tremendously important for IR. However, we cannot rigorously examine conflict patterns before the early twentieth century without sufficient data on wars throughout the world and the states that fought them.

As a brief but related pair of examples, consider two other conflict-related debates that suffer from insufficient data. As we discussed in chapter 4, the Confucian Peace thesis holds that the states of East Asia experienced few interstate wars during the five centuries prior to European colonialism.[10] Scholars explain this peace by stressing the importance of Confucian culture and its antiwar norms, the legitimacy at the heart of the Sinocentric tribute system, the pacifying role of Chinese hegemony, and the shrewd imperial policies of the Qing Dynasty. If the thesis is true, then it would have implications for Chinese global leadership, the merits of hegemonic stability, and the potential benefits of non-Western forms of international order. But without a comprehensive global list of state actors and the wars they fought, how can we mount a rigorous comparison of conflict patterns in East Asia with other regional state systems over time?

Consider the distinction between interstate wars and intrastate wars (i.e., civil wars). Some studies show a decline in interstate war after 1945, while the frequency of intrastate war has held constant or even potentially increased.[11] But we cannot establish a long-term trend that includes the years before 1920 without more complete data. Indeed, some scholars suggest

CONCLUSION

a more variable and complex relationship with respect to the kinds of war across different historical locales. For example, scholarship on the Confucian Peace notes that although war between the core states may have been relatively rare, both intrastate war and states' conflicts with nomadic tribes were quite common.[12] Our research in this book leads us to suspect that intrastate war during the nineteenth century was more common in regional systems composed of decentralized states with low levels of political reach.

There are several reasons why IR currently lacks the necessary data to study these questions and others systematically. First, there is a basic temporal problem insofar as some prominent datasets do not begin early enough. For example, the Uppsala Conflict Data Program is an industry standard, but its data begin in 1946.[13] Similarly, the Armed Conflict Event Dataset begins its coverage even later, in the late 1990s.[14]

Second, there is a "Europe problem" because many of the datasets that do include the nineteenth and early twentieth centuries possess a strong Eurocentric bias. A central data source used is the COW, a foundational project that kick-started data-driven quantitative work in IR some fifty years ago. However, as we know, the COW conflict data are pinned to a list of mostly European states in the nineteenth century and elide several hundred non-European states and the wars they fought. Moreover, as Jason Lyall notes, COW's early-mover status created a conflict-data monoculture because many new corollary datasets are wedded to COW's incomplete list of states.[15] Although these conflict datasets are useful for answering specific questions—for example, on the outcomes of great-power wars—they cannot be used to answer major questions like the ones we asked earlier.

Third, many useful datasets suffer from what we call the "denominator problem." As Bear Braumoeller demonstrates, calculating the rate of conflict over time requires not only a list of the wars (the numerator) but also an accurate list of the states that were potential combatants (the denominator).[16] Recent contributions such as the Historical Conflict Event Dataset go beyond COW but have done so by identifying and cataloging conflicts without a corresponding list of state actors and potential combatants.[17] Or they begin with a set of battles and identify only state actors that fought in them.[18] This conflict-first approach cannot resolve the denominator problem because it will naturally exclude the states that do not fight. Crucially, this approach generally relies on regional histories and war compendia such as Tony Jaques's *Dictionary of Battles and Sieges* (2006), which are much better at recording wars involving European actors. A different approach is to begin with a comprehensive list of states and trace their individual history with respect to conflict. This state-first approach not only solves the denominator problem but also picks up conflicts that are missed in datasets that rely on conflict compendia and are not formed through research on specific states.

In sum, there are many great conflict datasets out there, but none of them overcomes the temporal, the Europe, and the denominator problems. What is needed is not another undiscovered and unmined source—although such sources can be quite useful for specific regions[19]—but rather a different approach. A state-first approach can solve all three problems. It represents a different cut into conflict-data creation, one that can be easily integrated with the others to develop a truly comprehensive list of conflicts over time and space. We believe the ISD provides the ideal foundation for a state-first approach to conflict-data creation.

To illustrate this potential, we can utilize the ISD to probe the decline-of-war thesis. If interstate and intrastate wars can be fought only by states (per most definitions of these concepts in empirical conflict studies), the number of states is the baseline against which we should measure the risk of war. Just as a million COVID-19 infections mean something very different for individual risk in Australia (with 20 million people) and the United States (with more than 350 million people), so one hundred wars in a state system with forty states mean something very different from the same number of wars in a system with three hundred states.

The decline-of-war thesis is usually couched in terms of a declining risk that states experience armed conflict.[20] Most commonly, "armed conflict" in this assertion refers to interstate wars, but there are more general statements of this proposition that apply to all forms of violent conflict.[21] When the decline of war is discussed, it is usually stated in terms of how capitalism or development or norms of peace or increased investment in conflict resolution has reduced the risk of armed conflict between states, not the somewhat less interesting proposition that the number of wars may have declined simply because there are fewer states (which, of course, after the end of World War II, there are not).[22]

We are in a unique position to reassess these claims with a more accurate list of states at risk of fighting wars. We make a simple comparison.

CONCLUSION

What are the patterns in the per state risk of war using the number of COW states as the baseline versus what the patterns are when we use the number of ISD states? We first examine wars in general and then interstate wars in particular. We are careful to note that these data are far from conclusive. We are adding more complete information on statehood to the debate, but we are also adding states that are considerably less well studied than European or Asian states. As such, we are adding states where it is likely that wars are undercounted.

Figure 10.1 shows how trends in the per state-year risk of war change when we adjust for the number of states in the ISD, compared to adjusting for the number of COW states. This is something of an unfair comparison because nonstate wars in the COW data do not need a state as a participant to be recorded, and, therefore, the true underlying set of units for COW wars at risk is all territorial units capable of fighting conflicts. However, most wars do require at least one state entity to be recorded (interstate, intrastate, and extrastate), making the number of states in the system a reasonable baseline to compare war risk. In addition, we have excluded nonstate wars from this comparison. We also emphasize that without knowing how many units there are at risk of experiencing armed conflict (there are no data on the nonstate units at risk of war in the COW list),[23] it is not even possible to estimate per state war risk and whether it is changing over time for wars in general. We take a first step in this direction.

The dashed line shows the total number of state-war years divided by the number of COW states in the international system. The war-participation rate declines from a peak over 1 in 1821, implying that on average each state was participating in slightly more than one war, to a low of 0.067 wars per state in 1959 (similar to the end of the time series in 2007, with 0.073 wars per state). However, the trend is flatter and the decline of war less clear when the more inclusive ISD definition of statehood is used, as shown in the solid line. The peak is now around World War I, a period that combined a relatively low number of states (fifty-eight in ISD, forty-five in COW) with high war participation. The recent low point in total war risk in 2007 is similar to the estimated war-participation rate in 1823 or 1827. One possible conclusion is straightforward—the empirical observation that wars are declining reflects the dramatic decline in the number of states with the coming of colonialism, *not* necessarily a declining per state risk of war. The

CONCLUSION

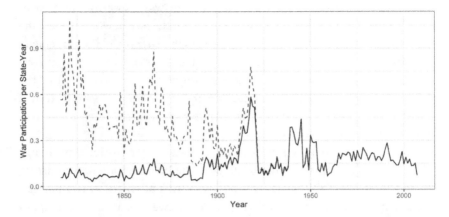

FIGURE 10.1. War participation per state-year per COW and ISD data, 1816–2007. *Note*: The dashed line shows the total number of state-war years divided by the number of COW states in the international system. The solid line shows the total number of state-war years divided by the number of ISD states in the international system. *Source*: COW data sourced from Correlates of War Project, "State System Membership List, v2016."

simplest conclusion is that there were many states between 1816 and around 1860 and consequently many wars. Overall, this simple analysis using more comprehensive data suggests that war has not declined.

Of course, our conclusions about the risk of any state participating in a war changes depending on who we count as members of state systems. Likewise, the notion that some regions of the world were historically more peaceful, such as East Asia, can be tested only with comprehensive data of states and the wars they fought. Whether there is a transhistorical trend in the ratio of intrastate-to-interstate wars requires data to make that judgment. These large questions and others in IR can be answered by following the course we have charted.

NOTES

1. BILLIARD BALLS AND BULL'S-EYES

1. Waltz, *Theory of International Politics*.
2. Tilly, *Coercion, Capital, and European States*.
3. Gilpin, *War and Change in World Politics*, 43.
4. Herbst, *States and Power in Africa*; Phillips, *War, Religion, and Empire*; Ringmar, "Performing International Systems"; Reus-Smit, "Cultural Diversity and International Order"; Zarakol, "A Non-Eurocentric Approach to Sovereignty," 509; Spruyt, *The World Imagined*.
5. To name a few, see Herbst, *States and Power in Africa*; Centeno, *War and the Nation-State in Latin America*; Hui, *War and State Formation in Ancient China and Early Modern Europe*; Kang, *East Asia Before the West*; Phillips, *War, Religion, and Empire*; Ringmar, "Performing International Systems"; Besley and Reynal-Querol, "The Legacy of Historical Conflict"; Suzuki, Zhang, and Quirk, eds., *International Orders in the Early Modern World*; Butcher and Griffiths, "Alternative International Systems?"; Phillips and Sharman, *International Order in Diversity*; Kwan, "Hierarchy, Status, and International Society"; Pella, *Africa and the Expansion of International Society*; Dunne and Reus-Smit, eds., *The Globalization of International Society*; Reus-Smit and Dunne, "The Globalization of International Society"; Phillips and Reus-Smit, *Culture and Order in World Politics*; Zarakol, *Before the West*.
6. Acharya, "Global International Relations (IR) and Regional Worlds," 647–49.
7. Griffiths, *Secession and the Sovereignty Game*.
8. Correlates of War Project, "State System Membership List, v2016."
9. We also do not mean there is no work in historical IR on these regions, rather that this work is often not explicitly comparative in its approach.

1. BILLIARD BALLS AND BULL'S-EYES

10. McNeill, *The Rise of the West*, 726–28.
11. Butcher and Griffiths, "States and Their International Relations Since 1816."
12. Phillips, *War, Religion, and Empire*; Suzuki, Zhang, and Quirk, eds., *International Orders in the Early Modern World*; Dunne and Reus-Smit, eds., *The Globalization of International Society*.
13. One would have to look back quite far into human history to find a similarly small number of states.
14. Tilly, *Coercion, Capital, and European States*, 1–2.
15. Phillips, *War, Religion, and Empire*; Spruyt, *The World Imagined*.
16. Tilly, *Coercion, Capital, and European States*, 5.
17. In *International Systems in World History*, this is what Buzan and Little call "structural differentiation" (87).
18. Waltz, *Theory of International Politics*.
19. MacDonald and Camara, "Segou, Slavery, and Sifinso."
20. Acharya, "Global International Relations (IR) and Regional Worlds."
21. We build on a long history of scholarship emphasizing that institutions are the outcome of bargaining processes between rulers and subordinates, especially over revenue. See, for example, North, *Institutions, Institutional Change, and Economic Performance*; Levi, *Of Rule and Revenue*; Acemoglu and Robinson, *Economic Origins of Dictatorship and Democracy*; Bueno de Mesquita et al., *The Logic of Political Survival*; Clark, Golder, and Golder, "The British Academy Brian Barry Prize Essay"; Ahmed and Stasavage, "Origins of Early Democracy"; Garfias and Sellars, "When State Building Backfires." Chapter 3 covers these approaches in more detail.
22. Following Hechter, *Containing Nationalism*, we are using the concepts of direct and indirect rule to describe political rule for not just empires but also states more generally.
23. For a history of the port of Ouidah, see Law, *Ouidah*.
24. Buzan and Little, *International Systems in World History*, 80.
25. Herbst, *States and Power in Africa*; Hechter, *Containing Nationalism*; Cederman and Girardin, "Growing Sovereignty."
26. Tilly, *The Formation of National States in Western Europe*, 42.
27. Spruyt, *The Sovereign State and Its Competitors*.
28. V. Lieberman, *Strange Parallels*, vol. 1: *Integration on the Mainland*; V. Lieberman, *Strange Parallels*, vol. 2: *Mainland Mirrors*.
29. E. Lieberman, "Nested Analysis as a Mixed Methods Strategy for Comparative Research."
30. Butcher and Griffiths, "States and Their International Relations Since 1816."
31. George and Bennet, *Case Studies and Theory Development in the Social Sciences*.
32. Pardesi, "Region, System, and Order"; Pardesi, "Mughal Hegemony and the Emergence of South Asia as a 'Region' for Regional Order-Building."
33. Sharman, "Something New out of Africa"; Herbst, *States and Power in Africa*; Adegbulu, "Pre-colonial West African Diplomacy"; Ejiogu, "State Building in the Niger Basin in the Common Era and Beyond, 1000–Mid 1800s"; Ejiogu, "State Building in Pre-colonial Sub-Saharan Africa"; Pella, *Africa and the Expansion of International Society*.
34. Acharya, *The Making of Southeast Asia*.
35. Sharman, "Something New out of Africa."

2. THE BIRTH AND DEATH OF STATES BEFORE THE LEAGUE OF NATIONS

1. Butcher and Griffiths, "States and Their International Relations Since 1816." For ISD, version 1, see Griffiths and Butcher, "Introducing the International System(s) Dataset (ISD), 1816–2011." Following the example set in version 1, we refer to international system(s) in a way that implies singular/plural ambiguity in the number of systems over time. Most readers will accept that in 2022 there was only one international system. Many will accept that in 1816 there were a number of loosely connected or even disconnected systems. That plurality gradually consolidated into a singularity over the past two hundred years.
2. Tilly, *Coercion, Capital, and European States*, 1.
3. Wittgenstein, *Philosophical Investigations*.
4. Works such as G. Anderson, "Was There Any Such Thing as a Nonmodern State?," and Skinner, "On the Person of the State," argue that the state is a social construct that only emerged in the nineteenth century as a product of a specific confluence of Western ideas.
5. Qin, *A Relational Theory of World Politics*, 3.
6. See Zarakol, *Before the West*, 221, for a discussion on this matter.
7. The logic of political survival is a reference to the work of Bruce Bueno de Mesquita and colleagues, who in *The Logic of Political Survival* assert that we can understand diverse outcomes across modern states by thinking about the central dilemmas of revenue extraction and how they affect and are affected by institutional design. Here, we extend these ideas to historical periods and regions not covered in their work and join a growing number of studies of historical IR starting from the premise that historical rulers were revenue-seeking agents aiming to survive in power, in similar fashion to modern rulers. See Blaydes and Chaney, "The Feudal Revolution and Europe's Rise"; Blaydes and Paik, "The Impact of Holy Land Crusades on State Formation"; and Blaydes and Paik, "Trade and Political Fragmentation on the Silk Roads."
8. Holm, "Conclusion," 514.
9. Simmel, *Sociology*; Erikson, "Formalist and Relationist Theory in Social Network Analysis." In some ways, our conception of the state is what relationists call "a project" (P. Jackson and Nexon, "Relations Before States").
10. See Zarakol, *Before the West*, 10–12, for a similar usage.
11. Poggi, *The Development of the Modern State*, 2–6.
12. Barry Buzan and Richard Little argue in *International Systems in World History* that the internal/external distinction emerged as early as ancient Sumer and was the defining characteristic of actors in systems (163).
13. These distinctions are developed further in Butcher and Griffiths, "States and Their International Relations Since 1816."
14. Watson, *The Evolution of International Society*, 15.
15. Olson, "Dictatorship, Democracy, and Development"; Donnelly, "The Elements of the Structures of International Systems."
16. M. Weber, "Politics as Vocation"; Tilly, *Coercion, Capital, and European States*; Elliott, "A Europe of Composite Monarchies"; Spruyt, *The Sovereign State and Its Competitors*; Agnew, "The Territorial Trap"; Ferguson and Mansbach, *Polities*;

2. THE BIRTH AND DEATH OF STATES BEFORE THE LEAGUE OF NATIONS

Ruggie, *Constructing the World Polity*; R. Jackson, *Sovereignty*; Nexon, *The Struggle for Power in Early Modern Europe*.
17. Nexon, *The Struggle for Power in Early Modern Europe*; Butcher and Griffiths, "Between Eurocentrism and Babel."
18. Farrant, *Tippu Tip and the East African Slave Trade*.
19. This is also an example of heteronomy, which we discuss in chapter 9, because Tippu Tip was subject to two sovereigns, the Belgians and the Sultanate of Zanzibar.
20. Laing, "Tippu Tip in the Late 19th-Century East and Central Africa."
21. Bennett, *Arab Versus European*, 225; Laing, "Tippu Tip in the Late 19th-Century East and Central Africa."
22. Horowitz, "Ba Karim"; Dewière, "The Kanem and Borno Sultanates (11th–19th Centuries)"; Gates, Akyeampong, and Niven, "Rabih, al-Zabayr Fadl Allah."
23. Acharya, *The Making of Southeast Asia*, 61; Spruyt, *The World Imagined*, 288.
24. Kathirithamby-Wells, "Siak and Its Changing Strategies for Survival," 221–22.
25. Schrauwers, "Houses, Hierarchy, Headhunting, and Exchange," 360.
26. Falola and Oguntomisin, *Yoruba Warlords of the Nineteenth Century*, 250; Law, *The Oyo Empire*.
27. Arhin, "The Structure of Greater Ashanti (1700–1824)," 82.
28. Barnett, *North India Between Empires*, 40, 22.
29. V. Lieberman, *Strange Parallels*, vol. 2: *Mainland Mirrors*, 441.
30. Winichakul, *Siam Mapped*.
31. Tilly, *Coercion, Capital, and European States*, 5.
32. Buzan and Little, *International Systems in World History*, 90–97; see also Phillips, "International Systems," 46.
33. Buzan and Little, *International Systems in World History*, 87. Also see Buzan and Albert, "Differentiation"; Donnelly, "The Differentiation of International Societies"; and Donnelly, *Systems, Relations, and the Structures of International Societies*.
34. In earlier developments of our model, we used the terms *structural differentiation* and *functional differentiation* (Butcher and Griffiths, "Between Eurocentrism and Babel"). Centralization is like Michael Mann's idea of infrastructural power, described in "The Autonomous Power of the State."
35. We do utilize the concept of structural differentiation in a slightly different way from Buzan and Little. For them, structural differentiation is conceived as a single measure for an entire system (*International Systems in World History*, 87). In contrast, we regard it as a measure for each state and thereby recognize the fact that structural differentiation can vary between states within the same system.
36. See Nexon, *The Struggle for Power in Early Modern Europe*, on composite polities.
37. Watson, *The Evolution of International Society*.
38. Lake, *Hierarchy in International Relations*; Buzan and Little, *International Systems in World History*.
39. Lake, *Hierarchy in International Relations*; Savage, *Political Survival and Sovereignty in International Relations*.
40. Savage, *Political Survival and Sovereignty in International Relations*; Savage, "Common-Pool Hierarchy."
41. A distinction also made in Mazzuca, *Latecomer State Formation*.

2. THE BIRTH AND DEATH OF STATES BEFORE THE LEAGUE OF NATIONS

42. In terms developed by Mann in "The Autonomous Power of the State," these states would be those with high despotic power but low infrastructural power.
43. Buzan and Little, *International Systems in World History*, 141, 161.
44. Krasner, *Sovereignty*; Philpott, *Revolutions in Sovereignty*.
45. Our conception of sovereignty is akin to Andrew Latham's historicist approach in "IR's Medieval-Sovereignty Debate."
46. Other dimensions of variation in state structures such as regime type are not captured in our model.
47. Correlates of War Project, "State System Membership List, v2016."
48. See, for example, Tambiah, "The Galactic Polity"; Wilks, *Asante in the Nineteenth Century*; Herbst, *States and Power in Africa*; Oliver and Atmore, *Medieval Africa, 1250–1800*; Kang, *East Asia Before the West*; Ringmar, "Performing International Systems"; Fenske, "Does Land Abundance Explain African Institutions?"; Besley and Reynal-Querol, "The Legacy of Historical Conflict"; Phillips and Sharman, *International Order in Diversity*; and Wig, "Peace from the Past."
49. Correlates of War Project, "State System Membership List, v2016." The second COW criterion for statehood in the pre-1920 period was having a population of at least 500,000.
50. Singer and Small, "The Composition and Status Ordering of the International System," 246.
51. Fagbule and Fawehinmi, *Formation*, 113.
52. Teorell, "Rules of Recognition?"
53. K. Gleditsch and Ward, "A Revised List of Independent States Since the Congress of Vienna." See also Bremer and Ghosn, "Defining States"; and Fazal, *State Death*.
54. In "The Economic Origins of the Territorial State," Scott Abramson's definition for identifying European states is similar in the lack of a requirement for external sovereignty.
55. Fazal, *State Death*, 14–17.
56. Coppedge et al., V-Dem [Country-Year/Country-Date] Dataset, vol. 9.
57. M. Weber, "Politics as Vocation," 78.
58. Spruyt, *The Sovereign State and Its Competitors*; Ruggie, *Constructing the World Polity*; Krasner, *Sovereignty*; Buzan and Little, *International Systems in World History*; Fazal, *State Death*; Lake, *Hierarchy in International Relations*; Donnelly, "The Elements of the Structures of International Systems"; Branch, *The Cartographic State*; Butcher and Griffiths, "Between Eurocentrism and Babel"; McConaughey, Musgrave, and Nexon, "Beyond Anarchy."
59. Moving the population threshold from 100,000 to 10,000 is one of the main differences between ISD version 1 and ISD version 2.
60. Nexon, *The Struggle for Power in Early Modern Europe*; McConaughey, Musgrave, and Nexon, "Beyond Anarchy."
61. Law, *The Oyo Empire*.
62. Buzan and Little, *International Systems in World History*, 87; Butcher and Griffiths, "Between Eurocentrism and Babel."
63. In some marginal cases, we did not include potential states that did not control leadership succession as states in the ISD.
64. Griffiths and Butcher, "Introducing the International System(s) Dataset (ISD), 1816–2011," 757.

2. THE BIRTH AND DEATH OF STATES BEFORE THE LEAGUE OF NATIONS

65. Even the British East India Company sought to be a vassal of the Mughal Empire.
66. Fazal, *State Death*.
67. Butcher and Griffiths, "States and Their International Relations Since 1816."
68. For example, Tim Besley and Marta Reynal Querol identified 19 states in Africa ("The Legacy of Historical Conflict"); Depetris-Chauvin identified 54 ("State History and Contemporary Conflict"); AfricaMap identified just 15 for 1840 (ArcGIS, "1840 CE," after McEvedy, *Atlas of African History*); and GeaCron identified 27 (GeaCron, "World History Maps & Timelines").
69. Fazal, *State Death*, 27–28.
70. See, for example, Buzan and Lawson, *The Global Transformation*.
71. See Mazzuca, *Latecomer State Formation*, for a discussion of latecomer state formation in the Americas.
72. Griffiths, *Age of Secession*.
73. Hudson, "The Formation of the North German Confederation"; Breuilly, *Nineteenth-Century Germany*.
74. Griffiths, *Age of Secession*.
75. Last, *The Sokoto Caliphate*, 37–40; P. Lovejoy, *Jihād in West Africa During the Age of Revolutions*; Fagbule and Fawehinmi, *Formation*, 13–28.
76. Falola and Heaton, *A History of Nigeria*, xxii.
77. Jeater, *Law, Language, and Science*, 23–26.
78. There are potential borderline examples, however. The Fante Confederation was a voluntary union of Fante chiefdoms, albeit under British supervision. See Gershoni, "The Fante Confederation and the Grebo Reunited Confederation," 18–19.
79. New Zealand is also an example of unification where the Maori states confederated as Aotearoa in 1835.
80. Boxberger, *On the Edge of Empire*, 35.
81. There are several examples, including the Oyo Empire, Gobir, Maradi, Arochokwu, and New Oyo.
82. Fagbule and Fawehinmi, *Formation*, 113.
83. In South Asia, Nepal remained an independent state.
84. Aspinall, *Islam and Nation*.
85. Last, *The Sokoto Caliphate*.
86. Gobir and Zaria are in the ISD as states that migrated to new territories but retained their elite structures.
87. Yamani, *Cradle of Islam*, 8; Al Rasheed, "Durable and Non-durable Dynasties," 152–55.
88. On Bukhara and Khiva, see Becker, *Russia's Protectorates in Central Asia*, 43; on Kokand, see Pierce, *Russian Central Asia, 1867–1917*, 34–37; and on Dagestan, see Yemelianova, *Russia and Islam*, 52.
89. Schaik, *Tibet*.
90. On Udaipur, see Lavania et al., *Rajasthan*, 10–11; on Jaipur, see Stern, *The Cat and the Lion*, 14. See also Tod, *Annals and Antiquities of Rajasthan*, 1092–94.
91. One possibility is that the decentralized nature of many African states made making credible commitments difficult. See Gerring, Ziblatt, et al., "An Institutional Theory of Direct and Indirect Rule"; and Fearon, "Rationalist Explanations for War."
92. Mahoney, *The Legacies of Liberalism*, 66.

3. THE COMPARATIVE DYNAMICS OF STATES AND SYSTEMS

93. On the North German Confederation, see Hudson, "The Formation of the North German Confederation."
94. On Italy, see Duggan, *The Force of Destiny*, 228; on Aotearoa, see Sinclair, *A History of New Zealand*, 49. Other actors signed the treaty to create Aotearoa, but only four are included as states in the ISD.
95. Holzinger, Kern, and Kromrey, "Explaining the Constitutional Integration and Resurgence of Traditional Political Institutions in Sub-Saharan Africa."
96. Lesotho is counted twice in the ISD since it expired in 1848, was resurrected in 1852, and then died again in 1868.
97. Nejd existed at two different periods in the nineteenth century and was later resurrected as Saudi Arabia.

3. THE COMPARATIVE DYNAMICS OF STATES AND SYSTEMS

1. Waltz, *Theory of International Politics*, 88.
2. See Keohane, ed., *Neorealism and Its Critics*; Milner, "The Assumption of Anarchy in International Relations Theory"; Spruyt, *The Sovereign State and Its Competitors*; Lake, "Anarchy, Hierarchy, and the Variety of International Relations"; Lake, *Entangling Relations*; Lake, *Hierarchy in International Relations*; Ruggie, *Constructing the World Polity*; Donnelly, "Rethinking Political Structures"; Donnelly, "The Differentiation of International Societies"; Donnelly, "The Elements of the Structures of International Systems"; Donnelly, "The Discourse of Anarchy in IR"; Donnelly, *Systems, Relations, and the Structures of International Societies*; Mattern and Zarakol, "Hierarchy in World Politics"; and Griffiths, "The Waltzian Ordering Principle and International Change."
3. Lake, "Anarchy, Hierarchy, and the Variety of International Relations"; Lake, *Entangling Relations*.
4. This is similar to the differences among dominion, suzerainty, and hegemony proposed in Watson, *The Evolution of International Society*, 15–16. See also Buzan and Little, *International Systems in World History*, 178; Cederman and Giradin, "Growing Sovereignty"; and Tilly, *Coercion, Capital, and European States*, 104.
5. Nexon, *The Struggle for Power in Early Modern Europe*.
6. Kratochwil, "Of Systems, Boundaries, and Territoriality"; Sahlins, *Boundaries*; Agnew, "The Territorial Trap"; Spruyt, *The Sovereign State and Its Competitors*; Winichakul, *Siam Mapped*; Ruggie, *Constructing the World Polity*; Adelman and Aron, "From Borderlands to Borders"; Krasner, *Sovereignty*; Sassen, *Territory, Authority, Rights*; Branch, *The Cartographic State*.
7. Winichakul, *Siam Mapped*, 101.
8. Winichakul, *Siam Mapped*, 64.
9. Winichakul, *Siam Mapped*, 96.
10. Longo, *The Politics of Borders*.
11. Ruggie, "Continuity and Transformation in the World Polity," 154. Ruggie borrowed the term *heteronomous* from Friedrich Meinecke, who in *Machiavellianism*, as Ruggie points out, "spoke of the heteronomous shackles of the Middle Ages, referring to the lattice-like network of authority relations" (154).

3. THE COMPARATIVE DYNAMICS OF STATES AND SYSTEMS

12. Costa Lopez, "Political Authority in International Relations"; Haldén, "Heteronymous Politics Beyond Anarchy and Hierarchy"; Spruyt, *The Sovereign State and Its Competitors*, 12.
13. Bean, "War and the Birth of the Nation State," 220.
14. Butcher and Griffiths, "Toward a Theory of Heteronomy."
15. Specifically, we call this configuration "interstitial heteronomy" and contrast it with "functional and personalistic heteronomy" (Butcher and Griffiths, "Toward a Theory of Heteronomy").
16. For a larger and more complex model for assessing the structures of systems, see Donnelly, *Systems, Relations, and the Structures of International Societies*.
17. This definition is given by Bentley Allan, who in *Scientific Cosmology and International Orders* goes on to say that orders are "historical periods characterized by distinct combinations of political, military, and economic practices" (5).
18. Bull, *The Anarchical Society*; Waltz, *Theory of International Politics*; Buzan and Little, *International Systems in World History*; Schweller, "The Problem of International Order Revisited"; Ikenberry, *After Victory*; Trachtenburg, "The Problem of International Order and How to Think About It"; Phillips, *War, Religion, and Empire*; Reus-Smit, *Individual Rights and the Making of the Modern International System*; Reus-Smith, *On Cultural Diversity*; Kissinger, *World Order*; Goddard, *When Might Makes Right*; Spruyt, *The World Imagined*; Lascurettes and Poznansky, "International Order in Theory and Practice"; Zarakol, *Before the West*.
19. Butcher and Griffiths, "Toward a Theory of Heteronomy"; Donnelly, *Systems, Relations, and the Structures of International Societies*.
20. Gerring, "Mere Description."
21. Tilly, *Coercion, Capital, and European States*; Spruyt, *The Sovereign State and Its Competitors*.
22. Gilpin, *War and Change in World Politics*, 4.
23. Cederman et al., "War Did Make States," 44. The literature on the subject includes Poggi, *The Development of the Modern State*; Levi, *Of Rule and Revenue*; Sahlins, *Boundaries*; Tilly, *The Formation of National States in Western Europe*; Tilly, *Coercion, Capital, and European States*; Olson, "Dictatorship, Democracy, and Development"; Spruyt, *The Sovereign State and Its Competitors*; Spruyt, "War and State Formation"; Ruggie, *Constructing the World Polity*; Herbst, *States and Power in Africa*; Philpott, *Revolutions in Sovereignty*; Centeno, *War and the Nation-State in Latin America*; Hui, *War and State Formation in Ancient China and Early Modern Europe*; Nexon, *The Struggle for Power in Early Modern Europe*; Scott, *The Art of Not Being Governed*; Branch, *The Cartographic State*; Abramson, "The Economic Origins of the Territorial State"; and Mazzuca, *Latecomer State Formation*.
24. Gerring, Ziblatt, et al., "An Institutional Theory of Direct and Indirect Rule."
25. Mann, "The Autonomous Power of the State."
26. Garfias and Sellars, "From Conquest to Centralization," 996.
27. On Buganda, see R. Reid, *Political Power in Pre-colonial Buganda*, 3–4.
28. Ahmed and Stasavage, "Origins of Early Democracy."
29. Stasavage, *The Decline and Rise of Democracy*; Clark, Golder, and Golder, "The British Academy Brian Barry Prize Essay."
30. Even Capetian France, for example, started as a conglomerate of subordinate vassal kingdoms (Spruyt, *The Sovereign State and Its Competitors*).

3. THE COMPARATIVE DYNAMICS OF STATES AND SYSTEMS

31. Pascali et al., "Wars, Taxation, and Representation." It was not uncommon for international systems to swing between periods of fragmentation where small, centralized city-states dominated and periods where large, decentralized empires dominated (Buzan and Little, *International Systems in World History*, 174–75).
32. Abramson, "The Economic Origins of the Territorial State." Modern European states vary enormously in size. Belgium, for example, is around 31,000 square kilometers, and the Netherlands around 41,500, but Germany is more than 350,000 square kilometers and France more than 500,000. City-states tend to be less 10,000 square kilometers. Singapore, for example, is 738 square kilometers, and Luxemburg around 5,000.
33. It is argued that the Catholic Church acted as a balancer and active competitor to European monarchs, stymieing the rise of a single empire and helping to maintain the fragmented and competitive international environment that eventually produced sovereign states. The church also provided administrative models and legal precedents that were emulated by monarchs; it also served as a source of literate bureaucrats and eventually of windfall revenues when church properties were appropriated. See Grzymala-Busse, "Beyond War and Contracts"; Gorski, "The Protestant Ethic Revisited"; Møller, "Why Europe Avoided Hegemony"; and Dincecco and Wang, "Violent Conflict and Political Development Over the Long Run."
34. In *The Struggle for Power in Early Modern Europe*, Daniel Nexon argues that the Protestant Reformation was an external shock that disturbed stable coalitions between rulers and vassals, creating opportunities for rulers to forge new alliances with religious actors and remove prerogatives from subordinate kingdoms. In "The Impact of Holy Land Crusades on State Formation," Lisa Blaydes and Christopher Paik argue that the Crusades enabled centralization in Europe.
35. Garfias and Sellars, "From Conquest to Centralization."
36. Huang and Kang, *State Formation Through Emulation*; Tilly, *Coercion, Capital, and European States*, 114.
37. Tilly, *The Formation of National States in Western Europe*, 42.
38. Tilly, *Coercion, Capital, and European States*, 105.
39. Tilly, *The Formation of National States in Western Europe*, 73.
40. In Tilly's account in *Coercion, Capital, and European States*, variations in economic structure (trade and city based versus agriculture based) produced different types of centralized states, but war drove centralization overall.
41. On Europe, see Dincecco and Prado, "Warfare, Fiscal Capacity, and Performance"; Hui, *War and State Formation in Ancient China and Early Modern Europe*; Tilly, *Coercion, Capital, and European States*; Hui, "How Tilly's State Formation Paradigm Is Revolutionizing the Study of Chinese State-making"; and Pascali et al., "Wars, Taxation, and Representation." On East Asia, see Hui, *War and State Formation in Ancient China and Early Modern Europe*.
42. Mazzuca, *Latecomer State Formation*, 35; Cederman et al., "War Did Make States."
43. For example, Spruyt, *The Sovereign State and Its Competitors*. For an application to Africa, see also Acharya and Lee, "Path Dependence in European Development"; Acharya and Lee, "Economic Foundations of the Territorial State System"; and Fenske, "Ecology, Trade, and States in Pre-colonial Africa."
44. Spruyt, *The Sovereign State and Its Competitors*.

3. THE COMPARATIVE DYNAMICS OF STATES AND SYSTEMS

45. Spruyt, *The Sovereign State and Its Competitors*. See also Abramson, "The Economic Origins of the Territorial State." There are also similarities to some Marxist approaches to the rise of the state (B. Anderson, *Imagined Communities*).
46. In *Latecomer State Formation*, Sebastian Mazzuca argues that international trade in Latin America created incentives to maintain decentralized forms of rule. Rulers might prefer more indirect forms of rule when vassals could more efficiently deliver resources and benefits that the state wanted (taxes, public order, military resources). Also see Gerring, Ziblatt, et al., "An Institutional Theory of Direct and Indirect Rule"; Garfias and Sellars, "From Conquest to Centralization," 996; and Riker, "Federalism."
47. Voigtländer and Voth, "Gifts of Mars"; Saylor and Wheeler, "Paying for War and Building States"; Pascali et al., "Wars, Taxation, and Representation"; Karaman and Pamuk, "Different Paths to the Modern State in Europe"; Møller, "Medieval Roots of the Modern State."
48. Stasavage, "Representation and Consent"; Gerring, Apfeld, et al., *The Deep Roots of Modern Democracy*.
49. Stasavage, *States of Credit*.
50. Dincecco and Onorato, "Military Conflict and the Rise of Urban Europe."
51. Feinstein and Wimmer, "Consent and Legitimacy."
52. Dincecco and Wang, "Violent Conflict and Political Development Over the Long Run."
53. In "Consent and Legitimacy," Yuval Feinstein and Andreas Wimmer also emphasize nationalism as a conditioning factor.
54. Abramson, "The Economic Origins of the Territorial State"; Spruyt, *The Sovereign State and Its Competitors*.
55. Goenaga and Hagen-Jamar, "When Does War Make States?"
56. Hui, *War and State Formation in Ancient China and Early Modern Europe*; Huang and Kang, *State Formation Through Emulation*.
57. Centeno, *War and the Nation-State in Latin America*; Mazzuca, *Latecomer State Formation*.
58. Herbst, *States and Power in Africa*; Clapham, *Africa and the International System*. See also Thies, "The Political Economy of State Building in Sub-Saharan Africa." On precolonial warfare in Africa, see Dincecco, Fenske, and Onorato, "Is Africa Different?"
59. On higher trade, see Fenske, "Ecology, Trade, and States in Pre-colonial Africa." On exogenous shocks, see Garfias and Sellars, "Fiscal Legibility and State Development," 996; Riker, "Federalism"; and Acharya and Lee, "Path Dependence in European Development."
60. V. Lieberman, *Strange Parallels*, vol. 1: *Integration on the Mainland*.
61. On early emergence, see Spruyt, *The Sovereign State and Its Competitors*; on late emergence, see Buzan and Lawson, *The Global Transformation*, 34; on competition as a driver of decentralization, see Teschke, "After the Tilly Thesis," 37. Even in Tilly's account, centralization in France did not take hold until the French Revolution. See A. Lee and Paine, "The Great Revenue Divergence." And war also does not seem to be a good explanation for state building after World War II, something that Tilly predicted.

3. THE COMPARATIVE DYNAMICS OF STATES AND SYSTEMS

62. There are exceptions for West Africa (Ejiogu, "State Building in the Niger Basin in the Common Era and Beyond, 1000–Mid 1800s") and Thailand (Paik and Vechbanyongratana, "Path to Centralization and Development").
63. On interaction capacity, see Buzan and Little, *International Systems in World History*, 80, 85. Ruggie made a similar argument when he identified dynamic density—"the aggregate quantity, velocity, and diversity of transactions that go on within society"—as the determinant of change within systems (*Constructing the World Polity*, 151). See also Buzan and Lawson, *The Global Transformation*.
    On the connection between trade and the projection of power, see Butcher and Griffiths, "States and Their International Relations Since 1816"; and Kochen and Deutsch, "A Note on Hierarchy and Coordination."
64. Studies in this area include Cederman and Girardin, "Growing Sovereignty"; Butcher and Griffiths, "Between Eurocentrism and Babel"; and Butcher and Griffiths, "War, Interaction Capacity, and the Structures of State Systems."
65. Tilly, *Coercion, Capital, and European States*, 25; Garfias and Sellars, "From Conquest to Centralization," 994. Successful centralization efforts have often increased state revenues (Garfias and Sellars, "From Conquest to Centralization").
66. Tilly, *Coercion, Capital, and European States*, 25.
67. Brambor et al., "The Lay of the Land"; M. Lee and Zhang, "Legibility and the Informational Foundations of State Capacity"; A. Lee and Paine, "The Great Revenue Divergence"; Scott, *The Art of Not Being Governed*; Mann, "The Autonomous Power of the State," 189; Giddens, "Time, Space, and Regionalisation," 266–67.
68. Mitchell and Yin, "Political Centralization, Career Incentives, and Local Economic Growth in Edo Japan."
69. Stasavage, "When Distance Mattered," 625.
70. Stasavage, *The Decline and Rise of Democracy*; Ahmed and Stasavage, "Origins of Early Democracy"; Scott, *The Art of Not Being Governed*.
71. M. Lee and Zhang, "Legibility and the Informational Foundations of State Capacity."
72. Scott, *The Art of Not Being Governed*, 71. See also M. Lee and Zhang, "Legibility and the Informational Foundations of State Capacity."
73. Garfias and Sellars, "From Conquest to Centralization."
74. Stasavage, *The Decline and Rise of Democracy*; Ahmed and Stasavage, "Origins of Early Democracy"; Garfias and Sellars, "Fiscal Legibility and State Development," 3.
75. Ahmed and Stasavage, "Origins of Early Democracy." This approach borrows much from Douglass North's work on transaction costs and institution building; see, for example, his book *Institutions, Institutional Change, and Economic Performance*.
76. Cederman and Giradin, "Growing Sovereignty"; Garfias and Sellars, "From Conquest to Centralization."
77. See, for example, Nexon, *The Struggle for Power in Early Modern Europe*; Blaydes and Paik, "Trade and Political Fragmentation on the Silk Roads"; and A. Lee and Paine, "The Great Revenue Divergence."
78. Doyle, *Empires*.
79. Abramson, "The Economic Origins of the Territorial State."
80. Buzan and Lawson, *The Global Transformation*, 128.

3. THE COMPARATIVE DYNAMICS OF STATES AND SYSTEMS

81. In *Coercion, Capital, and European States*, even Tilly notes that rapid shifts toward direct rule in France occurred between 1789 and 1793 (111).
82. A. Lee and Paine, "The Great Revenue Divergence."
83. Brambor et al., "The Lay of the Land."
84. A. Lee and Paine, "The Great Revenue Divergence," 375.
85. Luttwak, *The Grand Strategy of the Roman Empire*; Longo, *The Politics of Borders*.
86. Such theories are often explicit about these scope conditions. See Gerring, Ziblatt, et al., "An Institutional Theory of Direct and Indirect Rule"; and Garfias and Sellars, "From Conquest to Centralization."
87. European states gave concessions to their populations after World War I that deepened democracy (a form of decentralization) because mass mobilization increased the dependence of the state on its population. Women's rights also tend to increase after intense wars for the same reason. See Bakken and Buhaug, "Civil War and Female Empowerment"; and Webster, Chen, and Beardsley, "Conflict, Peace, and the Evolution of Women's Empowerment."
88. Gordon, *The Marathas 1600–1818*; Hägerdal, "Periphery and Bridgehead," 162.
89. It is possible, however, that these factors cause changes other than interaction capacity that drive state centralization, which can be alternative explanations for the results.
90. Michalopoulos, "The Origins of Ethnolinguistic Diversity"; Ashraf and Galor, "Genetic Diversity and the Origins of Cultural Fragmentation"; Ahlerup and Olsson, "The Roots of Ethnic Diversity"; V. Lieberman, *Strange Parallels*, vol. 1: *Integration on the Mainland*; Wimmer, *Nation Building*.
91. A. Reid, *Southeast Asia in the Age of Commerce 1450–1680*; Sharman, "Something New out of Africa."
92. Buzan and Lawson, *The Global Transformation*.

4. EAST ASIA

1. Woodside, "Territorial Order and Collective-Identity Tensions in Confucian Asia"; Zhang, "System, Empire, and State in Chinese International Relations"; Kang, *East Asia Before the West*; Kelly, "A 'Confucian Long Peace' in Pre-Western East Asia"; Zhou, "Equilibrium Analysis of the Tributary System"; Phillips, *War, Religion, and Empire*; Ringmar, "Performing International Systems"; Zhang and Buzan, "The Tributary System as International Society in Theory and Practice"; Park, *Sovereignty and Status in East Asian International Relations*; J. Lee, *China's Hegemony*; Mackay, "Rethinking Hierarchy in East Asian Historical IR"; Spruyt, *The World Imagined*; Huang and Kang, *State Formation Through Emulation*.
2. Woodside, "Territorial Order and Collective-Identity Tensions in Confucian Asia," 196.
3. Hwang, *A History of Korea*, 5; Seth, *A Concise History of Korea*, 7.
4. Schellinger and Salkin, eds., *International Dictionary of Historical Places*, s.v. "Ho Chi Minh City," 5:354.
5. Kang, *East Asia Before the West*, 10–11.
6. Johnston, *Cultural Realism*. For further discussion, see Barfield, *The Perilous Frontier*; Keene, *Beyond the Anarchical Society*; and J. Lee, *China's Hegemony*.

4. EAST ASIA

7. The Vietnamese monarchy retained nominal powers in the protectorate of Annam, and the French drew upon the Vietnamese bureaucracy during the colonial period. The emperor abdicated after World War II (Corfield, *The History of Vietnam*, 27–30).
8. Correlates of War Project, "State System Membership List, v2016."
9. Zhang, "Curious and Exotic Encounters," 65–68.
10. Park, *Sovereignty and Status in East Asian International Relations*, 51; Costa Lopez and De Carvalho, "Introduction," 491.
11. Kang, *East Asia Before the West*, 56.
12. Ringmar, "Performing International Systems"; Kang, *East Asia Before the West*, 56; Park, *Sovereignty and Status in East Asian International Relations*, 54.
13. J. Lee, *China's Hegemony*.
14. Kang, *East Asia Before the West*; Suzuki, "Europe at the Periphery of the Japanese World Order," 81.
15. J. Lee, *China's Hegemony*, 6, 16; Doyle, *Empires*.
16. Fairbank, "Tributary Trade and China's Relations with the West"; Fairbank, *The Chinese World Order*.
17. Millward et al., eds., *New Qing Imperial History*; Waley-Cohen, "The New Qing History."
18. For a rich coverage of these topics, see J. Lee, *China's Hegemony*.
19. Zhang and Buzan, "The Tributary System as International Society in Theory and Practice," 15; Reus-Smit, *The Moral Purpose of the State*, 7.
20. J. Lee, *China's Hegemony*, 12.
21. Woodside, "Territorial Order and Collective-Identity Tensions in Confucian Asia."
22. Ringmar, "Performing International Systems."
23. MacKay, "Rethinking Hierarchy in East Asian Historical IR"; A. Swidler, "Culture in Action." Also see Phillips, "Contesting the Confucian Peace."
24. Millward, "Qing and Twentieth-Century Chinese Diversity Regimes," 72.
25. J. Lee, *China's Hegemony*, 12.
26. Figures taken from "Demographics of China," Wikipedia, last edited November 21, 2024, https://en.wikipedia.org/wiki/Demographics_of_China#Census_data.
27. Kennedy, *The Rise and Fall of the Great Powers*, 99.
28. United Nations Population Division, "World Population Prospects 2019."
29. Woodside, *Vietnam and the Chinese Model*, 159.
30. Kang, *East Asia Before the West*, 63–65.
31. V. Leiberman, *Strange Parallels*, vol. 2: *Mainland Mirrors*, 462, 469, 488.
32. V. Lieberman, *Strange Parallels*, vol. 1: *Integration on the Mainland*.
33. Woodside, "Territorial Order and Collective-Identity Tensions in Confucian Asia"; Huang and Kang, *State Formation Through Emulation*, 102.
34. Ropp, *China in World History*, 91.
35. See V. Lieberman, *Strange Parallels*, vol. 2: *Mainland Mirrors*.
36. Ropp, *China in World History*, 100.
37. J. Lee, *China's Hegemony*, 32.
38. Kang, *East Asia Before the West*, 45.
39. Kang, *East Asia Before the West*; Kelly, "A 'Confucian Long Peace' in Pre-Western East Asia"; Doyle, "Three Pillars of the Liberal Peace."
40. Kang, Shaw, and Fu, "Measuring War in Early Modern East Asia, 1368–1841."

4. EAST ASIA

41. Using our ISD data, matched with the data given in Lyall, *Divided Armies*.
42. Kelly, "A 'Confucian Long Peace' in Pre-Western East Asia"; Kang, *East Asia Before the West*.
43. Kang, *East Asia Before the West*.
44. Gilpin, *War and Change in World Politics*; Ikenberry, *After Victory*.
45. Phillips, "Contesting the Confucian Peace," 744. In his argument, Phillips uses Daniel Nexon's concept of heterogenous contracting. See Nexon, *The Struggle for Power in Early Modern Europe*.
46. Kwan, "Hierarchy, Status, and International Society."
47. Johnston, *Cultural Realism*; Kang, Shaw, and Fu, "Measuring War in Early Modern East Asia, 1368–1841."
48. Kelly, "A 'Confucian Long Peace' in Pre-Western East Asia," 416. On this point, see also Perdue, "Military Mobilization in Seventeenth and Eighteenth-Century China, Russia, and Mongolia"; Woodside, "Territorial Order and Collective-Identity Tensions in Confucian Asia," 206; Phillips, "Contesting the Confucian Peace," 753; and Hui, "Cultural Diversity and Coercive Cultural Homogenization in Chinese History."
49. Perdue, *China Marches West*.
50. Sharman, "Power and Profit at Sea."
51. Ropp, *China in World History*, 102–6.
52. Jansen, "The Meiji Restoration," 311–12; Ko, Koyama, and Sng, "Unified China and Divided Europe."
53. Suzuki, "Europe at the Periphery of the Japanese World Order," 76; Jansen, "Japan in the Early Nineteenth Century," 97–103.
54. See Dutton, *The Tay Son Uprising*, for an account of the Tay Son state and rebellion.
55. In "Territorial Order and Collective-Identity Tensions in Confucian Asia," Alexander Woodside writes that Korean territoriality to the Yalu River was achieved by the end of the tenth century (201–2).
56. Kang, Shaw, and Fu, "Measuring War in Early Modern East Asia, 1368–1841," 770. Civil wars include rebellions, dynastic struggles, and intraelite fighting.
57. Kang, Shaw, and Fu, "Measuring War in Early Modern East Asia, 1368–1841," 773.
58. Kang, *East Asia Before the West*, 46.
59. Kang, *East Asia Before the West*, 26.
60. Vietnam's relations with Cambodia are an exception that we discuss later in the chapter. Japan during the Tokugawa Shogunate practiced vassalage through the *han* system. However, all *han* were subordinated to the shogun (and nominally to the emperor), but heteronomous forms of vassalage—common in Europe—were rare (Bolitho, "The Han," 183).
61. In "Political Centralization, Career Incentives, and Local Economic Growth in Edo Japan," Austin Mitchell and Weiwen Yin describe Edo Japan as a quasi-federal state (3).
62. Woodside, "Territorial Order and Collective-Identity Tensions in Confucian Asia."
63. B. Anderson, *Imagined Communities*; Fukuyama, *The Origins of Political Order*, 118.
64. Huang and Kang, *State Formation Through Emulation*, 35; Woodside, "Territorial Order and Collective-Identity Tensions in Confucian Asia," 196.
65. Kang, *East Asia Before the West*, 51.
66. Huang and Kang, *State Formation Through Emulation*, 143.

4. EAST ASIA

67. Li, "From Alien Land to Inalienable Parts of China."
68. Kang, *East Asia Before the West*, 63–65; Ropp, *China in World History*, 99; Li, "From Alien Land to Inalienable Parts of China"; Huang and Kang, *State Formation Through Emulation*, 40. On setting the Chinese-Korean border at the Yalu River, see Woodside, "Territorial Order and Collective-Identity Tensions in Confucian Asia," 201; and see Huang and Kang, *State Formation Through Emulation*, 80, for a description of how the border was finalized around Mount Paektu in the early 1700s. For the Chinese-Vietnamese border, see Huang and Kang, *State Formation Through Emulation*, 72.
69. Woodside, "Territorial Order and Collective-Identity Tensions in Confucian Asia," 202.
70. In "Cultural Diversity and Coercive Cultural Homogenization in Chinese History," Victoria Tin-Bor Hui argues that Chinese state practices tended to obliterate minority differences rather than accommodate them.
71. Woodside, "Territorial Order and Collective-Identity Tensions in Confucian Asia," 208.
72. Chandler, *A History of Cambodia*, 136; Simms, *The Kingdoms of Laos*, 193–94.
73. MacKay, "Rethinking Hierarchy in East Asian Historical IR," 606.
74. Huang and Kang, *State Formation Through Emulation*, 108.
75. Mitchell and Yin, "Political Centralization, Career Incentives, and Local Economic Growth in Edo Japan," 3. The shogunate was preceded by the Warring States Period (1467–1600), although the Tokugawa allies were ascendant and started centralizing policies in the sixteenth century.
76. Bolitho, "The Han," 202; Hall, "The Bakuhan System."
77. Ravina, "State-Building and Political Economy in Early-Modern Japan," 1000–1001. Local tax rates were, for example, lower in daimyo that experienced more severe rebellions; see Steele, Paik, and Tanaka, "Constraining the Samurai."
78. Ravina, "State-Building and Political Economy in Early-Modern Japan," 1000–1001; Bolitho, "The Han."
79. Ikegami, *The Taming of the Samurai*, 157.
80. Ikegami, *The Taming of the Samurai*, 182.
81. Bolitho, "The Han," 209; Ferejohn and Rosenbluth, "War and State Building in Medieval Japan," 1.
82. V. Lieberman, *Strange Parallels*, vol. 2: *Mainland Mirrors*, 443; Ikegami, *The Taming of the Samurai*, 182; Mitchell and Win, "Political Centralization, Career Incentives, and Local Economic Growth in Edo Japan."
83. In "The Han," Harold Bolitho dates the decline from 1651 (206).
84. Bolitho, "The Han," 205–8.
85. Jansen, "The Meiji Restoration," 336.
86. Jansen and Rozman, "Overview," in *Japan in Transition*, 7.
87. Jansen, "The Meiji Restoration," 325. Marius Jansen claims that the Satsuma, Chosu, Tosa, and Hinzen who led the Meiji Revolution were more remote, larger, and more autonomous than other han.
88. Jansen, "The Meiji Restoration," 335, 346.
89. Beasley, "Meiji Political Institutions," 640, 645–46.
90. Ferejohn and Rosenbluth, "War and State Building in Medieval Japan," 17.
91. V. Lieberman, *Strange Parallels*, vol. 1: *Integration on the Mainland*, 423.

4. EAST ASIA

92. Victor Lieberman rates the Ly state with the highest level of centralization, "Pattern D" (*Strange Parallels*, vol. 1: *Integration on the Mainland*, 382). The Ly monarch appointed officers down to the district level, expanded the Ming examination system, divided the country into a grid of circuits, prefectures, and districts, and conducted land and population registers.
93. V. Lieberman, *Strange Parallels*, vol. 1: *Integration on the Mainland*, 427.
94. Woodside, *Vietnam and the Chinese Model*, 102; V. Lieberman, *Strange Parallels*, vol. 1: *Integration on the Mainland*, 427–28.
95. V. Lieberman, *Strange Parallels*, vol. 1: *Integration on the Mainland*, 429.
96. Woodside, *Vietnam and the Chinese Model*, 103.
97. Dutton, "From Civil War to Uncivil Peace," 175.
98. V. Lieberman, *Strange Parallels*, vol. 1: *Integration on the Mainland*, 430, 429, 432, 454. Vietnamese rulers also removed the final vestiges of Champa autonomy (N. Weber, "The Destruction and Assimilation of Campā (1832–35) as Seen from Cam Sources").
99. V. Lieberman, *Strange Parallels*, vol. 2: *Mainland Mirrors*, 465. See also Jansen, "The Meiji Restoration," 339.
100. Jansen, "Japan in the Early Nineteenth Century," 65.
101. Ikegami, *The Taming of the Samurai*, 177.
102. Lieberman, *Strange Parallels*, vol. 1: *Integration on the Mainland*, 347.
103. Lieberman, *Strange Parallels*, vol. 1: *Integration on the Mainland*, 372.
104. Kang, *East Asia Before the West*.
105. Lieberman, *Strange Parallels*, vol. 1: *Integration on the Mainland*, 454.
106. Lieberman, *Strange Parallels*, vol. 2: *Mainland Mirrors*, 429.
107. Lieberman, *Strange Parallels*, vol. 1: *Integration on the Mainland*, 409–13.
108. Lieberman, *Strange Parallels*, vol. 1: *Integration on the Mainland*, 401, 406. Specifically in the 1657–1682 period in the North and after 1744 in the South.
109. Huang and Kang, *State Formation Through Emulation*, 36–37, 26–27.
110. Woodside, "Territorial Order and Collective-Identity Tensions in Confucian Asia"; Ropp, *China in World History*; Kelly, "A 'Confucian Long Peace' in Pre-Western East Asia"; Phillips, *War, Religion, and Empire*; Fukuyama, *The Origins of Political Order*; Ringmar, "Performing International Systems"; Zhang and Buzan, "The Tributary System as International Society in Theory and Practice"; Zhang, "Curious and Exotic Encounters"; Suzuki, "Europe at the Periphery of the Japanese World Order"; Park, *Sovereignty and Status in East Asian International Relations*; J. Lee, *China's Hegemony*; Dincecco and Wang, "Violent Conflict and Political Development Over the Long Run"; Spruyt, *The World Imagined*; Millward, "Qing and Twentieth-Century Chinese Diversity Regimes"; Li, "From Alien Land to Inalienable Parts of China."
111. Hui, *War and State Formation in Ancient China and Early Modern Europe*.
112. Huang and Kang, *State Formation Through Emulation*, 3.
113. Allan, *Scientific Cosmology and International Orders*, 5.
114. Huang and Kang, *State Formation Through Emulation*, 155.
115. J. Lee, *China's Hegemony*, 57–61.
116. Griffiths, *Secession and the Sovereignty Game*.
117. Woodside, *Vietnam and the Chinese Model*.
118. Huang and Kang, *State Formation Through Emulation*, 5.

119. Huang and Kang, *State Formation Through Emulation*, 69.
120. Jansen, "The Meiji Restoration," 340.
121. Beasley, "Meiji Political Institutions," 658.

5. SOUTH ASIA

1. See, for example, M. Roy, "Politics, War, and State Formation in Early Modern India."
2. Gordon, *The Marathas 1600–1818*; Richards, *The Mughal Empire*.
3. Bayly, *Rulers, Townsmen, and Bazaars*, 26; Bayly *Indian Society and the Making of the British Empire*, 8, 15.
4. In *The Indian Princes and Their States*, Barbara Ramusack places these states into three categories: successor states, antique states, and warrior states.
5. Pardesi, "Region, System, and Order"; Bayly, *Rulers, Townsmen, and Bazaars*, 148–49.
6. Pardesi, "Mughal Hegemony and the Emergence of South Asia as a 'Region' for Regional Order-Building"; Spruyt, *The World Imagined*.
7. Spruyt, *The World Imagined*.
8. The Maratha state of Baroda signed a separate treaty of protection with the British prior to 1816.
9. T. Roy, *An Economic History of India 1707–1857*, 100.
10. Raychaudhuri, "The Mid-Eighteenth-Century Background," 34–35.
11. Gordon, *The Marathas 1600–1818*, 23. See also Divekar, " Regional Economy (1757–1857): Western India," 339.
12. Kumar, "Regional Economy (1757–1857): South India," 353.
13. T. Roy, *An Economic History of India 1707–1857*, 108. For South India, see also Kumar, "Regional Economy (1757–1857): South India," 353, 364.
14. Kessinger, "Regional Economy (1757–1857): North India," 245, 247; T. Roy, *An Economic History of India 1707–1857*, 137.
15. Kessinger, "Regional Economy (1757–1857): North India," 245.
16. T. Roy, *An Economic History of India 1707–1857*, 92. See also Bayly, *Rulers, Townsmen, and Bazaars*, 98–99; and Bhattacharya and Chaudhuri, "Regional Economy (1757–1857): Eastern India," 271.
17. Bhattacharya and Chaudhuri, "Regional Economy (1757–1857): Eastern India," 272.
18. Herbst, *States and Power in Africa*.
19. The population-density figure for Africa is somewhat distorted by the Sahara and rainforests of the Congo. See Klein Goldewijk, "Three Centuries of Global Population Growth." These figures are similar to those Jeffrey Herbst recorded for population densities in 1750: South Asia, 24.1 people per square kilometer; sub-Saharan Africa, 2.7; and Europe, 26.9 (Herbst, *States and Power in Africa*, 16).
20. Bayly, *Rulers, Townsmen, and Bazaars*, 107; Visaria and Visaria, "Population (1757–1947)," 465.
21. Raychaudhuri, "The Mid-Eighteenth-Century Background," 32–33. In "Regional Economy (1757–1857): South India,", Kumar also notes that variations in population density and economic organization had "physical" causes, such as rainfall and areas suitable for cash cropping (353).

22. Bayly, *Rulers, Townsmen, and Bazaars*, 88.
23. In *The Marathas 1600–1818*, Stewart Gordon suggests that "exit" to find new lands was still possible for peasants in eighteenth-century Maharashtra, as in West Africa (23). See also T. Roy, *An Economic History of India 1707–1857*, 69.
24. T. Roy, *An Economic History of India 1707–1857*, 119.
25. Bayly, *Rulers, Townsmen, and Bazaars*, 135.
26. T. Roy, *An Economic History of India 1707–1857*, 125.
27. Divekar, "Regional Economy (1757–1857): Western India," 342–43.
28. Kessinger, "Regional Economy (1757–1857): North India," 246–47.
29. T. Roy, *An Economic History of India 1707–1857*, 119.
30. Murshidabad was also a large city during the eighteenth and early nineteenth centuries; in "Regional Economy (1757–1857): South India," Kumar notes the presence of many large towns in eighteenth-century South India (357).
31. T. Roy, *An Economic History of India 1707–1857*, 96.
32. Kessinger, "Regional Economy (1757–1857): North India," 246–49.
33. Bayly, *Rulers, Townsmen, and Bazaars*, 112–13.
34. T. Roy, *An Economic History of India 1707–1857*, 101–2. In "Regional Economy (1757–1857): North India," Kessinger notes that a shipment of almonds traveling from Kabul to Delhi in 1820 could expect duties "equal to 251 percent of the prime cost and transport costs equal to 142 percent" (245).
35. Kumar, "Regional Economy (1757–1857): South India," 353–54; Divekar, "Regional Economy (1757–1857): Western India," 339.
36. T. Roy, *An Economic History of India 1707–1857*, 100.
37. Metcalf and Metcalf, *A Concise History of Modern India*, 39.
38. See Phillips and Sharman, *Outsourcing Empire*.
39. K. Roy, *War, Culture, and Society in Early Modern South Asia, 1740–1849*, 97–99.
40. See Brecke, "Violent Conflicts 1400 AD to the Present in Different Regions of the World"; and Barua, *The State at War in South Asia*. In "The State and the Economy: The South," Burton Stein argues that in South India levels of warfare increased from the middle of the sixteenth century through to the end of the eighteenth (203, 211).
41. Hamilton, *The East Indian Gazetteer*, 238; Malleson, *An Historical Sketch of the Native States of India*, 114.
42. British Government of India, *Imperial Gazetteer of India, Provincial Series*, 211.
43. Codrington, "The Coinages of Cutch and Kathiawar," 62–63.
44. Data from Miller and Bakar, "Conflict Events Worldwide Since 1468 BC."
45. M. Roy, "Politics, War, and State Formation in Early Modern India," 22; Gordon, *The Marathas 1600–1818*, 148–50.
46. Lyall, *Divided Armies*, number of soldiers taken from the dataset that accompanies the book at https://dataverse.harvard.edu/dataset.xhtml?persistentId=doi:10.7910/DVN/DUO7IE.
47. T. Roy, *An Economic History of India 1707–1857*, 7; K. Roy, *War, Culture, and Society in Early Modern South Asia, 1740–1849*, 136, 146, 150; Bayly, *Rulers, Townsmen, and Bazaars*, 65–66; M. Roy, "Politics, War, and State Formation in Early Modern India," 51.
48. K. Roy, *War, Culture, and Society in Early Modern South Asia, 1740–1849*, 93, 129; Duff, *A History of the Mahrattas*, 35; Gordon, *The Marathas 1600–1818*, 168.

5. SOUTH ASIA

49. T. Roy, *An Economic History of India 1707–1857*, 17. See also M. Roy, "Politics, War, and State Formation in Early Modern India," 22–23; Fukazawa, "Agrarian Relations and Land Revenue: The Medieval Deccan and Maharashtra," 256, 260; Gordon, *The Marathas 1600–1818*, 148.
50. T. Roy, *An Economic History of India 1707–1857*, 18.
51. The indigenous institutions included the *amani* system in northern India (Barnett, *North India Between Empires*, 171) and the *kamavisdar*s in Maratha domains (Gordon, *Marathas, Marauders, and State Formation in Eighteenth-Century India*, 40).
52. Gordon, *The Marathas 1600–1818*, 144.
53. T. Roy, *An Economic History of India 1707–1857*, 68.
54. Our rendering of state centralization in this chapter is similar to the one given in Foa, "Ancient Polities, Modern States" (chapter 3), which also identifies Mysore and Pune as the most centralized states, along with Khalistan and Travancore as "concessionary" centralized regimes. Our conclusions are also similar to those given in T. Roy, "Rethinking the Origins of British India."
55. Richard Barnett dates Awadh's independence to 1754 (*North India Between Empires*, 40). It is unclear when Awadh lost its external sovereignty; the treaty of 1764 is one possibility, but Awadh appears to have acted independently of the EIC until 1775 and thereafter.
56. Barnett, *North India Between Empires*, 2–3.
57. Raychaudhuri, "The Mid-Eighteenth-Century Background," 8.
58. Barnett, *North India Between Empires*, 94.
59. Barnett, *North India Between Empires*, 166, 223.
60. Bayly, *Rulers, Townsmen, and Bazaars*, 117–29, 116–17.
61. In 1751, the raja of Satara "renounced all sovereign power and agreed to sanction the Peshwa's policies unconditionally" (Wink, *Land and Sovereignty in India*, 77). The raja at Satara remained the nominal sovereign throughout the eighteenth century, which created a type of heteronomy where an independent state such as Gwalior could be subordinate to the peshwa, the raja at Satara, and the Mughal Empire at the same time.
62. Gordon, *The Marathas 1600–1818*, 118–19; Metcalf and Metcalf, *A Concise History of Modern India*, 72.
63. The line between subordinate and autonomous was often blurry. The members of the confederacy negotiated treaties with neighboring states on their own behalf. Gordon, *The Marathas 1600–1818*, 167, 156.
64. Baroda is the fifth state but signed a treaty of protection with the British before the ISD begins in 1816.
65. Gordon, *The Marathas 1600–1818*, 165.
66. Gordon, *The Marathas 1600–1818*; Wink, *Land and Sovereignty in India*, 124; Duff, *A History of the Mahrattas*, 463.
67. Duff, *A History of the Mahrattas*, 463.
68. Wink, *Land and Sovereignty in India*, 315–16; Wink, "Maratha Revenue Farming."
69. Wink, *Land and Sovereignty in India*, 186–87. A core part of this argument is that shifting alliances created openings for rulers to back one side against the other and establish new suzerain relations, while providing openings for rivals to do the same thing. Governance was managed or institutionalized conflict.

5. SOUTH ASIA

70. Gordon, *The Marathas 1600–1818*, 32.
71. Contracts, or *sanad*s, between the center and *deshmukh*s were formal, often written out and made specific.
72. Wink, *Land and Sovereignty in India*, 202.
73. Wink, *Land and Sovereignty in India*, 303.
74. Wink, *Land and Sovereignty in India*, 112. In this instance, the nested hierarchies went at least three levels down (Pune → Nagpur → Kharda → local landed elites). See also Axelrod, *Living on the Edge*, 570, for examples of Maratha governance in the area surrounding Goa.
75. Wink, *Land and Sovereignty in India*, 193, 192; Wink, "Maratha Revenue Farming," 600; T. Roy, *An Economic History of India 1707–1857*, 34.
76. T. Roy, *An Economic History of India 1707–1857*, 78, with additional examples on 29, 33–36, 66, 68–69, 72–75, and 78.
77. Gordon, *The Marathas 1600–1818*, 119. To be clear, there are many examples of indigenous border making in India. See Gordon, *The Marathas 1600–1818*, 133; Ramusack, *The Indian Princes and Their States*, 27; and Barfield, *Afghanistan*, 99. Bhutan, Chamba, and Cutch, for example, had relatively well-defined borders on account of mountain ranges or coast. Boundaries between the Marathas and the Mughal Empire were sometimes precisely demarcated (in Orissa, for example), and the boundaries between the Nizam and the Marathas were also negotiated by treaty and agreed upon, especially after the 1760s during the rule of Ali Khan. There is evidence of border marking between the Durrani Empire and the Uzbek emir of Bukhara in 1768–1770, "recognizing the Amu Darya as Afghanistan's northern border" (Barfield, *Afghanistan*, 99).
78. Gordon, *The Marathas 1600–1818*, 135–39. It is unclear how this dual rule was organized, but both powers drew revenue from the same administrative unit (pargana). Dual sovereignty in revenue collection appears to have been quite common in marginal Maratha domains (Wink, *Land and Sovereignty in India*, 194).
79. Gordon, *The Marathas 1600–1818*, 127–28.
80. Lingen and Wiggins, *Coins of the Sindhias*.
81. Metcalf and Metcalf, *A Concise History of Modern India*, 53.
82. Barnett, *North India Between Empires*, 60.
83. Gordon, "The Slow Conquest," 8.
84. This acceleration in the amount of information required appears to have been confined mostly to the areas around Bhilsa and Sironj (Gordon, *Marathas, Marauders, and State Formation in Eighteenth-Century India*, 48).
85. Gordon, "The Slow Conquest," 26.
86. Bandyopadhyay, *From Plassey to Partition and After*, 23.
87. Gordon's study is limited to the 1720–1760 period. Also, in *An Economic History of India 1707–1857*, Tirthankar Roy mentions the development of a "multilayered tax administration" that developed in western Maharastra (34).
88. T. Roy, *An Economic History of India 1707–1857*.
89. See, for example, Duff, *A History of the Mahrattas*; Seshan, "The Maratha State," 42; Wink, *Land and Sovereignty in India*, 78.
90. Bandyopadhyay, *From Plassey to Partition and After*, 24.
91. Ogawa, "Socio-economic Study of Indapur Pargana (1761–1828)."

5. SOUTH ASIA

92. Ogawa, "The Spatial Analysis of the Transition of the Land Revenue System in Western India (1761–1836)," 37–38, 45; T. Roy, *An Economic History of India 1707–1857*, 74; Gordon, *The Marathas 1600–1818*, 156; Wink, *Land and Sovereignty in India*, 622.
93. T. Roy, *An Economic History of India 1707–1857*, 67–68, 75. The specific claim is that both peshwa archives and the early colonial reports suggest the state's and warlords' growing dependence on revenue farming arrangements in the later years of the regime.
94. Wink, *Land and Sovereignty in India*, 160, 161.
95. T. Roy, *An Economic History of India 1707–1857*, 53.
96. Bandyopadhyay, *From Plassey to Partition and After*, 29.
97. Leonard, "The Hyderabad Political System and Its Participants," 576; Grewal, *The Sikhs of the Punjab*, 105 (quote); Ramusack, *The Indian Princes and Their States*, 39; T. Roy, *An Economic History of India 1707–1857*, 43.
98. K. Roy, *War, Culture, and Society in Early Modern South Asia, 1740–1849*, 139. See also Alam, *The Crisis of Empire in Mughal North India*, 12.
99. Leonard, "The Hyderabad Political System and Its Participants," 576. See also Ramusack, *The Indian Princes and Their States*, 27; Faruqui, "At Empire's End," 42; and Bandyopadhyay, *From Plassey to Partition and After*, 17–18.
100. Ramusack, *The Indian Princes and Their States*, 41; see also Stern, *The Cat and the Lion*, 2.
101. Rudolph, "The Princely States of Rajputana"; Bandyopadhyay, *From Plassey to Partition and After*, 32.
102. Hamilton, *The East Indian Gazetteer*, 237.
103. N. Swidler, "Kalat," 554–55.
104. Barfield, *Afghanistan*, 102, 110, 37, 110, 161. The capital of the Durrani Empire was moved to Kabul in the eighteenth century.
105. Hunter et al., *Imperial Gazetteer of India*, 11, 360.
106. Guha, "The Ahom Political System," 22–23.
107. T. Roy, *An Economic History of India 1707–1857*, 73.
108. Stein, "State Formation and Economy Reconsidered"; Habib, *Confronting Colonialism*, 75. Mysore retained Mughal titles and insignia to legitimize domestic rule.
109. Yazdani, *India, Modernity, and the Great Divergence*, 11, 15.
110. Perlin, "Proto-industrialization and Pre-colonial South Asia."
111. M. Roy, "Politics, War, and State Formation in Early Modern India," 169.
112. Stein, "State Formation and Economy Reconsidered," 392.
113. Gopal, *Tipu Sultan's Mysore*, 75, 83. Tipu wrote to the nawab of Savanore (a vassal of Mysore) in 1786, for example, stating that eight lakhs of rupees were due and to the nawab of Karnool stating that four lakhs were owed.
114. Stein, "State Formation and Economy Reconsidered," 391.
115. Yazdani, *India, Modernity, and the Great Divergence*, 275. See also Gopal, *Tipu Sultan's Mysore*.
116. Gopal, *Tipu Sultan's Mysore*, 66.
117. Stein, "State Formation and Economy Reconsidered," 402.
118. Yazdani, *India, Modernity, and the Great Divergence*, 236.
119. Stein, "State Formation and Economy Reconsidered," 402, 392.

120. See Phillips and Sharman, *International Order in Diversity*. Orders from Britain took six months to reach Bengal, making direct control from London difficult. See Marshall, *Bengal*, 100.
121. We do not code the EIC as a state because its external sovereignty was removed after (at least) the India Act of 1784, before our dataset starts.
122. Lawson, *The East India Company*, 110. Clive believed the EIC should not directly intervene in the local revenue-collection process (Marshall, *Bengal*, 116–17).
123. Lawson, *The East India Company*, 133. The EIC's army was larger than the British army at the end of the eighteenth century.
124. Lawson, *The East India Company*, 120.
125. These revenue demands, however, were very high, and defaulting zamindars could lose these rights.
126. Marshall, *Bengal*, 127.
127. Lorge, *The Asian Military Revolution*.
128. See Barnett, *North India Between Empires*, 249.
129. Perlin, "Proto-industrialization and Pre-colonial South Asia." See also Gordon, *The Marathas 1600–1818*, 129.
130. See Barua, *The State at War in South Asia* .
131. T. Roy, *An Economic History of India 1707–1857*, 24; Wink, *Land and Sovereignty in India*, 112.
132. Yazdani, "Haidar 'Ali and Tipu Sultan," 114; Wink, *Land and Sovereignty in India*, 200.
133. As Hendrik Spruyt points out in *The Sovereign State and Its Competitors*, for example, when trade disproportionately empowers merchants over states, trading leagues and city-states are more common.

6. MARITIME SOUTHEAST ASIA

1. Geertz, *The Religion of Java*; Geertz, *Negara*; B. Anderson, *Imagined Communities*; Kulke, "The Early and Imperial Kingdom in Southeast Asia History"; A. Reid, *Southeast Asia in the Age of Commerce*, vol. 1: *The Lands Below the Winds*; Wolters, *History, Culture, and Region in Southeast Asian Perspectives*; Ricklefs, *A History of Modern Indonesia Since c. 1200* (3rd ed.); Day, *Fluid Iron*; V. Lieberman, *Strange Parallels*, vol. 2: *Mainland Mirrors*; Acharya, *The Making of Southeast Asia*; Tambiah, "The Galactic Polity in Southeast Asia."
2. Others see Southeast Asia as encompassing the mainland states of Myanmar, Thailand, Laos, Cambodia, and Vietnam.
3. Ricklefs, *A History of Modern Indonesia Since c. 1200* (3rd ed.), 22. Other notable empires include Srivijaya (eighth–twelfth centuries CE) and the Malacca Sultanate (1400 to approximately 1511).
4. Scott, *The Art of Not Being Governed*.
5. V. Lieberman, *Strange Parallels*, vol. 2: *Mainland Mirrors*, 763–70.
6. Ricklefs, *A History of Modern Indonesia Since c. 1200* (3rd ed.), 59.
7. V. Lieberman, *Strange Parallels*, vol. 2: *Mainland Mirrors*, 795.
8. Ricklefs, *A History of Modern Indonesia Since c. 1200* (3rd ed.), 23; V. Lieberman, *Strange Parallels*, vol. 2: *Mainland Mirrors*, 809.

6. MARITIME SOUTHEAST ASIA

9. Ricklefs, *A History of Modern Indonesia Since c. 1200* (3rd ed.), 80.
10. Vickers, *Bali*, 110; Hägerdal, "Candrasangkala," 128–29; Nordholt, *The Spell of Power*, 183.
11. Hägerdal, "Periphery and Bridgehead," 168; Pringle, *A Short History of Bali*, 100.
12. Van der Kraan, "Lombok Under the Mataram Dynasty, 1839–94," 405.
13. Andaya and Andaya, *A History of Malaysia*, 164–65, 109, 118, 125. Other examples of state creation include Tampin, which separated from Rembau from 1832 to 1886.
14. This was especially the case in the mid- and late eighteenth century.
15. Ricklefs, *A History of Modern Indonesia Since c. 1200* (4th ed.), 109; Ricklefs, *A History of Modern Indonesia Since c. 1200* (3rd ed.), 134. Surakarta was more borderline as it had a historically closer relationship to the VOC than Mataram.
16. Ricklefs, *A History of Modern Indonesia Since c. 1200* (3rd ed.), 153.
17. Tagliacozzo, *Secret Trades, Porous Borders*.
18. Warren, *The Sulu Zone, 1768–1898*, 112–25.
19. Laarhoven, "We Are Many Nations."
20. Ricklefs, *A History of Modern Indonesia Since c. 1200* (3rd ed.), 167.
21. Vickers, *Bali*, 89.
22. Geertz, *Negara*, 8.
23. Note that "Mataram" is also the name of the south-central region and historical kingdom in Java.
24. Ricklefs, *A History of Modern Indonesia Since c. 1200* (3rd ed.), 173–76, 163.
25. Tagliacozzo, *Secret Trades, Porous Borders*.
26. Tilly, *Coercion, Capital, and European States*, 1–2; Acharya, *The Making of Southeast Asia*, quoting Tilly, 67. See also McCloud, *System and Process in Southeast Asia*; and Day, *Fluid Iron*.
27. Koh, "Travel and Survival in the Colonial Malay World," 567.
28. Acharya, *The Making of Southeast Asia*, 68.
29. A. Reid, "The Structure of Cities in Southeast Asia, Fifteenth to Seventeenth Centuries," 239.
30. V. Lieberman, *Strange Parallels*, vol. 2: *Mainland Mirrors*, 803, 764.
31. In "The Structure of Cities in Southeast Asia, Fifteenth to Seventeenth Centuries," Anthony Reid also points out that fruit trees were considered more valuable than the land they were planted on (241).
32. V. Lieberman, *Strange Parallels*, vol. 2: *Mainland Mirrors*, 768.
33. Henley, "Population and the Means of Subsistence," 340.
34. A. Reid, *Southeast Asia in the Age of Commerce*, vol. 1: *The Lands Below the Winds*.
35. A. Reid, "The Structure of Cities in Southeast Asia, Fifteenth to Seventeenth Centuries."
36. Ricklefs, *A History of Modern Indonesia Since c. 1200* (3rd ed.); Tambiah, "The Galactic Polity in Southeast Asia."
37. Acharya, *The Making of Southeast Asia*, 76.
38. V. Lieberman, *Strange Parallels*, vol. 2: *Mainland Mirrors*, 823; A. Reid, "The Structure of Cities in Southeast Asia, Fifteenth to Seventeenth Centuries," 240.
39. A. Reid, "The Structure of Cities in Southeast Asia, Fifteenth to Seventeenth Centuries," 237. These Southeast Asian coastal cities were of comparable size to some larger European cities.

40. Kathirithamby-Wells, "Royal Authority and the 'Orang Kaya' in the Western Archipelago, Circa 1500–1800," 261; A. Reid, "The Structure of Cities in Southeast Asia, Fifteenth to Seventeenth Centuries," 249; McCloud, *System and Process in Southeast Asia*; McNeill, *The Rise of the West*, 378; Geertz, *Negara*.
41. Ricklefs, *A History of Modern Indonesia Since c. 1200* (3rd ed.), 20–21; Acharya, *The Making of Southeast Asia*, 68.
42. Spruyt, *The World Imagined*, 296–97; Tambiah, "The Galactic Polity in Southeast Asia"; Scott, *The Art of Not Being Governed*.
43. Most of the wars in Southeast Asia noted in the Brecke catalog also involved the Dutch. See Brecke, "Violent Conflicts 1400 AD to the Present in Different Regions of the World."
44. McCloud, *System and Process in Southeast Asia*; Day, *Fluid Iron*; Acharya, *The Making of Southeast Asia*; Manggala, "The Mandala Culture of Anarchy."
45. Spruyt, *The World Imagined*, 295, 286–89. However, Barbara Watson Andaya notes that borders between *negeri* (i.e., city-states) were accepted, albeit difficult to enforce. See Andaya, "The Installation of the First Sultan of Selangor in 1766."
46. Andaya and Andaya, *A History of Malaysia*, 71, 81–84. In 1823, Badung conquered Mengwi, and from 1838 to 1839 Karangasem and Mataram Lombok fought a series of wars that culminated in Mataram Lombok ascendency on Bali and Lombok (van der Kraan, "Lombok Under the Mataram Dynasty, 1839–94," 392–96).
47. A. Reid, "The Structure of Cities in Southeast Asia, Fifteenth to Seventeenth Centuries," 245. Similar claims are made in Wolters, *History, Culture, and Region in Southeast Asian Perspectives*, and Geertz, *Negara*.
48. Spruyt, *The World Imagined*, 285.
49. Ricklefs, *A History of Modern Indonesia Since c. 1200* (4th ed.), 165; Day, *Fluid Iron*. Reporting bias is a serious issue when collecting data on contemporary conflicts. See Weidmann, "A Closer Look at Reporting Bias in Conflict Event Data."
50. Ricklefs, *A History of Modern Indonesia Since c. 1200* (4th ed.), 120, 133. The Yogyakarta Sultanate could mobilize up to 100,000 soldiers.
51. The extent to which Yogyakarta participated on the rebel side in the Java War is complicated. Many of the "princes" joined the rebels, although the royal family sided with the VOC. Ricklefs, *A History of Modern Indonesia Since c. 1200* (4th ed.), 141.
52. The Dutch fought many smaller wars with other independent Southeast Asian states, including wars with Bone (in 1824 and 1858–1860), Banjarmasin, Palembang, Jambi, and Minankabau. Ricklefs, *A History of Modern Indonesia Since c. 1200* (4th ed.), 167–78.
53. Clodfelter, *Warfare and Armed Conflicts*, 254.
54. Scott, *The Art of Not Being Governed*, 58–59; Manggala, "The Mandala Culture of Anarchy," 6–7.
55. Geertz, *Negara*, 4; V. Lieberman, *Strange Parallels*, vol. 2: *Mainland Mirrors*, 803.
56. Geertz, *Negara*, 13.
57. Tambiah, "The Galactic Polity in Southeast Asia," 503–4.
58. Modelski, "Kautilya," 549–50. The classic texts mentioned were written by Sun Tzu and Machiavelli.
59. Spruyt, *The World Imagined*, chap. 8.
60. Wolters, *History, Culture, and Region in Southeast Asian Perspectives*, 29.

6. MARITIME SOUTHEAST ASIA

61. Geertz, *Negara*, 25; Acharya, *The Making of Southeast Asia*, 61; Spruyt, *The World Imagined*, 287–88.
62. Tambiah, *World Conqueror and World Renouncer*; V. Lieberman, *Strange Parallels*, vol. 2: *Mainland Mirrors*, 764; Moertono, *State and Statecraft in Old Java*, 112.
63. See Wolters, *History, Culture, and Region in Southeast Asian Perspectives*, 27–40.
64. Creese, "New Kingdoms, Old Concerns."
65. Hägerdal, "Periphery and Bridgehead," 154–55; Ricklefs, *A History of Modern Indonesia Since c. 1200* (4th ed.), 82–83.
66. Ricklefs, *A History of Modern Indonesia Since c. 1200* (4th ed.), 164.
67. Kathirithamby-Wells, "Achehnese Control Over West Sumatra up to the Treaty of Painan, 1663," 453. See also Kahin, "Review of Multiple Centres of Authority," 177, in relation to Siak, and Laarhoven, "We Are Many Nations," in relation to the Sultanate of Maguindanao.
68. Aspinall, *Islam and Nation*, 23, 22.
69. Kathirithamby-Wells, "Siak and Its Changing Strategies for Survival," 221–23.
70. Hooker, *A Short History of Malaysia*, 89. See also Andaya and Andaya, *A History of Malaysia*, 168, for decentralization in other Malay states, such as Pahang.
71. Mahmud, "The Population of Kedah in the Nineteenth Century"; Hooker, *A Short History of Malaysia*, 118 (quotes).
72. Keat Gin, *Historical Dictionary of Malaysia*, 86, s.v. "Kedah."
73. Andaya and Andaya, *A History of Malaysia*, 92.
74. Labi, "A Re-analysis of Negri Sembilan Socio-political Organization," 148; Hooker, "The Early Adat Constitution of Negri Sembilan (1773–1824)," 106–7.
75. Andaya and Andaya, *A History of Malaysia*, 95.
76. Ricklefs, *Jogjakarta Under Sultan Mangkubumi 1749–1792*, 23.
77. Van der Kraan, "Lombok Under the Mataram Dynasty, 1839–94"; Hägerdal, "Periphery and Bridgehead," 168, 149–50; Pringle, *A Short History of Bali*, 74, 81.
78. Hägerdal, "Periphery and Bridgehead," 149–50, 168, 171.
79. Schrauwers, "Houses, Hierarchy, Headhunting, and Exchange," 360, 364.
80. Sidhu, *Historical Dictionary of Brunei Darussalam*, 8; Ileto, *Magindanao, 1860–1888*; Warren, *The Sulu Zone, 1768–1898*; Black, "The 'Lastposten,'" 284–85.
81. Acharya, *The Making of Southeast Asia*, 76. See also V. Lieberman, *Strange Parallels*, vol. 2: *Mainland Mirrors*, 797, 819, 871.
82. V. Lieberman, *Strange Parallels*, vol. 2: *Mainland Mirrors*, 797, 823, 871. Lieberman argues that the older Srivijaya and Mahajapit Empires collapsed because increases in trade created new competitors and empowered subordinates to throw off imperial rule.
83. Van Meersbergen, "The Dutch East India Company in South Asia"; Ricklefs, *A History of Modern Indonesia Since c. 1200* (3rd ed.), 143.
84. Kathirithamby-Wells, "Siak and Its Changing Strategies for Survival," 224, 231, 235.
85. Acharya, *The Making of Southeast Asia*, 78; V. Lieberman, *Strange Parallels*, vol. 2: *Mainland Mirrors*, 893; Kathirithamby-Wells, "Siak and Its Changing Strategies for Survival," 234.
86. Kahin, *Historical Dictionary of Indonesia*, 245, s.v. "Kongsi Wars"; Heidhues, "Chinese Gold Mining Communities in Western Borneo"; Chan, "The Founding of Singapore and the Chinese Kongsis of West Borneo (ca. 1819–1840)."

87. Andaya and Andaya, *A History of Malaysia*, 150, 146.
88. Ileto, *Magindanao, 1860–1888*, 8.
89. Spruyt, *The World Imagined*, 285.
90. Ricklefs, *A History of Modern Indonesia Since c. 1200* (3rd ed.), 104, 133, 102–7.
91. Day, *Fluid Iron*, 231. See also Acharya, *The Making of Southeast Asia*, 71.
92. Spruyt, *The World Imagined*, 296–97; Acharya, *The Making of Southeast Asia*, 61.
93. Acharya, *The Making of Southeast Asia*, 61; see also Spruyt, *The World Imagined*, 285.
94. Spruyt, *The World Imagined*, 282.
95. Ricklefs, *Jogjakarta Under Sultan Mangkubumi 1749–1792*, 235.
96. V. Lieberman, *Strange Parallels*, vol. 2: *Mainland Mirrors*, 785, 764.
97. Ricklefs, *Jogjakarta Under Sultan Mangkubumi 1749–1792*, 22.
98. Andaya and Andaya, *A History of Malaysia*, 92–93.
99. Kathirithamby-Wells, "Royal Authority and the 'Orang Kaya' in the Western Archipelago, Circa 1500–1800," 262.
100. Ricklefs, *A History of Modern Indonesia Since c. 1200* (3rd ed.), 88–94, 25, 86. See also Ricklefs, *Jogjakarta Under Sultan Mangkubumi 1749–1792*, 25.
101. Kathirithamby-Wells, "Royal Authority and the 'Orang Kaya' in the Western Archipelago, Circa 1500–1800," 256, 264; V. Lieberman, *Strange Parallels*, vol. 2: *Mainland Mirrors*, 846. The supervision of governors was also potentially a strategy to undermine the growing power of these elites..
102. V. Lieberman, *Strange Parallels*, vol. 2: *Mainland Mirrors*, 892; Winichakul, *Siam Mapped*, 103; Paik and Vechbanyongratana, "Path to Centralization and Development."
103. Spruyt, *The World Imagined*, 281; Tambiah, "The Galactic Polity in Southeast Asia," 507.
104. Doyle, *Empires*; Barkey, *Empire of Difference*, 294; Kulke, "The Early and Imperial Kingdom in Southeast Asia History," 7.
105. Wolters, *History, Culture, and Region in Southeast Asian Perspectives*, 29.

7. WEST AFRICA

1. Oliver and Atmore, *Africa since 1800*, 12.
2. This distribution is skewed. The majority are small states with a handful of larger empires. The mean population in South Asia was 1.1 million, while in Europe it was 3.4 million.
3. The Mughal Empire, in contrast, ruled more than 1.0 million square miles.
4. On the Senegal and Guinea-Bissau area, see Wilfahrt, *Precolonial Legacies in Postcolonial Politics*.
5. Approximately 483,000 slaves embarked from the Bight of Benin from the 1750s to the 1790s, which fell to about 409,000 from 1800 to the 1840s. Authors' estimates based on Manning, Zhang, and Yi, "Volume and Direction of the Atlantic Slave Trade, 1650–1870," appendix 1.
6. Hopkins, *An Economic History of West Africa*, 67.
7. "Dual" because it had two centers: Nikki and Bussa.
8. Egypt and the North African states from Morocco in the East to Egypt in the North were also important players on the margins of the system.

7. WEST AFRICA

9. Brown, "Toward a Chronology for the Caliphate of Hamdullahi (Māsina)."
10. Oliver and Atmore, *Africa since 1800*, 135.
11. The exceptions were Liberia and Ethiopia.
12. Monroe, "Building the State in Dahomey."
13. Coquery-Vidrovitch and Baker, *Africa and the Africans in the Nineteenth Century*, 70–74.
14. Hopkins, *An Economic History of West Africa*, 72.
15. Law, *The Oyo Empire*, 209. Horses were not utilized for transport because of the tsetse fly and the high costs of purchasing and maintaining them.
16. Wilfahrt, *Precolonial Legacies in Postcolonial Politics*, 54.
17. Oliver and Atmore, *Africa since 1800*, 26. The Timbuktu, Djenne, Goa route was important, for example. Hopkins, *An Economic History of West Africa*, 72.
18. Hopkins, *An Economic History of West Africa*, 76.
19. Wilks, *Asante in the Nineteenth Century*, 36, 60–64, 40–41.
20. See Alsan, "The Effect of the TseTse Fly on African Development," 391.
21. Approximately twenty miles per day could be traveled on foot. Hopkins, *An Economic History of West Africa*, 72.
22. Alsan, "The Effect of the TseTse Fly on African Development," 387–88.
23. Hopkins, *An Economic History of West Africa*, 74.
24. See also Herbst, *States and Power in Africa*.
25. H. Lovejoy, "Mapping Uncertainty," 149; Fagbule and Fawehinmi, *Formation*, 77; MacDonald and Camara, "Segou, Slavery, and Sifinso," 177.
26. It is difficult to make a direct comparison of population densities in the Yoruba or Igbo regions to the population densities of other regions, but they are often described as being relatively high (Coquery-Vidrovitch, *The History of African Cities South of the Sahara*, 19 and 246).
27. Hopkins, *An Economic History of West Africa*, 49.
28. Hopkins, *An Economic History of West Africa*, 19, 48.
29. Coquery-Vidrovitch, *The History of African Cities South of the Sahara*, 238–43.
30. Adebayo and Falola, *Culture, Politics, and Money Among the Yoruba*, 132; Hopkins, *An Economic History of West Africa*, 19.
31. Coquery-Vidrovitch, *The History of African Cities South of the Sahara*, 245–46, 277. Ibadan and Abeokuta had probably 100,000 people.
32. See also Fenske, "Ecology, Trade, and States in Pre-colonial Africa."
33. Hopkins, *An Economic History of West Africa*, 63.
34. In *An Economic History of West Africa*, Hopkins cites one example where a kola nut purchased in Gonja for 5 cowries would sell for 250–300 cowries on Lake Chad, 1,250 miles away (58–59).
35. Hopkins, *An Economic History of West Africa*, 102.
36. Nunn, "The Long-Term Effects of Africa's Slave Trades."
37. Laitin, "Capitalism and Hegemony."
38. P. Lovejoy, *Jihād in West Africa During the Age of Revolutions*.
39. Howard, "Nodes, Networks, Landscapes, and Regions," 86.
40. Monteil, "The Wolof Kingdom of Kayor."
41. Howard, "Nodes, Networks, Landscapes, and Regions."
42. Brecke, "Violent Conflicts 1400 AD to the Present in Different Regions of the World"; Dincecco, Fenske, and Onorato, "Is Africa Different?"

43. Brecke, "Violent Conflicts 1400 AD to the Present in Different Regions of the World"; Fenske, "Ecology, Trade, and States in Pre-colonial Africa."
44. Kumase was conquered by the British in 1896 without resistance.
45. R. Smith, *Warfare and Diplomacy in Pre-colonial West Africa*, 35.
46. Sokoto and Bornu fought another war in 1824.
47. See H. Lovejoy, "Mapping Uncertainty." According to Henry Lovejoy, Oyo was attacked nine times by Ilorin between 1818 and 1836 (this number was calculated from the replication data for the article, now accessible at https://dataverse.harvard.edu/dataset.xhtml?persistentId=doi:10.7910/DVN/TALYQW). See also Morton-Williams, "The Yoruba Kingdom of Oyo."
48. Ejiogu, "State Building in the Niger Basin in the Common Era and Beyond, 1000–Mid 1800s"; Ejiogu, "State Building in Pre-colonial Sub-Saharan Africa," 24. See also Falola, "Slavery and Pawnship in the Yoruba Economy of the Nineteenth Century." The length and start date of the Ekiti conflict are debated, but there is consensus that it was long and continuous. See Fagbule and Fawehinmi, *Formation*, 169.
49. Fagbule and Fawehinmi, *Formation*, 93.
50. R. Smith, *Warfare and Diplomacy in Pre-colonial West Africa*, 331.
51. Forrest, *Lineages of State Fragility*, 56, 79.
52. Forrest, *Lineages of State Fragility*, 79.
53. See, for example, R. Smith, *Warfare and Diplomacy in Pre-colonial West Africa*, 30, 39; Ejiogu, "State Building in the Niger Basin in the Common Era and Beyond, 1000–Mid 1800s."
54. See, for example, the descriptions of warfare in Last, *The Sokoto Caliphate*; Wilks, *Asante in the Nineteenth Century*; R. Reid, *Political Power in Pre-colonial Buganda*; R. Reid, "The Fragile Revolution"; Forrest, *Lineages of State Fragility*; and O'Fahey, *The Darfur Sultanate*.
55. Fagbule and Fawehinmi, *Formation*, 286.
56. Falola and Oguntomisin, *Yoruba Warlords of the Nineteenth Century*, 189.
57. Wilks, *Asante in the Nineteenth Century*, 218.
58. Thornton, *Warfare in Atlantic Africa, 1500–1800*, 15, 82, 92. Dahomey had a standing army by the late 1700s.
59. Lyall, *Divided Armies*; R. Smith, *Warfare and Diplomacy in Pre-colonial West Africa*, Wilks, *Asante in the Nineteenth Century*, 82–83 (Asante); Falola and Oguntomisin, *Yoruba Warlords of the Nineteenth Century*, 58 (Ibadan, Abeokuta, and Ijaye).
60. Lyall, *Divided Armies*, average number of troops taken from the dataset that accompanies the book at https://dataverse.harvard.edu/dataset.xhtml?persistentId=doi:10.7910/DVN/DUO7IE; R. Reid, "The Fragile Revolution," 393.
61. Bradbury, *The Benin Kingdom and the Edo-Speaking Peoples of South-Western Nigeria*, 22. See also Awe, "The Ajele System," 51, in relation to Ibadan, and Little, "The Mende Cheifdoms of Sierra Leone," 247, in relation to Sierra Leone.
62. For example, the northern borders of Asante, the borders between the Mossi kingdoms, and the southern borders of the Darfur Sultanate. See Coquery-Vidrovitch and Baker, *Africa and the Africans in the Nineteenth Century*, 162; Wilks, "Ashanti Government"; and O'Fahey, *The Darfur Sultanate*.
63. See, for example, Branch, *The Cartographic State*, or Herbst, *States and Power in Africa*. For examples, see Last, *The Sokoto Caliphate*, 77–79; Hiribarren, *A History*

7. WEST AFRICA

of Borno, 35, 110; R. Smith, *Kingdoms of the Yoruba*, 90; Wilks, *Asante in the Nineteenth Century*; Monroe, "Building the State in Dahomey"; Ejiogu, "State Building in the Niger Basin in the Common Era and Beyond, 1000–Mid 1800s"; and Howard, "Nodes, Networks, Landscapes, and Regions," 78.

64. Monteil, "The Wolof Kingdom of Kayor"; Hopkins, *An Economic History of West Africa*.
65. Forrest, *Lineages of State Fragility*, 41.
66. Coquery-Vidrovitch and Baker, *Africa and the Africans in the Nineteenth Century*, 30.
67. MacDonald and Camara, "Segou, Slavery, and Sifinso," 174.
68. Zahan, "The Mossi Kingdoms," 160; Englebert, *Burkina Faso*, chap. 2. "Mossi" refers to a ruling class, not an ethnic group specifically.
69. Ejiogu, "State Building in Pre-colonial Sub-Saharan Africa," 13, 21–23.
70. Oliver and Atmore, *Africa since 1800*, 67.
71. Abubakar, "The Emirate-Type of Government in the Sokoto Caliphate."
72. Hiribarren, *A History of Borno*, 50–51.
73. Coquery-Vidrovitch and Baker, *Africa and the Africans in the Nineteenth Century*, 100.
74. O'Fahey, *The Darfur Sultanate*, 179.
75. Law, *Ouidah*, 75.
76. Stewart, *African States and Their Rulers*. The king of Dahomey also attempted to restore the Hueda Kingdom as a tributary several times from the 1720s to the 1740s.
77. Monroe, *The Precolonial State in West Africa*.
78. Monroe, "Building the State in Dahomey"; Monroe, *The Precolonial State in West Africa*, 21.
79. Coquery-Vidrovitch and Baker, *Africa and the Africans in the Nineteenth Century*, 110; Akinjogbin, *Dahomey and Its Neighbours, 1708–1818*.
80. In *Asante in the Nineteenth Century*, Ivor Wilks notes that it is "permissible" to speak of Asante by 1680. The most powerful *amanhene* were Dwaben, Mampon, Kokofu, and Bekwae (405–6).
81. Wilks, *Asante in the Nineteenth Century*, 93, 113, 117–19 (quoting Bowditch). The nature of the Dwaben-Asante hierarchy was still contested by both sides in the 1820s.
82. The Asantemanhyiamu also contained representatives from the northern provinces. See Wilks, *Asante in the Nineteenth Century*, 547.
83. Boahen, "The States and Cultures of the Lower Guinea Coast," 420.
84. Wilks, *Asante in the Nineteenth Century*, 129–31.
85. Arhin, "The Structure of Greater Ashanti (1700–1824)," 78–83. The coastal Akan states regularly rebelled against Asante rule. In *Asante in the Nineteenth Century*, Wilks records rebellions in 1785–1787 (Wassa), 1805–1807 (Assin), 1806–1807 (Fante), and 1810–1811 (Akyem, Akwapim) (146–53).
86. Wilks, *Asante in the Nineteenth Century*, 264–66, 267.
87. Wilks, *Asante in the Nineteenth Century*, 468. Asante also had highway police and border guards in addition to state-run and state-approved traders.
88. Wilks, *Asante in the Nineteenth Century*, 476, 407–8. See also Wilks, "Aspects of Bureaucratization in Ashanti in the Nineteenth Century"; and Coquery-Vidrovitch and Baker, *Africa and the Africans in the Nineteenth Century*, 113.

7. WEST AFRICA

89. McCaskie, "Ahyiamu—'A Place of Meeting,'" quoted in Howard, "Nodes, Networks, Landscapes, and Regions," 82.
90. Wilks, "Ashanti Government," 232.
91. Oba were royal, hereditary town rulers, whereas *bale* were lesser, nonroyal town rulers.
92. See Law, *The Oyo Empire*, 96-112.
93. See Law, *The Oyo Empire*, 113-18; and Morton-Williams, "The Yoruba Kingdom of Oyo," 40-42. Oyo also practiced colonization strategies on its frontier (Usman, "On the Frontier of Empire").
94. The few comparative studies of state centralization in Africa that take ethnic groups as their starting point have found that while centralization does not correlate well with population density in Africa, proxies for trade diversity explain centralization better. See Fenske, "Ecology, Trade, and States in Pre-colonial Africa"; and Osafo-Kwaako and Robinson, "Political Centralization in Pre-colonial Africa." There are several limitations to these studies. Centralization is defined in a way that equates states such as Asante and Oyo, which, however, varied considerably in their centralization, and elides multiethnic empires such as Sokoto.
95. E. C. Ejiogu's article "State Building in the Niger Basin in the Common Era and Beyond, 1000–Mid 1800s" is the only direct application of Tilly's theory to precolonial West Africa, but the focus is on state formation rather than on centralization.
96. Ekiti and New Oyo could also be seen as "new states" following in the wake of the Oyo Empire.
97. The Ibadan Empire was about 25,500 square kilometers, about the size of modern-day Rwanda.
98. Falola and Oguntomisin, *Yoruba Warlords of the Nineteenth Century*, 167.
99. Falola and Oguntomisin, *Yoruba Warlords of the Nineteenth Century*, 64.
100. Alagoa, Elango, and N'Nah, "The Niger Delta and the Cameroon Region," 734.
101. R. Smith, *Warfare and Diplomacy in Pre-colonial West Africa*, 35.
102. Wilks, *Asante in the Nineteenth Century*, 53, 407, 530.
103. Bekwae, Kokofu, and Denyase, specifically. Wilks, *Asante in the Nineteenth Century*, 540-43.
104. Wilks, *Asante in the Nineteenth Century*, 586.
105. Wilks, *Asante in the Nineteenth Century*, 122-23, 296.
106. Quoted in Wilks, *Asante in the Nineteenth Century*, 280.
107. Wilks, *Asante in the Nineteenth Century*, 703.
108. Falola and Oguntomisin, *Yoruba Warlords of the Nineteenth Century*, 166-67.
109. Sharman, "Something New out of Africa"; Sharman and Zarakol, "Global Slavery in the Making of States and International Orders."
110. Asiwaju, "Dahomey, Yorubaland, Borgu, and Benin in the Nineteenth Century."
111. This is similar to Ejiogu's argument in "State Building in the Niger Basin in the Common Era and Beyond, 1000–Mid 1800s"—that slave trading had both state-building and state-disintegrating effects.
112. Ejiogu, "State Building in Pre-colonial Sub-Saharan Africa," 8; Ejiogu, "State Building in the Niger Basin in the Common Era and Beyond, 1000–Mid 1800s," 609. It is possible, however, that Oyo was centralizing toward the end of the eighteenth century.
113. Laitin, "Capitalism and Hegemony."

114. Laitin, "Capitalism and Hegemony." Some studies find that slavery undermined strong states. See, for example, Bezemer, Bolt, and Lensink, "Slavery, Statehood, and Economic Development in Sub-Saharan Africa."
115. Monroe, *The Precolonial State in West Africa*, 98–99. Female state officials were also used to limit exploitative tax-farming practices; see Bay, *Wives of the Leopard*.
116. See Hopkins, *An Economic History of West Africa*, map 9.
117. Quoted in Wilks, *Asante in the Nineteenth Century*, 685.
118. Bates, *Essays on the Political Economy of Rural Africa*; Herbst, *States and Power in Africa*; Fenske, "Ecology, Trade, and States in Pre-colonial Africa."
119. Goody, "The Over-Kingdom of Gonja," 183; Adeleye, *Power and Diplomacy in Northern Nigeria, 1804–1906*, 6–7.
120. In "Militarism and Economic Development in Nineteenth Century Yoruba Country," Bolanle Awe estimates that "trade routes radiated from Ibadan in virtually all directions: to the north, through Oyo, Ogbomosho and Ilorin; to Lagos through Abeokuta and the Ijebu country; and to Porto Novo also through Abeokuta. These were the major routes, supplying the main articles of exchange between the forest and the savannah zones, and were the most frequented by traders; for example, there were at least two large caravans containing not less than a thousand traders from Abeokuta and Ijebu country reaching Ibadan every month during peace time, and many more from Ibadan went to these places" (71–72).
121. Awe, "The Ajele System," 53.
122. Wilks, *Asante in the Nineteenth Century*, 30, 61–63.
123. Law, *Ouidah*, 50–53.
124. Lombard, "The Kingdom of Dahomey," 76.
125. Wilks, *Asante in the Nineteenth Century*, chap. 3.

8. LESSONS FROM THE CASE STUDIES

1. If we were more expansive, we could also include Awadh and Oyo for some periods of their rule. Had the ISD started earlier, we would also have included Travancore. See Foa, "Ancient Polities, Modern States," 118; T. Roy, "Rethinking the Origins of British India"; and Ramusack, *The Indian Princes and Their States*.
2. Ibadan, for example, used governors, whereas princes of the royal court were more common in Java.
3. For example, the Ajnapatra, a Marathi treatise for the regulation of Maratha domains, advised against land grants and noted that salaries provide greater incentives to loyalty (Wink, *Land and Sovereignty in India*, 216). Maratha leaders were also aware of, for example, the importance of rotating governors and administrators so that they couldn't develop local power bases (Gordon, "Forts and Social Control in the Maratha State").
4. The *oyo mesi* were based largely in the capital, Oyo Ile, and were the members of the key council upon which the *alafin* depended.
5. See Law, *The Oyo Empire*, 249–51, for an account of this event.
6. This is closely related to the idea that indirect rule is employed where vassals are strong (see Gerring, Ziblatt, et al., "An Institutional Theory of Direct and

Indirect Rule"). But we also note acephalous regions were rarely the target of centralization projects in general.
7. Had we adopted a more expansive definition of Southeast Asia, we would have included the Irrawaddy and Salween Basins, where Burma and Siam completed fairly successful centralization projects.
8. A recent study of armed groups in the eastern Democratic Republic of Congo suggests that indirect rule is a strategy used by conquering actors to overcome a deficit of local legitimacy. See Henn et al., "Indirect Rule."
9. See Ricklefs, *Jogjakarta Under Sultan Mangkubumi 1749–1792*, chapter 11, for a discussion of relations between Jogjakarta and the VOC.
10. See V. Lieberman, *Strange Parallels*, vol. 1: *Integration on the Mainland*, for a detailed discussion of centralization in Burma and Siam, and Winichakul, *Siam Mapped*, for a discussion of Siam.
11. Sharman, "Something New out of Africa."
12. Seen from a very broad perspective, the higher-capacity regions of East Asia and South Asia produced more centralized states. If we accept the basic premise that more people lower the marginal costs of economic and political interactions, as some do (e.g., Herbst in *States and Power in Africa*), then East and South Asia had the highest population densities, the highest capacity for interactions, and more extensive adoption of direct rule. The depth of centralization was also higher in these regions. Mysore and Pune probably employed more governors and bureaucrats over wider land areas than Asante did, for example.
13. Our claim is similar to Michael Hechter's argument in *Containing Nationalism* that poor communications were a background condition that led to the widespread adoption of indirect rule by premodern states (42).
14. For example, Herbst, *States and Power in Africa*.
15. Foa, "Ancient Polities, Modern States."
16. Abramson, "The Economic Origins of the Territorial State"; Spruyt, *The Sovereign State and Its Competitors*.
17. See Dalrymple, *The Anarchy*.
18. Stein, "State Formation and Economy Reconsidered."
19. This is how Robin Law describes how the *alafin* ruled his vassals (*The Oyo Empire*, 100).
20. Wilks, *Asante in the Nineteenth Century*, 53.
21. Barnett, *North India Between Empires*; K. Roy, *War, Culture, and Society in Early Modern South Asia, 1740–1849*, 3, 11. See also Wink, *Land and Sovereignty in India*, 159.
22. Spruyt, *The World Imagined*, 285. See also Chandler, *A History of Cambodia*, 133.
23. Ricklefs, *A History of Modern Indonesia Since c. 1200* (4th ed.), 115.
24. Vassals in Mysore were pensioned off by the state, for example (Stein, "State Formation and Economy Reconsidered").
25. Feinstein and Wimmer, "Consent and Legitimacy."
26. Wimmer, *Nation Building*; Spruyt, "War and State Formation," 91.
27. Bayly, *Rulers, Townsmen, and Bazaars*, 116–17.
28. Bayly, *Rulers, Townsmen, and Bazaars*, 112–13.
29. Sharman, "Something New out of Africa"; Sharman and Zarakol, "Global Slavery in the Making of States and International Orders."

9. SYSTEMS OF DECENTRALIZED STATES

30. The Aro Confederacy was essentially an alliance of interior merchants—trading mostly in slaves but also other in products—who agreed to cooperate on matters of war and trade but were otherwise independent of one another.
31. For the point that slavery coexisted equally with strong states, collapsing states, and areas with very thin state presence, see also Manning, "Slaves, Palm Oil, and Political Power on the West African Coast," and Laitin, "Capitalism and Hegemony," 711.
32. Laitin, "Capitalism and Hegemony."
33. See Law, *The Oyo Empire*, 309; Sharman, "Something New out of Africa."
34. Law, *The Oyo Empire*, 311. Law also points to strong descent groups, the use of slaves in the bureaucracy, and the difficulties of centralizing a cavalry army as explanations for Oyo's comparative decentralization (312).
35. Laitin, "Capitalism and Hegemony."
36. V. Lieberman, *Strange Parallels*, vol. 1: *Integration on the Mainland*.

9. SYSTEMS OF DECENTRALIZED STATES

1. Tilly, *Coercion, Capital, and European States, AD 990–1992*, 1–2.
2. MacDonald and Camara, "Segou, Slavery, and Sifinso," 174, which includes information on the Toeda.
3. Van der Kraan, "Lombok Under the Mataram Dynasty"; Hägerdal, "Periphery and Bridgehead," 168; Pringle, *A Short History of Bali*, 74, 81; V. Lieberman, *Strange Parallels*, vol. 2: *Mainland Mirrors*, 764; Tambiah, "The Galactic Polity in Southeast Asia," 503–4.
4. Modelski, "Kautilya," 549–50.
5. Doyle, *Empires*; Motyl, *Imperial Ends*; Nexon and Wright, "What's at Stake in the American Empire Debate"; Barkey, *Empire of Difference*; Luttwak, *The Grand Strategy of the Roman Empire*.
6. Laitin, "The National Uprisings in the Soviet Union"; Tilly, *Coercion, Capital, and European States, AD 990–1992*; Tilly, "How Empires End"; Motyl, "Thinking About Empire"; Beissinger, "1. Rethinking Empire in the Wake of Soviet Collapse."
7. Spruyt, *The Sovereign State and Its Competitors*; Buzan and Little, *International Systems in World History*; Reus-Smit, "Struggles for Individual Rights and the Expansion of the International System"; Phillips and Sharman, *International Order in Diversity*.
8. Lieven, *Empire*; Maier, *Among Empires*.
9. In "How Empires End," Tilly writes that the difference between national states and empires is a matter of degree (3).
10. Barkey, *Empire of Difference*, 294.
11. Doyle, *Empires*.
12. Kulke, "The Early and Imperial Kingdom in Southeast Asia History," 7.
13. Allan, *Scientific Cosmology and International Orders*.
14. Bull, *The Anarchical Society*; Waltz, *Theory of International Politics*; Buzan and Little, *International Systems in World History*; Schweller, "The Problem of International Order Revisited"; Ikenberry, *After Victory*; Trachtenburg, "The Problem of International Order and How to Think About It"; Phillips, *War, Religion, and Empire*; Reus-Smit, *Individual Rights and the Making of the Modern International*

9. SYSTEMS OF DECENTRALIZED STATES

System; Reus-Smith, *On Cultural Diversity*; Kissinger, *World Order*; Goddard, *When Might Makes Right*; Spruyt, *The World Imagined*; Lascurettes and Poznansky, "International Order in Theory and Practice"; Zarakol, *Before the West*.

15. Geertz, *Negara*, 13.
16. Spruyt, *The World Imagined*, 281.
17. Tambiah, "The Galactic Polity in Southeast Asia," 507.
18. As a matter of intellectual genealogy, it is interesting to note that many of the Southeast Asianists referenced in this book, including Benedict Anderson, Stanley Tambiah, Anthony Day, M. C. Ricklefs, and O. W. Wolters, were educated at Cornell University or taught there. One specialist on the region suggested to us that the mandala concept may have coalesced among and been promulgated by the Southeast Asianists at that institution.
19. Geertz, *Negara*, 20–21.
20. Griffiths, *Secession and the Sovereignty Game*.
21. Bayly, *Rulers, Townsmen, and Bazaars*, 178.
22. See, for example, Herbst, *States and Power in Africa*; and Clapham, *Africa and the International System*.
23. Branch, *The Cartographic State*; Goettlich, "The Rise of Linear Borders in World Politics"; Herbst, *States and Power in Africa*; Spruyt, *The World Imagined*.
24. Some borderlands in Europe were still poorly defined even in the nineteenth century. See Sahlins, *Boundaries*; and Holborn, *A History of Modern Germany*, 441.
25. Holborn, *A History of Modern Germany*, 441.
26. Fabry, *Recognizing States*, 81, 107.
27. Burns, *Patriarch and Folk*, 19.
28. Hiribarren, *A History of Borno*, 25.
29. R. Reid, *Political Power in Pre-colonial Buganda*.
30. Beattie, *The Nyoro State*, 254.
31. Green, "Ethnicity and Nationhood in Precolonial Africa," 7.
32. Coquery-Vidrovitch and Baker, *Africa and the Africans in the Nineteenth Century*, 18.
33. Winichakul, *Siam Mapped*, 64. See also Leach, "The Frontiers of 'Burma'"; and Renard, "The Delineation of the Kayah States Frontiers with Thailand."
34. Wilks, *Asante in the Nineteenth Century*, 53.
35. Butcher and Griffiths, "Toward a Theory of Heteronomy." John Ruggie popularized the concept of heteronomy in describing the European medieval order as a patchwork of overlapping, crosscutting, and entangled forms of political authority. He borrowed the term *heteronomous* from Friedrich Meinecke, who in *Machiavellianism*, Ruggie points out, "spoke of the heteronomous shackles of the Middle Ages, referring to the lattice-like network of authority relations." See Ruggie, "Continuity and Transformation in the World Polity," 154. Also see Spruyt, *The Sovereign State and Its Competitors*, 3; and Branch, *The Cartographic State*, 25.
36. In our article "Toward a Theory of Heteronomy," we argue that heteronomy has taken different forms historically. In this book, we focus on interstitial heteronomy, where polities with limited capacity in low-density regions experience zones of informal mixed rule on the frontier. In the article, we outline two other forms of heteronomy: functional heteronomy and personalistic heteronomy.
37. Herbst, *States and Power in Africa*, 44.

9. SYSTEMS OF DECENTRALIZED STATES

38. Little, "The Mende Chiefdoms of Sierra Leone," 247.
39. M. Smith, "A Hausa Kingdom," 102.
40. Coquery-Vidrovitch and Baker, *Africa and the Africans in the Nineteenth Century*, 100.
41. Goody, "The Over-Kingdom of Gonja."
42. Gordon, *The Marathas 1600–1818*, 135–39.
43. Scott, *The Art of Not Being Governed*, 61.
44. Some forms of heteronomy were formal. Pune and Hyderabad probably agreed that both would collect taxes from Khandesh villages.
45. Adelman and Aron, "From Borderlands to Borders."
46. Tambiah, "The Galactic Polity"; Geertz, *Negara*; Oliver and Atmore, *Medieval Africa, 1250–1800*, 37; Scott, *The Art of Not Being Governed*; Spruyt, *The World Imagined*.
47. Pitts, "Political Theory of Empire and Imperialism."
48. Bueno de Mesquita et al., *The Logic of Political Survival*; Fearon, "Rationalist Explanations for War"; Walter, "Bargaining Failures and Civil War"; Acemoglu and Robinson, *Economic Origins of Dictatorship and Democracy*.
49. Spruyt, "War and State Formation." Another exception is Daniel Nexon, who argues in *The Struggle for Power in Early Modern Europe* that centralized states emerged in Europe because of an external religious shock (the Protestant Reformation) that undermined old ways of managing decentralized (or, in his description, "composite") states, creating new crosscutting alliances and reshaping states. This insight is derived from a theory that explicitly models one of the core dilemmas of decentralized rule—how to keep autonomous subordinates from allying, defecting, and overthrowing the ruler. Recent works that emphasize the power of substate elites include Garfias and Sellars, "From Conquest to Centralization"; Garfias and Sellars, "Fiscal Legibility and State Development"; Garfias and Sellars, "When State Building Backfires"; Garfias, "Elite Coalitions, Limited Government, and Fiscal Capacity Development"; Garfias, "Elite Competition and State Capacity Development"; Gerring, Ziblatt, et al., "An Institutional Theory of Direct and Indirect Rule"; and Mazzuca, *Latecomer State Formation*.
50. Garfias and Sellars, "From Conquest to Centralization."
51. Arias, "Building Fiscal Capacity in Colonial Mexico."
52. See Ahmed and Stasavage, "Origins of Early Democracy," in relation to early democracy.
53. Clark, Golder, and Golder, "The British Academy Brian Barry Prize Essay."
54. Brittlebank, "Curiosities, Conspicuous Piety, and the Maker of Time"; Andaya, "The Installation of the First Sultan of Selangor in 1766."
55. Exit has played an important role in explaining democratization whereby rulers are more likely to grant inclusion to groups that have strong exit options. See, for example, Clark, Golder, and Golder, "The British Academy Brian Barry Prize Essay"; Freeman and Quinn, "The Economic Origins of Democracy Reconsidered"; and Ahmed and Stasavage, "Origins of Early Democracy."
56. Ricklefs, *Jogjakarta Under Sultan Mangkubumi 1749–1792*.
57. Stasavage, "When Distance Mattered"; Ahmed and Stasavage, "Origins of Early Democracy"; Stasavage, *The Decline and Rise of Democracy*.
58. Tilly, *The Formation of National States in Western Europe*.

9. SYSTEMS OF DECENTRALIZED STATES

59. Feinstein and Wimmer, "Consent and Legitimacy."
60. Gellner, *Nations and Nationalism*.
61. Gilpin, *War and Change in World Politics*.
62. Spruyt, *The Sovereign State and Its Competitors*.

CONCLUSION

1. See, for example, Nexon, *The Struggle for Power in Early Modern Europe*.
2. In a way like others, such as Charles Tilly in *Coercion, Capital, and European States*, and Scott Abramson in "The Economic Origins of the Territorial State."
3. Butcher and Griffiths, "States and Their International Relations Since 1816."
4. In "After the Tilly Thesis," Benno Teschke argues that inside/outside distinctions did not exist in medieval Europe (38).
5. Costa Lopez, "Political Authority in International Relations."
6. Ruggie, *Constructing the World Polity*; Teschke, "After the Tilly Thesis."
7. R. Smith, *Warfare and Diplomacy in Pre-colonial West Africa*; R. Smith, "Peace and Palaver."
8. Gaddis, "The Long Peace"; Mueller, "The Obsolescence of Major War"; Mueller, "War Has Almost Ceased to Exist"; Jervis, "Theories of War in an Era of Leading-Power Peace"; Pinker, *The Better Angels of Our Nature*; Goldstein, *Winning the War on War*; Clauset, "Trends and Fluctuations in the Severity of Interstate Wars"; Gat, "Is War Declining—and Why?"
9. Fazal, "Dead Wrong?"; N. Gleditsch et al., "The Forum: The Decline of War"; Cirillo and Taleb, "On the Statistical Properties and Tail Risk of Violent Conflicts"; Braumoeller, *Only the Dead*.
10. Kang, *East Asia Before the West*; Kelly, "A 'Confucian Long Peace' in Pre-Western East Asia"; Kang, Shaw, and Fu, "Measuring War in Early Modern East Asia, 1368–1841"; Phillips, "Contesting the Confucian Peace."
11. Fearon and Laitin, "Ethnicity, Insurgency, and Civil War"; Walter, "Bargaining Failures and Civil War"; Harbom, Melander, and Wallensteen, "Dyadic Dimensions of Armed Conflict, 1946–2007"; Guillen, "Wars Between States Are Down, but Civil Wars Are Up."
12. Johnston, *Cultural Realism*; Perdue, "Military Mobilization in Seventeenth- and Eighteenth-Century China, Russia, and Mongolia"; Woodside, "Territorial Order and Collective-Identity Tensions in Confucian Asia"; Kang, *East Asia Before the West*; Kelly, "A 'Confucian Long Peace' in Pre-Western East Asia"; Kwan, "Hierarchy, Status, and International Society"; Kang, Shaw, and Fu, "Measuring War in Early Modern East Asia, 1368–1841"; Phillips, "Contesting the Confucian Peace"; Hui, "Cultural Diversity and Coercive Cultural Homogenization in Chinese History."
13. Sundberg and Melander, "Introducing the UCDP Georeferenced Event Dataset."
14. Raleigh et al., "Introducing ACLED."
15. Lyall, *Divided Armies*, 4.
16. Braumoeller, *Only the Dead*, xii–xv.
17. Miller and Bakar, "Conflict Events Worldwide Since 1468 BC"; Brecke, "Violent Conflicts 1400 AD to the Present in Different Regions of the World"; Clodfelter, *Warfare and Armed Conflicts*.

CONCLUSION

18. Lyall, *Divided Armies*.
19. Kang, Shaw, and Fu, "Measuring War in Early Modern East Asia, 1368–1841"; Dincecco and Onorato, "Military Conflict and the Rise of Urban Europe"; Dincecco and Wang, "Violent Conflict and Political Development Over the Long Run"; Dincecco, Fenske, and Onorato, "Is Africa Different?"; N. Anderson, "Introducing the Warring States Japan Battle Data."
20. Braumoeller, *Only the Dead*.
21. Pinker, *The Better Angels of Our Nature*; Spagat and van Weezel, "The Decline of War Since 1950."
22. N. Gleditsch et al., "The Forum: The Decline of War."
23. One option is to use the COW list, but start and end dates are hard to infer from this list.

BIBLIOGRAPHY

Abramson, Scott F. "The Economic Origins of the Territorial State." *International Organization* 71, no. 1 (2017): 97–130.

Abubakar, Sa'ad. "The Emirate-Type of Government in the Sokoto Caliphate." *Journal of the Historical Society of Nigeria* 7, no. 2 (1974): 211–29.

Acemoglu, Daron, and James A. Robinson. *Economic Origins of Dictatorship and Democracy*. New York: Cambridge University Press, 2005.

Acharya, Amitav. "Global International Relations (IR) and Regional Worlds: A New Agenda for International Studies." *International Studies Quarterly* 58, no. 4 (2014): 647–59.

———. *The Making of Southeast Asia*. Ithaca, NY: Cornell University Press, 2012.

Acharya, Avidit, and Alexander Lee. "Economic Foundations of the Territorial State System." *American Journal of Political Science* 62, no. 4 (2018): 954–66.

———. "Path Dependence in European Development: Medieval Politics, Conflict, and State Building." *Comparative Political Studies* 52, nos. 13–14 (2019): 2171–206.

Adebayo, Akanmu, and Toyin Falola. *Culture, Politics, and Money Among the Yoruba*. New Brunswick, NJ: Transaction, 2000.

Adegbulu, Femi. "Pre-colonial West African Diplomacy: It's Nature and Impact." *Journal of International Social Research* 4, no. 18 (2011): 170–82.

Adeleye, Rowland A. *Power and Diplomacy in Northern Nigeria, 1804–1906: The Sokoto Caliphate and Its Enemies*. London: Longman, 1971.

Adelman, Jeremy, and Stephen Aron. "From Borderlands to Borders: Empires, Nation-States, and the Peoples in North American History." *American Historical Review* 104, no. 3 (1999): 814–41.

Agnew, John. "The Territorial Trap: The Geographical Assumptions of International Relations Theory." *Review of International Political Economy* 1, no. 1 (1994): 53–80.

BIBLIOGRAPHY

Ahlerup, Pelle, and Ola Olsson. "The Roots of Ethnic Diversity." *Journal of Economic Growth* 17, no. 2. (2012): 71–102.

Ahmed, Ali T., and David Stasavage. "Origins of Early Democracy." *American Political Science Review* 114, no. 2 (2020): 502–18.

Akinjogbin, I. A. *Dahomey and Its Neighbours, 1708-1818.* Cambridge: Cambridge University Press, 1967.

Alagoa, E. J., L. Z. Elango, and M. Metegue N'Nah. "The Niger Delta and the Cameroon Region." In *General History of Africa*, vol. 6: *Africa in the Nineteenth Century Until the 1880s*, ed. J. F. Ade Ajayi, 724–48. Berkeley, CA: UNESCO, 1989.

Alam, Muzaffar. *The Crisis of Empire in Mughal North India Awadh and the Punjab, 1707-48.* 2nd ed. New Delhi: Oxford University Press, 2013.

Allan, Bentley. *Scientific Cosmology and International Orders.* Cambridge: Cambridge University Press, 2018.

Alsan, Marcella. "The Effect of the TseTse Fly on African Development." *American Economic Review* 105, no. 1 (2015): 382–410.

Andaya, Barbara Watson. "The Installation of the First Sultan of Selangor in 1766." *Malaysian Branch of the Royal Asiatic Society* 47, no. 1 (1974): 41–57.

Andaya, Barbara Watson, and Leonard Y. Andaya. *A History of Malaysia.* New York: St. Martin's, 1982.

Anderson, Benedict. *Imagined Communities: Reflections on the Origin and Spread of Nationalism.* London: Verso, 1983.

Anderson, Greg. "Was There Any Such Thing as a Nonmodern State?" In *State Formations: Global Histories and Cultures of Statehood*, ed. John L. Brooke, Julia C. Strauss, and Greg Anderson, 58–70. Cambridge: Cambridge University Press, 2018.

Anderson, Nicholas D. "Introducing the Warring States Japan Battle Data." *International Interactions* 49, no. 1 (2022): 147–62.

ArcGIS. "1840 CE." ArcGIS map. January 14, 2021; updated April 8, 2021. https://worldmap.maps.arcgis.com/home/item.html?id=5192284ad3084a2bb3be6138ca49a216.

Arhin, Kwame. "The Structure of Greater Ashanti (1700–1824)." *Journal of African History* 8, no. 1 (1967): 65–85.

Arias, Luz Marina. "Building Fiscal Capacity in Colonial Mexico: From Fragmentation to Centralization." *Journal of Economic History* 73, no. 3 (2013): 662–93.

Ashraf, Quamrul, and Oded Galor. "Genetic Diversity and the Origins of Cultural Fragmentation." *American Economic Review* 103, no. 3 (2013): 528–33.

Asiwaju, A. I. "Dahomey, Yorubaland, Borgu, and Benin in the Nineteenth Century." In *General History of Africa*, vol. 6: *Africa in the Nineteenth Century Until the 1880s*, ed. J. F. Ade Ajayi, 279–91. Berkeley, CA: UNESCO, 1989.

Aspinall, Edward. *Islam and Nation: Separatist Rebellion in Aceh, Indonesia.* Studies in Asian Security. Stanford, CA: Stanford University Press, 2009.

Awe, Bolanle [Awẹ, Bọlanle]. "The Ajele System: A Study of Ibadan Imperialism in the Nineteenth Century." *Journal of the Historical Society of Nigeria* 3, no. 1 (1964): 47–60.

———."Militarism and Economic Development in Nineteenth Century Yoruba Country: The Ibadan Example." *Journal of African History* 14, no. 1 (1973): 65–77.

Axelrod, Paul. "Living on the Edge: The Village and the State on the Goa-Maratha Frontier." *Indian Economic & Social History Review* 45, no. 4 (2008): 553–80.

BIBLIOGRAPHY

Bakken, Ingrid Vik, and Halvard Buhaug. "Civil War and Female Empowerment." *Journal of Conflict Resolution* 65, no. 5 (2021): 982–1009.

Bandyopadhyay, Sekhar. *From Plassey to Partition and After: A History of Modern India.* Hyderabad, India: Orient Longman, 2004.

Barfield, Thomas. *Afghanistan: A Cultural and Political History.* Reprint ed. Princeton, NJ: Princeton University Press, 2012.

———. *The Perilous Frontier: Nomadic Empires and China, 221 BC to AD 1757.* Oxford: Blackwell, 1989.

Barkey, Karen. 2008. *Empire of Difference: The Ottomans in Comparative Perspective.* Cambridge: Cambridge University Press.

Barnett, Richard B. *North India Between Empires: Awadh, the Mughals, and the British, 1720–1801.* Berkeley: University of California Press, 1980.

Barua, Pradeep. *The State at War in South Asia.* Lincoln: University of Nebraska Press, 2005.

Bates, Robert H. *Essays on the Political Economy of Rural Africa.* Cambridge: Cambridge University Press, 1983.

Bay, Edna G. *Wives of the Leopard: Gender, Politics, and Culture in the Kingdom of Dahomey.* ACLS Humanities E-Book. Charlottesville: University of Virginia Press, 1998.

Bayly, C. A. *Indian Society and the Making of the British Empire.* Cambridge: Cambridge University Press, 1988.

———. *Rulers, Townsmen, and Bazaars: North Indian Society in the Age of British Expansion, 1770–1870.* 3rd ed. Oxford: Oxford University Press; Cambridge: Cambridge University Press, 2012.

Bean, Richard. "War and the Birth of the Nation State." *Journal of Economic History* 33, no. 1 (1973): 203–21.

Beasley, W. G. "Meiji Political Institutions." In *The Cambridge History of Japan*, vol. 5: *The Nineteenth Century*, ed. Marius B. Jansen, 618–73. Cambridge: Cambridge University Press, 1989.

Beattie, John. *The Nyoro State.* Oxford: Oxford University Press, 1971.

Becker, Seymour. *Russia's Protectorates in Central Asia: Bukhara and Khiva, 1865–1924.* 2nd ed. London: Routledge, 2004.

Beissinger, Mark R. "1. Rethinking Empire in the Wake of Soviet Collapse." In *Rethinking Empire in the Wake of Soviet Collapse*, ed. Zoltan Barany and Robert Moser, 14–45. Ithaca, NY: Cornell University Press, 2005.

Bennett, Norman R. *Arab Versus European: Diplomacy and War in Nineteenth-Century East Central Africa.* New York: Africana, 1986.

Besley, Tim, and Marta Reynal-Querol. "The Legacy of Historical Conflict: Evidence from Africa." *American Political Science Review* 108, no. 2 (2014): 319–36.

Bezemer, Dirk, Jutta Bolt, and Robert Lensink. "Slavery, Statehood, and Economic Development in Sub-Saharan Africa." *World Development* 57 (2014): 148–63.

Bhattacharya, S., and B. Chaudhuri. "Regional Economy (1757–1857): Eastern India." In *The Cambridge Economic History of India*, vol. 2: *C. 1757–c. 1970*, ed. Dharma Kumar, with Meghnad Desai, 270–331. Cambridge: Cambridge University Press, 1983.

Black, Ian. "The 'Lastposten': Eastern Kalimantan and the Dutch in the Nineteenth and Early Twentieth Centuries." *Journal of Southeast Asian Studies* 16, no. 2 (1985): 281–91.

Blaydes, Lisa, and Eric Chaney. "The Feudal Revolution and Europe's Rise: Political Divergence of the Christian West and the Muslim World Before 1500 CE." *American Political Science Review* 107, no. 1 (2013): 16–34.

Blaydes, Lisa, and Christopher Paik. "The Impact of Holy Land Crusades on State Formation: War Mobilization, Trade Integration, and Political Development in Medieval Europe." *International Organization* 70, no. 3 (2016): 551–86.

———. "Trade and Political Fragmentation on the Silk Roads: The Economic Effects of Historical Exchange Between China and the Muslim East." *American Journal of Political Science* 65, no. 1 (2021): 115–32.

Boahen, A. Adu. "The States and Cultures of the Lower Guinea Coast." In *General History of Africa*, vol. 5: *Africa from the Sixteenth to the Eighteenth Century*, ed. Bethwell A. Ogot, 399–433. London: Heinemann, 1992.

Bolitho, Harold. "The Han." In *The Cambridge History of Japan*, vol. 4: *Early Modern Japan*, ed. John Whitney Hall, 183–234. Cambridge: Cambridge University Press, 1991.

Boxberger, Linda. *On the Edge of Empire: Hadramawt, Emigration, and the Indian Ocean, 1880s–1930s*. Albany: State University of New York Press, 2002.

Bradbury, Robert Elwyn. *The Benin Kingdom and the Edo-Speaking Peoples of South-Western Nigeria*. Western Africa Part XIII. London: Routledge, 2017.

Brambor, Thomas, Agustín Goenaga, Johannes Lindvall, and Jan Teorell. "The Lay of the Land: Information Capacity and the Modern State." *Comparative Political Studies* 53, no. 2 (2020): 175–213.

Branch, Jordan. *The Cartographic State: Maps, Territory, and the Origins of Sovereignty*. Cambridge: Cambridge University Press, 2014.

Braumoeller, Bear F. *Only the Dead: The Persistence of War in the Modern Age*. Oxford: Oxford University Press, 2019.

Brecke, Peter. "Violent Conflicts 1400 AD to the Present in Different Regions of the World." Paper presented at the Peace Science Society meeting, Ann Arbor, MI, October 8–10, 1999.

Bremer, Stuart A., and Faten Ghosn. "Defining States: Reconsiderations and Recommendations." *Conflict Management and Peace Science* 20, no. 1 (2003): 21–41.

Breuilly, John. *Nineteenth-Century Germany: Politics, Culture, and Society 1780–1918*. London: Bloomsbury, 2019.

British Government of India. *Imperial Gazetteer of India, Provincial Series: North-West Frontier Province*. Calcutta: Government of India, 1908.

Brittlebank, Kate. "Curiosities, Conspicuous Piety, and the Maker of Time: Some Aspects of Kingship in Eighteenth-Century South India." *South Asia: Journal of South Asian Studies* 16, no. 2 (1993): 41–56.

Brown, William A. "Toward a Chronology for the Caliphate of Hamdullahi (Māsina)." *Cahiers d'études africaines* 8, no. 31 (1968): 428–34.

Bueno de Mesquita, Bruce, Alastair Smith, James D. Morrow, and Randolph M. Siverson. *The Logic of Political Survival*. Cambridge, MA: MIT Press, 2005.

Bull, Hedley. *The Anarchical Society: A Study of Order in World Politics*. New York: Columbia University Press, 1977.

Burns, E. Bradford. *Patriarch and Folk: The Emergence of Nicaragua, 1798–1858*. Cambridge, MA: Harvard University Press, 2013.

BIBLIOGRAPHY

Butcher, Charles R., and Ryan D. Griffiths. "Alternative International Systems? System Structure and Violent Conflict in 19th Century West Africa, Southeast Asia, and South Asia." *Review of International Studies* 41, no. 4 (2015): 715–37.

———. "Between Eurocentrism and Babel: A Framework for the Analysis of States, State Systems, and International Orders." *International Studies Quarterly* 61, no. 2 (2017): 328–36.

———. "States and Their International Relations Since 1816: Introducing Version 2 of the International System(s) Dataset (ISD)." *International Interactions* 46, no. 2 (2020): 291–308.

———. "Toward a Theory of Heteronomy." *International Studies Quarterly* 66, no. 1 (2022): 1–9.

———. "War, Interaction Capacity, and the Structures of State Systems." *International Theory* 13, no. 2 (2021): 372–96.

Buzan, Barry, and Mathias Albert. "Differentiation: A Sociological Approach to International Relations Theory." *European Journal of International Relations* 16, no. 3 (2010): 315–37.

Buzan, Barry, and George Lawson. *The Global Transformation: History, Modernity, and the Making of International Relations*. Cambridge: Cambridge University Press, 2015.

Buzan, Barry, and Richard Little. *International Systems in World History: Remaking the Study of International Relations*. Oxford: Oxford University Press, 2000.

Cederman, Lars-Erik, and Luc Girardin. "Growing Sovereignty: Modelling the Shift from Direct to Indirect Rule." *International Studies Quarterly* 54, no. 1 (2010): 27–48.

Cederman, Lars-Erik, Paola Galano Toro, Luc Girardin, and Guy Schvitz. "War Did Make States: Revisiting the Bellicist Paradigm in Early Modern Europe." *International Organization* 77, no. 2 (2023): 324–62.

Centeno, Miguel. *War and the Nation-State in Latin America*. University Park: Pennsylvania State University Press, 2003.

Chan, Ying-kit. "The Founding of Singapore and the Chinese Kongsis of West Borneo (ca. 1819–1840)." *Journal of Cultural Interaction in East Asia* 7, no. 1 (2016): 99–121.

Chandler, David. *A History of Cambodia*. 4th ed. London: Routledge, 2007.

Cirillo, Pasquale, and Nassim Nicholas Taleb. "On the Statistical Properties and Tail Risk of Violent Conflicts." *Physica A: Statistical Mechanics and Its Applications* 452 (2016): 29–45.

Clapham, Christopher. *Africa and the International System: The Politics of State Survival*. Cambridge: Cambridge University Press, 1996.

Clark, William Roberts, Matt Golder, and Sona N. Golder. "The British Academy Brian Barry Prize Essay: An Exit, Voice, and Loyalty Model of Politics." *British Journal of Political Science* 47, no. 4: (2017): 719–48

Clauset, Aaron. "Trends and Fluctuations in the Severity of Interstate Wars." *Science Advances* 4, no. 2 (2018): 1–9.

Clodfelter, Michael. *Warfare and Armed Conflicts: A Statistical Encyclopedia of Casualty and Other Figures, 1494–2007*. 3rd ed. London: McFarland, 2008.

Codrington, O. "The Coinages of Cutch and Kathiawar." *Numismatic Chronicle and Journal of the Numismatic Society* 15 (1895): 59–88.

BIBLIOGRAPHY

Coppedge, Michael, John Gerring, Carl Henrik Knutsen, Staffan I. Lindberg, Jan Teorell, David Altman, Michael Bernhard, et al. V-Dem [Country-Year/Country-Date] Dataset, vol. 9. Varieties of Democracy (V-Dem) Project, 2019. https://doi.org/10.23696/vdemcy19.

Coquery-Vidrovitch, Catherine. *The History of African Cities South of the Sahara: From the Origins to Colonization*. Princeton, NJ: Markus Wiener, 2005.

Coquery-Vidrovitch, Catherine, and Mary Baker. *Africa and the Africans in the Nineteenth Century: A Turbulent History*. New York: M. E. Sharpe, 2009.

Corfield, Justin J. *The History of Vietnam*. Greenwood Histories of the Modern Nations Westport, CT: Greenwood Press, 2008.

Correlates of War Project. "State System Membership List, v2011." 2011. https://correlatesofwar.org.

———. "State System Membership List, v2016." 2017. https://correlatesofwar.org.

Costa Lopez, Julia. "Political Authority in International Relations: Revisiting the Medieval Debate." *International Organization* 74, no. 2 (2020): 222–52.

Costa Lopez, Julia, and Benjamin De Carvalho. "Introduction: The Emergence of Sovereignty: More Than a Question of Time." In "Forum: In the Beginning There Was No Word (for It): Terms, Concepts, and Early Sovereignty." *International Studies Review* 20, no. 3 (2018): 490–94.

Creese, Helen. "New Kingdoms, Old Concerns: Balinese Identities in the Eighteenth and Nineteenth Centuries." In *The Last Stand of Asian Autonomies: Responses to Modernity in the Diverse States of Southeast Asia and Korea, 1750–1900*, ed. Anthony Reid, 345–66. London: Routledge.

Dalrymple, William. *The Anarchy: The East India Company, Corporate Violence, and the Pillage of an Empire*. Illus. ed. London: Bloomsbury, 2019.

Day, Anthony. *Fluid Iron: State Formation in Southeast Asia*. Honolulu: University of Hawaiʻi Press, 2002.

Depetris-Chauvin, Emilio. "State History and Contemporary Conflict: Evidence from Sub-Saharan Africa." Posted online October 26, 2015. https://papers.ssrn.com/abstract=2679594.

Dewière, Rémi. "The Kanem and Borno Sultanates (11th–19th Centuries)." In *Oxford Research Encyclopedia of African History* (online). Oxford: Oxford University Press, 2024. https://oxfordre.com/africanhistory/display/10.1093/acrefore/9780190277734.001.0001/acrefore-9780190277734-e-1147?rskey=zW213K&result=1.

Dincecco, Mark, James Fenske, and Massimiliano Gaetano Onorato. "Is Africa Different? Historical Conflict and State Development." *Economic History of Developing Regions* 34, no. 2 (2019): 209–50.

Dincecco, Mark, and Massimiliano Gaetano Onorato. "Military Conflict and the Rise of Urban Europe." *Journal of Economic Growth* 21, no. 3 (2016): 259–82.

Dincecco, Mark, and Mauricio Prado. "Warfare, Fiscal Capacity, and Performance." *Journal of Economic Growth* 17, no. 3 (2012): 171–203.

Dincecco, Mark, and Yuhua Wang. "Violent Conflict and Political Development Over the Long Run: China Versus Europe." *Annual Review of Political Science* 21, no. 1 (2018): 341–58.

Divekar, V. D. "Regional Economy (1757–1857): Western India." In *The Cambridge Economic History of India*, vol. 2: *C. 1757–c. 1970*, ed. Dharma Kumar, with Meghnad Desai, 332–51. Cambridge: Cambridge University Press, 1983.

BIBLIOGRAPHY

Donnelly, Jack. "The Differentiation of International Societies: An Approach to Structural International Theory." *European Journal of International Relations* 18, no. 1 (2019): 151–76.

———. "The Discourse of Anarchy in IR." *International Theory* 7, no. 3 (2015): 393–425.

———. "The Elements of the Structures of International Systems." *International Organization* 66, no. 4 (2012): 609–44.

———. "Rethinking Political Structures: From 'Ordering Principles' to 'Vertical Differentiation'—and Beyond." *International Theory* 1, no. 1 (2009): 49–86.

———. *Systems, Relations, and the Structures of International Societies*. Cambridge: Cambridge University Press, 2024.

Doyle, Michael W. *Empires*. Ithaca, NY: Cornell University Press, 1986.

———. "Three Pillars of the Liberal Peace." *American Political Science Review* 99, no. 3 (2005): 463–66.

Duff, James Grant. *A History of the Mahrattas*. Vol. 3. London: R.Cambray, 1918.

Duggan, Christopher. *The Force of Destiny: A History of Italy Since 1796*. Boston: Houghton Mifflin Harcourt, 2008.

Dunne, Tim, and Christian Reus-Smit, eds. *The Globalization of International Society*. Oxford: Oxford University Press, 2017.

Dutton, George. "From Civil War to Uncivil Peace: The Vietnamese Army and the Early Nguyễn State (1802–1841)." *South East Asia Research* 24, no. 2 (2016): 167–84.

———. *The Tay Son Uprising: Society and Rebellion in Eighteenth-Century Vietnam*. Honolulu: University of Hawai'i Press, 2006.

Ejiogu, E. C. "State Building in the Niger Basin in the Common Era and Beyond, 1000–Mid 1800s: The Case of Yorubaland." *Journal of Asian and African Studies* 46, no. 6 (2011): 593–614.

———. "State Building in Pre-colonial Sub-Saharan Africa: The Case of Yorubaland." *Political Power and Social Theory* 18 (2007): 3–40.

Elliott, J. H. "A Europe of Composite Monarchies." *Past and Present* 37, no. 1 (1992): 48–71.

Englebert, Pierre. *Burkina Faso: Unsteady Statehood in West Africa*. Boulder, CO: Westview Press, 1996.

Erikson, Emily. "Formalist and Relationist Theory in Social Network Analysis." *Sociological Theory* 31, no. 3 (2013): 219–42.

Fabry, Mikulas. *Recognizing States: International Society and the Establishment of New States Since 1776*. Oxford: Oxford University Press, 2010.

Fagbule, Fola, and Feyi Fawehinmi. *Formation: The Making of Nigeria from Jihad to Amalgamation*. London: Cassava Republic Press, 2021.

Fairbank, John K. *The Chinese World Order: Traditional China's Foreign Relations*. Cambridge, MA: Harvard University Press, 1968.

———. "Tributary Trade and China's Relations with the West." *Far Eastern Quarterly* 1, no. 2 (1942): 129–49.

Falola, Toyin. "Slavery and Pawnship in the Yoruba Economy of the Nineteenth Century." *Slavery & Abolition* 15, no. 2 (1994): 221–45.

Falola, Toyin, and Matthew M. Heaton. *A History of Nigeria*. Cambridge: Cambridge University Press, 2008.

Falola, Toyin, and Dare Oguntomisin. *Yoruba Warlords of the Nineteenth Century*. Trenton, NJ; Asmara, Eritrea: Africa World Press, 2001.

Farrant, Leda. *Tippu Tip and the East African Slave Trade*. London: Hamilton, 1975.
Faruqui, Munis D. "At Empire's End: The Nizam, Hyderabad, and Eighteenth-Century India." *Modern Asian Studies* 43, no. 1 (2009): 5–43.
Fazal, Tanisha M. "Dead Wrong? Battle Deaths, Military Medicine, and Exaggerated Reports of War's Demise." *International Security* 39, no. 1 (2014): 95–125.
——. *State Death: The Politics and Geography of Conquest, Occupation, and Annexation*. Princeton, NJ: Princeton University Press, 2007.
Fearon, James D. "Rationalist Explanations for War." *International Organization* 49, no. 3 (1995): 379–414.
Fearon, James D., and David D. Laitin. "Ethnicity, Insurgency, and Civil War." *American Political Science Review* 97, no. 1 (2003): 75–90.
Feinstein, Yuval, and Andreas Wimmer. "Consent and Legitimacy: A Revised Bellicose Theory of State-Building with Evidence from Around the World, 1500–2000." *World Politics* 75, no. 1 (2023): 188–232.
Fenske, James. "Does Land Abundance Explain African Institutions?" *Economic Journal* 123, no. 573 (2013): 1363–90.
——. "Ecology, Trade, and States in Pre-colonial Africa." *Journal of the European Economic Association* 12, no. 3 (2014): 612–40.
Fenske, James, and Namrata Kala. "1807: Economic Shocks, Conflict, and the Slave Trade." *Journal of Development Economics* 126 (2017): 66–76.
Ferejohn, John A., and Frances McCall Rosenbluth. "War and State Building in Medieval Japan." In *War and State Building in Medieval Japan*, ed. John A. Ferejohn and Frances McCall Rosenbluth, 1–20. Stanford, CA: Stanford University Press, 2010.
Ferguson, Yale H., and Richard W. Mansbach. *Polities: Authorities, Identities, and Change*. Columbia: University of South Carolina Press, 1996.
Foa, Roberto. "Ancient Polities, Modern States." PhD diss., Graduate School of Arts and Sciences, Harvard University, 2016.
Forrest, Joshua B. *Lineages of State Fragility: Rural Civil Society in Guinea-Bissau*. Athens: Ohio University Press, 2003.
Freeman, John R., and Dennis P. Quinn. "The Economic Origins of Democracy Reconsidered." *American Political Science Review* 106, no. 1 (2012): 58–80.
Fukazawa, H. 1982. "Agrarian Relations and Land Revenue: The Medieval Deccan and Maharashtra." In *The Cambridge Economic History of India*, vol. 1: *C. 1200–c. 1750*, ed. Tapan Raychaudhuri and Irfan Habib, 193–202. Cambridge: Cambridge University Press, 1982.
Fukuyama, Francis. *The Origins of Political Order: From Prehuman Times to the French Revolution*. 2011. Reprint. New York: Farrar, Straus and Giroux, 2012.
Gaddis, John Lewis. "The Long Peace: Elements of Stability in the Postwar International System." *International Security* 10, no. 4 (1986): 99–142.
Garfias, Francisco. "Elite Coalitions, Limited Government, and Fiscal Capacity Development: Evidence from Bourbon Mexico." *Journal of Politics* 81, no. 1 (2019): 94–111.
——. "Elite Competition and State Capacity Development: Theory and Evidence from Post-revolutionary Mexico." *American Political Science Review* 112, no. 2 (2018): 339–57.
Garfias, Francisco, and Emily A. Sellars. "Fiscal Legibility and State Development: Theory and Evidence from Colonial Mexico." *American Journal of Political Science*, online first, September 2024. https://doi.org/10.1111/ajps.12901.

———. "From Conquest to Centralization: Domestic Conflict and the Transition to Direct Rule." *Journal of Politics* 83, no. 3 (2021): 992–1009.

———. "When State Building Backfires: Elite Coordination and Popular Grievance in Rebellion." *American Journal of Political Science* 66, no. 4 (2022): 977–92.

Gat, Azar. "Is War Declining—and Why?" *Journal of Peace Research* 50, no. 2 (2013): 149–57.

Gates, Henry Louis, Jr., Emmanuel K. Akyeampong, and Steven J. Niven. "Rabih, al-Zabayr Fadl Allah." In *The Oxford Dictionary of African Biography*, 6 vols., ed. Henry Louis Gates Jr. and Emmanuel K. Akyeampong. Oxford: Oxford University Press, 2012. https://www.oxfordreference.com/display/10.1093/acref/9780195382075.001.0001/acref-9780195382075-e-1723

GeaCron. "World History Maps & Timelines." http://geacron.com/home-en/. Accessed December 19, 2024.

Geertz, Clifford. *Negara: The Theatre State in Nineteenth-Century Bali*. Princeton, NJ: Princeton University Press, 1980.

———. *The Religion of Java*. London: Free Press of Glencoe, 1960.

Gellner, Ernest. *Nations and Nationalism*. Ithaca, NY: Cornell University Press, 1983.

George, Alexander L., and Andrew Bennett. *Case Studies and Theory Development in the Social Sciences*. Cambridge, MA: MIT Press, 2005.

Gerring, John. "Mere Description." *British Journal of Political Science* 42, no. 4 (2012): 721–46.

Gerring, John, Brendan Apfeld, Tore Wig, and Andreas Forø Tollefsen. *The Deep Roots of Modern Democracy: Geography and the Diffusion of Political Institutions*. Cambridge: Cambridge University Press, 2022.

Gerring, John, Daniel Ziblatt, Johan Van Gorp, and Julian Arevalo. "An Institutional Theory of Direct and Indirect Rule." *World Politics* 63, no. 3 (2011): 377–433.

Gershoni, Yekutiel. "The Fante Confederation and the Grebo Reunited Confederation: A Political History of West African Confederations in the Nineteenth Century." *Liberian Studies Journal* 29, no. 2 (2004): 16–32.

Giddens, Anthony. "Time, Space, and Regionalisation." In *Social Relations and Spatial Structures*, ed. Derek Gregory and John Urry, 265–95. London: Macmillan Education UK, 1985.

Gilpin, Robert. *War and Change in World Politics*. Cambridge: Cambridge University Press, 1981.

Gleditsch, Kristian S., and Michael D. Ward. "A Revised List of Independent States Since the Congress of Vienna." *International Interactions* 25, no. 4 (1999): 393–413.

Gleditsch, Nils Petter, Steven Pinker, Bradley A. Thayer, Jack S. Levy, and William R. Thompson. "The Forum: The Decline of War." *International Studies Review* 15, no. 3 (2013): 396–419.

Goddard, Stacie E. *When Might Makes Right: Rising Power and World Order*. Ithaca, NY: Cornell University Press, 2018.

Goenaga, Agustín, and Alexander von Hagen-Jamar. "When Does War Make States? War, Rivalries, and Fiscal Extraction in the Nineteenth and Twentieth Centuries." In *De-centering State Making: Comparative and International Perspectives*, ed. Jens Bartelson, Martin Hall, and Jan Teorell, 85–111. Cheltenham, UK: Edward Elgar, 2018.

Goettlich, Kerry. "The Rise of Linear Borders in World Politics." *European Journal of International Relations* 25, no. 1 (2019): 203–28.

BIBLIOGRAPHY

Goldstein, Joshua S. *Winning the War on War: The Decline of Armed Conflict Worldwide*. 2011. Reprint. New York: Plume, 2012.

Goody, Jack. "The Over-Kingdom of Gonja." In *West African Kingdoms in the Nineteenth Century*, ed. Daryll Forde and P. M. Kaberry, 179–205. Oxford: Oxford University Press, 1967.

Gopal, Mysore Hatti. *Tipu Sultan's Mysore: An Economic Study*. Bombay: Popular Prakashan, 1971.

Gordon, Stewart. "Forts and Social Control in the Maratha State." *Modern Asian Studies* 13, no. 1 (1979): 1–17.

———. *The Marathas 1600–1818*. Cambridge: Cambridge University Press, 1993.

———. *Marathas, Marauders, and State Formation in Eighteenth-Century India*. Delhi: Oxford University Press, 1994.

———. "The Slow Conquest: Administrative Integration of Malwa Into the Maratha Empire, 1720–1760." *Modern Asian Studies* 11, no. 1 (1977): 1–40.

Gorski, Philip S. "The Protestant Ethic Revisited: Disciplinary Revolution and State Formation in Holland and Prussia." *American Journal of Sociology* 99, no. 2 (1993): 265–316.

Green, Elliott. "Ethnicity and Nationhood in Precolonial Africa: The Case of Buganda." *Nationalism and Ethnic Politics* 16, no. 1 (2010): 1–21.

Grewal, J. S. *The Sikhs of the Punjab*. Cambridge: Cambridge University Press, 1998.

Griffiths, Ryan D. *Age of Secession: The International and Domestic Determinants of State Birth*. Cambridge: Cambridge University Press, 2016.

———. *Secession and the Sovereignty Game: Strategy and Tactics for Aspiring Nations*. Ithaca, NY: Cornell University Press, 2021.

———. "The Waltzian Ordering Principle and International Change: A Two-Dimensional Model." *European Journal of International Relations* 24, no. 1 (2018): 130–52.

Griffiths, Ryan D., and Charles R. Butcher. "Introducing the International System(s) Dataset (ISD), 1816–2011." *International Interactions* 35, no. 5 (2013): 748–68.

Grzymala-Busse, Anna. "Beyond War and Contracts: The Medieval and Religious Roots of the European State." *Annual Review of Political Science* 23, no. 1 (2020): 19–36.

Guha, Amalendu. "The Ahom Political System: An Enquiry Into the State Formation Process in Medieval Assam (1228–1714)." *Social Scientist* 11, no. 12 (1983): 3–34.

Guillen, Mauro. "Wars Between States Are Down, but Civil Wars Are Up." *New York Times*, September 6, 2016. https://www.nytimes.com/roomfordebate/2016/09/06/is-the-world-becoming-safer/wars-between-states-are-down-but-civil-wars-are-up.

Habib, Irfan. *Confronting Colonialism: Resistance and Modernization Under Haidar Ali & Tipu Sultan*. London: Anthem Press, 2002.

Hägerdal, Hans. "Candrasangkala: The Balinese Art of Dating Events." Unpublished manuscript, 2006. https://urn.kb.se/resolve?urn=urn:nbn:se:vxu:diva-488.

———. "Periphery and Bridgehead: A Synthesis of West Balinese History." *Indonesia and the Malay World* 30, no. 87 (2002): 145–92.

Haldén, Peter. "Heteronymous Politics Beyond Anarchy and Hierarchy: The Multiplication of Forms of Rule 750–1300." *Journal of International Political Theory* 13, no. 3 (2017): 266–81.

Hall, John Whitney. "The Bakuhan System." In *The Cambridge History of Japan*, vol. 4: *Early Modern Japan*, ed. John Whitney Hall, 128–82. Cambridge: Cambridge University Press, 1991.

BIBLIOGRAPHY

Hamilton, Walter. *The East Indian Gazetteer: Containing Particular Descriptions of the Empires, Kingdoms, Principalities, Provinces, Cities, Towns, Districts, Fortresses, Harbours, Rivers, Lakes, &c. of Hindostan, and the Adjacent Countries, India Beyond the Ganges, and the Eastern Archipelago; Together with Sketches of the Manners, Customs, Institutions, Agriculture, Commerce, Manufactures, Revenues, Population, Castes, Religion, History, &c. of Their Various Inhabitants*. London: Parbury, Allen, 1828.

Harbom, Lotta, Erik Melander, and Peter Wallensteen. "Dyadic Dimensions of Armed Conflict, 1946–2007." *Journal of Peace Research* 45, no. 5 (2008): 697–710.

Hechter, Michael. *Containing Nationalism*. Oxford: Oxford University Press, 2001.

Heidhues, Mary Somers. "Chinese Gold Mining Communities in Western Borneo." In *Southeast Asia: A Historical Encyclopedia, from Angkor Wat to East Timor*, 3 vols., illus. ed., ed. Keat Gin Ooi, 1:343. Santa Barbara, CA: ABC-CLIO, 2004.

Henley, David. 2005. "Population and the Means of Subsistence: Explaining the Historical Demography of Island Southeast Asia, with Particular Reference to Sulawesi." *Journal of Southeast Asian Studies* 36, no. 3 (2005): 337–72.

Henn, Soeren J., Gauthier Marchais, Christian Mastaki Mugaruka, and Raúl Sánchez de la Sierra. "Indirect Rule: Armed Groups and Customary Chiefs in Eastern DRC." WIDER Working Paper Series, no. 18 (2024).

Herbst, Jeffrey. *States and Power in Africa: Comparative Lessons in Authority and Control*. Princeton, NJ: Princeton University Press, 2000.

Hiribarren, Vincent. *A History of Borno: Trans-Saharan African Empire to Failing Nigerian State*. Illus. ed. London: Hurst, 2017.

Holborn, Hajo. *A History of Modern Germany: 1840–1945*. Princeton, NJ: Princeton University Press, 1982.

Holm, Minda. "Conclusion: What, When, and Where, Then, Is the Concept of Sovereignty?" In "Forum: In the Beginning There Was No Word (for It): Terms, Concepts, and Early Sovereignty." *International Studies Review* 20, no. 3 (2018): 513–16.

Holzinger, Katharina, Florian Kern, and Daniela Kromrey. "Explaining the Constitutional Integration and Resurgence of Traditional Political Institutions in Sub-Saharan Africa." *Political Studies* 68, no. 4 (2020): 973–95.

Hooker, M. B. "The Early Adat Constitution of Negri Sembilan (1773–1824)." *Journal of the Malaysian Branch of the Royal Asiatic Society* 44, no. 1 (219) (1971): 104–16.

Hooker, Virginia Matheson. *A Short History of Malaysia: Linking East and West*. Crows Nest, Australia: Allen & Unwin, 2003.

Hopkins, A. G. *An Economic History of West Africa*. London: Routledge, 2014.

Horowitz, M. M. "Ba Karim: An Account of Rabeh's Wars." *African Historical Studies* 3, no. 2 (1970): 391–402.

Howard, Allen M. "Nodes, Networks, Landscapes, and Regions: Reading the Social History of Tropical Africa 1700s–1920." In *The Spatial Factor in African History: The Relationship of the Social, Material, and Perceptual*, ed. Allen M. Howard and Richard Matthew Shain, 21–140. Leiden, Netherlands: Brill, 2005.

Huang, Chin-Hao, and David C. Kang. 2022. *State Formation Through Emulation: The East Asian Model*. Cambridge: Cambridge University Press.

Hudson, Richard. "The Formation of the North German Confederation." *Political Science Quarterly* 6, no. 3 (1981): 424–38.

Hui, Victoria Tin-Bor. "Cultural Diversity and Coercive Cultural Homogenization in Chinese History." In *Culture and Order in World Politics*, ed. Andrew Phillips and Christian Reus-Smith, 93–112. Cambridge: Cambridge University Press, 2020.

———. "How Tilly's State Formation Paradigm Is Revolutionizing the Study of Chinese State-making." In *Does War Make States? Investigations of Charles Tilly's Historical Sociology*, ed. Jeppe Strandsbjerg and Lars Bo Kaspersen, 268–95. Cambridge: Cambridge University Press, 2017.

———. *War and State Formation in Ancient China and Early Modern Europe*. Cambridge: Cambridge University Press, 2005.

Hunter, William Wilson, James Sutherland Cotton, Richard Burn, William Stevenson Meyer, and Great Britain India Office. *Imperial Gazetteer of India*. Vol. 11. Oxford: Clarendon Press, 1908. https://dsal.uchicago.edu/reference/gazetteer/.

Hwang, Kyung Moon. *A History of Korea: An Episodic Narrative*. New York: Palgrave Macmillan, 2010.

Ikegami, Eiko. *The Taming of the Samurai: Honorific Individualism and the Making of Modern Japan*. Cambridge, MA: Harvard University Press, 1997.

Ikenberry, G. John. *After Victory: Institutions, Strategic Restraints, and the Rebuilding of Order After Major Wars*. Princeton, NJ: Princeton University Press, 2001.

Ileto, Reynaldo Clemeña. *Magindanao, 1860–1888: The Career of Datu Utto of Buayan*. Mandayulong, Philippines: Anvil, 2007.

Jackson, Patrick Thaddeus, and Daniel H. Nexon. "Relations Before States: Substance, Process, and the Study of World Politics." *European Journal of International Relations* 5, no. 3 (1999): 291–332.

Jackson, Robert. *Sovereignty: The Evolution of an Idea*. Cambridge, UK: Polity Press, 2007.

Jansen, Marius B. "Japan in the Early Nineteenth Century." In *The Cambridge History of Japan*, vol. 5: *The Nineteenth Century*, ed. Marius B. Jansen, 50–115. Cambridge: Cambridge University Press, 1989.

———. "The Meiji Restoration." In *The Cambridge History of Japan*, vol. 5: *The Nineteenth Century*, ed. Marius B. Jansen, 308–66. Cambridge: Cambridge University Press, 1989.

Jansen, Marius B., and Gilbert Rozman. "Overview." In *Japan in Transition: From Tokugawa to Meiji*, ed. Marius B. Jansen and Gilbert Rozman, 3–26. Princeton, NJ: Princeton University Press, 2014.

Jaques, Tony. *Dictionary of Battles and Sieges: A Guide to 8,500 Battles from Antiquity Through the Twenty-First Century*. Westport, CT: Greenwood, 2006.

Jeater, Diana. *Law, Language, and Science: The Invention of the Native Mind in Southern Rhodesia, 1890–1930*. Santa Barbara, CA: Greenwood, 2006.

Jervis, Robert. "Theories of War in an Era of Leading-Power Peace." Presidential Address, American Political Science Association Conference, 2001. *American Political Science Review* 95, no. 1 (2002): 1–14.

Johnston, Alastair Iain. *Cultural Realism: Strategic Culture and Grand Strategy in Chinese History*. Princeton, NJ: Princeton University Press, 1995.

Kahin, Audrey. *Historical Dictionary of Indonesia*. Lanham, MD: Rowman & Littlefield, 2015.

———. "Review of Multiple Centres of Authority: Society and Environment in Siak and Eastern Sumatra, 1674–1827." *Indonesia*, no. 79 (2005): 175–77.

BIBLIOGRAPHY

Kang, David C. *East Asia Before the West: Five Centuries of Trade and Tribute.* New York: Columbia University Press, 2010.

Kang, David C., Meredith Shaw, and Ronan Tse-Min Fu. "Measuring War in Early Modern East Asia, 1368–1841: Introducing Chinese and Korean Language Sources." *International Studies Quarterly* 60, no. 4 (2016): 766–77.

Karaman, K. Kivanç, and Şevket Pamuk. "Different Paths to the Modern State in Europe: The Interaction Between Warfare, Economic Structure, and Political Regime." *American Political Science Review* 107, no. 3 (2013): 603–26.

Kathirithamby-Wells, Jeyamalar. "Achehnese Control Over West Sumatra up to the Treaty of Painan, 1663." *Journal of Southeast Asian History* 10, no. 3 (1969): 453–79.

——. "Royal Authority and the 'Orang Kaya' in the Western Archipelago, Circa 1500–1800." *Journal of Southeast Asian Studies* 17, no. 2 (1986): 256–67.

——. "Siak and Its Changing Strategies for Survival: C. 1700–1870." In *The Last Stand of Asian Autonomies: Responses to Modernity in the Diverse States of Southeast Asia and Korea, 1750–1900*, ed. Anthony Reid, 217–43. London: Palgrave Macmillan, 1997.

Keat Gin, Ooi. *Historical Dictionary of Malaysia.* Lanham, MD: Rowman & Littlefield, 2017.

Keene, Edward. *Beyond the Anarchical Society: Grotius, Colonialism, and Order in World Politics.* Cambridge: Cambridge University Press, 2002.

Kelly, Robert E. "A 'Confucian Long Peace' in Pre-Western East Asia." *European Journal of International Relations* 18, no. 3 (2011): 407–30.

Kennedy, Paul. *The Rise and Fall of the Great Powers: Economic Change and Military Conflict from 1500 to 2000.* New York: Vintage, 1987.

Keohane, Robert, ed. *Neorealism and Its Critics.* New York: Columbia University Press, 1986.

Kessinger, Tom G. "Regional Economy (1757–1857): North India." In *The Cambridge Economic History of India*, vol. 2: *C. 1757–c. 1970*, ed. Dharma Kumar, with Meghnad Desai, 242–69. Cambridge: Cambridge University Press, 1983.

Kissinger, Henry. *World Order.* New York: Penguin, 2014.

Klein Goldewijk, Kees. "Three Centuries of Global Population Growth: A Spatial Referenced Population (Density) Database for 1700–2000." *Population and Environment* 26, no. 4 (2005): 343–67.

Klein Goldewijk, Kees, Arthur Beusen, Gerard van Drecht, and Martine de Vos. "The HYDE 3.1 Spatially Explicit Database of Human-Induced Global Land-Use Change Over the Past 12,000 Years." *Global Ecology and Biogeography* 20, no. 1 (2011): 73–86.

Ko, Chiu Yu, Mark Koyama, and Tuan-Hwee Sng. "Unified China and Divided Europe." *International Economic Review* 59, no. 1 (2018): 285–327.

Kochen, Manfred, and Karl W. Deutsch. "A Note on Hierarchy and Coordination: An Aspect of Decentralization." *Management Science* 21, no. 1 (1974): 106–14.

Koh, Keng We. "Travel and Survival in the Colonial Malay World: Mobility, Region, and the World in Johor Elite Strategies, 1818–1914." *Journal of World History* 25, no. 4 (2014): 559–82.

Krasner, Stephen D. *Sovereignty: Organized Hypocrisy.* Princeton, NJ: Princeton University Press, 1999.

Kratochwil, Friedrich. "Of Systems, Boundaries, and Territoriality: An Inquiry Into the Formation of the State System." *World Politics* 39, no. 1 (1986): 27–52.

BIBLIOGRAPHY

Kulke, Hermann. "The Early and the Imperial Kingdom in Southeast Asia History." In *Southeast Asia in the 9th to 14th Centuries*, ed. David G. Marr and Anthony C. Milner, 1–22. Singapore: Institute of Southeast Studies; Canberra: Australian National University, Research School of Pacific Studies, 1986.

Kumar, Dharma. "Regional Economy (1757–1857): South India." In *The Cambridge Economic History of India*, vol. 2: *C. 1757–c. 1970*, ed. Dharma Kumar, with Meghnad Desai, 352–75. Cambridge: Cambridge University Press, 1983.

Kwan, Alan Shiu Cheung. "Hierarchy, Status, and International Society: China and the Steppe Nomads." *European Journal of International Relations* 22, no. 2 (2016): 362–83.

Laarhoven, Ruurdje. "We Are Many Nations: The Emergence of a Multi-ethnic Maguindanao Sultanate." *Philippine Quarterly of Culture and Society* 14, no. 1 (1986): 32–53.

Labi, Maria L. C. "A Re-analysis of Negri Sembilan Socio-political Organization." *Journal of the Malaysian Branch of the Royal Asiatic Society* 42, no. 2 (1969): 145–54.

Laing, Stuart. "Tippu Tip in the Late 19th-Century East and Central Africa." In *Oxford Research Encyclopedia of African History* (online). Oxford: Oxford University Press, 2022. https://oxfordre.com//africanhistory/display/10.1093/acrefore/9780190277734.001.0001/acrefore-9780190277734-e-967?d=%2F10.1093%2Facrefore%2F9780190277734.001.0001%2Facrefore-9780190277734-e-967&p=emailAkKPIeYCDCjbM.

Laitin, David D. "Capitalism and Hegemony: Yorubaland and the International Economy." *International Organization* 36, no. 4 (1982): 687–713.

——. "The National Uprisings in the Soviet Union." *World Politics* 44, no. 1 (1991): 139–77.

Lake, David A. "Anarchy, Hierarchy, and the Variety of International Relations." *International Organization* 50, no. 1 (1996): 1–33.

——. *Entangling Relations: American Foreign Policy in Its Century*. Princeton, NJ: Princeton University Press, 1999.

——. *Hierarchy in International Relations*. Ithaca, NY: Cornell University Press, 2009.

Lascurettes, Kyle, and Michael Poznansky. "International Order in Theory and Practice." In *The Oxford Research Encyclopedia of International Studies* (online), posted August 31, 2021. Oxford: Oxford University Press. https://oxfordre.com/internationalstudies/view/10.1093/acrefore/9780190846626.001.0001/acrefore-9780190846626-e-673.

Last, Murray. *The Sokoto Caliphate*. London: Longmans, 1967.

Latham, Andrew A. "IR's Medieval-Sovereignty Debate: Three Rival Approaches." *International Studies Review* 20, no. 3 (2018): 494–98.

Lavania, B. K., D. K. Samanta, S. K. Mandal, and N. N. Vyas. *Rajasthan*. Parts 1 and 2. People of India, vol. 38. Gen. ed. K. S. Singh. Mumbai: Popular Prakashan, 1998.

Law, Robin. *Ouidah: The Social History of a West African Slaving Port, 1727–1892*. Athens: Ohio University Press, 2005.

——. *The Oyo Empire: The History of a Yoruba State, c. 1600–c. 1836*. Oxford: Clarendon, 1977.

Lawson, Philip. *The East India Company: A History*. London: Routledge, 2013.

Leach, E. R. "The Frontiers of 'Burma.'" *Comparative Studies in Society and History* 3, no. 1 (1960): 49–68.

Lee, Alexander, and Jack Paine. "The Great Revenue Divergence." *International Organization* 77, no. 2 (2023): 363–404.

BIBLIOGRAPHY

Lee, Ji-Young. *China's Hegemony: Four Hundred Years of East Asian Domination.* New York: Columbia University Press, 2017.
Lee, Melissa M., and Nan Zhang. "Legibility and the Informational Foundations of State Capacity." *Journal of Politics* 79, no. 1 (2017): 118–32.
Leonard, Karen. "The Hyderabad Political System and Its Participants." *Journal of Asian Studies* 30, no. 3 (1971): 569–82.
Levi, Margaret. *Of Rule and Revenue.* Berkeley: University of California Press, 1989.
Li, Andy Hanlun. "From Alien Land to Inalienable Parts of China: How Qing Imperial Possessions Became the Chinese Frontiers." *European Journal of International Relations* 28, no. 2 (2022): 237–62.
Lieberman, Evan. "Nested Analysis as a Mixed Methods Strategy for Comparative Research." *American Political Science Review* 99, no. 3 (2005): 435–52.
Lieberman, Victor. *Strange Parallels: Southeast Asia in Global Context, c. 800–1830.* Vol. 1: *Integration on the Mainland.* New York: Cambridge University Press, 2003.
——. *Strange Parallels: Southeast Asia in Global Context, c. 800–1830.* Vol. 2: *Mainland Mirrors: Europe, Japan, China, South Asia, and the Islands: Southeast Asia in Global Context, c. 800–1830.* New York: Cambridge University Press, 2009.
Lieven, Dominic. *Empire: The Russian Empire and Its Rivals.* New Haven, CT: Yale University Press, 2002.
Lingen, Jan, and Kenneth W. Wiggins. *Coins of the Sindhias.* London: Hawkins, 1978.
Little, Kenneth. "The Mende Chiefdoms of Sierra Leone." In *West African Kingdoms in the Nineteenth Century,* ed. Daryll Forde and P. M. Kaberry, 239–59. London: Oxford University Press, 1967.
Lombard, J. "The Kingdom of Dahomey." In *West African Kingdoms in the Nineteenth Century,* ed. Daryll Forde and P. M. Kaberry, 70–92. London: Oxford University Press, 1967.
Longo, Matthew. *The Politics of Borders: Sovereignty, Security, and the Citizen After 9/11.* Cambridge: Cambridge University Press, 2018.
Lorge, Peter A. *The Asian Military Revolution: From Gunpowder to the Bomb.* Cambridge: Cambridge University Press, 2008.
Lovejoy, Henry B. "Mapping Uncertainty: The Collapse of Oyo and the Trans-atlantic Slave Trade, 1816–1836." *Journal of Global Slavery* 4, no. 2 (2019): 127–61.
Lovejoy, Paul E. *Jihād in West Africa During the Age of Revolutions.* Athens: Ohio University Press, 2016.
Luttwak, Edward N. *The Grand Strategy of the Roman Empire: From the First Century CE to the Third.* Rev. ed. Baltimore, MD: Johns Hopkins University Press, 2016.
Lyall, Jason. *Divided Armies: Inequality and Battlefield Performance in Modern War.* Princeton, NJ: Princeton University Press, 2020.
MacDonald, Kevin, and Seydou Camara. "Segou, Slavery, and Sifinso." In *Power and Landscape in Atlantic West Africa,* ed. J. Cameron Monroe and Akinwumi Ogundiran, 169–90. Cambridge: Cambridge University Press, 2012.
MacKay, Joseph. "Rethinking Hierarchy in East Asian Historical IR." *Journal of Global Security Studies* 4, no. 4 (2019): 598–611.
Mahmud, Zaharah. "The Population of Kedah in the Nineteenth Century." *Journal of Southeast Asian Studies* 3, no. 2 (1972): 193–209.
Mahoney, James. *The Legacies of Liberalism: Path Dependence and Political Regimes in Central America.* Baltimore, MD: Johns Hopkins University Press, 2002.

Maier, Charles S. *Among Empires: American Ascendancy and Its Predecessors*. Cambridge, MA: Harvard University Press, 2006.

Malleson, George Bruce. *An Historical Sketch of the Native States of India in Subsidiary Alliance with the British Government: With a Notice of the Mediatized and Minor States*. London: Longmans, Green, 1875.

Manggala, Pandu Utama. "The Mandala Culture of Anarchy: The Pre-colonial Southeast Asian International Society." *Journal of ASEAN Studies* 1, no. 1 (2013): 1–13.

Mann, Michael. "The Autonomous Power of the State: Its Origins, Mechanisms, and Results." *European Journal of Sociology* 25, no. 2 (1984): 185–213.

Manning, Patrick. "Slaves, Palm Oil, and Political Power on the West African Coast." *African Historical Studies* 2, no. 2 (1969): 279–88.

Manning, Patrick, Yun Zhang, and Bowen Yi. 2015. "Volume and Direction of the Atlantic Slave Trade, 1650–1870: Estimates by Markov Chain Carlo Analysis." *Journal of World-Historical Information* 2–3, no. 2 (2015): 127–49.

Marshall, P. J. *Bengal: The British Bridgehead: Eastern India 1740–1828*. Cambridge: Cambridge University Press, 1987.

Mattern, Janice Bially, and Ayşe Zarakol. "Hierarchy in World Politics." *International Organization* 70, no. 3 (2016): 623–54.

Mazzuca, Sebastian. *Latecomer State Formation: Political Geography and Capacity Failure in Latin America*. New Haven, CT: Yale University Press, 2021.

McCaskie, T. C. "Ahyiamu—'A Place of Meeting': An Essay on Process and Event in the History of the Asante State." *Journal of African History* 25, no. 2 (1984): 169–88.

McCloud, Donald G. *System and Process in Southeast Asia: The Evolution of a Region*. Boulder, CO: Westview Press, 1986.

McConaughey, Meghan, Paul Musgrave, and Daniel H. Nexon. "Beyond Anarchy: Logics of Political Organization, Hierarchy, and International Structure." *International Theory* 10, no. 2 (2018): 181–218.

McEvedy, Colin. *Penguin Atlas of African History*. Rev. ed. New York: Penguin, 1995.

McNeill, William H. *The Rise of the West: A History of the Human Community*. 1963. Reprint. Chicago: University of Chicago Press, 1991.

Meersbergen, Guido van. "The Dutch East India Company in South Asia." In *Oxford Research Encyclopedia of Asian History*, published online April 19, 2023. https://oxfordre.com/asianhistory/view/10.1093/acrefore/9780190277727.001.0001/acrefore-9780190277727-e-64.

Meinecke, Friedrich. *Machiavellianism*. New Haven, CT: Yale University Press, 1957.

Metcalf, Barbara D., and Thomas R. Metcalf. *A Concise History of Modern India*. 3rd ed. Cambridge: Cambridge University Press, 2012.

Michalopoulos, Stelios. "The Origins of Ethnolinguistic Diversity." *American Economic Review* 102, no. 4 (2012):1508–39.

Miller, Charles, and K. Shuvo Bakar. "Conflict Events Worldwide Since 1468 BC: Introducing the Historical Conflict Event Dataset." *Journal of Conflict Resolution* 67, nos. 2–3 (2023): 522–54.

Millward, James A. "Qing and Twentieth-Century Chinese Diversity Regimes." In *Culture and Order in World Politics*, ed. Andrew Phillips and Christian Reus-Smit, 71–92. Cambridge: Cambridge University Press, 2020.

BIBLIOGRAPHY

Millward, James, Ruth Dunnell, Mark Elliott, and Philippe Foret, eds. *New Qing Imperial History: The Making of Inner Asian Empire at Qing Chingde*. London: Routledge, 2004.
Milner, Helen. "The Assumption of Anarchy in International Relations Theory: A Critique." In *Neorealism and Neoliberalism*, ed. David Baldwin, 143–69. New York: Columbia University Press, 1993.
Mitchell, Austin M., and Weiwen Yin. "Political Centralization, Career Incentives, and Local Economic Growth in Edo Japan." *Explorations in Economic History* 85 (July 2022): art. 101446. https://doi.org/10.1016/j.eeh.2022.101446.
Modelski, George. "Kautilya: Foreign Policy and International System in the Ancient Hindu World." *American Political Science Review* 58, no. 3 (1964): 549–60.
Moertono, Soemarsaid. *State and Statecraft in Old Java: A Study of the Later Mataram Period, Sixteenth to Nineteenth Century*. Ithaca, NY: Cornell University Press, 1968.
Møller, Jørgen. "Medieval Roots of the Modern State: The Conditional Effects of Geopolitical Pressure on Early Modern State Building." *Social Science History* 42, no. 2 (2018): 295–316.
——. "Why Europe Avoided Hegemony: A Historical Perspective on the Balance of Power." *International Studies Quarterly* 58, no. 2 (2014): 660–70.
Monroe, J. Cameron. "Building the State in Dahomey: Power and Landscape on the Bight of Benin." In *Power and Landscape in Atlantic West Africa: Archaeological Perspectives*, ed. Akinwumi Ogundiran and J. Cameron Monroe, 191–221. Cambridge: Cambridge University Press, 2012.
——. *The Precolonial State in West Africa: Building Power in Dahomey*. New York: Cambridge University Press, 2014.
Monteil, Vincent. "The Wolof Kingdom of Kayor." In *West African Kingdoms in the Nineteenth Century*, ed. Daryll Forde and P. M. Kaberry, 260–82. London: Oxford University Press, 1967.
Morton-Williams, Peter. "The Yoruba Kingdom of Oyo." In *West African Kingdoms in the Nineteenth Century*, ed. Daryll Forde and P. M. Kaberry, 36–69. London: Routledge, 1967.
Motyl, Alexander. *Imperial Ends: The Decay, Collapse, and Revival of Empires*. New York: Columbia University Press, 2001.
——. "Thinking About Empire." In *After Empire: The Soviet Union and the Russian, Ottoman, and Habsburg Empires*, ed. Karen Barkey and Mark Von Hagen, 19–29. Oxford: Westview Press, 1997.
Mueller, John. "The Obsolescence of Major War." *Bulletin of Peace Proposals* 21, no. 3 (1990): 321–28.
——. "War Has Almost Ceased to Exist: An Assessment." *Political Science Quarterly* 124, no. 2 (2009): 297–321.
Nexon, Daniel H. *The Struggle for Power in Early Modern Europe: Religious Conflict, Dynastic Empires, and International Change*. Princeton, NJ: Princeton University Press, 2009.
Nexon, Daniel H., and Thomas Wright. "What's at Stake in the American Empire Debate." *American Political Science Review* 101, no. 2 (2007): 253–71.
Nordholt, H. G. C. Schulte. *The Spell of Power: A History of Balinese Politics, 1650–1940*. Leiden, Netherlands: Brill, 2010.

North, Douglass C. *Institutions, Institutional Change, and Economic Performance.* New York: Cambridge University Press, 1990.

Nunn, Nathan. "The Long-Term Effects of Africa's Slave Trades." *Quarterly Journal of Economics* 123, no. 1 (2008): 139–76.

O'Fahey, R. S. *The Darfur Sultanate: A History.* London: Hurst, 2008.

Ogawa, Michihiro. "Socio-economic Study of Indapur Pargana (1761–1828)." PhD diss., Pune University, 2012.

——. "The Spatial Analysis of the Transition of the Land Revenue System in Western India (1761–1836), with Special Reference to Indapur Pargana." In *Spaces and Places in Western India,* ed. Bina Sengar and Laurie Hovell McMillin, 35–50. London: Routledge, 2019.

Oliver, Roland, and Anthony Atmore. *Africa since 1800.* 5th ed. Cambridge: Cambridge University Press, 2005.

——. *Medieval Africa, 1250–1800.* Cambridge: Cambridge University Press, 2001.

Olson, Mancur. "Dictatorship, Democracy, and Development." *American Political Science Review* 87, no. 3 (1993): 567–76.

Osafo-Kwaako, Philip, and James A. Robinson. "Political Centralization in Pre-colonial Africa." *Journal of Comparative Economics* 41, no. 1 (2013): 6–21.

Paik, Christopher, and Jessica Vechbanyongratana. "Path to Centralization and Development: Evidence from Siam." *World Politics* 71, no. 2 (2019): 289–331.

Pardesi, Manjeet S. "Mughal Hegemony and the Emergence of South Asia as a 'Region' for Regional Order-Building." *European Journal of International Relations* 25, no. 1 (2019): 276–301.

——. "Region, System, and Order: The Mughal Empire in Islamicate Asia." *Security Studies* 26, no. 2 (2017): 249–78.

Park, Seo-Hyun. *Sovereignty and Status in East Asian International Relations.* Cambridge: Cambridge University Press, 2017.

Pascali, Luigi, Sascha O. Becker, Andreas Ferrara, and Eric Melander. "Wars, Taxation, and Representation: Evidence from Five Centuries of German History." CEPR Discussion Papers no. 15601, 2020. https://ideas.repec.org/p/cpr/ceprdp/15601.html.

Pella, John A. *Africa and the Expansion of International Society: Surrendering the Savannah.* London: Routledge, 2016.

Perdue, Peter C. *China Marches West: The Qing Conquest of Central Eurasia.* Cambridge, MA: Harvard University Press, 2005.

——. "Military Mobilization in Seventeenth- and Eighteenth-Century China, Russia, and Mongolia." *Modern Asian Studies* 30, no. 4 (1996): 757–93.

Perlin, Frank. "Proto-industrialization and Pre-colonial South Asia." *Past and Present* 98, no. 1 (1983): 30–95.

Phillips, Andrew. "Contesting the Confucian Peace: Civilization, Barbarism, and International Hierarchy in East Asia." *European Journal of International Relations* 24, no. 4 (2018): 740–64.

——. "International Systems." In *The Globalization of International Society,* ed. Tim Dunne and Christian Reus-Smit, 43–62. Oxford: Oxford University Press, 2017.

——. *War, Religion, and Empire: The Transformation of International Orders.* Cambridge: Cambridge University Press, 2011.

Phillips, Andrew, and Christian Reus-Smit, eds. *Culture and Order in World Politics.* Cambridge: Cambridge University Press, 2020.

BIBLIOGRAPHY

Phillips, Andrew, and Jason C. Sharman. *International Order in Diversity: War, Trade, and Rule in the Indian Ocean*. Cambridge: Cambridge University Press, 2015.

———. *Outsourcing Empire: How Chartered Company-States Spearheaded European Expansion and Helped Create the World's First Genuinely Global Order*. Princeton, NJ: Princeton University Press, 2020.

Philpott, Daniel. *Revolutions in Sovereignty: How Ideas Shaped Modern International Relations*. Princeton, NJ: Princeton University Press, 2001.

Pierce, Richard Austin. *Russian Central Asia, 1867–1917: A Study in Colonial Rule*. Whitefish, MT: Literary Licensing, 2012.

Pinker, Steven. *The Better Angels of Our Nature: Why Violence Has Declined*. New York: Penguin, 2011.

Pitts, Jennifer. "Political Theory of Empire and Imperialism." *Annual Review of Political Science* 13, no. 1 (2010): 211–35.

Poggi, Gianfranco. *The Development of the Modern State: A Sociological Introduction*. Stanford, CA: Stanford University Press, 1978.

Pringle, Robert. *A Short History of Bali: Indonesia's Hindu Realm*. Crows Nest, Australia: Allen & Unwin, 2004.

Qin, Yaqing. *A Relational Theory of World Politics*. Cambridge: Cambridge University Press, 2018.

Raleigh, Clionadh, Andrew Linke, Håvard Hegre, and Joakim Karlsen. "Introducing ACLED: An Armed Conflict Location and Event Dataset: Special Data Feature." *Journal of Peace Research* 47, no. 5 (2010): 651–60.

Ramusack, Barbara N. *The Indian Princes and Their States*. Cambridge: Cambridge University Press, 2004.

Al Rasheed, Madawi. "Durable and Non-durable Dynasties: The Rashidis and Sa'udis in Central Arabia." *British Journal of Middle Eastern Studies* 19, no. 2 (1992): 144–58.

Ravina, Mark. "State-Building and Political Economy in Early-Modern Japan." *Journal of Asian Studies* 54, no. 4 (1995): 997–1022.

Raychaudhuri, Tapan. "The Mid-Eighteenth-Century Background." In *The Cambridge Economic History of India*, vol. 2: *C. 1757–c. 1970*, ed. Dharma Kumar, with Meghnad Desai, 3–35. Cambridge: Cambridge University Press, 1983.

Reba, M., F. Reitsma, and K. C. Seto. "Spatializing 6,000 Years of Global Urbanization from 3700 BC to AD 2000." *Scientific Data* 3, no. 1 (2016): 1–16.

Reid, Anthony. *Southeast Asia in the Age of Commerce 1450–1680*. Vol. 1: *The Lands Below the Winds*. New Haven, CT: Yale University Press, 1988.

———. "The Structure of Cities in Southeast Asia, Fifteenth to Seventeenth Centuries." *Journal of Southeast Asian Studies* 11, no. 2 (1980): 235–50.

Reid, Richard. "The Fragile Revolution: Rethinking War and Development in Africa's Violent Nineteenth Century." In *Africa's Development in Historical Perspective*, ed. Emmanuel Akyeampong, James Robinson, Nathan Nunn, and Robert H. Bates, 393–423. Cambridge: Cambridge University Press, 2014.

———. *Political Power in Pre-colonial Buganda: Economy, Society, and Warfare in the 19th Century*. Oxford: James Currey, 2002.

Renard, Ronald D. "The Delineation of the Kayah States Frontiers with Thailand: 1809–1894." *Journal of Southeast Asian Studies* 18, no. 1 (1987): 81–92.

Reus-Smit, Christian. "Cultural Diversity and International Order." *International Organization* 71, no. 4 (2017): 851–85.

——. *Individual Rights and the Making of the Modern International System.* Cambridge: Cambridge University Press, 2013.
——. *The Moral Purpose of the State.* Princeton, NJ: Princeton University Press, 1999.
——. *On Cultural Diversity: International Theory in a World of Difference.* Cambridge: Cambridge University Press, 2018.
——. "Struggles for Individual Rights and the Expansion of the International System." *International Organization* 65, no. 2 (2011): 207–42.
Reus-Smit, Christian, and Tim Dunne. "The Globalization of International Society." In *The Globalization of International Society*, ed. Tim Dunne and Christian Reus-Smit, 18–42. Oxford: Oxford University Press, 2017.
Richards, John F. *The Mughal Empire.* Cambridge: Cambridge University Press, 1995.
Ricklefs, M. C. *A History of Modern Indonesia Since c. 1200.* 3rd ed. Stanford, CA: Stanford University Press, 2001.
——. *A History of Modern Indonesia Since c. 1200.* 4th ed. Stanford, CA: Stanford University Press, 2008.
——. *Jogjakarta Under Sultan Mangkubumi 1749–1792: A History of the Division of Java.* London: Oxford University Press, 1974.
Riker, William H. "Federalism." In *Handbook of Political Science*, ed. Fred I. Greenstein and Nelson W. Polsby, 93–172. Reading, MA: Addison-Wesley, 1975.
Ringmar, Erik. "Performing International Systems: Two East-Asian Alternatives to the Westphalian Order." *International Organization* 66, no. 1 (2012): 1–26.
Ropp, Paul S. *China in World History.* Oxford: Oxford University Press, 2010.
Roy, Kaushik. *War, Culture, and Society in Early Modern South Asia, 1740–1849.* New York: Routledge, 2011.
Roy, Madhabi. "Politics, War, and State Formation in Early Modern India." PhD diss., Graduate School of Arts and Sciences, Harvard University, 1994.
Roy, Tirthankar. *An Economic History of India 1707–1857.* 2nd ed. New York: Routledge, 2021.
——. "Rethinking the Origins of British India: State Formation and Military-Fiscal Undertakings in an Eighteenth Century World Region." *Modern Asian Studies* 47, no. 4 (2013): 1125–56.
Rudolph, Susanne Hoeber. "The Princely States of Rajputana: Ethic, Authority, and Structure." *Indian Journal of Political Science* 24, no. 1 (1963): 14–32.
Ruggie, John Gerard. *Constructing the World Polity: Essays on International Institutionalization.* New York: Taylor and Francis Group, 1998.
——. "Continuity and Transformation in the World Polity: Toward a Neorealist Synthesis." In *Neorealism and Its Critics*, ed. Robert Keohane, 131–57. New York: Columbia University Press, 1986.
Sahlins, Peter. *Boundaries: The Making of France and Spain in the Pyrenees.* Berkeley: University of California Press, 1989.
Sarkees, Meredith Reid, and Frank Whelon Wayman. *Resort to War: 1816–2007.* Washington, DC: CQ Press, 2010.
Sassen, Saskia. *Territory, Authority, Rights: From Medieval to Global Assemblages.* Princeton, NJ: Princeton University Press, 2008.
Savage, Jesse Dillon. "Common-Pool Hierarchy: Explaining the Emergence of Cooperative Hierarchies." *International Studies Quarterly* 65, no. 3 (2021): 712–23.

———. *Political Survival and Sovereignty in International Relations*. Cambridge: Cambridge University Press, 2020.
Saylor, Ryan, and Nicholas C. Wheeler. "Paying for War and Building States: The Coalitional Politics of Debt Servicing and Tax Institutions." *World Politics* 69, no. 2 (2017): 366–408.
Schaik, Sam van. *Tibet: A History*. Illus. ed. New Haven, CT: Yale University Press, 2013.
Schellinger, Paul E., and Robert M. Salkin, eds. *International Dictionary of Historical Places*. Vol. 5: *Asia and Oceania*. London: Taylor and Francis, 1996.
Schrauwers, Albert. "Houses, Hierarchy, Headhunting, and Exchange: Rethinking Political Relations in the Southeast Asian Realm of Luwu." *Bijdragen Tot de Taal-, Land- en Volkenkunde* 153, no. 3 (1997): 356–80.
Schweller, Randall L. "The Problem of International Order Revisited." *International Security* 26, no. 1 (2001): 161–86.
Scott, James C. *The Art of Not Being Governed: An Anarchist History of Upland Southeast Asia*. New Haven, CT: Yale University Press, 2010.
Seshan, Radhika. "The Maratha State: Some Preliminary Considerations." *Indian Historical Review* 41, no. 1 (2014): 35–46.
Seth, Michael J. *A Concise History of Korea: From Antiquity to the Present*. 2nd ed. Lanham, MD: Rowman and Littlefield, 2016.
Sharman, Jason C. "Power and Profit at Sea: The Rise of the West in the Making of the International System." *International Security* 43, no. 4 (2019): 163–96.
———. "Something New out of Africa: States Made Slaves, Slaves Made States." *International Organization* 77, no. 3 (2023): 497–526.
Sharman, Jason C., and Ayşe Zarakol. "Global Slavery in the Making of States and International Orders." *American Political Science Review* 118, no. 2 (2024): 802–14.
Sidhu, Jatswan S. *Historical Dictionary of Brunei Darussalam*. 3rd ed. Lanham, MD: Rowman and Littlefield, 2016.
Simmel, Georg. *Sociology: Inquiries Into the Construction of Social Forms*. Vol. 1. Trans. and ed. Anthony J. Blasi, Anton K. Jacobs, and Mathew Kanjirathinkal. Boston: Brill, 2009.
Simms, Sanda. *The Kingdoms of Laos*. London: Routledge, 2013.
Sinclair, Keith. *A History of New Zealand*. 5th ed. New York: Penguin, 2000.
Singer, David, and Melvin Small. "The Composition and Status Ordering of the International System: 1815–1940." *World Politics* 18, no. 2 (1966): 236–82.
Skinner, Quentin. "On the Person of the State." In *State Formations: Global Histories and Cultures of Statehood*, ed. John L. Brooke, Julia C. Strauss, and Greg Anderson, 25–44. Cambridge: Cambridge University Press, 2018.
Smith, M. G. "A Hausa Kingdom: Maradi Under Dan Baskore, 1854–1875." In *West African Kingdoms in the Nineteenth Century*, ed. Daryll Forde and P. M. Kaberry, 93–122. London: Oxford University Press, 1967.
Smith, Robert S. *Kingdoms of the Yoruba*. Madison: University of Wisconsin Press, 1988.
———. "Peace and Palaver: International Relations in Pre-colonial West Africa." *Journal of African History* 14, no. 4 (1973): 599–621.
———. *Warfare and Diplomacy in Pre-colonial West Africa*. 2nd ed. Madison: University of Wisconsin Press, 1989.

Spagat, Michael, and Stijn van Weezel. "The Decline of War Since 1950: New Evidence." In *Lewis Fry Richardson: His Intellectual Legacy and Influence in the Social Sciences*, ed. Nils Petter Gleditsch, 129–42. Cham, Switzerland: Springer International, 2020.

Spruyt, Hendrick. *The Sovereign State and Its Competitors*. Princeton, NJ: Princeton University Press, 1994.

——. "War and State Formation: Amending the Bellicist Theory of State Making." In *Does War Make States? Investigations of Charles Tilly's Historical Sociology*, ed. Jeppe Strandsbjerg and Lars Bo Kaspersen, 73–97. Cambridge: Cambridge University Press, 2017.

——. *The World Imagined: Collective Beliefs and Political Order*. Cambridge: Cambridge University Press, 2020.

Stasavage, David. *The Decline and Rise of Democracy: A Global History from Antiquity to Today*. Princeton, NJ: Princeton University Press, 2020.

——. "Representation and Consent: Why They Arose in Europe and Not Elsewhere." *Annual Review of Political Science* 19 (2016): 145–62.

——. *States of Credit: Size, Power, and the Development of European Polities*. Princeton, NJ: Princeton University Press, 2011.

——. "When Distance Mattered: Geographic Scale and the Development of European Representative Assemblies." *American Political Science Review* 104, no. 4 (2010): 625–43.

Steele, Abbey, Christopher Paik, and Seiki Tanaka. "Constraining the Samurai: Rebellion and Taxation in Early Modern Japan." *International Studies Quarterly* 61, no. 2 (2017): 352–70.

Stein, Burton. "The State and the Economy: The South." In *The Cambridge Economic History of India*, vol. 1: *C. 1200–c. 1750*, ed. Tapan Raychaudhuri and Irfan Habib, 203–13. Cambridge: Cambridge University Press, 1982.

——. "State Formation and Economy Reconsidered." *Modern Asian Studies* 19, no. 3 (1985): 387–413.

Stern, Robert W. *The Cat and the Lion: Jaipur State in the British Raj*. Leiden, Netherlands: Brill Academic, 1988.

Stewart, John. *African States and Their Rulers*. 3rd ed. Jefferson, NC: McFarland, 2006.

Sundberg, Ralph, and Erik Melander. "Introducing the UCDP Georeferenced Event Dataset." *Journal of Peace Research* 50, no. 4 (2013): 523–32.

Suzuki, Shogo. "Europe at the Periphery of the Japanese World Order." In *International Orders in the Early Modern World: Before the Rise of the West*, ed. Shogo Suzuki, Yongkin Zhang, and Joel Quirk, 76–93. New York: Routledge, 2014.

Suzuki, Shogo, Yongjin Zhang, and Joel Quirk, eds. *International Orders in the Early Modern World: Before the Rise of the West*. London: Routledge, 2014.

Swidler, Ann. "Culture in Action: Symbols and Strategies." *American Sociological Review* 51, no. 2 (1986): 273–86.

Swidler, Nina. "Kalat: The Political Economy of a Tribal Chiefdom." *American Ethnologist* 19, no. 3 (1992): 553–70.

Tagliacozzo, Eric. *Secret Trades, Porous Borders: Smuggling and States Along a Southeast Asian Frontier, 1865–1915*. New Haven, CT: Yale University Press, 2005.

Tambiah, Stanley J. "The Galactic Polity in Southeast Asia." *HAU: Journal of Ethnographic Theory* 3, no. 3 (2013): 503–34. Reprinted from Stanley J. Tambiah, *Culture, Thought, and Social Action*, 3–31. Cambridge, MA: Harvard University Press, 1985.

BIBLIOGRAPHY

———. "The Galactic Polity: The Structures of Traditional Kingdoms in Southeast Asia." *Annals of the New York Academy of Sciences* 293 (1977): 69–97.

———. *World Conqueror and World Renouncer: A Study of Buddhism and Polity in Thailand Against a Historical Background*. Cambridge: Cambridge University Press, 1976.

Teorell, Jan. "Rules of Recognition? Explaining Diplomatic Representation in the Long Nineteenth Century." STANCE Working Paper Series, no. 3, Lund University, 2017.

Teschke, Benno. "After the Tilly Thesis: Social Conflict, Differential State-Formation, and Geopolitics in the Construction of the European System of States." In *Does War Make States? Investigations of Charles Tilly's Historical Sociology*, ed. Jeppe Strandsbjerg and Lars Bo Kaspersen, 25–51. Cambridge: Cambridge University Press.

Thies, Cameron G. "The Political Economy of State Building in Sub-Saharan Africa." *Journal of Politics* 69, no. 3 (2007): 716–31.

Thornton, John K. *Warfare in Atlantic Africa, 1500–1800*. New York: Routledge, 1999.

Tilly, Charles. *Coercion, Capital, and European States, AD 990–1992*. Hoboken, NJ: Wiley-Blackwell, 1992.

———. *The Formation of National States in Western Europe*. Princeton, NJ: Princeton University Press, 1975.

———. "How Empires End." In *After Empire: The Soviet Union and the Russian, Ottoman, and Habsburg Empires*, edited by Karen Barkey and Mark Von Hagen, 1–11. Oxford: Westview Press, 1997.

Tod, James. *Annals and Antiquities of Rajasthan*. 8th ed. Ed. William Crooke. Calcutta: Rupa Publications India, 1997.

Trachtenburg, Marc. "The Problem of International Order and How to Think About It." *The Monist* 89, no. 2 (2006): 207–31.

United Nations Population Division. "World Population Prospects 2019." 2019. https://www.un.org/development/desa/pd/news/world-population-prospects-2019-0.

Usman, Aribidesi A. "On the Frontier of Empire: Understanding the Enclosed Walls in Northern Yoruba, Nigeria." *Journal of Anthropological Archaeology* 23, no. 1 (2004): 119–32.

van der Kraan, Alfons. "Lombok Under the Mataram Dynasty, 1839–94." In *The Last Stand of Asian Autonomies: Responses to Modernity in the Diverse States of Southeast Asia and Korea, 1750–1900*, ed. Anthony Reid, 389–408. London: Routledge, 1997.

Vickers, Adrian. *Bali: A Paradise Created*. 2nd ed. Tokyo: Tuttle, 2012.

Visaria, Leela, and Pravin Visaria. "Population (1757–1947)." In *The Cambridge Economic History of India*, vol. 2: *C. 1757–c. 1970*, ed. Dharma Kumar, with Meghnad Desai, 463–532. Cambridge: Cambridge University Press, 1983.

Voigtländer, Nico, and Hans-Joachim Voth. "Gifts of Mars: Warfare and Europe's Early Rise to Riches." *Journal of Economic Perspectives* 27, no. 4 (2013): 165–86.

Waley-Cohen, Joanna. "The New Qing History." *Radical History Review* 88 (Winter 2004): 193–206.

Walter, Barbara F. "Bargaining Failures and Civil War." *Annual Review of Political Science* 12 (2009): 243–61.

Waltz, Kenneth N. *Theory of International Politics*. Boston: McGraw Hill, 1979.

Warren, James Francis. *The Sulu Zone, 1768–1898: The Dynamics of External Trade, Slavery, and Ethnicity in the Transformation of a Southeast Asian Maritime State*. Singapore: NUS Press, 2007.

BIBLIOGRAPHY

Watson, Adam. *The Evolution of International Society: A Comparative Historical Analysis*. New York: Routledge, 1992.

Weber, Max. "Politics as Vocation." In *From Max Weber: Essays in Sociology*, ed. H. H. Gerth and C. Wright Mills, 77–128. New York: Oxford University Press, 1946.

Weber, Nicolas. "The Destruction and Assimilation of Campā (1832–35) as Seen from Cam Sources." *Journal of Southeast Asian Studies* 43, no. 1 (2012): 158–80.

Webster, Kaitlyn, Chong Chen, and Kyle Beardsley. "Conflict, Peace, and the Evolution of Women's Empowerment." *International Organization* 73, no. 2 (2019): 255–89.

Weidmann, Nils B. "A Closer Look at Reporting Bias in Conflict Event Data." *American Journal of Political Science* 60, no. 1 (2016): 206–18.

Wiens, Ashton, Henry B. Lovejoy, Zachary Mullen, and Eric A. Vance. "A Modelling Strategy to Estimate Conditional Probabilities of African Origins: The Collapse of the Oyo Empire and the Transatlantic Slave Trade, 1817–1836." *Journal of the Royal Statistical Society, Series A: Statistics in Society* 185, no. 3 (2022): 1247–70.

Wig, Tore. "Peace from the Past: Pre-colonial Political Institutions and Civil Wars in Africa." *Journal of Peace Research* 53, no. 4 (2016): 509–24.

Wilfahrt, Martha. *Precolonial Legacies in Postcolonial Politics: Representation and Redistribution in Decentralized West Africa*. Cambridge: Cambridge University Press, 2021.

Wilks, Ivor. *Asante in the Nineteenth Century: The Structure and Evolution of a Political Order*. Paperback ed. with added introductory material. New York: Columbia University Press, 1989.

———. "Ashanti Government." In *West African Kingdoms in the Nineteenth Century*, ed. Daryll Forde and P. M. Kaberry, 206–38. London: Oxford University Press, 1967.

———. "Aspects of Bureaucratization in Ashanti in the Nineteenth Century." *Journal of African History* 7, no. 2 (1966): 215–32.

Wimmer, Andreas. *Nation Building: Why Some Countries Come Together While Others Fall Apart*. Princeton, NJ: Princeton University Press, 2018.

Winichakul, Thongchai. *Siam Mapped: A History of the Geo-body of a Nation*. Honolulu: University of Hawai'i Press, 1994.

Wink, André. *Land and Sovereignty in India: Agrarian Society and Politics Under the Eighteenth-Century Maratha Svarājya*. Cambridge: Cambridge University Press, 1986.

———. "Maratha Revenue Farming." *Modern Asian Studies* 17, no. 4 (1983): 591–628.

Wittgenstein, Ludwig. *Philosophical Investigations*. Oxford: Basil Blackwell, 1958.

Wolters, O. W. *History, Culture, and Region in Southeast Asian Perspectives*. Rev. ed. Ithaca, NY: Southeast Asia Program, Cornell University, 1999.

Woodside, Alexander. "Territorial Order and Collective-Identity Tensions in Confucian Asia: China, Vietnam, Korea." *Daedalus* 127, no. 3 (1998): 191–220.

———. *Vietnam and the Chinese Model: A Comparative Study of Nguyen and Ch'ing Civil Government in the First Half of the Nineteenth Century*. Cambridge, MA: Asia Center, Harvard University, 1988.

Yamani, Mai. *Cradle of Islam: The Hijaz and the Quest for an Arabian Identity*. London: I. B. Tauris, 2009.

Yazdani, Kaveh. "Haidar 'Ali and Tipu Sultan: Mysore's Eighteenth-Century Rulers in Transition." *Itinerario* 38, no. 2 (2014): 101–20.

BIBLIOGRAPHY

———. *India, Modernity, and the Great Divergence: Mysore and Gujarat (17th to 19th C.).* Leiden, Netherlands: Brill, 2017.

Yemelianova, Galina M. *Russia and Islam: A Historical Survey.* 2nd ed. New York: Palgrave Macmillan, 2002.

Zahan, Dominique. "The Mossi Kingdoms." In *West African Kingdoms in the Nineteenth Century*, ed. Daryll Forde and P. M. Kaberry, 152–78. London: Oxford University Press, 1967.

Zarakol, Ayşe. *Before the West: The Rise and Fall of Eastern World Orders.* Cambridge: Cambridge University Press, 2022.

———. "A Non-Eurocentric Approach to Sovereignty." *International Studies Review* 20, no. 3 (2018): 506–9.

Zhang, Yongjin. "Curious and Exotic Encounters: Europeans as Supplicants in the Chinese Imperium, 1513–1793." In *International Orders in the Early Modern World: Before the Rise of West*, ed. Shogo Suzuki, Yongkin Zhang, and Joel Quirk, 55–75. New York: Routledge, 2014.

———. "System, Empire, and State in Chinese International Relations." *Review of International Studies* 27, no. 5 (2001): 43–63.

Zhang, Yongjin, and Barry Buzan. "The Tributary System as International Society in Theory and Practice." *Chinese Journal of International Politics* 5, no. 1 (2012): 3–36.

Zhou, Fangyin. "Equilibrium Analysis of the Tributary System." *Chinese Journal of International Politics* 4, no. 2 (2011): 147–78.

INDEX

Abeokuta Kingdom, 173, 175, 177, 181
Aceh, 10, 45, *51*, *139*, 145, 148, 152, 213; centralization attempts in, 198, 202–3; pepper trade and, 154–55
Acharya, Amitav, 2–3, 144, 154–55
Adeleye, Roland, 187
administrative centralization, 85, 105
Afghanistan, 38, *51*, 116, 120
African states, 17–18, 32–33, 38, 244, 258n91; Central, 27–28, 33, 41–42, *44*, 45; centralization in, 228, 282n94; East Africa, 18, 27–28, *44*, 45, 227; North Africa, *44*, 228; population-density, 42, 269n19; precolonial, 28–29, 42, 66; South Africa, 38, *44*, 45, 227; state births in, 40, *41*; state deaths in, 7, 40, *41*, 45–46, 47, 48–49, 50, 167; sub-Saharan Africa, 50. *See also* West Africa
Agaja (King), 12–13, 188
agriculture, 112, 115, 133, 169, 185
Ahom Kingdom, 127–28
Ali, Haider (ruler), 128–29
alien rule, 212
Allada Kingdom, 12–13, 176–78, 182, 188
Amangkurat I, Susuhunan, 159

Americas, 40, *41*, *44*, 46, 50, *53*, 86, 171
anarchy, 2, 9, 56, 59, 205
Andaya, Barbara Watson, 158–59
Andaya, Leonard, 158–59
Anglo-Dutch Treaty of 1824, 144
Ankole, *48*, 228
Annam, 42, *51*, 79. *See also* Vietnam
Aotearoa, 46, *51*, 258n79, 259n94
aristocracy, 102–3, 126, 130, 146, 159–60
armed conflicts, 14, 249–51. *See also* war, warfare and
Aro Confederacy, *48*, *166*, 185–86, 215, 285n30
Arthasastra (ancient Indian text), 151, 221
Asante Kingdom, 29, 229–31, 281n85, 281n88, 281nn80–82, 282n94; centralization in, 178–79, 182–89, 195–98, 216; defecting vassals and, 210; interaction capacity for, 168; taxation in, 167; wars in, 174–75
Assam, 108, *109*, 127–28
assimilation, 85, 99, 205–6
asymmetries, information, 234, 237–38
Atlantic slave trade, 163–64, 170–71, 184–86, 206, 213–17

INDEX

Austria-Hungary, 50, 53
autocracy, 31, 167, 188
autonomy, 29, 36–37, 67–68, 152, 179, 217, 221, 227; internal, 47, 108, 179; vassal, 57, 60–62, 70, 95, 138, 153, 164, 190–91, 196–202, 211–12, 219, 224, 229, 233–37, 245–47
Awadh, 114–15, 123, 130, 132, 213, 271n55; as a decentralized kingdom, 119–21; standing army for, 117
Awe, Bolanle, 187, 283n120
Awole, Alafin (king), 201–2

Badung, 51, 276n46
Bagirmi, 28, *48*, *166*, 177, 231
Baker, Mary, 231
Bali and Balinese kingdoms, 1, 18, 41, 70, 140–41, 196–98, 208; Dutch and, 33, 35, 144, 157–58; interaction capacity in, 150; power projection and, 224; slavery and, 137, 144; wars and, 137–38, 147–48, 150
Barfield, Thomas, 127
bargaining power, vassal, 12, 65–68, 70, 123, 180, 229, 233, 235
Barnett, Richard, 29, 120, 210–11, 271n55
Batavia, 142
Battle of Buksar (1764), 120, 132
Battle of Panipat (1761), 116–17, 208
Bayly, C. A., 112, 213, 225
Beasley, W. G., 105–6
Belgium, 27–28, 227, 256n19, 261n32
Benares, 213
Bengal, 1, 107, 115, 119–20, 129–30, 132–35, 274n120
Benin, 12, *48*, *170*, 171, 176, 191, 196; population density of, 169; slavery and, 163–64
biases, 32, 37, 147–48, 172, 276n49
billiard ball model, of centralization, 10–12, 18, 55–60, *57*, 233, 236, 238–39, 245; East Asia as, 9, 77, 92, 104–5
births, state, 5, 16, 18, 23, 38, *40*, *41*, 41–43, 241; in Africa, 40, *41*; in South Asia, 107; in Southeast Asia, 40, *44*; in West Africa, 33, 40, 44, 45–46, 163

Black Death, 66
Bone, *51*, *139*, 143, 148, 276n52
borders and border making, *44*, 151, 175, 272n77, 276n45, 280n62, 286n24; colonialism and, 137; frontiers *vs.*, 9, 57–58, 93–94, 123, 153, 220, 225–30, 232, 236; fuzzy, 16, 19, 29, 36–37, 176, 225–30, 236–37, 246–47; Indonesia-Malaysia, 137, 144; linear, 9–10, 28, 56, 92, 220, 226, 228–30, 232, 236, 238; in West Africa, 175, 227
Borgu Kingdom, 165
Borneo, 3, 141–43, 153, 155
Bornu Empire, 3, 28, 167, 228–29
Bowditch, Thomas, 178
Boxer Rebellion (1900), 90
Brakna Emirates, 165
Braumoeller, Bear, 249
Brecke, Peter, 172
Britain, 28, 33, 37, 81, 87, 90, 274n120; British colonialism, 1, 19, 45–47, 108, 110, 116, 120, 126–31, 137, 143–44, 156–57, 161, 168, 172, 174, 176, 179; EIC, 107, 110, 114, 116, 119–21, 123, 129–34, 205, 208–11, 225, 274nn121–23
Brooke, James, 141, 143
Brunei, 137, *139*, 143
Buddhism, 100
Buganda, 33, *48*, 61, 228
Bukhara, *113*, 227
bull's-eye model, for decentralization, 9–12, 18, 55–60, *58*, 220, 221, 233, 236, 245–46; heteronomy and, 230–31, *231*; systems change and, 238; in West Africa, 176
Bunyoro, *48*, 228
bureaucracies, 14, 28, 64, 69, 71, 144–45, 213; centralization and, 197–201; East Asian, 92–95, 101, 105–6; slavery and, 216; South Asian, 122, 124, 127–29; taxes and, 56, 61; West African, 167, 178–79, 185
Burma, 42, 58, 206, 216–17, 228
Busogu, 228
Buzan, Barry, 30, 32, 66–67, 83, 254n17, 255n12, 256n35, 263n63

INDEX

Calcutta, 129
Camara, Seydou, 176
Cambodia, 51, 58, 90, 94, 98, 100, 102, 266n60
Cameroon, 177
capitalism, 66, 128, 250
capitals, state, 43, 169, 175, 196, 201–2, 233
caravans, trading, 115, 170
cartographic revolution, 226
caste system, 126, 128–29
Catholic Church, 62, 261n33
cavalry warfare, 116
Cederman, Lars-Erik, 60, 63
Centeno, Miguel, 66
Central Africa, 27–28, 33, 41–42, 44, 45
Central America, 50, 227
Central Asia, 44, 45–47
centralized states and centralization, 11–16, 232–33, 242, 261n34, 261n40, 263n65, 264n89, 271n54; administrative, 85, 105; in Africa, 228, 282n94; in the Asante Kingdom, 178–79, 182–89, 195–98, 216; Beasley on, 105–6; bureaucracies and, 197–201; in China, 77–78, 94, 101, 195, 204; in the Dahomey Kingdom, 154, 177–78, 182, 184–86, 188–89, 195–98, 202–3, 206, 208–9, 215–16; decentralized states compared to, 55–60, 57, 58, 67–68, 196–218; in East Asia, 17, 77–81, 98–106, 195, 204, 218; in Europe, 60, 195, 203, 207, 211–12, 218, 239, 247, 287n49; in India, 207, 271n54; interaction capacity and, 14–15, 66–73, 200–203, 211; in Japan, 77–78, 96, 98–99, 101–3, 105–6, 133, 209; in Korea, 77–78, 94, 101, 195; in maritime Southeast Asia, 137, 159–60; in Mysore, 107, 119, 128–29, 133–36, 154, 195–96, 198, 207, 209; in the Oyo Empire, 31, 180, 198, 202–3, 209–10; in South Asia, 107, 119, 127–36, 195–96, 284n12; taxes and, 94, 105, 128–29, 196–203; theories of, 60–73; trade and, 15, 19, 138, 203, 213–18; vassals and, 233–37, 239; in Vietnam, 77–78, 97–102, 104–6, 133, 236; warfare and,

203, 207–13; in West Africa, 31, 163–64, 177–91, 195–96. *See also* billiard ball model, of centralization
chiefdoms, 32, 42, 58
China and the Chinese state 3, 18–19, 35, 46, 267n70; centralization in, 77–78, 94, 101, 195, 204; Confucianism, 78, 80–81, 238, 248–49; Han, 78, 89; interaction-capacity in, 204; Japan and, 84, 88–89, 91; Ming Dynasty, 140, 268n92; Parabellum paradigm for, 81, 89; political centralization in, 92–93; population of, 79, 84–85; Qin Dynasty, 93, 102–3; Qing Dynasty, 1, 80–83, 87–90, 104, 225, 248; road system in, 72; state-building in, 65–66; Taiping Rebellion, 90, 92; Tang Dynasty, 78, 104; trade and, 86–87, 90; trading republics, 155; Vietnam invaded by, 88, 102; Warring States Period, 24–25, 65–66; wars and, 88–92; westward expansion of, 89, 93–94
city-states, 3, 27, 64, 213, 261n32, 276n45; in West Africa, 163, 172–73, 184–85
civil wars, 179, 266n56
Clapham, Christopher, 66
Clive, Robert, 129
Coercion, Capital, and European States (Tilly), 64, 261n40, 264n81
coercion-wielding organizations, states as, 24, 26–27, 220
collective beliefs, 211–12
colonialism, 38, 40, 69, 106, 216, 251; British, 1, 19, 45–47, 108, 110, 116, 120, 126–31, 137, 143–44, 156–57, 161, 168, 172, 174, 176, 179; Dutch, 1, 45, 137, 140–44, 146, 148–49, 152, 156–58, 161, 205–6; European, 43, 45–47, 77, 144, 172, 177, 241, 248; French, 31, 80, 172, 177; global enclosure by, 4, 7, 18, 23, 40, 106, 219, 243; Spanish, 61; state deaths and, 43, 44, 45–47, 53, 54
commercial revolution, 15, 63–64
commitment problems, decentralization and, 16, 101, 200–203, 233–35

INDEX

communication, 66–67, 85, 105, 199, 202–4, 207, 214, 237–38; electronic, 219, 225; in Southeast Asia, 158–59, 161–62; telecommunications and, 69; in West Africa, 168–69, 187–88
comparative analysis, 2, 5, 7–10, 17, 55, 59–60, 241–48
competition, international, 14, 65–66, 70–71, 207–11; Japan and, 101–2; in Southeast Asia, 154; in West Africa, 172, 182, 189–90
Confederation of German States, 46
conflict datasets, 248–50
Confucian governance, 238
Confucianism, 78, 80–81, 238, 248–49
conquest/annexation, as state death, 43, *44*, 45–46
constitutional monarchies, 177, 196
constructivism, 89
Containing Nationalism (Hechter), 284n13
Coquery-Vidrovitch, Catherine, 169–70, 231
Correlates of War (COW) project, 3, 6, 6–7, 27, 81, 243, 249, 251, 252; on pre–League of Nations period, 32–33, *34*, *36*, 37–38
cosmology, 151, 160–62, 198, 224
Costa Rica, 227
COW project. *See* Correlates of War
cultural integration, 71, 105

Dagomba, 179, 229–30
Dahomey Kingdom, 3, 12–13, 31, 176, 230, 244, 281n76; centralization in, 154, 177–78, 182, 184–86, 188–89, 195–98, 202–3, 206, 208–9, 215–16; slave trade and, 215; taxation in, 167
Dan Fodio, Usman, 42, 165, 172
Darfur, 177
Day, Anthony, 148, 156
deaths, states, 5, 16, 18–19, 23, 35, *41*, 241; in Africa, 47, *48*–49, 50, 167; in Asia, 44, 46–47, 50, *51*–52, 106, 107, 108;

colonialism and, 43, *44*, 45–47, *53*, 54; in Europe, 50, *53*, 54; in the ISD, 38, *39*, *40*, 40–43, *41*, *44*, 45–47, *48*–50, 50, *51*–53, 54; mass state-extinction event and, 6, 6, 40, 43, 47, 243; unification and, 43, *44*, 45–47, 50; West Africa and, 33, 40, *44*, 45–46, 163
decentralization trap, 200–203, 209, 211, 246
decentralized states and decentralization, 219, 221–23, 244, 262n46, 262n61, 264n87, 285n34, 287n49; Atlantic slave trade and, 213; bull's-eye model for, 9–12, 18, 55–60, *58*, 218, 220, *221*, 230–31, *231*, 233, 236, 238, 245–46; centralization compared to, 55–60, *57*, *58*, 67–68, 196–218; frontiers in, 57, 220, 225–30; fuzzy borders and, 225–30, 246–47; heteronomy and, 10, 19, 57–59, 220, 227, 230–32, *231*, *237*; interaction capacity and, 14–15, 19, 199–208, 212–13, 218, 224–25, 230, 233–37, 246; international change and, 232–39; Japan and, 85, 87, 92, 94–96, 100–102; Maratha Empire as, 121–22, 124, 208–9; in maritime Southeast Asia, 138, 147, 151–62; migration and, 42–43; Oyo Empire as, 180, 197–98, 216; prevalence of, 195–99; as radial rule, 161–62, 220–21, *221*, 223, 230, 233, 236–39; slave trade and, 215; Sokoto Caliphate as, 196, 198; in South Asia, 107–8, 121, 124, 127–28, 130–36; structure and order in, 223–25; Vietnam as, 94, 100–102; waterborne transportation and, 203–4; in West Africa, 175–77, 181–91, 263. *See also* mandala states
decision-making processes, 8–9, 31–32, 36–37, 60, 68, 135, 188, 190
decline-of-war debate, 19, 242, 248–52, 252
decolonization era, 7, 38, 46, 54, 66, 243; state birth and, 40; West Africa and, 163

INDEX

defection and exit options, vassal kingdoms, 15, 61, 70–71, 158, 196, 210–11, 234–35, 237–38; secession and, 29, 41–43, *44*, 45, 58, 61–62, 141, 157, 172–73, 183, 197–98, 202
Delhi, 108, *113*, 113–14, 130
democracy, 31, 264n87
Democratic Republic of Congo, 27
democratization, 287n55
development, state, 62, 100, 188
Dictionary of Battles and Sieges (Jaques), 249–50
diplomacy, 5, 29, 33, 35, 37, 81–82, 90, 145
direct rule, 12, 60–61, 198, 219, 238, 254n22, 264n81, 284n12; in East Asia, 77, 96–99, 105; interaction capacity and, 14, 67–68, 71, 207; in South Asia, 119; taxes and, 120–21, 178–79; in West Africa, 177–78, 189. *See also* centralized states
diseases, 66, 68, 72
dissolution, state deaths, 45
diversity, 3, 10, 72, 212
divine ancestry, 196
division of labor, 56
domestic legitimacy, 84, 225
Dominican Republic, 31, *53*
Doyle, Michael, 82
dual vassalage, 92
Durrani Empire (Afghanistan), 108, 116, 126–27, 227, 272n77, 273n104
Dutch-Aceh War (1904 and 1907), 149
Dutch-Bali war, 141
Dutton, George, 98
Dyuet, Le Van, 97–98

East Africa, 18, 27–28, 44, 45, 227
East Asia, 11, 19, *44*, 66, 94, 232, 245–46; billiard ball model in, 9, 77, 92, 104–5; bureaucracies in, 92–95, 101, 105–6; centralization in, 17, 77–81, 98–106, 204, 218; Confucianism in, 83–85, 87–89, 92, 94, 101, 104, 106, 248–49; direct rule in, 77, 96–99, 105; Europe and, 77, 90–92; interaction capacity in, 77–78, 84–92, 98, 105, 204, 206, 225, 238; interstate conflicts in, 87–88, 91–92, 248; political centralization, 92–98; population density in, 79, *85*, 98–100, 105, 207; trade in, 77–78, *86*, 86–87, 90, 98–101, 105–6; tributary relationships in, 80–84, 89, 94, 100, 103–4; vassalage in, 78, 92–97, 105; war in, 78, 87–92, *88*, *91*, *106*. *See also specific states*
Eastern Turkistan, 89–90
East India Company (EIC), British, 107, 110, 205, 208–11, 225, 274nn121–23; South Asia and, 114, 116, 119–21, 123, 129–34
East Timor, 137
Egbado province, 180, 198, 203
Egypt, 28, 31, 38, *48*, 167, 278n8
EIC. *See* East India Company
Ejiogu, E. C., 282n95
Ekiti conflict, 280n48
emulation thesis, 62–63, 102–4
Ethiopia, 38, 45
ethnic groups, 94, 142–43, 171
Eurocentrism, 2–3, 5–7, 32, 37, 81, 243–45, 249–50
European states and Europe, 14, *44*, 50, 62, 66, 257n54, 261n32, 278n2; border and, 226–27; centralization in, 60, 195, 203, 207, 211–12, 218, 239, 247, 287n49; colonialism and, 43, 45–47, 77, 144, 172, 177, 241, 248; Concert of Europe, 7, 54, 55; the Crusades impacting, 261b34; gunboat diplomacy by, 90; hierarchical vassalage relations in, 58–59; Industrial Revolution, 69; medieval, 288n4; Middle Ages, 15; population density in, 207, 269n19; Roman influence in, 78, 80; sovereign state system in, 239; state births in, 41; state deaths in, 50, *53*, 54; West Africa and, 163, 167; after World War I, 264n87
European state system, 2, 9, 28, 33, 35, 62, 129, 241
European Union, 31
executive power, 64–65

INDEX

external relations, states controlling, 2, 25–26, 37–38, 57, 220
external sovereignty, 27, 37–38, 257n54, 271n55
external validity, external recognition and, 2, 25–28, 241
extraction rights, 30–31

Fagbule, Fola, 174
Fairbank, John King, 83
Falola, Toyin, 174
Fante Confederation, 258n78
Fawehinmi, Feyi, 174
Fazal, Tanisha, 35, 38, 40
Feinstein, Yuval, 211–12, 262n53
Fenske, James, 172
feudalism, 2, 63–64, 127–28, 152. *See also* vassal kingdoms
First Opium War (1839–1842), 90
fiscal institutions, 96, 115, 128, 131, 133, 156, 207
Foa, Roberto, 207
foreign policy, 95–96, 174–76, 179–81
foreign rule, 205, 212
fragmentation, 64–65, 71–72, 205–8, 214–17, 261n31; in maritime Southeast Asia, 141, 154–55, 158–59, 162; in South Asia, 121, 125–27; in West Africa, 164, 173, 184, 187
France, 33, 37, 93, 195, 260n30, 261n32, 262n61, 264n81; colonialism by, 31, 80, 172, 177; trade and, 35; Vietnam and, 80–81, 90, 265n7
free-trade capitalism, 66
French Revolution, 69, 262n61
frontiers: borders *vs.*, 9, 57–58, 93–94, 123, 153, 220, 225–30, 232, 236; fuzzy, 16, 19, 29, 36–37, 176, 225–30, 236–37, 246–47
Fu, Ronan Tse-Min, 88–89, 91
Fuladu, 165, *166*
functional differentiation, 30, 256n34
fuzzy borders and frontiers, 16, 19, 29, 36–37, 176, 225–30, 236–37, 246–47

galactic polities, 221
Gaza Empire, 42, *48*

Geertz, Clifford, 143, 151
Gelgel Empire, 151–52
geography, 17, 81, 84–85, 110–11, 164–65, 168, 176; interaction capacity and, 72, 105; maritime Southeast Asia, 140, 142–45
Germany and German states, 41, 50, 207, 226, 261n32
Ghana, 29, 174, 178
Ghezo (King), 178
Gianyar, *51*, *139*, 141
Gilpin, Robert, 2, 203, 238–39
Gleditsch, Kristian, 35
Gobir, 42, 45, 165, *166*, 167, 227–28, 258n86
Gonja Kingdom, *48*, 179, 187, 229–31
Goody, Jack, 187
Gordon, Stewart, 111, 123–25, 270n23, 272n87
governance systems, 11–14, 19, 24, 27–28, 36–37, 196–207, 219–20, 245–47. *See also* centralized states; decentralized states; direct rule; indirect rule; *specific types of rulers*
Gowa, *139*, 140, 143, 145
Gran-Colombia, 41–42
Great Indian Peninsular Railway, 111
Guinea-Bissau, 173, 176
gunboat diplomacy, 90

Hägerdal, Hans, 153
Hamilton, Walter, 127
Han China, 78, 89
Hanseatic League, 64
Hausa, Nigeria, 35–36, 45, 165, 167, 169, 171–72, 184–85, 213
Hawai'i, 50, *53*
headman (authority), 124, 203
Hechter, Michael, 284n13
hegemonic-stability theory, 89
hegemony, 221, 248
Henley, David, 145–46
Herbst, Jeffrey, 66
hereditary monarchies, 190
hereditary rights, 130
hereditary rulers, 180

INDEX

heteronomy, 256n19, 259n11, 271n61, 286n35, 287n44; centralization and, 238; decentralization and, 10, 19, 57–59, 220, 227, 230–32, 231, 237; interstitial, 16, 260n15, 286n36; vassalage and, 230–32, 231, 247, 266n60
hierarchies, 2, 3, 9, 12, 28–29, 31, 152, 176, 220, 230; administrative, 26; Mazzuca on, 66; in tributary networks, 80–83, 106, 190–91, 196; Waltz on, 56, 58–59
Hinduism, 140, 143, 197
Historical Conflict Event Dataset, 249
Holy Roman Empire, 64
Honduras, 227
Hong Kong, 90
Hopkins, A. G., 165, 279n34
Howard, Allen, 171
Huang, Chin-Hao, 65–66, 93, 102–4
Hueda Kingdom, 12–13, 176, 182, 188, 281n76
Hui, Victoria Tin-Bor, 65–66, 101, 103, 267n70
hunter-gatherers, 27
Hyderabad, 113, 114, 116, 196

Ibadan Empire, Nigeria, 29, 48, 166, 170, 184, 186, 282n97, 283n2, 283n120; decentralization of, 196–97; Ijaye and, 181–82; standing army for, 174–75, 177, 187
Ijaye, 166, 167, 175, 182
Ikegami, Eiko, 95, 98
Ilorin, 42, 45, 48, 166, 202, 210, 280n47; Oyo Empire and, 172, 180; war and, 184
Imjin War (1592–1598), 88–89
imperialism, 29, 82, 94, 124, 174, 225, 248
indeterminate zones, 29, 58, 227
India, 29, 41, 107, 271n51, 271n69, 272n71; British colonialism in, 45–46; centralized states in, 207, 271n54; China and, 86; Northern, 119–20, 135, 205–6, 210–12; regional economies in, 270n34; South, 11, 270n40. *See also* Maratha Empire
India Act (1784), 129–30, 132–33

Indian Ocean, 115, 143, 216
indigenous institutions, 119, 271n51, 272n77
indigenous rulers, 28, 163
indigenous states, 129–31; in South Asia, 108, 125–26, 132–34; in Southeast Asia, 138, 147–50, 158–59; in West Africa, 167, 171–74
indirect rule, 60–61, 107, 151–52, 238, 254n22, 284n8, 284n13; interaction capacity and, 14–16, 67; vassals and, 9, 57, 178–79, 219, 233–37, 262n46, 283n6. *See also* decentralized states
Indonesia, 1, 19, 29, 41, 45, 86, 137, 144
industrialization, 87, 128
Industrial Revolution, 69
information, 124, 197, 199–200; asymmetries, 234, 237–38; problems, 67–68, 101, 233–34, 237–38, 247
infrastructure and infrastructural power, 98–99, 133, 167, 190, 203–4, 256n34, 257n42; interaction capabilities and, 85; railways as, 69, 111, 203; road systems as, 72, 85, 98, 112, 129, 203–4; vassals and, 61. *See also* transportation, transport costs and; waterborne transportation, maritime transit and
institutional reform, 204
interaction capacity, 13, 16–17, 239, 241–42, 263n63, 264n87; in the Asante Kingdom, 168; in Bali, 150; centralization and, 14–15, 66–73, 200–203, 211; decentralization and, 14–15, 19, 199–208, 212–13, 218, 224–25, 230, 233–37, 246; in maritime Southeast Asia, 138, 145–50, 154, 158, 160; in South Asia, 107–8, 111–18, 133–34; in West Africa, 145–46, 164, 168–75, 187
internal autonomy, 47, 108, 179
internal/external distinction, of states, 2, 29, 32, 230, 255nn12–13, 288n4
international change, theory of, 16, 19, 220, 232–39
international orders, 8–9, 83–84, 103–6, 138, 154, 161, 204, 214–15, 260n17

INDEX

international system(s), 4–6, 18, 36–37, 56–57, 81, 224–25, 241–42, 255n1, 261n31
International System(s) Dataset (ISD), 16, 226, 243, 248, 257n59, 257n63, 258n86, 259n94, 259nn96–97, 283n1; state birth and state death in, 38, *39*, *40*, 40–43, *41*, *44*, 45–47, *48*–*50*, *50*, *51*–*53*, *54*; state-first approach of, 5–7, 6, 23, 32–33, 35–38, *39*, *44*, 250–52, *252*
International Systems in World History (Buzan, Little), 255n12
interstate conflicts, wars and, 65, 87–88, 91–92, 116, 173, 248–52
interstitial heteronomy, 16, 260n15, 286n36
intrastate wars, 87–92, 148, 248–50, 252
investiture, 81–84, 129, 177, 234–35, 247
ISD. *See* International System(s) Dataset
Islamic culture, states and, 8, 10, 140, 143, 165, 167, 172, 190, 196–97
Italy, 46, 50, 64

Jammal Shammar, 45
Jansen, Marius, 96, 99, 267n87
Japan, 17, 29, 35, 37, 66, 81, 197, 205, 236; Boxer Rebellion, 90; Bunkuyu Reforms, 96; Bunsei reforms, 96; centralization in, 77–78, 96, 98–99, 101–3, 105–6, 133, 209; China and, 84, 88–89, 91; decentralization in, 85, 87, 92, 94–96, 100–102; interaction-capacity in, 105, 204, 206; linguistic homogeneity, 212; Meiji Revolution, 80, 87, 90–91, 95–96, 111, 209, 267n87; population of, 79, 85, 98–99; Taika Reforms, 94; Tokugawa Shogunate, 90–91, 94–96, 98–99, 209, 266n60, 267n70
Jaques, Tony, 197, 249–50
Java, 1, 150, 156, 158–59, 198, 205–6, 208, 213, 235–36, 276n51; Java War, 142, 148, 157; rice production and, 140, 145
Java War (1825–1830), 142, 148, 157
Jembrana, 141, 153
jihadism, 42, 165, 167, 171
Johnston, Alastair, 81, 89
Johor-Riau Empire, 141

Kaabu Empire, 165, 186
Kaarta, 45, 165, *166*, 167
Kanem-Bornu Empire, 28, *48*, 231
Kanemi Dynasty, 172
Kang, David, 65–66, 80–82, 87–89, 91–93, 100, 102–4
Kano, 169, 171
Karangasem, 1, *51*, 158, 196
Kathirithamby-Wells, Jeyamalar, 155, 159–60
Katsina, 231
Kautilya (statesman), 151, 221, 224
Kayah states, 58
Kelly, Robert, 87, 89
Kessinger, Tom, 112, 270n34
Khalistan, 108, 116–17, 119, 126, 195–97
Kingdom of Westphalia, 41
kin networks, 42, 171, 238
Klungkung, 1, *52*, 141, 151–52, 158
Kofi Kakari (king), 183
Kokand, 89–90
Kongsi Wars, 155
Korea, 52, 66, 81, 91, 104, 266n55, 267n68; centralization in, 77–78, 94, 101, 195; interaction-capacity in, 204; as a Japanese protectorate, 80, 87, 90; population of, 79, 85
Kosovo, 3
Kulke, Hermann, 161
Kumar, Dharma, 111, 269n21, 270n30
Kumasi, 168, 178–79, 183, 188
Kurunmi (ruler), 182
Kwaku Dua I, 179, 182

Lagos, 176, 185–86
Laing, Stuart, 28
laissez-faire, 87
Laitin, David, 186
Lake, David, 56
Laos, 58, 94, 98, 100
Latham, Andrew, 257n45
Latin America, 66, 227, 262n46
Law, Robin, 285n34
League of Nations, 4–5, 23, 33. *See also* United Nations
Lee, Alexander, 69
Lee, Ji-Young, 82 104

INDEX

legitimacy, 89, 104–5, 126, 197, 212; domestic, 84, 225
Leonard, Karen, 126
Lesotho, *49*, 259n96
Li, Andy Hanlun, 93
Liberia, 38, 165, 167
Libya, *49*, 228
Lieberman, Victor, 15, 66, 97–99, 101, 151, 155, 160, 216–17, 277n82
Little, Kenneth, 231
Little, Richard, 30, 32, 66–67, 254n17, 255n12, 256n35, 263n63
local elites, 67–68, 121–22, 131, 135, 196, 198, 244. *See also* vassal kingdoms
Lombok, *52*, *139*, 141, 143–44
London Conference (1830), 227
Lovejoy, Henry, 280n47
Luba Kingdom, 33
Lunda Empire, 33
Luwu, *139*, 143, 153, 196
Lyall, Jason, 116, 175, 249
Ly state, 97, 268n92

MacDonald, Kevin, 176
Macina Caliphate, 45, 165, 167
MacKay, Joseph, 84, 94
Madar, 227–28
Madhav Rao (peshwa), 124
Madras, 107
Mahajapit Empire, 277n82
Maharashtra, 70, 111, 270n23, 272n87
Mahdist state, 167
Majapahit Empire, 41, 138, 143, 158
Malacca Strait (Sunda Strait), 138
Malaysia, 19, 45, 137, 140–41, 144, 196–97, 204, 217
mandala states (decentralized governance model), 3–4, 10, 197–98, 208, 220, 222, 224, 236; East Asian, 93, 104; Southeast Asian, 151, 153–54, 160–62, 246
Mangkunegaran, 205
Mann, Michael, 256n34, 257n42
Maori states, 42, 46, 258n79
Maratha Empire, 3, 46, 133, 206, 229, 272n74, 272nn77–78, 273n93, 283n3; centralization, 119; decentralization of, 121–22, 124, 208–9; decline of, 121–22, 130; successor kingdoms for, 108; tributaries and, 122–23, 131; war and, 116–17, 125–26
Marathas 1600–1818, The (Gordon), 270n23
mass state-extinction event, 6, *6*, 40, 43, 47, 243
Mataram Empire, 41, *52*, 143–44, 156, 203, 213, 275n23
Mauritania, 165
Mazzuca, Sebastian, 63, 66, 262n46
McCaskie, T. C., 179
McNeill, William, 4
Meiji Revolution, Japan, 80, 87, 90–91, 95–96, 111, 209, 267n87
Mensa Bonsu (ruler), 179, 183–84
Mexico, 61, 82
Middle East, 42, 44, 45, 227
migration and migratory states, 42–43, 72, 150, 169, 258n86
militaries and militias, 3, 14, 26, 64, 68, 93, 133, 135; slave trade and, 216–17; standing armies and, 88, 95, 105, 116–17, 126, 128, 131, 174–75, 187, 201, 207, 209–10, 216; vassal, 12, 61, 67, 197–98, 200–201, 210, 233–35
military elites, 125, 130, 135, 200–203, 209–10, 216–17
military revolution, 116, 131
Millward, James, 84
Minangkabau kingdom, *52*, *139*, 141–42, 152–53
Ming Dynasty, China, 140, 268n92
misinformation, 234
modern states, 4, 242–2243, 255n7
monarchies, 3, 15, 64, 121, 190, 261n33, 265n7; constitutional, 177–78, 196
monopolies, 36, 105, 146, 154–55, 171, 185, 214, 216–18; black pepper, 129; foreign policy, 95; vassals and, 16, 71–72
Monroe, J. Cameron, 186
Montenegro, 50
Montevideo Declaration on the Rights and Duties of States (1933), 27
Morocco, 38, *49*, 228
Mossi kingdoms, 176–77, 281n68

INDEX

Mount Tambora eruption (1815), 144
Mozambique, 42
Mthetwa Kingdom, 45, *49*
Muda, Iskandar, 159
Mughal Empire, 1, 37, 41, 58, 72, 108, 110, 225, 272n77, 278n3; decline of, 107, 112, 114–16, 118–19, 131, 135, 196–97, 205, 208; EIC and, 129; ports, 115; road system, 203; successor states, 126
Muhammad Bello (Caliph), 228
Murshidabad, India, 270n30
Myanmar, 86, *109*
Mysore, 15, 110, 116–17, 130, 208, 244, 284n12, 284n24; centralization in, 107, 119, 128–29, 133–36, 154, 195–96, 198, 207, 209; military fiscalism in, 133, 209

Napoleonic Empire, 41
Napoleonic Wars, 144, 226
nationalism, 211–12, 262n53
Ndwandwe Kingdom, 45, *49*
Nejd, 45, 52, 259n97
neo-Confucianism, 92–93, 97
neofeudal shogunate rule, Japan, 94–95
Nepal, 38, *109*, 258
Netherlands, 33, 35, 261n32; Dutch colonialism by, 1, 45, 137, 140–44, 146, 148–49, 152, 156–58, 161, 205–6; Southeast Asia and, 1, 140–42, 148–49, 276n43, 276n52; VOC, 142, 144, 148, 156–59, 205–6, 275n15, 276n51; West Africa and, 168. *See also* Vereenigde Oostindische Compagnie
New Guinea, 142
New Zealand, 42, 258n79
Nexon, Daniel, 261n34, 287n49
Nguyen Dynasty, Vietnam, 90
Nicaragua, 37, 227
Nigeria, 12, 28, 29, 163–64, 191, 208, 215; Hausa, 35–36, 45, 165, 167, 169, 171–72, 184–85, 213; Ibadan Empire, 29, *48, 166, 170,* 174–75, 177, 181–82, 184, 186–87, 196–97, 282n97, 283n2, 283n120. *See also* Oyo Empire; Yoruba kingdoms

Nizam, 126
nomadic groups, 164, 249
nonstate actors, 27
nonstate wars, 251
North, Douglass, 263n75
North Africa, 44, 228
Northern Cyprus, 225
Northern India, 119–20, 135, 205–6, 210–12
North German Confederation, 46
North India, 11
Nupe, 45, *49*, 165, *166*

Oceania, 227
O'Fahey, R. S., 177
Ogawa, Michihiro, 125
Oguntomisin, Dare, 174
oligarchies, 196
Oman, 35, 42, 52
omission, state erasure and, 7, 32–33, *34*, 35–36, 50
Opium Wars, 87, 90
Osei Bonsu (king), 174, 179
Osei Kwadwo, 179
Osei Kwame, 179
Ottoman Empire, 42, 45
Ouidah, slave-trading port, 12–14, 171, 177, 184, 198, 202–3, 213, 215
Oyo Empire, 1, 10, 49, 280n47, 282n96, 282nn93–94, 283n4, 285n34; centralization in, 31, 180, 198, 202–3, 209–10; collapse of, 43, 45, 167, 172–73, 180–82, 184, 202, 208, 210, 216; decentralization in, 180, 197–98, 216; imperial rule in, 29; political centralization and, 37; population, *166, 170;* secession and, 42, 45; slave trade and, 185, 215–16; successor states of, 177, 208; transportation costs for, 168; tributaries, 176; vassalage in, 200–202, 209–10

Pahang, Malaysia, 196
Paine, Jack, 69
Pakistan, 127, 135, 196
Palestine, 3
palm-oil production, 178, 186

INDEX

Parabellum paradigm, 81, 89
pepper trade, 129, 154–55, 213–14
Perdue, Peter, 89
Permanent Settlement Act, 130, 132, 134
Perry, Matthew, 90–91, 96, 101–2, 209
Persia, 108
Peru-Bolivian Confederation, 41–42, 50, 53
Philippines, 138–39, 143, 153
Phillips, Andrew, 8, 89
pilgrimages, 165
pluralistic universalism, 3
Poggi, Gianfranco, 25–26
political centralization, 8–9, 11–12, 23, 37, 164
political survival, 24–25, 255n7
polities, 2, 26, 93, 220–21, 221, 225–26, 230
population, 84–85, 278n2, 279n31; statehood and, 36, 257n49, 257n59
population density, 13, 67, 203–8, 269n19, 269n21, 279n26, 282n94, 284n12; in Africa, 42, 269n19; in East Asia, 79, 85, 98–100, 105, 207; in European states, 207, 269n19; in maritime Southeast Asia, *139*, 140, 145–47, *147*, 150; in South Asia, *109*, 110–12, *113*, 113–15, 134–35, 207; in West Africa, 145, *166*, 169–70, 172, 181–82, 184, 190, 206–7
Portugal, 40, 141, 146
precolonial state systems, precolonial period and, 2, 32; non-Western, 5, 28–29, 66, 115, 120, 168, 171, 175, 213
principal–agent problems, 16, 62, 233–34, 237–38, 246–47
problems, information, 67–68, 101, 233–34, 237–38, 247
projected power, distance and, 9, 16, 42, 69, 162, 199–221, *221*, 229–30, 236–39
property rights, 15, 63–64, 130
Protestant Reformation, 62, 261n34, 287n49
protonationalism, 15, 71, 78, 205
provincial rule, 93, 178–79, 181–89, 200
Pune, *113*, 113–14, 121, 123–24, 195–97, 203, 207–9, 244

Qin, Yaqing, 24
Qin Dynasty, China, 93, 102–3
Qing Dynasty, China, 1, 80–83, 87–90, 104, 225, 248

Rabih az-Zubayr (slave trader), 28–29, 167
radial rule, 161–62, 220–21, *221*, 223, 230, 233, 236–39
railways, 69, 111, 203
Rajasthan, 108
Rajput states, 12, 108, 110, 116, 229
Ramusack, Barbara, 269n4
Ravina, Mark, 95
Raychaudhuri, Tapan, 111
regional subsystems, 4, 18
Reid, Richard, 148, 175
religion, 72, 126, 129, 155, 165, 171. *See also specific religions*
Rembau, 153, 275
Republic Texas, 50
resource extraction, 13–14, 26–27, 29–31, 57, 130–31, 135, 234, 247
Reus-Smit, Christian, 83
revenue extraction, 30–31, 73, 115, 120–23, 126–32, 164, 207, 255n7
revenue farming, 120, 123, 125, 273n93
Rhine Confederation, 41
Riau, 141–42, 145
Ricklefs, M. C., 140–41, 148, 153, 155–57, 159, 235–36
road systems, 72, 85, 98, 112, 129, 203–4
Roy, Kaushik, 210–11
Roy, Tirthankar, 111, 117–18, 125, 272n87
Ruggie, John, 259n11, 286n35
Russia, 45–47, 90
Russo-Japanese War (1904–1905), 90

Safdar Jang (nawab of Awadh), 29
Sahell, 17, 164, 171
Sarawak, *52*, *139*, 141, 143
Satara, India, 271n61
Saudi Arabia, 259n97
Scott, James, 67, 147
secession, state, 29, 41–43, *44*, 45, 58, 61–62, 141, 183, 197–98, 202; in Southeast Asia, 157; in West Africa, 172–73, 183

INDEX

Second Opium War (1856–1860), 90
Segou Kingdom, 165, *166*, 167, 169, 176
Selangor, *52*, *139*, 155
Senegal, 165, 171, 173, 176, 186, 196
Shah, Nadir, 108
Sharman, Jason, 17, 90, 185, 214
Shaw, Meredith, 88–89, 91
Siak, *139*, 152, 155, 214
Siam, 29, 58, 94, 97, 142, 160, 206, 228
Sikh states, 126
Sind, Pakistan, 196
Singapore, 137, 144, *147*, 261n32
Singh, Ranjit, 108
Sinocentrism, 1, 8, 80–89, 102–4, 138, 140, 248
slavery and the slave trade, 1, 12–13, 202, 213, 278n5, 282n111, 283n114, 285n34; Atlantic slave trade, 163–64, 170–71, 184–86, 206, 213–17; attempts at centralization and, 198–99; Oyo Empire and, 185, 215–16; West Africa and, 17, 145, 163–65, 167, 170, 172–74, 178, 180, 184–86, 214–15, 217
Sokoto Caliphate, 1, 35, 42, 45, *49*, 172, 199, 208, 213, 227–28; advent of, 165, 167; decentralization of, 196, 198; on defection, 244; Islam and, 171, 177; Oyo Empire and, 180; slave trade and, 215; tributary systems and, 231
solar polities, 92, 151, 221–22
Somaliland, 225
South Africa, 38, *44*, 45, 227
South America, 41, 66, 227
South Asia, 9, 15, 32–33, 258n83, 276n43, 278n2, 284n12; borders in, 227; bureaucracies in, 122, 124, 127–29; centralization in, 107, 119, 127–36, 195–96; colonialism in, 1, 19, 43, 45, 108, 110, 127–29; decentralization in, 107–8, 121, 124, 127–28, 130–36; defecting vassals in, 210; fragmentation in, 121, 125–27; indirect rule in, 107; interaction capacity in, 107–8, 111–18, 133–34; political centralization in, 108, 118–30; population density in, *109*, 110–12, *113*, 113–15, 134–35, 207; port cities in, 114–15; precolonial, 66; state birth, 107; state deaths in, *44*, 46–47, 50, 107; trade in, 107–8, 112–15, *113*, 121, 129, 131–32, 134–35, 145; tributary relationships in, 113–14, 122–23, 124, 126–31; vassalage in, 107, 119–23, 127–28, 130–32, 135–36, 231; wars in, 107–8, 115–19, *117*, *118*, 125–28, 131, 133–34, 149, 208, 210–11, 236; West Africa compared to, 164. *See also* Mughal Empire; *specific states*
Southeast Asia, maritime, 3–4, 8, 9, 18–19, 28–29, 32–33, 224, 275n39, 284n7; absence of centralization in, 196; borders in, 227–28, 232; centralization in, 137, 159–60; colonialism in, 137, 140–43; decentralized rule in, 138, 147, 151–62; fragmentation in, 141, 154–55, 158–59, 162; governance in, 196–97; heteronomy in, 231; interaction capacity in, 138, 145–50, 154, 158, 160; mandala system in, 138, 246; political centralization and, 150–54; population density in, *139*, 140, 145–47, *147*, 150; ports, 146; slavery and, 137, 144–45; state births in, 40, 44; state deaths in, 50; trade in, 137–38, 140, 144, 146–47, *147*, 154–56, 161, 216–17; tributary relationships in, 145, 148, 152, 157, 160; vassalage in, 138, 156–59, 161–62; wars in, 88, 108, 137–38, 141, 147–50, *149*, *150*, 156–57; waterborne transportation in, 138, 204. *See also specific states*
South India, 11, 270n40
sovereign integration, 30–32
sovereign rights, 26, 30–31, 122
sovereignty, 12, 25–26, 32, 228, 242–43, 257n45, 271n61, 272n78, 285n31; in the contemporary international system, 224–25; in the European system, 62; external, 27, 37–38, 47, 257n54, 271n55; ruler claims to, 196–97; Spruyt on, 239; in tribute systems, 81–83; vassals and, 229–32, *231*

INDEX

Spain, 40–41, 61, 149
Spanish-Philippines War (1896–1898), 149
spice trade, 138, 146, 216; pepper in, 129, 154–55, 213–14
Spruyt, Hendrick, 8, 15, 64, 71, 157, 211, 218, 233; on the mandala model, 151; on population density, 146–47; on soverignty, 239
Srivijaya Empire, 277n82
standardization, 15, 63–64
standing armies, 88, 105, 126, 128, 131, 201, 207, 209–10, 216; for Awadh, 117; for Ibadan Empire, 174–75, 177, 187; for Japan, 95; Lyall on, 116
state formation, 19, 31, 40, 44, 100, 155–56, 213–18; bellicist theory of, 65–66, 101–2, 107, 170, 233; decolonization and, 162; slave trade and, 214; state building and, 60, 64–66, 71–72, 85, 163–64, 174, 187, 214, 217, 262n61
statehood, 5, 23–28, 197, 204, 242–44, 251, 257n49, 257n59
statelessness, 2–3, 6, 10, 32–33, 41, 241
states, state systems and. *See specific topics*
Stein, Burton, 129, 270n40
Strange Parallels (Lieberman), 15
structural differentiation, 30, 254n17, 256nn34–35
Struggle for Power in Early Modern Europe, The (Nexon), 261n34, 287n49
subordinate states, subordinate relations and, 10, 56, 59, 82–84, 151–53, 157, 198, 271n61, 271n63
sub-Saharan Africa, 50, 269n19
successor states, 29, 41, 58, 112, 132, 135, 208, 225, 269n4; South Asian, 108, 110–11, 114–18, 126, 128; in Southeast Asia, 147, 150; West African, 165, 167, 177
Sudan, 28, 49, 167
Sulawesi, 3, 29, 138, 140, 143, 153, 196
Sultanate of Maguindanao, 143
Sultanate of Zanzibar, 28, 256n19
Sumatra, 138, 141–42, 152, 154–55

Surakarta, 142, *147*, 148, 154, 156–58, 205, 225, 275n15
survival, political, 24–25, 255n7
Sweden, 226, 230
Swidler, Ann, 84
Swidler, Nina, 127
systems change, 16, 238–39

Taiping Rebellion, China, 90, 92
Taiwan, 3, 91
Tambiah, Stanley, 147, 160
Tampin, 52, *139*, 142, 153, 275n13
Tang Dynasty, China, 78, 104
Tanzania, 27
taxes, 11–12, 30–31, 37, 56–58, 61–67, 127, 234–35, 245–46, 287n44; centralization and, 94, 105, 128–29, 196–203; direct rule and, 120–21, 178–79
tax farming, 87, 128–30, 132–33, 198, 283n115
Tay Son Rebellion, Vietnam, 90
technology, 13–14, 67–69, 72, 203, 219, 226, 248
territoriality: China and, 89–90, 93, 97; decentralized states and, 58–59, 199; EIC and, 130; land and, 9, 25, 27, 36, 124, 182, 220, 266n55; succession and, 41–43; trade and, 213
textile manufacturing, 169
Thailand, 86, 138, *139*, 141
thalassocracy, 146
Thani, Iskandar, 160
Tibet, 46, 89–90
Tilly, Charles, 7, 64, 101, 214, 220, 261n40, 262n61, 282n95; on states, 24, 25, 29, 144
Timor, 144
Tippu Tip (slave trader), 27–29, 198, 256n19
Tipu Sultan, 117, 128–29, 197, 273n113
Togo, 12
Tokolor Empire, 10, *49*, 165, 167, 173, 215
Tokugawa Shogunate, Japan, 90–91, 94–96, 98–99, 209, 266n60, 267n70

INDEX

trade, 3, 13, 15–16, 19, 28, 231, 241–42, 247; Atlantic slave, 163–64, 170–71, 184–86, 206, 213–17; caravan, 115, 170; centralization and, 15, 19, 203, 213–18; China and, 86–87, 90; in East Asia, 77–78, 86, 86–87, 90, 98–101, 105–6; international, 101, 146, 155, 262n46; pepper, 129, 154–55, 213–14; Vietnam and, 87, 100–101; war and, 62–66, 69–73, 218; in West Africa, 164–65, 168–72, *170*, 178, 187. *See also* slavery, slave trade and

trading leagues, 163, 274n133

transportation: railways and, 69, 111, 203; road systems and, 72, 85, 98, 112, 129, 203–4; in South Asia, 111–12, 114, 133; transport costs and, 85, 99, 115, 145, 202–4, 207, 214, 270n34; in West Africa, 168–71. *See also* waterborne transportation, maritime transit and

trans-Saharan trade network, 170–71

Trarza Emirates, 165

Travancore, 110

Treaty of Bassein (1803), 122

Treaty of Giyanti (1755), 148, 156

Treaty of Seringapatam (1792), 129

tribute payments and tributary relationships, 10, 28, 57–58, 197–98, 229, 234, 244, 245–48; in East Asia, 80–84, 89, 94, 100, 103–4; hierarchies and, 80–83, 106, 190–91, 196; as revenue extraction, 113–14, 164; in South Asia, 113–14, 122–23, 124, 126–31; in Southeast Asia, 145, 148, 152, 157, 160; in West Africa, 165, 167, 173, 175–77, 182–91

Trondheim, 226

Tukolor Empire, 45

Tunisia, 38, *50*

Udaipur, 46, 52, 109

unification, state death and, 43, *44*, 45–47, 50

United Kingdom, 31, 171, 183–84

United Nations, 3–5, 33, 36, 50, 82, 224–25

United Provinces of Central America, 41–42, 46, 50, 53

United States, 31, 82, 149

Uppsala Conflict Data Program, 249

urbanization, 63–64, 112–13, 115, 169–70, 182, 184, 186

vassal kingdoms, 13–14, 29, 73, 242, 260n30, 261n34, 266n60; autonomy of, 57, 60–62, 70, 95, 138, 153, 164, 190–91, 196–202, 211–12, 219, 224, 229, 233–37, 245–47; bargaining power of, 12, 65–68, 70, 123, 180, 229, 233, 235; bribery and, 210–11; defection and exit options for, 15, 61, 70–71, 157–58, 183, 196, 210–11, 234–35, 237–38; in East Asia, 78, 92–97, 105; in European states, 58–59; governors vs., 200–203, 207, 209; heteronomy and, 230–32, 231, 247, 266n60; indirect rule and, 9, 57, 178–79, 219, 233–37, 262n46, 283n6; in maritime Southeast Asia, 138, 156–59, 161–62; militaries of, 12, 61, 67, 197–98, 200–201, 210, 233–35; of the Mughal Empire, 37, 205; in the Oyo Empire, 200–202, 209–10; political centralization and, 11–12; in South Asia, 107, 119–23, 127–28, 130–32, 135–36, 231; trade and, 216–17; in West Africa, 164, 175–80, 182–84, 186–91

Vereenigde Oostindische Compagnie (VOC, Dutch East India Company), 142, 144, 148, 156–59, 205–6, 275n15, 276n51

Vietnam (Annam), 42, *51*, 58, 197, 216–17, 232, 266n60, 268n98; centralization in, 77–78, 97–102, 104–6, 133, 236; China invading, 88, 102; decentralization in, 94, 100–102; direct rule in, 97–99; France and, 80–81, 90, 265n7; interaction-capacity in, 105, 204, 206; monarchies in, 265n7, 268n92; population of, *79*, 85, 93, 99–100; Tay Son Rebellion, 97, 100, 102; trade in, 87, 100–101; war and, 87, 90, 92, 102

Vijayanagara Empire, 128

VOC. *See* Vereenigde Oostindische Compagnie

INDEX

Wadai, 28, 50, 166, 177, 231
Waltz, Kenneth, 56–59
war and warfare, 3, 196, 227–28, 236, 241–42, 247; in the Asante Kingdom, 174–75; in Balinese kingdoms and, 137–38, 147–48, 150; bellicism, 14, 15, 63, 65–66, 101–2, 131, 156, 170, 181, 233, 237; centralization and, 203, 207–13; Chinese, 88–92; civil wars, 179, 266n56; decline-of-war debate and, 19, 242, 248–52, *252*; East Asia and, 78, 87–92, *88*, *91*, *106*; interstate conflicts and, 65, 116, 250–52; intrastate, 87–92, 148, 248–50; in maritime Southeast Asia, 88, 108, 137–38, 141, 147–50, *149*, *150*, 156–57; nonstate, 251; in South Asia, 107–8, 115–19, *117*, *118*, 125–28, 131, 133–34, 149, 208, 210–11, 236; state centralization and, 19, 62–66, 77; trade and, 62–66, 69–73, 215, 218; vassal kingdoms and, 29; Vietnam and, 87, 90, 92, 102; West Africa and, 88, 149, 163, 172–75, *173*, *174*, 183–84, 189, 208, 215–16. *See also specific wars*
Ward, Michael, 35
Warring States Period, China, 24–25, 65–66
Wassulu Empire, 167
waterborne transportation, maritime transit and, 85, 105, 111–12, 114, 134, 203–5; Southeast Asian, 138, 140, 145–46, 161
Watson, Adam, 26–27
Watson Andaya, Barbara, 276
West Africa, 3–4, 17, 19, 221, 236, 245–46, 263n62, 270n23, 282n95; borders in, 175, 227; bull's-eye model in, 9–10, 163; bureaucracies in, 167, 178–79, 185; centralization in, 31, 163–64, 175, 177–91, 195–96; colonization and, 163, 165, 168, 172, 177, 180, 190; cosmology in, 198; decentralization in, 175–77, 181–91, 263; decolonization and, 163; fragmentation in, 164, 173, 184, 187; heteronomy in, 231; interaction capacity, 145–46, 164, 168–75, 187;

Islamic states in, 10; political centralization and, 164, 175–81; population, 164, 169, *170*; population density in, 145, *166*, 169–70, 172, 181–82, 184, 190, 206–7; ports, 171; slavery, slave trade and, 17, 145, 163–65, 167, 170, 172–74, 178, 180, 184–86, 214–15, 217; sovereign states in, 12; state birth and state death in, 33, 40, *44*, 45–46, 163; trade in, 164–65, 168–72, *170*, 178, 187; tributary relationships in, 165, 167, 173, 175–77, 182–91; vassalage in, 164, 175–80, 182–84, 186–91; wars in, 88, 149, 163, 172–75, *173*, *174*, 183–84, 189, 208, 215–16. *See also specific countries; specific empires; specific states*
Wilks, Ivor, 168, 178–79, 182–83, 187–88, 229, 281n80
Wimmer, Andreas, 211–12, 262n53
Wink, André, 122, 125, 133
Wittgenstein, Ludwig, 24
Wolters, O. W., 151, 161
Woodside, Alexander, 78, 83–84, 92–93, 266n55
World War I, 6, 251
World War II, 6, 262n61

Xiang Khouang, 94

Yazdani, Kaveh, 133
Yemen, 42
Yogyakarta Sultanate, 1, 142, *147*, 148, 154, 156–59, 205, 276nn50–51
Yoruba kingdoms, 18, 174, 176–77, 185, 187, 196, 208; Oyo Empire collapse and, 167; population density of, 169–70; vassals of, 29

Zanzibar, 27–28, 50, 256n19
Zarakol, Ayşe, 185, 214
Zaria, 45, 57, *170*, 258n86
Zheng He, 140
Zimbabwe, 42
Zinder, 229
Zulu Empire, 45

GPSR Authorized Representative: Easy Access System Europe, Mustamäe tee 50, 10621 Tallinn, Estonia, gpsr.requests@easproject.com

www.ingramcontent.com/pod-product-compliance
Lightning Source LLC
LaVergne TN
LVHW091042180925
821343LV00024B/381